Composers of North America

Series Editors: John Beckwith, Sam Dennison, William C. Loring, Jr., Margery M. Lowens, Martha Furman Schleifer

Arthur Foote

A Musician in the Frame of Time and Place

Nicholas E. Tawa

1923-2011

*Composers of North America
Series, No. 22*

The Scarecrow Press, Inc.
Lanham, Md., & London
1997

SCARECROW PRESS, INC.

Published in the United States of America
by Scarecrow Press, Inc.
4720 Boston Way
Lanham, Maryland 20706

4 Pleydell Gardens, Folkestone
Kent CT20 2DN, England

British Library Cataloguing in Publication Information Available

Library of Congress Cataloging-in-Publication Data

Tawa, Nicholas E.
    Arthur Foote : a musician in the frame of time and place /
Nicholas E. Tawa.
        p. cm. — (Composers of North America series ; no. 22)
    Includes bibliographical references.
    ISBN 0-8108-3295-X (cloth : alk. paper)
        1. Foote, Arthur, 1853-1937. 2. Composers—United States—
Biography. I. Title. II. Series: Composers of North America ; no. 22.
ML410.F75T38 1997
780'.92—dc21   97-10070
[B]   CIP
MN
ISBN 0–8108–3295–X (cloth : alk. paper)

This volume is dedicated to
Rev. Arthur Foote II,
who has worked tirelessly to advance
the music of his granduncle.

Contents

Part IV: The Modern Era (1901–1937)

Series Note

This series, Composers of North America, is designed to focus attention on the development of art music and folk music from colonial times to the present. Few of our composers had their works performed frequently enough during their lifetimes to establish them in the standard repertoire of soloists, chamber groups, orchestras, or choruses. Their compositions, therefore, even when published, have often suffered undeserved neglect.

Each volume begins with the life and works of a given composer, placing that person in the context of the musical world of the period, providing comments by contemporary critics, and noting those compositions that today's listeners might enjoy. Each volume includes a catalog of the composer's works with publication details and locations of unpublished works.

The series will have served its purpose if it draws attention to the large body of work that has so long been treated with benign neglect. The editors firmly believe that a number of these compositions are worthy of being regularly performed today. They hope these works will be considered for performance by planners and conductors of concert programs and that performers will add some of these works to their repertoire.

John Beckwith, Sam Dennison,
William C. Loring, Jr., Margery M. Lowens,
Martha Furman Schleifer, Series Editors

Preface

Arthur Foote was one of the most important American composers in the last quarter of the nineteenth century and first two decades of the twentieth century. Contemporaneous with him were the composers John Knowles Paine, George Chadwick, Horatio Parker, and Edward MacDowell in the United States, and Antonin Dvořák, Edvard Grieg, Paul Dukas, Nicolai Rimsky-Korsakov, and Giacomo Puccini in Europe. He shared with these composers the tonal system and common practices developed over three centuries that none of his generation was inclined to reject.

Foote was nine years older than Claude Debussy, nineteen years older than Alexander Scriabin, twenty-one years older than Arnold Schoenberg, and twenty-nine years older than Igor Stravinsky. These younger composers, at the cutting edge of musical composition, would drastically modify the heretofore shared tradition and propose novel creative methods that revolutionized musical thinking. Thus Foote's style was abreast of his own time and should not be considered reactionary because it did not delve into atonality, primitivism, machine music, neoclassicism, or other movements. These radical musical innovations were instituted by younger composers just as he was reaching the end of his creative career.

Several circumstances encouraged a decline in Foote's musical standing after World War I. Forceful objection to the Germanic ascendancy in American art music grew, a disapproval strongly abetted by anti-German feelings caused by the war and, later, by the advance and threat of Nazism. Then came World War II. However much Foote's mature style had evolved away from its Central European beginnings, he was still seen as allied to the Teutonic camp. American critics consistently relegated Foote to the ranks of the sentimental, second-rate composers of the nineteenth century, despite his well-conceived ideas and lack of gush. In addition, Foote's empathy with the American music public and his music's ability to gratify the public's taste was considered to be pandering to the ignorant and a violation of artistic principles.

In contrast, the musical world of Foote's day highly respected him as an educator, keyboard performer, and choral music director and could not praise his music highly enough. This high regard for his music is now returning. Since the beginning of the 1990s, a renewed interest in his compositions has grown steadily. Listeners are struck by how coherent the music is, both in its general form and in its details. They note a command of craft that allowed Foote to integrate his tones with his desired expression. Moreover, they hear an honest, straightforward sound that brooked no pretentious complexities, no enigmas of meaning.

Yet, no reliable study of Foote's life and music exists. Of the three dissertations listed in my bibliography, Douglas Moore's, excellent as it is, deals with only the cello music, and Doric Alviani's with only the choral church music. Frederick Kopp's dissertation, "Arthur Foote," is incomplete and frequently inaccurate, and it contains negligible insight concerning his life. The discussion of the music is mostly limited to a quasi-statistical summation of Foote's stylistic propensities. Regrettably, Kopp says very little about why the music is worth knowing. Convinced of the impact that Foote had had on music in America and of the excellence of his compositions, I was amazed to find that no thorough and reliable examination of the composer, his works, and his importance in American culture exists. This study hopes to offer such an examination.

In creating this work, I have had the invaluable advice of Rev. Arthur Foote II, the composer's grandnephew and namesake, who read and commented on the chapters as they were completed. He is one of the very last living persons to have known the composer well. Through meetings and correspondence, Rev. Foote and I resolved most of the questions that arose during my investigations. When I became discouraged about obstacles impeding my research, Rev. Foote urged me on with unfailing enthusiasm and optimism.

My labors were lightened by the excellent work *A Catalog of the Works of Arthur Foote* by Wilma Reid Cipolla.[1] Any reader desiring a complete and annotated listing of Foote's published and unpublished music will find it here. Additionally, it includes a bibliography of Foote's published writings and of writings on Foote. I have seen no need to duplicate her efforts in what follows. Cipolla also edited a reprint of Arthur Foote's *An Autobiography*, complete with an introduction and notes.[2]

For primary sources, the recently established "Arthur Foote Collection" of Williams College contains a rich lode of music, newspaper clippings, letters, family documents, and so on, gathered by Rev. Arthur Foote II and Katharine Foote Raffy, the composer's daughter. Douglas Moore, the director of the collection, put himself to considerable trouble to help further my research. When I visited Williams College, he had everything that I had requested ready for study. In addition, Moore cheerfully responded to all my queries, photocopied a tremendous amount of material for me, and sent me taped copies of what recorded music he had.

A second important source of primary sources is the New England Conservatory of Music. Music in manuscript, published music, a scrapbook, and a wealth of letters are located in the library. Jean Morrow, director of libraries, and Patrick Maxfield, catalog librarian, have been extraordinarily helpful in searching out and photocopying music for me and in having the conservatory's Foote holdings on hand for my visits. Maxfield also took time to search the conservatory's archives in order to provide me with accurate information about Foote's activities at the conservatory.

A third source for essential information on Foote is the Harvard Musical Association. Its librarian, Natalie Palme, enthusiastically located published and manuscript music for me and made certain I did not overlook any of the volumes bound by the composer and presented to the association. She kindly offered to photocopy anything I desired to take away with me, even though she had to carry the material to a photocopy establishment a distance from the association's building.

The Music Department of the Boston Public Library harbors a wealth of scrapbooks that were put together either by Foote, Allan Brown, or members of the library staff. A great deal of music published and in manuscript is also found. The collection is indispensable for an understanding of the composer. Unfortunately for the researcher, there are strict limits on what may be photocopied.

Moreover, access to original documents is often denied and only microfilm viewing is allowed. Otherwise, the staff of the library is helpful in finding whatever is housed in its department.

Although the Music Division of the Library of Congress holds many Foote items and, of course, the copyrighted music, its catalog listings are incomplete or inaccurate. I must thank Wayne D. Shirley, librarian in the Music Division, for his special efforts on my behalf in discovering where much of the Foote material was hiding.

For documents related to a history of the Foote family, including his ancestors, parents, and siblings, and to Arthur Foote's pre-adult years, the Archives of Harvard University and the library of the Essex Institute, in Salem, Massachusetts, offer information not available from any other source.

Assiduous as he was in preserving various aspects of his public life in his several scrapbooks, Foote strove to keep his private life out of the public eye. He discouraged the publication of his more personal letters and, when grown old, even desired their destruction. What information I give about his domestic existence and his private thoughts was difficult to come by and, I am afraid, less complete than I would have liked. It is in this area that my discussions with Rev. Foote were extremely valuable. He talked with me about his family and granduncle, about what was said and (offering great insight to me) what was left unsaid.

This book is just a beginning. It is meant to encourage others to explore the rich lode of American art music from the past. Their reward will be the discovery of many compositions that merit attention and satisfy our desire for well-made, nourishing sounds, grateful to the ear and exciting aesthetic delight.

Notes

1. Wilma Reid Cipolla, *A Catalog of the Works of Arthur Foote*, Bibliographies in American Music, 6 (Detroit: Published for the College Music Society by Information Coordinators, 1980).

2. Arthur Foote, *An Autobiography* (1946; reprint, with introduction and notes by Wilma Reid Cipolla, New York: Da Capo, 1979).

Part I

Emerging from the
New England Matrix

1

Antecedents

Throughout his lifetime (1853–1937), Arthur Foote exemplified the artist who is well integrated into his community. As such, he offers us an informative contrast to today's usual concept of the artist as unappreciated by and often in conflict with society. Foote's community included mostly cultivated and informed New Englanders descended from the first English settlers. It also included German Americans and, to a lesser degree, men and women of other European origins (British, Irish, Italian, Polish, French, and so on), most of whom lived in the Salem and Greater Boston area. Not only sophisticated listeners but also ordinary concertgoers, usually from the middle class and sometimes from the working class, came to appreciate Foote's work.

From the 1880s on, the circle that interacted with Arthur Foote gradually expanded to include residents of all six New England states. Later, New Yorkers, inhabitants of other regions of the United States, Canadians, and even a number of Europeans came to know him well. Few American composers of his time were able to win the high respect, even love, accorded Foote by contemporary musicians, educators, and audiences. This is worth analysis if only to learn how an artist can retain his or her integrity and how art can prosper in a democracy.

Foote existed within a difficult artistic environment, though he never expressed hostility toward it. Instead, he probed and conceptualized, by means of his art, the inarticulate mental and

spiritual leanings of the New England community that had mold-
ed him. His faculty for embodying these leanings into musical
expressions gave his work important social meaning in his day
and increases our comprehension of that community today.
Foote composed music without a deliberate awareness of the
public implications of his activities. Yet, the music was true to his
own and other contemporary Americans' vision of America. Owing to this, his compositions had serious social meaning. For this
reason, too, he is worthy of study.

In addition, Foote deserves study because of the influence
that he exerted on his contemporaries through his role as educator, musical entrepreneur, and performer. Moreover, his activities as a composer are significant, for he created finely crafted
compositions with outstanding musical content. They would retain their artistic significance for audiences beyond his own era.
American music lovers of the late nineteenth and early twentieth
centuries were proud of his creative achievements. They saw him
as contributing vitally to their civilization and to a lasting musical
literature. Anyone with real interest in the cultural roots of the
United States must take into consideration the accomplishments
of Arthur Foote.

Because Foote was a preeminent composer whose career
and mode of living has significance for human and artistic reasons, familiarity with his life is as important as gaining a better
perception of his music. Therefore, I wish to examine the practical and existential link between his creative work and being.[1] I
address three essential questions. First, what forces shaped the
man and the musician? Second, how did he view himself and his
community and how did his community view him? Third, why
did his society accept him and receive his music as sympathetically as it did?

General Background

Several threads connect Foote with his New England—Puritanism, Unitarianism, Transcendentalism, Germanic idealism and
art, and local social history. The earliest thread joins him to his
Puritan ancestors, for the first Foote arrived in the Boston area in

1635.[2] When examining the Puritan characteristics handed down to later generations, including eminent figures such as Ralph Waldo Emerson, Nathaniel Hawthorne, William James, Henry Wadsworth Longfellow, and Emily Dickinson, we find evidence of deeply felt and imaginative thought processes whose external display was carefully controlled. We find also a desire to hold their emotions and yearning for mental lucidity in equilibrium. We encounter in them a high regard for education and scholarship. As well as a dedication to discovering truths that extend beyond mere earthly existence, laborers in the arts like Foote, who also exhibited these characteristics, would score creative achievements that were thoughtful and solidly American.[3]

Puritans of the seventeenth century and New Englanders of the next two centuries did not try to bar music or dancing, writes Walter Spalding. For several generations the harsh realities of New England life left little time for music. Nevertheless, "the Puritan blood . . . was a potent source of creative imagination, albeit sometimes in suspended animation." This "is shown by the fact that the majority of original composers in our country for the last seventy-five years [from 1860] are of Puritan descent." He cites composers such as Paine, Foote, Chadwick, Parker, Whiting, Converse, Hill, Mason, and Carpenter.[4]

The second thread leads from Puritanism to Unitarianism and then to Transcendentalism. Although nineteenth-century New England society was beholden to Puritan attitudes, religion, and preoccupation with moral truths, it was a modification of Puritanism in the form of Christian humanism, Unitarianism, that Arthur Foote experienced more directly. Several men closely related to him were Unitarian ministers—his brother Henry, his nephew Henry II, and his grandnephew Arthur II, to name three; his parents and sister took seriously the teachings of their faith. Unitarianism cast aside the rigid dogma of man's depravity and propensity for evil but retained the moralistic and reason-oriented constituents of Puritanism. It tried to see the ethical problems of the world more as predicaments visited on helpless humans that required compassion and an effort by all Christians to aid those unable to aid themselves and less as afflictions from God for sinfulness. But the apparent stress on objectivity and rationality led to an offshoot of Unitarianism, Transcendentalism.[5] As we shall see, Foote unconsciously merged his Unitarian faith with Transcendentalism's broadly defined mix of beliefs. These beliefs deemphasized even more the concept of an inherently flawed and needy mankind, taking greater interest in the individual as a distinctive and feeling being. To Transcendentalists, God permeated nature. He was an immediate presence in every man and woman, and thus personal intuition was a fundamental means to knowledge. The comprehension gained through perceptive insight was an important component of the creative act. Foote instinctively and clear-sightedly translated his deeply felt imaginings into actual sounds, thus realizing higher reaches of himself through such self-exploration. This way of seeing himself was to some degree a response to a new but not necessarily better America, that supplanted what Foote valued with an inordinate love of material things and an excessive acquisitiveness. His way of life was threatened by a sometimes ruthless breed of entrepreneur who had set out to subjugate the western frontier and to produce railroads, machinery, manufactories, and metropolises. Foote was not always sympathetic toward the changes taking place in American society. But when it came to other races, religions, and cultures, Foote was unprejudiced.

His parents were friends with or at least followed with great interest the careers of several New Englanders who articulated the Transcendentalist view of humanity, among them Emerson in his philosophic tracts, Hawthorne with his symbolist stories, the music-loving John Sullivan Dwight who (with Hawthorne) tried to practice a form of communism at Brook Farm, Margaret Fuller expounding her ardent feminism, and Elizabeth Peabody endeavoring to reform education. An abiding faith in the Christian God and a ready responsiveness to things of beauty were evident in his parents' behavior. In addition, they were concerned for the needy and dispirited. They themselves experienced life's tragedies through the deaths of three of their children.[6]

Foote's parents had lived out their younger lives in a region where the Puritan tradition, however modified by Unitarianism and Transcendentalism, was still dominant. The New England citizenry of the early nineteenth century remained culturally raw and unschooled. If additional stimuli, which came from Central Europe, had not begun to enter the austere New England society about the time Arthur Foote was born, it would have remained far less receptive to the native art composer. Indeed, Arthur Foote might have realized his musicianship in an utterly different configuration, if he realized it at all. In short, the third thread is one that joins New England and Foote to continental Europe's culture.

Most of these additional stimuli were brought from Central Europe by the influx of German immigrants to the Salem-Boston area, beginning at mid-century. Among these German immigrants were trained musicians. However, Foote and other New Englanders like him did not just learn or imitate Central European values; they accepted these values because they paralleled and could be integrated with New England ones. Central Europe's impressive contributions to philosophy corresponded to those of Emerson. Indeed, Transcendentalism was also a German manifestation. In music, there were the awesome works from the past of Bach, Handel, Mozart, Beethoven, Schubert, and Schumann, and from the present of Brahms, Wagner, and Liszt. Here was a serious, sophisticated, and exalted art, which was articulated in persuasive structures—something to which New Englanders could relate. Americans who had the money to do so flocked to Europe to study and absorb its culture. Those who stayed home could exchange views with and learn from the educated Europeans who had migrated to the New World. Cultivated Americans hoped that out of this ferment would emerge an advanced art capable of representing the New World. When American composers after the Civil War were taking their fledgling steps in music, they found a number of these Europeans ready to support their every step. Foote, for example, spoke highly of Central Europeans resident in America who taught him a great deal about his craft and helped him win the recognition of his countrymen. He named musicians like the conductor Theodore Thomas, the violinist Franz Kneisel, and the music publisher Arthur P. Schmidt, among others.[7]

Rupert Hughes, born in 1872, once wrote that it took a long time for a new art such as music to emerge in America. Inevitably Americans had to resort to European methods. A distinctively native art music in the nineteenth century was not possible because Americans had no advanced musical traditions of their

own. Moreover, they were mostly of English descent and contemporary England had little to offer in the way of art music of
the first rank. It was continental Europe, especially Germany and
the Austro-Hungarian nations, that had a great deal to teach
Americans, he concluded.[8]

A last thread has to do with the town of Salem itself, Foote's
birthplace, and its influence on him. Writing in 1936 about the
Salem of his boyhood, Foote states that the town "was a quiet,
prosperous, self-contained place, not dependent for music and
theatre on Boston. It had tradition and cultivation; life there was
simple and easy, and it is a pleasant thing to look back upon in
these restless, anxious times."[9] Growing up then was delightful.
Salem's population of twenty thousand was of mostly English
and Irish descent. Labor friction was absent. The town was well
governed and experienced "contentment and good average
prosperity." "We had one series of first-rate lectures and another
consisting partly of lectures and partly of good concerts."[10] His
mother confirms this in a letter dated 6 March 1852, writing of a
lecture and concert series and other social activities she was en-
joying: "R. W. Emerson lectures for us this week, which will be a
treat. We have had Wendell Phillips, H. W. Beecher, Starr King,
and many other interesting people. Then, every fortnight, [the
Mendelssohn] Quintette Club for the music. Every week a tea-
party. . . . Then some splendid balls and many little tea-nights
made the winter gay."[11]

In 1911 her son Arthur recalled the "Salem witchcraft delusion" and added that "the house [later destroyed by fire] in
which I lived when a boy, by the way, was within a stone's throw
or at least a golf drive of Gallows Hill [to the west], whose name
has obvious derivation."[12] The house at 44 Warren Street and
close to the Chestnut-Street district, he told Olin Downes, was a
prototype of the one described by Joseph Hergesheimer, in his
book *Java Head* (1919).[13] He was acutely aware of the town's
grim past, yet withal experienced only happiness as he grew up.

To conclude this general survey, we find Foote occupying the
land of his ancestors and acted upon by its values, attitudes, and
long-standing institutions. His environment was comfortable
and unthreatening. He was secure in the knowledge of who he
was, where he came from, and, in a broad sense, where he might
go and how to get there. What remained was the need for him to

establish specific goals for himself. All of this engendered a pride of place and a reduction in inner conflict. He had no need to rebel against his ancestry, assert his complete independence from any tradition or carve out a completely different and individual realm for himself. Nor would he and his generation have agreed that rebellion was necessary to the creation of durable artistic works.

Arthur Foote's Parents

A "Pasco Foot" arrived from England around 1635–37 and eventually settled in Salem.[14] Pasco died in 1671.[15] Several of Pasco's descendants were seamen. One of them, Caleb Foot (1750–87), the great-grandfather of Arthur Foote, served under Washington during the siege of Boston in 1775 and then shipped on several privateers. He was Prize Master on the sloop *Gates*, when it was captured by the British in 1778. Caleb was imprisoned in Forton Prison in Portsmouth, England, until he escaped to Amsterdam on 14 October 1780. Ill health, probably brought on by the hardships of prison life, resulted in death when he was thirty-seven years of age.[16]

Arthur's father, also named Caleb and the son of a sea captain, was born in 1803. His father's mother died in 1802, and his father's father was lost at sea in 1808. Caleb was then cared for by his grandmother, Mary Dedman Foot. Caleb was the first of the family to add the letter *e* to the name "Foot," making it "Foote." He began his autobiography (later published by his daughter) with: "My history has really been common and uneventful. It is the short and simple story of early orphanage, poverty, and lack of education, followed by a life of moderate industry, perseverance, and economy, and, by the natural result, a degree of success, which, without any great stroke of fortune or remarkable capacity, brought me in my old age to an ample competency."[17] The unpretentiousness revealed here would also be found in the son.

A few days after her engagement to Caleb, the future Mary Wilder Foote wrote to her sister Eliza A. Dwight on 3 February 1835 describing her husband-to-be, a description that with few adjustments could have fitted her future son Arthur:

> One of the most striking features in his character and manner
> is his simplicity and ease of feeling, which always prompts to
> the most natural and agreeable movement of thought, word,
> and deed. He has a mingling of contrasts in his character
> which is very striking,—a very quick perception of the ludi-
> crous, which always makes him laugh at the right place, with
> an extreme tenderness about other people,—a decision of
> character, and an energy which acts immediately upon the
> decision, and yet a gentleness of manner and of feeling which
> dreads giving pain to anything alive . . . and a charity and for-
> bearance in judging of others which reminds me of my dear
> minister.[18]

His grandson, Henry Foote II, states that he was "a small,
lightly built man, a bit under five feet six inches tall, with little
muscular strength, but healthy and well preserved both physically and mentally to a great old age."[19] We note similarities to
Arthur in this description.

When young, Caleb Foote educated himself through ceaseless reading even as he worked as a kitchen boy, then a shop boy,
and then a bookstore salesman. In 1817, he went as apprentice
to the biweekly *Salem Gazette*, and eight years later bought a
half-share in the paper and assumed the editorship. He was its
sole editor and proprietor in 1833 and continued his connection
with the *Gazette* until 1888. Caleb Foote always maintained that
the newspaper was founded in 1768 as the *Essex Gazette*. The
Revolutionary War interrupted publication, which was resumed
in 1786, when the paper was renamed the *Salem Gazette*.[20] In
1830, he was elected Master of the Essex Lodge of Freemasons,
and in the early 1830s he became president of a debating society
and joined a literary club, among whose members was Judge
Daniel A. White, father of his future wife. Both he and Judge
White at one time "officiated at a public meeting to take into
consideration the wrongs of the Indians," Caleb states.[21]

Music came into Caleb's life in 1826, with a new partner in
the *Gazette*, William Brown. Brown showed more interest in his
bass voice and more commitment to his musical engagements
than to the paper. He was bought out in 1833. Caleb Foote
boarded with Brown's mother for a year or two and then with

the Parsons family, where again music entered his life: "Mr. Parsons was the leader of the singing in the North Church, and got me to join the choir, of which I remained a member till after my marriage."[22] He also became librarian and teacher at the Sunday school, where his future wife "took a class." They soon became close friends, Caleb writes, especially after the two went to "the music meetings which were then given by leading members of the First [Church] and North [Church] Societies and by the public meetings of the Salem Glee Club and the Mozart Society, in both of which I held membership."[23] Their wedding took place on 21 October 1835.

Besides his editorship, he was a member of the Salem School Committee (1820–21), an elected "Representative to the General Court" (a term that comprehends both the Massachusetts Senate and the House of Representatives) in 1832–33 and the House of Representatives in 1838.[24] In 1841, he was appointed Salem postmaster. Politically, he began as a Whig and then joined the Republicans. He always took special pride in his children, as in his comment in the autobiography on "the birth of Mary on the 20th of August, 1843, and of Arthur, March 5, 1853, who have since filled a most important place in my life, and are beloved and honored heads of families of their own."[25] He died in 1894.

Mary Wilder Tileston's book, *Caleb and Mary Wilder Foote,* contains the letters and reminiscences of Arthur's and her parents. The frontispiece shows Mary Wilder Foote, as she looked in 1841, when she was thirty-one. She appears with her hair parted in the middle, cut short and straight across, about an inch below her ears. Gentle eyes gaze modestly from the page. She seems reluctant to be on view. Mary Wilder Foote (*née* White) was born in Newburyport, Massachusetts, in 1810. Six months later, her mother died and her father moved to Salem. She and her sister Eliza attended boarding school at first. When she was thirteen, her father, Daniel Appleton White, a judge of the probate court, ended their formal education. He had decided to keep his daughters at home and teach them himself, because he feared the coarsening influence of school life.[26] Arthur's mother was described as extremely intelligent, affectionate, unselfish, and a devout Unitarian.[27] She wrote in her journal on 17 May 1829 that she had heard Ralph Waldo Emerson lecture on "Christian grace and gentleness." Then he and his brother Charles visited her father. Her future husband's name enters her journal on 11 November 1831: "In the evening the singers met here. There were few of them, but we had a very good sing. After they had gone, Mr. and Mrs. Upham, David Mack, and Mr. Foote remained, and I sang several songs to them." She had joined the choir of the First Church in November 1830 and was described as having "a voice of great range and sweetness." Her grandnephew Arthur Foote II comments in a letter dated 27 May 1993, that she had "musical interests and talent." Although she died while Arthur "was just an infant, he inherited his love of music from her."[28] She also had literary abilities and after her marriage edited a column on books for her husband's *Gazette*.

In a letter she wrote on 7 January 1834, she says: "The evening I spent with Elizabeth Peabody, where I met Charles Emerson and Miss Hoar, and I don't know when I have spent so delightful an evening. He is extremely agreeable and interesting in conversation, even more so than his fascinating brother Waldo, and she is altogether lovely." After her marriage to Caleb Foote, she continued her friendship with the Emersons and the Peabodys. For example, on 7 April 1840, she visited the Peabodys, taking great pleasure in her conversation with Elizabeth Hoar and Sophia Peabody. She was delighted when Sophia and Nathaniel Hawthorne became engaged. In a congratulatory letter dated 23 April 1842 she writes to Sophia: "It has always been a peculiar pleasure to us [she and Caleb Foote] that we have sympathized in our enthusiasm about everything that Mr. Hawthorne has written, and you know, too, how much it has added to my happiness to find how he immediately adopted your friends as his own."[29]

Arthur's mother rarely let gentility or idealism cloud her vision. She was annoyed with people who refused to see the ugly realities of the world that caused human suffering: "There are some things that, after you once see, you can never *unsee*, and, when you have once *rubbed your eyes*, and seen things as they are, you can never hope to have that gentle mist come over them again, which shall conceal deformities so gracefully." She was disturbed by the Brook Farm experiment, which she considered "a grand mistake." It was ridiculous to her that Sophia Ripley washed everybody's clothes and scrubbed floors when she could be more useful aiding the intellectual development of people and imparting an "elevated view" to society.[30]

As for herself, "The question I often ask—Who is wiser or better for my life? That some are happier for it does not prove much in my favor because their own loving, long-suffering natures 'make the virtue they confide in.' But one ought not to come into God's world with a particular gift (which every one has), without making a mark there. We should not live in the world, and leave it just as we found it." She favored religious tolerance for the countless number of lowly Americans who went to camp meetings and for Catholics and the Irish. She abhorred the institution of slavery but tried to understand the slaveowner, rather than seeing him as a monster, in order to more effectively conduct a dialogue with him.[31]

She and her husband Caleb rejected the Know-Nothing movement. It represented a drift toward anti-immigrant and anti-Catholic sentiments and proslavery sympathies. Know-Nothingism split the Whig party apart and in 1855 seemed to be on the verge of winning consequential national power. Caleb, she writes, was unhappy about the direction the Whigs were taking and uncertain about the leadership of the new Republican party. Yet, he did not "fall back upon the rum and pro-slavery Whigs, but . . . really succeeded in maintaining an independent position." The next year, Caleb went over to the Republicans, and she wrote excitedly to Margaret E. White: "We are all for 'Free speech, free press, free soil, free men, *Fremont* and victory!' It is the first electioneering campaign that I ever felt like going into, and I do it with my whole heart."[32]

When she died in 1857, an obituary published in the 29 December *Salem Gazette*, written by her minister, Rev. Charles Lowe, praised her "uncommon powers of intellect . . . vigorous imagination, sound judgment, and retentive memory." It took note of her remarkably extensive reading, saying she was "acquainted with most of the literature of the day, and her estimate of books was singularly accurate and reliable." Hers was a "large and loving heart and eminently religious nature."[33] A great deal of his mother would rub off on Arthur Foote, either through natural inheritance or through her nurturing during his first four years of life.

In addition, both his father and his grandfather, Judge White, were worthy of emulation. Both men, as Doric Alviani writes, were prominent members of Salem society and actively involved in strengthening its cultural institutions—its libraries, museums, musical groups, literary societies, lecture series, and concerts. Alviani then concludes: "The impact of these two men on Arthur Foote revealed itself in his sensitivity to community service, respect for the individual differences of people, awareness of patterns for gracious living, and, most of all, an interest in the humanities."[34]

Brother and Sister

Henry Wilder Foote (1838–1889) was a kind and loving mentor to his much younger brother Arthur during his growing years. Arthur would come to trust him and accept his guidance as he grew up. Immediately after graduating from Harvard Divinity School in 1861, Henry served as minister to King's Chapel in Boston until his death on 29 May 1889. King's Chapel, as his son Henry Foote II explains, clung to the "conservative Channing Unitarianism" in which Henry had been brought up. William Ellery Channing (1780–1842) was a founder of the American Unitarian Association in 1825, and an advocate of humanitarianism, religious tolerance, and the abolition of slavery. He had an influence on Emerson and other Transcendentalists.

Henry Foote was never strong or vigorous. He was described as easily fatigued and afflicted with what was called a "weak throat."[35] His son, Henry Foote II, also a Unitarian minister, portrays him as "a painstaking scholar, gentle, warmhearted and wise." Winslow Warren writes that he held liberal views but in many ways was conservative and cautious. Although prepared to courageously accept the findings of modern science, he arrived slowly at decisions if they necessitated a renunciation of one or more of his prior convictions. Anything he accepted came as a result of much thought. Above all, says Warren, he would follow "no guide but that of his own honest head and heart."[36] In these descriptions of Henry's character, we find much that accurately describes Arthur, who adored and may have modeled himself after his older brother. In short, father, mother, and brother made contributions to the formation of Arthur's character and foreshadowed his love of music.

In 1863, Henry married Frances Anne Eliot, daughter of Samuel Atkins Eliot, congressman, mayor of Boston, and a founder of the Boston Academy of Music. She was sister to Charles Eliot, president of Harvard. They had four children. She and Henry loved music and compiled a hymnbook for use in King's Chapel. After Henry died, his widow, brother Arthur, and sister Mary completed *Hymns of the Church Universal*, on which Henry had started work. It was published in 1890.[37] Here are other possible influences on the musical direction the young Arthur was to take.

Mary Wilder Foote (1843–1934) conscientiously took over the upbringing of her brother Arthur after their mother died. She was a young girl of fourteen at the time. Like the rest of the Foote family, her Christian faith was strong and served to guide her life. Her rule over her brother was gentle hearted, understanding, and sensitive to his needs. She married John Boies Tileston in 1865 and, owing to her husband's poor health, had to contribute largely to her own family's living by editing books, writes her grandson John T. Edsall. He adds that she prepared books for publication "made up of selections from classical authors. The best known was 'Daily Strength for Daily Needs,' [1882] which had a wide sale and was reprinted a number of times. She had seven children."[38]

Arthur always spoke with love of his two siblings, Henry and Mary, and with gratitude over their sympathetic concern for him. He never hesitated to turn to them with his problems and respected the guidance they offered him.

Arthur Foote's First Years in Salem

In a letter to her brother Henry, dated Sunday, 6 March 1853, nine-year-old Mary wrote in excitement: "I went to Mr. Treadwell's, Miss Ward's, Mrs. Hoppen's, Mrs. Frothingham's and many other places in order to tell them that we had got a baby [*sic*]. He is a boy, and was born last night [Saturday, 5 March] between 8 and 9 o'clock. Father went to Lynn to get a wet nurse."[39] Arthur's mother was forty-three at the time and had already lost three of her children—Eliza, born in 1836, died at fourteen months; William, born in 1841, died at eighteen months; Martha, born in 1842, died at eight weeks. Only Henry and Mary had lived beyond babyhood. Almost ten years after Mary, Arthur was born.

The happy mother wrote in her journal on 27 March: "It is exquisitely delightful to me again to press a little satin cheek that is all my own, and it seems to me as if the floods of tenderness had accumulated instead of drying up."[40] In a letter to her sister Eliza in October she continues in a state of delight: "My baby has been much worried by coming teeth this week, and is a great *moth* of time and strength, but it is happily put into me to like the creature and *call it fun.*"[41] As the weeks went by, she decided: "He is not going to be pretty, his features are too faulty but he has a good look of sweetness and sense when you fairly look into his face and the sweetest thing about him is the total absence of sullenness."[42]

By two years of age, Arthur had become quite attached to his parents. If his mother wanted "to get away from Artie," she had to distract him with a piece of gingerbread or with his blocks; otherwise he complained vociferously. At times Arthur overslept and his father left for work before he awakened. On one occasion when this happened, the child came down for breakfast, but turned "away disgusted even from the pears he [his father] has left for a souvenir, and sits looking like a forsaken lover," says his mother. "I always delight in every triumph of mind and soul over the more animal nature, and to see a child love his father more than a Seckel pear is charming."[43] She was pleased at Arthur's developing sense of compassion when he was three years of age: "Saturday morning, a little girl came into the kitchen to ask for charity while he was eating his dinner. He picked up the import of her message, and, jumping down from his high chair, carried his plate of rice to her, saying, 'Little girl, take Artie's dinner. Artie is sorry you are cold.'" Nevertheless, he was not always good at three. Once he left home without permission, exhibiting a will of his own. His mother wrote into her journal: "I was at Mrs. Cole's, and, looking out of the window, saw a cotton umbrella going by which seemed to belong to a *short* person. Who should be beneath it but my Arthur, followed by a train of little boys and girls! I seized him by the hand, and peremptorily led him home."[44]

Apparently, little Arthur misbehaved more than once or twice. When he was five years of age, he received a letter from his brother Henry,[45] who advised him:

My dear little boy.
   BE GOOD AND LOVING.
   DO WHAT AUNTIE PEIRSON SAYS.
   TRY NOT TO BE *NAUGHTY*
   SO AS TO BE SENT INTO THE STUDY.
   GET YOUR LESSONS AT SCHOOL.
   IF YOU ARE GOOD I SHALL
LOVE YOU.
   KISS YOUR LITTLE MAMMA
   AND GIVER HER THE LETTER.
      YOUR BROTHER,
      HENRY W. FOOTE

The first hint of a bent toward music came when he was almost four. His mother wrote in a letter dated 22 February 1857: "This bright, hopeful Sunday morning puts a new spirit within me. My heart dances with joy, as unconscious of *why* as Arthur is when he moves to the music of his brother's whistling."[46] But her joy was short-lived. In the fall, her son Henry became seriously ill with typhoid fever, and for weeks she watched over his sick bed, exhausting herself as she did so. At the end, "the descending Angel of Death came slowly down—not, as it had been feared, to the cherished son but to the beloved mother." She died of typhoid fever on 23 December 1857, at the age of forty-seven.[47]

"There were, as I grew up," Arthur says, "only my father and sister Mary, who, though in 1857 a girl of fourteen, was my 'little mamma.'"[48] He spoke proudly of his father. He praised his "able and fearless" editorials in the *Gazette*, in particular his courageous exposé of Ben Butler's corruption, something the Boston papers feared to run. "I remember the campaign of Butler against Dana (father of my classmate). For some time (after having abandoned my plan of being a railroad engineer) I expected eventually to succeed my father as editor. Indeed, I did not think of music as a profession until after leaving college." He said his father led a secluded life, devoting much of his time to the paper. Yet, on Sundays he did find time to take "a good walk" with young Arthur, "not seldom to the cemetery at Harmony Grove [where his mother was buried]. I look back and realize how little I understood of my father's solitary life for almost forty years. If we only had in early youth something of the sympathy and understanding that comes to us later!"[49]

We have watched as the baby grew into boyhood under his mother's special care and sway. From diaper days on, Arthur responded to his family and surroundings, acquiring patterns of behavior and being advised how to deal with the variety of sentiments arising within him. He could not help but be influenced by the manners and opinions of his parents and his siblings. Certainly his experiences were mostly benign, and the people with whom he interacted were kind and solicitous. Inner and outer forces were combining to affect an early outlook upon which his future might be predicated.

Growing Up in Salem

In his autobiography, Foote speaks nostalgically about the modest but comfortable house in which he was raised. He liked its large garden, fruit trees, berry bushes, and box borders. Caleb Foote gave little Arthur three of the pear trees to be his very own. Only the smell of the Boston Street tanneries marred the recollection. The Footes could reach Boston by railroad in forty-five minutes. They attended the North [Unitarian] Church, although his nurse Bridget occasionally took Arthur to a Catholic church on Federal Street. Every Saturday, he remembered, he would go out through the garden, cross the street, and leave a pot of beans to be baked for Sunday's breakfast. He enjoyed the fire fighters' Saturday afternoon practice and would show up to pull on the bar that pumped the water. Boyhood amusements were few. Golf, tennis, and football were unknown to him. (He took up golf and tennis as an adult.) He did play "kick-a-ball" and a kind of baseball. Sailing and rowing a dory to Beverly or Danversport was fun for him. He enjoyed practicing on a trapeze in a nearby gymnasium (where he "grew rather expert," although he had "small muscular ability"). He also took dancing lessons at Papanti's.

Arthur's first schooling was at Ma'am Baker's children's school on Chestnut Street, then at Daddy Waters' boys' school close by Salem Common. He learned little here and when he was "between eleven and twelve" was placed in the Hacker Grammar School. The new school offered better instruction and showed up the deficiencies in his earlier education. Later, in Salem High School, he had "one fine teacher," John W. Perkins, who helped him acquire some further knowledge. He played the piano for the classes when they marched in to their desks. In addition, Arthur formed a small students' society, assisted in editing a "quasi-newspaper," and tried his hand at musical and theatrical criticism for this juvenile journal. Meanwhile, his grades were excellent. However, "I was never taught to think or observe, these qualities, to whatever degree I possess them, coming later in life. The truth is that we merely learned to recite, retaining little when classes were over." A benefit from attending high school was the little shop across the street, where he could buy and enjoy "three-cent turnovers, mince and apple," and an assortment of candies.

He of course had boyhood friends. Among his earliest playmates were Jack and Frank Peabody, George Silsbee, "Chad" Tuckerman, and Dudley Pickman. In high school, his companions were Ernest and Billy Fenollosa (whose father was a locally respected pianist), Fred Emerton, Frank Spinney, George Jewett, and Lewis Osborne.[50]

His letters to brother Henry afford glimpses into his adolescent life. He wrote, on 23 July 1869, of giving a comic declamation, "Daniel and Dishclout," at a school exhibition: "I noticed one man in particular who 'didn't laugh when he ought to' and said to myself, 'Well, old fellow! I'm going to make you laugh before I get through anyway!' And at last, after a good deal of winking, I succeeded." About two years later, in a letter dated "Aug. 2nd" only, he said: "I am having a very good time, even if it is a little slow—I have hired, with another fellow, a dory for the rest of vacation for $5 apiece, very reasonable—as the old man charged $15 at first till he was talked down." He went on to write that he had taken a steamer excursion to Provincetown: "It was really quite rough, quite two-thirds [on board] were sick. It also rained most of the time quite hard. I enjoyed it very much, though, as I always do such scrapes." He ended by telling his brother that he was debating joining "a schooner sail of about a week." On 30 July 1872, he wrote about visiting the Rev. William White, in Keene, New Hampshire: "The Church Centennial was more successful than anybody had expected and Dr. Loring had the cheek to say emphatically that the North was a parochial paradise (like Mr. Bumble) and no minister had ever been obliged to leave. . . . The speeches were good but some of the very old ministers were dreadfully long winded."[51]

What we learn from the letters of Arthur Foote and his family is that father, mother, brother, and sister shared a love and concern for each other. Already as a youngster, Arthur was showing signs of loyalty, humor, and charity toward others. That he had a high intelligence and a capacity for learning was quite evident. He had demonstrated some ability to look at himself and others objectively, whatever his convictions. Moreover, he had a mind of his own, which could cause him, if he was so inclined, to refuse to conform to one or more of Salem's standards or to refuse to accept things as they are.

Notes

1.   See Edward W. Said, *Musical Elaborations* (New York: Columbia University Press, 1991), 37.

2.   Mary Wilder Tileston, ed., *Caleb and Mary Wilder Foote* (Boston: Houghton Mifflin, 1918), 295. The date of arrival is given as 1634 in *The National Cyclopedia of American Biography*, vol. 27 (New York: White, 1939), s.v. "Foote, Arthur." Frederick Edward Kopp, "Arthur Foote: American Composer and Theorist" (Ph.D. diss., Eastman School of Music, University of Rochester, 1957), 294, gives the date as around 1630.

3.   Alfred North Whitehead, *The Aims of Education* (New York: Macmillan, 1929), 151–52; Henry Bamford Parkes, *The American Experience* (New York: Vintage, 1959), 191–92, 195–96; Henry Steele Commager, *The American Mind* (New Haven: Yale University Press, 1950), 23.

4. Walter Raymond Spalding, *Music at Harvard* (New York: Coward-McCann, 1935), 21–22.

5. For an informative discussion of Unitarianism and Transcendentalism, see Merle Curti, "Psychological Theories in American Thought," in *Dictionary of the History of Ideas*, vol. 4, ed. Philip P. Wiener (New York: Scribner's Sons, 1973), 23–24.

6. Their letters and reminiscences, as found in Tileston, ed., *Caleb and Mary Wilder Foote*, support what I have just written.

7. Arthur Foote, "Music in the United States," (lecture delivered at the University of California at Berkeley, 1911; MS at the Boston Public Library, shelf no. **M.472.134, no. 1042; see pp. 1, 24.

8. Rupert Hughes, *Contemporary American Composers* (Boston: Page, 1900), 14.

9. Arthur Foote, "A Bostonian Remembers," *Musical Quarterly* 23 (1937), 37.

10. Arthur Foote, *An Autobiography* (Norwood, Mass.: Plimpton Press, 1946), 13.

11. Tileston, ed., *Caleb and Mary Wilder Foote*, 179.

12. Foote, "Music in the United States," 5.

13. Olin Downes, "Works of Arthur Foote," *New York Times,* 18 April 1937, 5.

14. Kopp, "Arthur Foote," 27, states that Pasco and his brothers Caleb and Nathaniel came from Colchester, England, to Watertown, Massachusetts, in 1635. He states further that they had a genealogy that went back to landowners of the early fifteenth century and to Thomas Foote, Lord Mayor of London in the seventeenth century. Shortly after arriving in Watertown, Nathaniel left for Connecticut and Pasco for Salem. However, in a letter dated 9 May 1995, Arthur Foote II states that he doubts "if Kopp got Pasco's ancestry right, or that he was Nathaniel's brother, or that there was a third brother named Caleb. Pasco and Nathaniel may have been brothers but it seems unlikely. In any case they promptly went their separate ways. Nathaniel's descendants from Wethersfield, CT. are legion. Their genealogical albums mention the Pasco line as a separate one, only possibly related."

15. "Abstracts from Wills, Inventories, etc. on file in the Office of Clerk of Courts, Salem, Mass.," comp. Ira J. Patch, in *Historical Collections of the Essex Institute*, vol. 2 (Salem: Essex Institute, 1860), 70: "Pasca Foot, 4th mo. 1671. Will of Pasca ffoot senior of Salem, dated 21 Sept. 1670,

mentions son ——, daughters Elizabeth, Mary ffoot, sons Samuel and Pasco, dau. Abigail ffoot, in court 30 4, '71."

16.   "Reminiscences of the Revolution, Prison Letters and Sea Journal of Caleb Foot: Born, 1750, Died 1787," compiled by his grandson and namesake, Caleb Foote, in *Historical Collections of the Essex Institute*, vol. 26 (Salem: Essex Institute, 1889), 90–93. An unidentified clipping, from 1889 that discusses the life of Caleb Foote is contained in the first of three scrapbooks compiled by Arthur Foote, now in the Boston Public Library, shelf no. *ML.46.F65. Henry Foote II, in an unpublished MS that gives an account of the Foote family's history, states on p. 9 that Caleb died in the West Indies, possibly of yellow fever.

17.   In Tileston, ed., *Caleb and Mary Wilder Foote*, 291. The name change is mentioned by Henry Foote II in his unpublished MS, p. 15.

18.   Ibid., 47–48. She had become engaged to Caleb on 21 January 1835. They married 21 October 1835; see Tileston, ed., *Caleb and Mary Wilder Foote*, 46, 49.

19.   Henry Foote II, unpublished MS, p.12.

20.   Harriet Silvester Tapley, *Salem Imprints, 1768–1825* (Salem, Mass.: Essex Institute, 1927), 76–77. Henry Foote II, in his unpublished MS, p. 12, states that his grandfather at age 17 became office boy at the *Salem Gazette*.

21.   Tileston, 331–32. The date of his becoming the master is given as 1829 in Tileston, 332, but William Leavitt, "History of the Essex Lodge of Freemasons," in *Historical Collections of the Essex Institute*, vol. 18 (Salem, Mass.: Essex Institute, 1881), 255, writes, "Admitted to the Lodge 4th Jan., 1825, and its Master 1830, 1831, and 1832."

22.   Ibid., 330.

23.   Ibid., 334.

24.   This is what Caleb states in his autobiography, ibid., 322, 337. His wife wrote to her sister Eliza, 7 January 1838, that he was elected to the Governor's Council, "which will oblige him to go to Boston on Tuesday, for two or three months." Arthur Foote saved a newspaper clipping from around the fall of 1888, in Scrapbook I, now in the Boston Public Library, shelf no. *ML.46.F65, which notes his father's retirement from the *Gazette* and adds that "he has been a member of the State Senate, and filled other offices to the perfect acceptance of his fellow citizens."

25.   Tileston, 347. Henry Foote II, in his unpublished MS, p. 12, says that Caleb served the term 1833–34 in the Massachusetts House of Repre-

sentatives and for short periods was member of the Governor's Council and was postmaster of Salem.

26. Edith Lane, "Arthur Foote, Massachusetts' Own Musician," MS now at the Essex Institute, shelf no. E F688.3L 19–. A copy may be found in the Arthur Williams Collection, Williams College, Williamstown, Massachusetts. Edith Lane was a student of Foote, studying harmony with him in 1907, piano in the 1920s and again in 1937, just before he died.

27. Tileston, ed., *Caleb and Mary Wilder Foote*, 3, 7.

28. Ibid., 31, 33. In a letter to Douglas Moore dated 27 May 1993 and now in the Arthur Foote Collection, Arthur Foote II also writes that he has found several parlor songs by British musicians that had once belonged to Arthur's mother, three of them signed "Mary W. White."

29. Ibid., 39–40, 41, 71, 90–91, respectively.

30. Ibid., 41–42, 121–22.

31. Ibid, 179, 102, 165, 167-68, respectively.

32. Ibid., 222, 237–38.

33. "Mrs. Mary W. Foote, *Salem Gazette*, 29 December 1857," clipping at the Essex Institute and included in a folder, shelf no. BR 920.F68.

34. Doric Alviani, "The Choral Church Music of Arthur William Foote" (S.M.D. diss., Union Theological Seminary, 1962), 3.

35. Henry Foote II, unpublished MS, 18, 20.

36. Winslow Warren, "Memoir of Rev. Henry W. Foote," *Publication of the Massachusetts Historical Society* (May 1893), 250.

37. Arthur Foote II, *Henry Wilder Foote, Hymnologist* (New York: Hymn Society of America, 1968), 3–4. Arthur Foote II has also supplied me with detailed family trees of the descendants of Caleb Foote.

38. A letter of John T. Edsall dated 15 September 1982, which Arthur Foote II contributed to the Arthur Foote Collection in November 1994.

39. The letter is in the Arthur Foote Collection.

40. Tileston, ed., *Caleb and Mary Wilder Foote*, 187.

41. Ibid., 192. The letter is dated 29 October 1853. "Moth" refers to something or someone that little by little eats or, as in this instance, uses up a person.

42. Quoted in Lane, "Arthur Foote, Massachusetts' Own Musician."

43. Tileston, ed., *Caleb and Mary Wilder Foote*, 221–22. The first quote is from a letter dated 25 February 1855, sent to Margaret E. White; the second, from a letter dated 14 October 1855, sent to Catherine E. Frothingham.

44. Ibid., 227–28, 231–32, respectively. The first quotation is from a letter dated 28 January 1856, sent to William O. White; the second, a journal entry, dated 23 April 1856.

45. The letter was sent in 1858, day and month unknown, and is in the Arthur Foote Collection.

46. Tileston, ed., *Caleb and Mary Wilder Foote*, 261. The letter was sent to Caroline E. Frothingham.

47. "In Memoriam," *Salem Register*, around the end of December 1857, clipping included in a folder at the Essex Institute, Shelf no. BR 920.F68. The date of death, 23 December 1857, is given by Henry Foote II in his unpublished MS, p. 16.

48. Arthur Foote, *An Autobiography*, 11.

49. Ibid., 26–28. Many Americans during and after the Civil War regarded Benjamin Butler as a notoriously corrupt demagogue.

50. Ibid., 12, 14–19, for the sources of this and the previous paragraph.

51. These letters are in the Arthur Foote Collection.

2

Salem Days

The first indication that Arthur Foote was taking an interest in musical study came in a letter that Caleb Foote sent to his son Henry on 17 July 1865: "We are all very well. Arthur is passing through another stage. Having passed through astronomy, locomotives, and rebuses, he is just plunging into music, which absorbs him, for the moment, like a passion. I have engaged lessons for him on the piano which he is to begin tomorrow."[1] Arthur's father was skeptical about his son's new interests and expected music to be a thing of the moment. Nothing in the family's or Arthur's previous background indicated a strong musical strain or a firm disposition to take up a musical career.

Arthur's sister Mary had received piano lessons from Manuel Fenollosa, born in Spain and father of Arthur's chums Ernest and Billy. Her example undoubtedly stimulated him, possibly exciting envy. Whatever the cause, his interest in music endured. However, for an unexplained reason, Arthur did not study with Manuel Fenollosa. His piano teacher was Fanny Paine (not related to the composer John Knowles Paine). She had been a student of Benjamin Johnson Lang of Boston. She gave Arthur *Richardson's New Method* to study and stressed finger dexterity, but taught him next to nothing about phrasing, pedaling, and expression. The piano on which he practiced was a square Chickering with a very light action.[2]

His interest in music was not "for the moment," as his father expected. On 5 March 1866, Arthur wrote to his brother Henry

and sister-in-law Frances, thanking them for the (birthday?)
present of Mendelssohn's *Songs without Words*, which he found
"very pretty, and are none too hard." He planned to take them
up "for lessons," and would play selections for them when they
came to Salem. He sent them kisses, marked:

At the end of the year he persisted with his music. In addition, he was avidly reading issues of *Dwight's Journal of Music*,
which arrived every week in his father's office in exchange for
copies of the *Salem Gazette*. Its editor, John Sullivan Dwight of
Boston, had conservative tastes and a regard mostly for the utterly serious Germanic music of elevated expression from the
past—Bach, Handel, and Beethoven, especially. He rejected operatic and programmatic music completely, whether of Wagner,
Verdi, Berlioz, or Liszt, and looked askance at the increased
chromaticism, harmonic complexity, and emotionality found in
most contemporary music, not excluding that of Brahms. His
prejudices ran deep, but his sincere love for the music that attracted him had a profound effect on the tastes of educated and
culturally aspiring Americans of the time. In the eighties, his day
would be over. He would be regarded as a rigid reactionary
whose views were not in keeping with the times.

As an adolescent, Foote was fascinated by the information
and opinions expressed in *Dwight's Journal*:

> I cannot be too grateful for its influence on my taste and
> knowledge. Dwight (a retired parson) was not a thor-
> oughly educated musician but a man of sensibility and
> cultivation, with a sincere appreciation of what was best in
> music, and with the advantage of having as counselor,
> Otto Dresel. Dresel was a man of thorough knowledge,
> real talent in composition, a pianist of exquisite taste and
> feeling, profound convictions as to what was best and

what was negligible, and consequently with pretty strong prejudices, as later against Brahms and Wagner (He used to say that he would not sleep in the same room with a Wagner score). Dresel in after years was to be for me an inspiration.[3]

When his musical tastes were in the formative stage, Foote received an early introduction to the views and values of two archtraditionalists through *Dwight's Journal*. Later, when he moved to Boston, he met and exchanged views with both men directly. He may have first met Dwight during the 1869–70 season of symphony concerts sponsored by the Harvard Musical Association. An admission pass from that time, issued by Dwight, reads, "Admit Mr. F. H. Lee & friend [Foote] to Symphony Concert Rehearsal."[4] It was only at a later date (around 1874) that more forward-looking musicians, especially B. J. Lang, would counteract this overly conservative influence.

Foote discovered the music of Robert Schumann through a selection of pieces from *Kreisleriana* ("which I thought was the most beautiful music I had ever seen"). It had come as a supplement to a New York musical journal, which the *Gazette* received in a reciprocal arrangement. During 1867, his father, accompanied by Henry, was in London. He returned to Salem with the E-flat Nocturne (op. 9) of Chopin and a few Beethoven sonatas as presents for his younger son. Arthur later said that one of the sonatas was "Op. 10, No. 3, the slow movement of which made an impression that has lasted through the years. And how I did revel in the slow movement of the Fifth Symphony when I discovered it a little later."[5] The statement is significant in the light of later comments on his own compositions from contemporary writers on music, who often observed that Foote had a penchant for slow movements and that even his allegros could at times sound more like andantes.[6]

A letter from Caleb Foote to his sister-in-law, Mrs. William Dwight, dated 2 December 1867, admits that the boy's musical interests had not flagged. He writes: "Arthur is much interested in music, just now, and plays with ease and pleasure the difficult pieces of Mendelssohn and Beethoven." Apparently, his father, far from objecting to Arthur's music making, was rather proud of it.

No written record exists that shows him or anybody else trying to discourage Arthur's growing engrossment in music. On the contrary, his father and siblings provided him with music and whatever other materials he needed for his musical studies. This encouragement is somewhat surprising, given the contemporary prejudices against the pursuit of music as an occupation, especially for males.

The youngster had also become interested in attending concerts, whether in Salem or Boston. He wrote to his brother Henry, on 7 November 1867, about having taken up Greek in addition to Latin and tells him that his friends have nicknamed him "doughnut Foote." Then follows an attempt to write "doughnut Foote" in Greek. He continues with a wistful lament: "The Harvard Symphony concerts began today. I wish I could go." It is evident that he wanted his admired brother's approval of his school studies, especially when he concludes his letter with "my average for September and October were 3.64 and 3.65"; declamation earned him a 3.5; composition, a 3.55—"which are quite good." One also detects an attempt to convince his brother Henry (and, through Henry, his father), that his devotion to his studies was worthy of reward. At any rate, Arthur did go to concerts. On 5 March 1870, he wrote to his brother, saying that he has heard and now thinks "the concerto in *F* minor of Freddie Chopin is a superb thing."[7] The nonchalance of the adolescent shows through this comment.

Further awakening his interest in music were the Peace Jubilee of 1869 and the World Peace Jubilee and International Music Festival of 1872, both held in Boston and organized by Patrick Gilmore. These celebrations featured "monster" concerts performed by massive numbers of choralists and instrumentalists. Talking about the Jubilees, in 1911, Foote said: "These monstrosities were counterbalanced by the immense amount of good done through the formation of choruses in towns everywhere, that came together and spread familiarity, with works like the 'Creation' and 'Messiah.'"[8] Arthur had joined the Salem Oratorio Society, which participated in the Jubilees, and learned to sing in oratorios like Handel's *Messiah*, Haydn's *Creation*, and Mendelssohn's *Elijah*. Foote said later: "I sang in the Salem [Oratorio Society] chorus, and, as one of it, was present at the concerts of this Jubilee [of 1869], as also at those of its successor in 1872. . . . They had a marked effect in awakening a real interest in good music."[9] The Society, consisting of 260 members, had been formed in 1868 under Carl Zerrahn. It had presented its first concert in February 1869 with a presentation of *The Creation*. An unidentified newspaper clipping from 1899, which Foote preserved, claims: "At fourteen, his [Foote's] enthusiasm for Mendelssohn's 'Elijah' constrained him to try his hand at writing new music—which he now calls 'funny'—for the first chorus of that work."[10] I have not been able to locate this music.

Two Salem men, musically somewhat on the conservative side, befriended the young Arthur. John Francis Tuckerman and Henry Kemble Oliver, better known as General Oliver, also encouraged his involvement with music. John Tuckerman, a medical doctor whom Arthur describes as a gifted amateur musician, came to Salem in 1852 and was a persuasive advocate for the "cultivation of a purer and higher style of music." He composed some sacred compositions, sang tenor, and led the choir of first the North Church and later of Grace Church until his death in 1885. Because Dr. Tuckerman was father of his friend "Chad," Arthur would surely have seen him often. Nevertheless, General Oliver (1800–1885) had a far more significant effect on Arthur's musical life. He forcefully urged the cultivation of music other than the popular variety on Salemites, including Arthur. He involved himself with the Salem Glee Club, supervised Salem's Mozart Society, and was president of the Salem Oratorio Society. As if this were not enough, he also played organ at three churches, taught in Salem's public and private schools, found time to go to Boston and sing with the Handel and Haydn Society, and contributed to the activities of the Harvard Musical Association. General Oliver was said to have a thorough knowledge of theory and composition, and, of even more interest, "his advice was often sought by and always most cheerfully given to the younger and less experienced in the domain of music," writes George Whipple, in an article on Salem's musical history. Arthur Foote says of the two men: "They were both extremely kind to me, and I now see that their encouragement had great influence on my future."[11]

General Oliver was born in Beverly, Massachusetts. As he grew up, he attended Boston Latin School, Phillips Academy, Har-

vard College, and Dartmouth College. He was mayor for a time of
Lawrence and then Salem, Massachusetts; later, from 1861 to
1865, he was Treasurer of Massachusetts and, still later, head of
the state's Department of Labor. In music his tastes seem to have
run the gamut from the old choral works of William Billings to a
few midcentury compositions by European artists. He was the
composer of the well-known hymn tune "Federal Street," in 1832,
as well as other hymn tunes that were also highly regarded in
their time—"Beacon Street," "Grove," "Harmony," "Hudson," and
"Morning." At the Peace Jubilee of 1872, Oliver conducted a chorus of twenty thousand in "Federal Street." He and Dr. Tuckerman put out the hymn tune collection *The National Lyre* in 1848,
in which appear many tunes by Oliver himself. In 1860, he issued
Oliver's Collection of Hymn and Psalm Tunes; in 1875, *Oliver's
Original Hymn-Tunes*.[12] In his old age, Foote acknowledged Oliver's interest in him and said of his hymn-tunes: "There was little
of harmonic interest in them (mostly I, IV, V), but they still hold
their own in our New England churches, and are from association
dear to many."[13]

We cannot doubt that the boy Arthur heard and sang hymn
tunes, whether recently written or traditional to New England,
both in church and in his home, although he does not definitely
say so. His mother's letters and journal entries show his parents
engaged in such singing, and there is every reason to believe similar activities continued as Arthur grew up. His brother, Rev. Henry Foote, devoted a great deal of his attention to hymn tunes,
gathering and carefully studying them. Arthur and his sister Mary
would eventually complete and publish a collection of hymn
tunes that Henry had left unfinished at his death. The two would
also issue their own hymn tune collection.[14]

Arlo Bates, a friend from Arthur's adult years, describes in
The Pagans (which was published in 1888) an evening in a New
England home that must have closely paralleled some evenings
in the Foote household:

> They fell into silence . . . the twilight deepening until only
> the glow of the fire lighted the room. Edith went to the
> piano and played a bit of Mozart, wandering off then into

the hymn-tunes which she loved and which were familiar
in all orthodox homes of the last generation: plaintive
Olmutz and stately *Geneva*, aspiring *Amsterdam* and
resonant *St. Martin's*, placid *Boylston* and grand *Hamburg*, *Nuremberg*, *Benevento*, *Turner* and *Old Hundred*;
the times of our fathers, the melodies which embody the
spirit of the old time New England Sabbath, a day heavy,
constrained and narrow, it may be; but, too, a day calm,
unworldly and pure.[15]

The Beginning of Music Studies in Boston

Foote states that after he had studied piano for two years (around
1867), Fanny Paine took him to her old teacher, B. J. Lang, for an
audition. We must have reservations about her pedagogic abilities, for Foote says of this event: "After performing the Chopin A-
flat Ballade to her and my satisfaction, I remember asking Lang
what those curved line (slurs) above the notes meant." Assuredly
the question flabbergasted Lang. Yet, no record was made of
Lang's reaction to the boy's playing, except that he advised him to
go to Stephen A. Emery for lessons in harmony.

Stephen Emery (1841–1891) was born in Paris, Maine. He
had traveled to Leipzig in 1862 in order to study in its conservatory of music under Ernst Friedrich Richter, Moritz Hauptmann, and
Benjamin Papperitz. In 1864, he was in Portland, Maine. Three
years later, he was in Boston teaching at the newly established
New England Conservatory of Music. He also would teach at Boston University's college of music. The New England Conservatory
had its inauguration concert on 30 January 1867 and opened its
doors on 20 February 1867 with thirteen in its faculty. Among Emery's other students were the composers Horatio Parker, Ethelbert Nevin, and Henry Hadley. Emery himself would compose
mostly songs and piano compositions, as well as some string
quartets. Moreover, he would publish *Elements of Harmony* in
1880 and *Foundation Studies in Pianoforte Playing* in 1882.[16]

An undated slip of paper that Foote pasted into one of his
scrapbooks contains a laconic handwritten reminder:

N.E. Cons. From Mr. Emery
Monday Th 2 PM Wed 9 AM

Richter Harmony trans. By Morgen

Cherubini Counterpoint trans. By Novello.[17]

Lehrbuch der Harmonie by Ernst Friedrich Richter was first published in 1853; *Cours de Contrepoint et de la Fugue* by Luigi Cherubini in 1835. Foote disliked the Richter text, calling it "dry and with nothing but figured basses for exercises. It was a book so full of rules about what to do and what not to do as to make one giddy."[18] An unidentified clipping, with the date "1899" in Foote's handwriting appearing at the top of it, informs us:

> He soon began study with Stephen A. Emery in harmony. Mr. Foote remarks that the difference between that day and this is shown in the fact that the progress of the class of three was abruptly ended by the withdrawal of two of its members—I am sorry to say they were girls—because when Suspensions were reached, they literally had enough of musical theory.[19]
>
> Foote himself comments: "At the Conservatory there were three in my class (one of them a colored girl), but by the time we got half-way through the book [Richter] I was left alone."[20]

Two compositions by Foote are extant that were supposed to have been written while he was studying with Emery but probably date from an earlier time. They are now in the Arthur Foote Collection, Williams College—a four-page "Andante" for piano with a legend written in the left margin: "Arthur W. Foote. May 15th, 1869" and a five-page "The Sands of Dee," a song with an "Alto-Baritone" part in the treble clef and a piano accompaniment below it. At the top of the first page, "A. W. Foote" appears on the left, the song's title in the middle, and "Words by Charles Kingsley" on the right; at the bottom of the page, Foote writes the date "July 16th, 1869." Neither piece is complimentary to Emery as a teacher or to Foote as a composer. One looks in vain for signs of precociousness in the adolescent. Both compositions break off before they are completed. Examples 1a and 1b reproduce the first page of each work.

The "Andante" has no time signature, although the piece is evidently in ³/₄ time. The key signature contains four sharps (E-major). Foote is uncertain of the order of the sharps, since the C-sharp and the D-sharp are transposed. Dynamics are indicated. A first section closes with a perfect cadence in E-major, a double bar, and the word *Fine*. A second section, incomplete, has only the music for the right hand sketched in and is evidently in B-major. The treble has the five-sharp key signature F-sharp, C-sharp, G-sharp, F-sharp (!), D-sharp; the bass also has a five-sharp signature: F-sharp, C-sharp, A-sharp, G-sharp, D-sharp. The entire piece is awkwardly written. It makes an uncertain attempt at carrying out a musical idea and handling chromatics. Nor do any of the ideas have much musical merit. Nothing hangs together. The sixteenth-note chordal stream in measure 3 makes liberal use of seventh chords but does not sound correct. The ensuing trill on the high B tone, with the sixteenth-note passage in thirds below, is ineffective. A lyrical idea begins in the fourth brace but is abandoned after eight measures. Clearly, he does not know how to expand on an idea and write convincing continuations. He constantly breaks off and begins anew. Yet, the "Andante" does show his desire to compose music at the very start of his musical studies, however limited his technical knowledge and experience.

"The Sands of Dee," dated two months later, is marginally better written. Notes are set down less as scratches and more distinctly as notes. Again, there is no time signature, but the piece is definitely in ⁴/₄. As with the "Andante," it is in E-major, although the sharps of the key signature are frequently set down in an incorrect order—the C-sharp often occurs first in the sequence (as in the order C-sharp, F-sharp, D-sharp, G-sharp). He demonstrates somewhat greater skill in handling harmony, as in the opening chords of tonic major, lowered submediant major, subdominant minor, and tonic major, and also in the alighting on the mediant minor at measure 11. The vocal melody holds together fairly well. At least the text, which calls on him to write a lengthier and more coherent tune, forces some discipline on him. The chromaticisms make more sense. Nevertheless the accompaniment is clumsily done, choppy, and uncongenial to the text.

Did Foote actually submit these pieces to Emery? No evidence of correction exists, even of the most obvious blunders. In his autobiography, Foote indicates that he may have shown these pieces to Lang or Emery in 1867.[21] Yet, the date 1869 on both works seems to contradict his statement. A most imperfect acquaintance with music, revealed in the manuscripts, would be more consistent with the earlier date. Interestingly, Caleb writes to "Artie boy" from Salem on 15 August 1869, telling him that he had obtained and sent to Arthur the book on thoroughbass that he desired. The cost, two dollars, was money well spent if his son came back "a tolerable swimmer."[22] Apparently Arthur was away on vacation, possibly with his Uncle William, in Keene, New Hampshire.

Harvard and John Knowles Paine

In 1869, Dr. Charles William Eliot (1834–1926) assumed the presidency of Harvard and immediately started developing it into a genuine university. When Foote entered as a freshman in 1870, the expansion was still in the future. The total number of students was less than eight hundred, and around seventy-five faculty members ministering to them. President Eliot was no stranger to Arthur Foote, since he was the brother of Henry Foote's wife Frances. However casual their relationship may have been previous to Foote's freshman year, Arthur would have appreciated the older man's positive views of music and his academic sponsorship of it as head of Harvard. Arthur's sister-in-law and her brother had grown up surrounded by music and had participated in domestic music making from childhood. When their father, Samuel, was mayor of Boston he helped Lowell Mason to introduce music into the Boston public schools. President Charles Eliot himself believed music to be of utmost value in exercising one's intellectual abilities, emancipating the imagination, and deepening the emotions.[23]

After Foote graduated from Harvard, he and Charles Eliot had a great deal to do with each other, especially in relation to music at Harvard. Eliot later said that he knew how important music was to America's culture and that he had tried as much as he could, "with admirable supporters," to strengthen Harvard's music department, "hoping that the influence of that department might spread through all the walks of life."[24] One of those supporters was Arthur Foote.

Foote, with his friend Ernest Fenollosa as roommate, lodged at Harvard's College House during his first year. For the next three years he lived alone at 49 Grays. He describes his board as costing around four dollars a week and being very plain. He did not mind this as much as he did the other students in the dining hall, whom he found to be "an ill-mannered lot." During his last two years, he dined "at a club table, which was fairly good, at six dollars a week, and more pleasant." Although his grandfather, Daniel A. White, had been a founder of Hasty Pudding, he did not opt for it. Instead, he chose to join the Pi Eta Society (11 October 1872), which gave mostly comic plays and musicals.[25] Some performances took place in neighboring towns, with Arthur at the piano and going by the name "Ernest Fabian." He says tongue in cheek about such performances (given by Pi Eta and the Harvard Glee Club, which he also joined), "The more alcoholic the town, the better its standing with us." Therefore New Bedford was a favorite.[26]

During his last two years, he led the twenty-member Harvard Glee Club, selecting "good" but not "highbrow" music for it.[27] At one time, his club joined with Harvard's Pierian Sodality to give a concert in Portland, Maine. Afterwards there was dancing. Foote writes:

> I shall probably never feel as proud as when, at that concert, Devens warbled "Seeing Nellie Home" in the most fetching manner, doing great execution among the girls, while I played the most fascinating accompaniments I could think up.[28]

Nevertheless, Walter Spalding states that under Foote's direction, the Glee Club achieved its "first high level of excellence both in type of music and in its rendering."[29] Foote, of course, appeared several times in his home town, Salem, both as pianist and as director of the Glee Club. In a concert given by Manuel

Fenollosa at the Essex Institute, Salem, on 26 January 1873, Ernest Fenollosa, bass, William Fenollosa, piano, and the Glee Club directed by Foote are listed "as assisting."[30]

The rank list for the Harvard freshmen of 1870–71 enters Foote as having an 86 percent average and standing tenth in a class of 91. In the sophomore year of 1871–72 his grades dropped. Greek and German are in the mid-nineties; Latin, rhetoric and history in the seventies; mathematics a poor 52 percent and elocution a miserable 40 percent. The junior-year lists marks in the sixty and fifty percentiles. Perhaps he was devoting too much time to his extracurricular activities. At any rate, his marks rose to the upper seventies and eighties during his senior year. Interestingly, this was the year he and another student enrolled in Paine's Music 3, in which he earned a 90 percent.[31]

A Harvard tuition bill, dated 15 March 1873, gives us some idea of the cost of a Harvard education for Foote:

Mr. A. W. Foote	To Harvard College, Dr.
Instruction and Library	100.00
Rent and Care of Room	50.00
Special repairs, by average	.40
Cash paid Cambridge Gas-light	
Company for Gas	3.58
Cash paid for Board at Thayer Club	63.64
Total	217.62

This bill is payable on or before 5th April, 1873.[32]

The bill above apparently includes a two-thirds annual charge for rent and tuition. There were, of course, music expenses. For example, Oliver Ditson billed him $24.33 for a four-month piano rental that ended on 4 May 1873. There was also a Ditson bill of $50.30, dated 17 May 1873, for a music purchase that included a volume of Schubert's songs, one of Schumann's, and two volumes of Chopin's piano music. Foote also purchased tickets for music performances like those of Anton Rubinstein in May 1873.[33]

Apparently, Arthur's brother Henry kept a watchful eye over his expenses at college, for we find Arthur somewhat guiltily writing to him from Cambridge, on 6 October 1873:

I went carefully yesterday over my acc. book which I shall
bring in tomorrow in order to show you. I found there
between $50 and $60 absolutely unnecessary expenditure
besides a large bill for music (of which I don't intend to
buy any this yr.) $45 for summer clothes for which won't
be nearly as much this yr. My piano also is going to cost
less this yr. And I intend to go to concerts and the theatre
much less. So with shirts, I shall not have to get one this yr.
While having very few last yr. I had to spend about $20 for
them. However, I shall see you again tomorrow AM and
we shall be able to speak about it with a more clear understanding on all points. You may think I don't appreciate
your kindness but I do, and if I ever *do* amount to anything it will be a great deal owing to you.[34]

An indication that he might amount to something came
when, at the end of his Harvard studies, he was elected Phi Beta
Kappa.[35]

Luckily for Foote, the composer John Knowles Paine (1839–
1906) was on the faculty of Harvard College, teaching a limited
number of music courses. Paine was born in Portland, Maine,
and studied music there under Hermann Kotschmar. He then
had studied organ in Berlin with Karl August Haupt and composition with Friedrich Wilhelm Wieprecht. He returned to Portland in 1861 as a thoroughly trained musician. A year later, he
won a teaching position at Harvard. This position he maintained,
despite some prominent faculty members' opposition to music
as an academic subject. Among Paine's students coming after
Foote were the composers Edward Burlingame Hill, Daniel Gregory Mason, Frederick S. Converse, and John Alden Carpenter.
Paine himself would gain renown as a composer for his *Mass in
D* (1865), oratorio *St. Peter* (1872), Symphony no. 1 and Symphony no. 2 (1875, 1879), Prelude and Incidental Music to *Oedipus Rex* (1881), and opera *Azara* (1903). Whatever their debt to
Germanic music, Paine's works were intended to blaze the way
toward a self-sustaining native art. He stated his ambition for
America in the *North American Review* (1873):

Who knows but that the musical sceptre may pass into the
hands of another and a younger people? As art-loving

Americans let us hope that it will be the mission of our own country to rejuvenate the life of music; may it be vouchsafed to her to lift the veil that now shrouds the future of this beautiful art![36]

Because he was fond of music, not because he had decided to take it up as his life's work, Foote enrolled in Paine's music courses. He still assumed he would eventually succeed his father as editor of the *Salem Gazette*. Of this period in his life, Foote observes:

I was unwise enough not to work at piano-playing in college, not realizing my inadequacy because I read rapidly and with understanding. But I did take Prof. John Knowles Paine's courses, and I owe him a great deal. In later years I came to know him intimately and to be fond of him. He was not one of the born teachers, but certainly he could give generously. Looking back at some of the fugues, etc., of which I have preserved the manuscripts, I am surprised to find how good the result of our work was. His influence was always for what was strong and good in music. After graduation I studied with him for another year, receiving in 1875 the degree of A.M. for work in music, the first time it was given in this country for excellence in that subject.[37]

Paine took great interest in teaching any student who wanted to study music seriously. Foote was such a student, and his relationship with Paine helped steer him "in the right direction at a critical time." For his first studies in harmony and the history of music Foote (and the other enrolled students) met with Paine in a large space in the basement of University Hall, which was furnished with a piano. He alone went to Paine's home for advanced lessons in counterpoint and fugue, since no other student had reached his stage of advancement.[38]

Paine's biographer, John C. Schmidt, writes that the Harvard catalog of courses for 1871–72 lists as an elective study a course in music theory and free composition (small forms) that included some counterpoint instruction. The next year, two courses appear—the one just described and a more advanced course in imitative counterpoint, canon, and thematic treatment. In 1873–74, a third course was added, in fugue and instrumentation. By the time Foote graduated with an M.A. in 1875, Paine was also giving instruction in sonata and symphonic forms.[39]

A quiz on counterpoint that Foote submitted to Paine, including written-out music examples, is extant (a "Canon in 5th, Free Bass" and "Fugue, 3 voices"). A three-page handwritten explanation of a fugue accompanies these pieces.[40] What immediately strikes the present-day observer is the increased technical knowledge demonstrated here—worlds apart from that of the youngster who composed the crude "Andante" and "Sands of Dee" of 1869. Foote writes a clarification of fugal structure directly onto the music manuscript. The music is on the *recto* side; the writing in ink, on the *verso* side of the page. There are also two penciled-in criticisms, not in Foote's handwriting and presumably by Paine, occurring in the margin and to the left of Foote's explanation; the first, "*Answer* not mentioned"; the second, "*Answer* not described." Indeed, Foote has failed to discuss the fugue answer. Nevertheless, the young man is clearly no longer a novice. One wonders if these pages contain part of the final examination for the M.A., which was given in counterpoint, fugue, and music history.[41]

His competence is established beyond a doubt with "Class Song, 1874," music by "A. W. Foote, Chorister, words by Nathan Haskell Dole." It was written as a contribution to the commencement exercises for his graduating class and printed in the *Harvard Advocate*,[42] thus making it his first published piece. There is a single vocal line in C major, except for three measures in E minor written in the treble clef. A simple keyboard accompaniment occurs below. Nothing exceptional resides in the tune, but it is pleasant, appropriately dignified, and easy to sing, save for one moment when the melody rises to a high E, which would prove troublesome for the basses.

In order to complete the requirements for the master's degree in June 1875, Foote wrote a thesis, "The Development of the Secular Style in Music," now in the Harvard University Archives. It is a lucid, succinct forty-six-page handwritten survey of vocal music's evolution from the ancient Hindus and Greeks to Gluck. No notes or musical examples are found. Nothing truly unique or intellectually penetrating is set down. Secondary sources could easily have supplied all of the subject matter. On page 45 of the thesis, Foote says: "I have omitted to discuss the development of instrumental music for the reason that it is really of less consequence in the growth of the secular style than vocal music, and that any adequate statement of it would require a separate thesis." One wonders about this. What is written down strikes the twentieth-century reader as an undemanding pro forma performance. On the other hand, the fact of his being the first person to earn an M.A. in music has been remarked innumerable times.[43]

Boston and B. J. Lang

When Foote graduated from college in June 1874, he returned to Salem. He considered teaching Latin and playing the organ at St. Mark's School in Southboro for a year, then perhaps entering law school. He also debated joining his father at the *Salem Gazette*. For the summer, he thought he should get a few organ lessons. For this purpose, he had B. J. Lang take him on as a student. Lang, Foote says, was a talented organist and keyboard extemporizer and "was a Salem boy like myself (this last point decided me, queerly enough)." He went to Boston weekly for lessons at "Dr. E. E. Hale's church on Union Park Street."[44] It was a momentous decision for Foote because it was Lang who convinced him of his gifts as a musician and urged him to give his attention completely to music. Lang also urged the young man to return to Harvard and earn his M.A. in music.

Benjamin Johnson Lang (usually known as B. J. Lang) was born in Salem in 1837. After some preliminary musical study with his father and Boston's Francis Hill, he left for Berlin in 1855 to study with Alfred Jaëll. He also took some instruction from Franz Liszt. Immediately after returning to America in 1858, he located in Boston. He soon won respect as an outstanding organist, pianist, music educator, and conductor of choruses and orchestras. He also produced concerts, both modest chamber ventures and ambitious ones calling for vocal soloists, chorus, and orchestra. Louis Elson could not say enough in his praise. To him and other nineteenth-century New Englanders involved with music, Lang was "one of the most typically American figures that we can find in our musical history. He was a man of enterprise beyond any European comprehension—a man who was a perfect organizer."[45]

Lang nursed back to health a Handel and Haydn Society that was almost moribund. He led the male chorus of the Apollo Club from its formation in 1868 until 1901. He conducted the mixed chorus of the Cecilia Club from its first concert in 1874 until 1907. He was an antidote to the conservatism of Dwight and Dresel, introducing many new works to Bostonians, including Berlioz's *Damnation of Faust* and *Requiem*, Brahms's *Requiem*, Bach's *Mass in B Minor*, Wagner's opera *Parsifal*, and Tchaikovsky's Piano Concerto no. 1. He was a powerful mentor. In one way or another composers like Foote, Ethelbert Nevin, and Lang's daughter Margaret, as well as writers like William F. Apthorp, reflected his training and views. Lang was also a champion of American composers, bringing out works like Dudley Buck's *The Nun of Nidros*, George Whiting's *March of the Monks of Bangor*, and George Chadwick's *The Viking's Last Voyage.*[46]

In 1909 Lang died, and Foote wrote about him in the *Boston Evening Transcript*:

> It was in the summer of 1874 (just after graduating at Harvard) that began for me a long and close companionship with B. J. Lang. That summer, as sometimes in subsequent years, he came into town once or twice a week, and gave a few lessons. We used to meet for organ lessons at Dr. Hale's church on Union Park street. . . . When any of us younger people went to him with our manuscripts, we never came away without keen and sympathetic criticism that had to be heeded. He had a remarkable feeling for perfection of detail (the absence of which is the great defect of most of our music here); for him there were no trifles, for they make perfection. . . .
>
> In his lessons, it was not only the music and the playing, but other things quite as important, that we got. He was willing to take the trouble and the risk of giving advice and direction about outside things: about manners, habits, business questions . . . so that we felt the friend as well as the teacher. . . . He was by nature an optimist; and he

taught us . . . that encouragement is better than fault-find-
ing, and that achievement comes partly from a belief that
the thing can be done.[47]

Lang made a far stronger impression on Foote than Paine
did. His contributions to Foote's technical training in keyboard
performance were limited, but he gave his student invaluable advice on starting and strengthening his career. Lang introduced
him to influential cultural leaders, helped him obtain church positions, and gave him exposure as a performer in public concerts. The older man's support was crucial when Foote was first
gaining his sea legs in the musical world.

A letter printed in the *Philharmonic Journal* sometime during the winter of 1880–81 identifies "the powers" controlling
music in Boston. Named were Dwight, the "educated music critic," Otto Dresel, B. J. Lang, J. C. D. Parker, Chickering, and institutions like the Handel and Haydn Society, the Apollo Club, and
the Cecilia Club. It declares Lang to be the head of "this
clique."[48] Constant attacks on Lang were launched by Benjamin
Edward Woolf, an English-born and exceedingly right-wing musician who wrote mainly for the *Saturday Evening Gazette*. Woolf
found Lang's musical tastes too radical and his dominance too
insidious.[49]

Foote did not agree. He thought Lang was exactly what Boston needed to overcome its conservatism. He praised the "foun-
dation-principles" and advanced ideas that Lang imparted to
him, on which he could build. He wished his own music studies
had been longer and more thorough, admitting that although "in
recitals I think my musical side carried me through, I never felt
wholly secure technically." Everything had come too easily to
him. When he was young, Boston had next to no musical standards against which he could measure himself. Yet, he did learn
much from Lang, as he would later from Franz Kneisel, George
Henschel, and Wilhelm Gericke. Nevertheless, most of his
knowledge in music came through independent study and close
attention to the musical practices of others. For the rest of his
life, he would solicit and assimilate the counsel and critiques of
musicians who had won his respect.[50]

During the years that young Arthur pursued his music studies, no indication is found that his family—whether father, brother, or sister—ever opposed what was to become his vocation. The three enjoyed and valued music and perceived in it no danger either to Arthur's person or to his future. They probably suspected early on that Arthur's musical abilities exceeded the average. Certainly, they provided him with the best available musical literature and with what keyboard instruction was available in Salem. One wonders if they consoled him when he received the inevitable teasing from the other Salem boys about the hours he had to spend in piano practice. They did not interfere when he took advice from Lang and studied theory under Emery or when at Harvard he looked to Paine for instruction in musical composition. They paid without hesitation whatever expenses were involved for musical materials and in fees.

Arthur Foote had taken his first steps into the world of music in the summer of 1865. Ten years later, in the summer of 1875, he had completed his formal studies and was poised to commence his professional life in music. He never continued his education in Germany although nothing and nobody would have prevented him from doing so. He realized that he would have to relocate permanently in Boston, since Salem provided him with few opportunities for furthering his career. One way or another, he would have to try to make his living. Teaching and performing were two likely avenues for him to pursue. As for musical composition, it would have to await whatever leisure moments were available. No means of livelihood came from being a composer in the United States.

Notes

1. Letter in the Arthur Foote Collection, Williams College, Williamstown, Massachusetts.

2. Foote, *An Autobiography*, (Norwood, Massachusetts: Plimpton Press, 1946), 21.

3. Ibid., 23–24.

4. In Arthur Foote, Scrapbook, 1869-76, Harvard University Archives, shelf no. HUD 874.27F.

5. Ibid., 22; see also, Arthur Foote, "A Bostonian Remembers," *Musical Quarterly* 23 (1937): 38.

6.   This aspect of Foote's musical style will be taken up fully in part 2 of the book.

7.   These letters are in the Arthur Foote Collection. See also *An Autobiography*, 22–23.

8.   Arthur Foote, "Music in the United States," MS, p. 16, lecture delivered at the University of California, Berkeley, in 1911; now in the Boston Public Library, shelf no. **M. 472.134, no. 1042.

9.   Foote, *An Autobiography*, 24–25.

10.   George N. Whipple, "A Sketch of the Musical Societies of Salem," in *Historical Collections of the Essex Institute*, 23 (Salem, Mass.: Essex Institute, 1886), 122–23.

11.   Whipple, "A Sketch," 129–131. Foote's comments may be found in *An Autobiography*, 37–38.

12.   Several books detail the career of Henry Kemble Oliver; see especially Frank J. Metcalf, *American Writers and Compilers of Sacred Music* (New York: Russell & Russell, 1925), 230–32; Leonard Ellinwood, *The History of American Church Music*, rev. ed. (New York: Da Capo, 1970), 229; F. O. Jones, ed., *A Handbook of American Music and Musicians* (Canaseraga, N. Y.: Jones, 1886), s.v. "Oliver, Henry Kemble"; John W. Moore, *Appendix to the Encyclopaedia of Music* (Boston: Ditson, 1875), s.v. "Oliver, Henry Kemble." In Arthur Foote, Scrapbook I, Boston Public Library, shelf no. **ML.46.F65, we find newspaper reports of a dinner in honor of Liszt that Foote attended, where Oliver was the main speaker.

13.   Foote, "A Bostonian Remembers," 38.

14.   Henry Wilder Foote, *Hymns of the Church Universal*, rev. and ed. Arthur W. Foote and Mary W. Tileston (Boston: Wilson & Son, 1890); Arthur W. Foote and Mary W. Tileston, *Hymns for Church and Home* (Boston: American Unitarian Association, 1896); twenty years later Arthur Foote was a member of the Editorial Board responsible for *The New Hymn and Tune Book* (Boston: American Unitarian Association, 1914).

15.   Arlo Bates, *The Pagans* (Boston: Ticknor, 1888), 162–63.

16.   F. O. Jones, ed., *A Handbook of American Music and Musicians* (Canaseraga, N. Y.: Jones, 1886), s.v. "Emery, Stephen Albert"; John C. Schmidt, *The Life and Works of John Knowles Paine* (Ann Arbor, Mich.: UMI Research Press, 1980), 74. Joseph Rezits in *The New Grove Dictionary of American Music*, vol. 2, ed. H. Wiley Hitchcock and Stanley Sadie, (London: Macmillan, 1986), s.v. "Emery, Stephen Albert," names Alfred Richter, son of Ernst Friedrich Richter, as Emery's teacher. Since Alfred

was born in 1846 and would have been only 16 years of age when Emery arrived in Leipzig, Rezits cannot be correct.

17. Arthur Foote, Scrapbook, New England Conservatory of Music. On the verso of the cover in Foote's handwriting is the note "Arthur Foote, 1875–1881."

18. Foote, "A Bostonian Remembers," 37.

19. The clipping is in the Arthur Foote Collection.

20. Foote, *An Autobiography*, 21.

21. Ibid., 21.

22. The letter is in the Arthur Foote Collection.

23. Walter Raymond Spalding, *Music at Harvard* (New York: Coward-McCann, 1935), 145-46.

24. Henry T. Finck, *My Adventures in the Golden Age of Music* (New York: Funk & Wagnalls, 1926), 75.

25. Foote, Scrapbook, 1869–76, Harvard University Archives, contains several of the Pi-Eta theatrical programs; for example, that of 15 April 1873 comprised *A Cup of Tea* and *Travestie, Black-Eyed Susan*, with Foote listed as the pianist.

26. Foote, *An Autobiography*, 29–31.

27. Ibid., 30. His friend Ernest Fenollosa is numbered among the basses in the membership lists for 1872–73 and 1873–74—see Foote, Scrapbook, 1869–76, Harvard University Archives.

28. Ibid., 31. Foote might have played either of two popular ballads: Patrick C. Gilmore's "When I Saw Sweet Nelly Home" (Boston: Reed, 1856) or John Fletcher's "Seeing Nellie Home" (New York: Pond, 1859). An accompaniment by Foote for the melody is said to have been put out in a Harvard songbook in 1874. It has not been located.

29. Spalding, *Music at Harvard*, 125.

30. Foote, Scrapbook, 1869–76, Harvard University Archives.

31. The rank lists are in Foote, Scrapbook, 1869–87, Harvard University Archives.

32. Foote, Scrapbook, New England Conservatory of Music.

33. The two Ditson items are in Foote, Scrapbook, 1869–87, Harvard University Archives.

34. The letter is in the Arthur Foote Collection.

35. Foote, Scrapbook, New England Conservatory of Music, contains a notice of his election to the society, billing him an initiation fee of $5 for the privilege.

36.   John Knowles Paine, "The New German School of Music," *North American Review* 16 (1873): 245.

37.   Foote, *An Autobiography*, 32–33.

38.   Foote, "A Bostonian Remembers," 38–39. The information about meeting at University Hall comes from Finck, *My Adventures in the Golden Age of Music*, 76–77.

39.   John C. Schmidt, *The Life and Works of John Knowles Paine* (Ann Arbor, Mich.: UMI Research Press, 1980), 92–94, 235.

40.   The two pieces are in the Arthur Foote Collection. Arthur Foote II identifies the handwriting as belonging to his granduncle, in a letter to Douglas Moore, 20 August 1988.

41.   The examination questions, handwritten probably by Paine, are in the Foote, Scrapbook, 1869–87, Harvard University Archives.

42.   *Harvard Advocate* 17, (18 June 1874), 153.

43.   To give an early instance, John Sullivan Dwight took pride in naming Foote as "one of the few who have taken a Master's degree at Harvard on the strength of special studies in music." See *Dwight's Journal of Music* 39 (March 1879): 39. The thesis itself is in Harvard University Archives, shelf no. HU 88.22.

44.   Foote, *An Autobiography*, 34–35.

45.   Louis C. Elson, *The History of American Music*, rev. to 1925 by Arthur Elson (New York: Macmillan, 1925), 259–60.

46.   Ibid., 261; for a more recent and informative article, see Steven Ledbetter, in *The New Grove Dictionary of American Music*, vol. 3, ed. H. Wiley Hitchcock and Stanley Sadie, (London: Macmillan, 1986), s.v. "Lang, B(enjamin) J(ohnson)."

47.   Arthur Foote, "A Near View of Mr. Lang," *Boston Evening Transcript*, (1 May 1909), pt. 3, p. 4.

48.   Arthur Foote, Scrapbook II, Boston Public Library, shelf no. **ML.46.F65.

49.   The first and second Scrapbooks in the Boston Public Library, shelf no. **ML.46.F65, contain several periodical clippings that feature the hostile remarks of Woolf about Lang and those seen as his disciples. Foote does not always come off unscathed in Woolf's reviews of his keyboard playing and music.

50.   Foote, *An Autobiography*, 35.

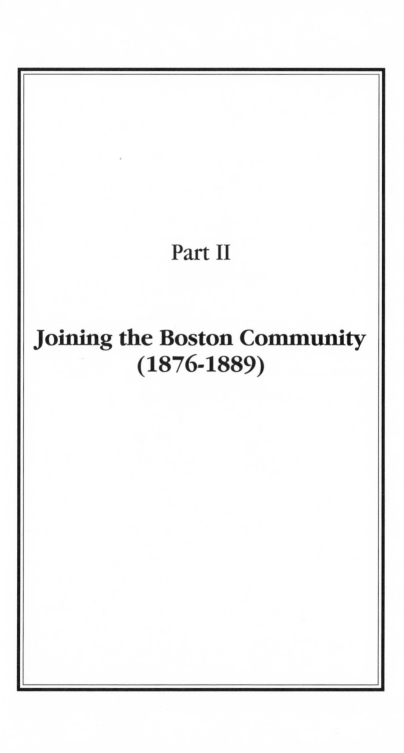

Part II

Joining the Boston Community
(1876-1889)

3

The Boston Community

In the decades after the Civil War, the United States was greatly
lacking in art music lovers and musical institutions. Advocates
for art music, however, like the excellent German orchestra director Theodore Thomas, considered Americans on the whole to
be fond of music. He said that they were open to at least the sensuous delights afforded by fine compositions. In the seventies,
he had seen an increase in general culture and in the hunger for
serious music. Thomas thought that the endless demands of the
workplace prevented men from giving much attention to music.
This situation would eventually change. At the same time, he
sadly admitted that as yet (he was writing in 1881) the musical
standards of the public were low and that the worthiest music
appealed only to a limited group of people. The average American, he said, was "so entirely absorbed in his work that when he
goes out in the evening he looks for relaxation in some kind of
amusement which makes little or no demand upon his intellect,
and he had no difficulty finding it."[1]

Although most Bostonians matched Thomas's description,
there was a group, usually affluent or educated or both, who supplied part of the audience for art music. But the reason for their
professed interest in art music lay in the fact that it distinguished
them from the herd and supplied them with a certain exclusive-
ness; thus it had little to do with the art itself. A second audience,
larger than the one just mentioned, knew little about music but
enjoyed it viscerally. Regrettably, its attendance at concerts was

unpredictable. This audience was made up of men and women from all walks of life, though it drew mostly from the middle class. It was fond of attractive tunes, invigorated by appealing rhythms, and beguiled by colorful and not overly obtrusive harmonies. What is more, its numbers grew throughout the century. This was especially true in New England after Patrick Gilmore organized the National Peace Jubilee of 1869 and the World Peace Jubilee of 1872, both extravaganzas held in Boston. Thousands of Americans participated as performers and spectators. They came away with a taste, however inchoate, for music beyond the popular. Owing to the interest of their readership, Boston newspapers and periodicals had to retain writers who regularly occupied themselves with art music. Most of them had musical training (as did several writers in a few other major cities), unlike the run-of-the-mill music critics in the rest of the United States. The latter crowd, said the respected Boston writer on music William Apthorp, was musically ignorant, not even knowing the meaning of words like *score*, *instrumentation*, and *intonation*. They were unable to differentiate between the different orchestral instruments "by sight or name" and were uninformed about terms like *fugue*, *canon*, *sonata*, and *rondo*.[2]

Finally, a third audience, the smallest, was made up of dedicated music lovers. Most of them were well educated, some of them well-to-do, and all of them with more than a smattering of musical knowledge. A civilized life, to them, was not only what they chose to lead but something they ardently believed they ought to lead. Their heritage encompassed a New England, British, and continental European past. It included traditional knowledge, interest in scientific developments, love of literature in general, and a high regard for the arts. This audience included professional people, academics, musicians, and the artistic and literary population. Among those active during Foote's student days were John Fiske, Benjamin Peirce, George Bancroft, Oliver Wendell Holmes, John Sullivan Dwight, Henry Wadsworth Longfellow, Celia Thaxter, Henry Lee Higginson, James and Annie Fields, and Mr. and Mrs. Montgomery Sears. None of them was a professional musician. Yet, this last audience had a strong desire to make art music a going concern. Fortunately for Boston's music, a significant percentage of its total citizenry belonged in this category of music lover. We note Oliver Wendell Holmes's tongue-in-cheek comment:

> Boston is just like other places of its size;—only, perhaps, considering its excellent fish-market, paid fire-department, superior monthly publications, and correct habit of spelling the English language, it has some right to look down on the mob of cities. . . . It drains a large watershed of its intellect, and will not itself be drained.[3]

Arthur Foote would be one of those drained from the Boston watershed into the city itself.

Fortunately, too, Boston was surrounded by a number of close-by towns. It helped swell the membership in this third audience, especially as more and more people collected in the urban area, disposable income increased, and transportation into the central city improved. In the second half of the nineteenth century, Boston had a spectacular era of expansion. The population grew from the original two hundred thousand in mid-century, enclosed mainly on a peninsula, "to a sprawling metropolitan area covering a ten-mile radius and encompassing thirty-one cities and towns, with over one million inhabitants."[4] When I speak about Boston and Bostonians, I have in mind this Greater Boston, which included places like Cambridge, Brookline, Newton, Milton, and Dedham, and which writers then and now also considered to extend to localities like Salem, Andover, and Worcester. These places were a few miles distant from the core city but linked to it by good roads and fine railroad and trolley service. Boston's population growth was a factor needed to allow musicians like Foote to thrive.

The Champions of Art Music

This third audience had supported Gottlieb Graupner when he established the Philo-Harmonic Society in 1809, which had stayed alive for about fifteen years. The third audience was crucial to the Handel and Haydn Society, founded in 1815, an organization that continues to this day. These Bostonians were undaunted by the demise of Graupner's band. They persisted in their efforts to lay the foundation for a permanent instrumental ensemble. The orchestra of the Boston Academy of Music began in 1833, only to be supplanted in 1847 by the orchestra of the Musical Fund Society, both conducted by George Webb. The latter ensemble lasted until 1855. The Germania Musical Society (1849–1854), made up of professional musicians from Berlin, found a ready audience for its offerings until its members broke up to seed other music groups. From 1857 to 1863, Carl Zerrahn, who had been a member of the Germania, was conducting the instrumentalists of a philharmonia society. To accommodate this music making, the Boston Music Hall, which seated three thousand people, was erected in 1852. Musician Thomas Ryan writes that up until the appearance of the Germania, the several Boston orchestras had to include many amateur players of deficient technical ability; therefore, "we could have no lightning-express trains in *tempo*; most music was played *tempo commodo*."[5]

The Harvard Musical Association then initiated a more sustained struggle to maintain an orchestra. Fifty Harvard alumni had founded the association in 1837, all of them had been members of the undergraduate Harvard Pierian Sodality. From 1865 to 1882, the association sponsored an orchestra led by Zerrahn. (A Philharmonic Society orchestra, directed by Bernhard Listemann, would make a brief appearance around 1880.) These were years when aestheticism became a matter of great debate for informed Bostonians. Artistic works attained a weightiness that attracted the attention of the exclusive class. Possessors of new wealth increasingly expressed themselves "by treasuring art objects as the most refined kind of valuables." They took pride in being connoisseurs, whether of painting, sculpture, or music.[6] Emboldened by this ferment, the members of the Harvard Musical Association attempted to promote good taste through its orchestra. It presented eight concerts a season during the first three years; ten concerts a season over the next ten years; eight concerts a season for another three years, and only five concerts in its last season.[7] The association elected Foote to be a member on 17 January 1875.[8] Regrettably, even though Foote eventually got on the program committee of the organization and tried to promote contemporary music, he did not completely succeed. As before, the orchestral offerings consisted mainly of German works of the past that were approved by a highly conservative clique, especially Dwight and Dresel. The clique only "grudgingly allowed a very little of Berlioz, Wagner, or other musical anarchists, to appear upon its programmes."[9] Yet, Brahms, Berlioz, Liszt, Grieg, Tchaikovsky, and Rubinstein did find their way onto the programs, thanks to people like Foote and Lang. George Chadwick had his Overture to *Rip Van Winkle* and Symphony in C done by the orchestra. Significantly, Foote's program for 11 December 1879, which lists the overture, has a pencil mark circling the Chadwick piece.[10] Did it signify respect for Chadwick's achievement, a wonder it was there at all, or an encouragement for Foote to try to do likewise? He did not hurry to follow in Chadwick's footsteps. His first public offering of a work for full orchestra, the Overture *In the Mountains*, was not completed until 1886.

The Boston audience had grumbled over the lack of variety and contemporary music on the programs, yet it "turned up its nose when it got them."[11] Moreover, visits by the superbly trained Theodore Thomas orchestra from New York exposed the Boston orchestra by pointing up its playing deficiencies. Attendance at association concerts dropped. Inspired in part by the Thomas orchestra, a permanent orchestra was established in 1881—the Boston Symphony Orchestra. Its instrumentalists were outstanding, its conductors highly competent, and the musical works drawn from a broader repertoire, past and present.

Foote says the excellence of the Thomas orchestra seriously undermined support for the association's orchestral series, "but the *coup de grâce* was given" the series "by the start of the Boston Symphony Orchestra."[12] On his program of the Harvard Musical Association concert, given at the Boston Museum on 9 March 1882, Foote wrote, "The very last!" The end of sponsorship was officially recognized on 20 November 1882. Foote was one of four committee members of the association who announced a revival of five musical and social meetings a year: "A simple supper at a moderate price will be provided, the expense of which will be divided among those present. It is hoped that these meetings may be the means of preserving and strengthening the life of the Association, now that our public work has been (at least *temporarily*) abandoned."[13]

Chamber music had an equally difficult time becoming established. However, Boston was fortunate to have the long-lived Mendelssohn Quintette Club begin its activities in December 1849. Thomas Ryan, a member of the club, wrote that they gave regular concerts in Boston, and sets of four or more concerts a season in nearby places like Salem, Lowell, Lawrence, Haverhill, Taunton, New Bedford, Providence, and Worcester. They were able to survive, despite the initiation of few men and women into chamber music, because within a radius of one hundred miles there were many cities and towns with hardly any diversions; they welcomed the club. Concerts in private homes also helped keep them going: "In Cambridge, for instance, we had for fifteen consecutive seasons a set of eight parlor concerts, given in the houses of the professors or other friends of music. The programmes were of good music only. We also had, for years, sets of parlor concerts in places like Milton and New Bedford."[14]

In the Foote scrapbook, now at the New England Conservatory of Music, is a clipping, beside which he has written "of 1879."[15] It reviews six seasons of music in Boston as follows:

Year	Number of Concerts
1874	60
1875	49
1876	62
1877	53
1878	43
1879	61

Ten or fewer each year were orchestral concerts.

Further information about music in Boston has come from the English singer Clara Doria, daughter of the composer John Barnett. She came to New York in 1871 and appeared in recitals and on the operatic stage until 1878, when she married the Boston lawyer Henry M. Rogers. She became convinced of Boston's advanced culture in the spring of 1873 after she appeared in

Mozart's *Don Giovanni* in that city, singing the part of Donna Elvira. She then realized, she says, that Boston had an audience of relatively advanced taste, and that songs of Schubert, Schumann and Franz "were greatly in vogue in amateur circles." In her memoirs of 1919, she recalled the "Old Boston" of "1873 to 1889." She went on to say:

> Simple living and high thinking were the order of the day; when people were valued for what they *were* and not for what they *possessed*; when Boston was still the hotbed of literature, art and science in America. In those days Boston had a social atmosphere quite its own. . . . It was restricted in its outlook; it might in fact have ben called provincial but for its obvious aspiration to be familiar with and to appreciate the better thing. But then, of course, as a natural concomitant of these virtues, Boston was self-conscious—as a sort of self-constituted advance guard of advanced thought![16]

Her estimation was rose colored, but reinforces the idea that some Bostonians took scientific, literary, and artistic matters seriously. To such Bostonians, Foote owed thanks for the concerts he was able to attend as he grew up in Salem and acquired an education at Harvard. And these were the Bostonians Foote would come to know when he lived in Boston. In the seventies, he would also become acquainted with three centers of musical activity. Oliver Ditson's publishing firm and retail store on Washington Street had all sorts of music teachers entering its doors to purchase sheet music and scores. Church singers met here regularly for a chat, and occasionally John Sullivan Dwight made his appearance: "A real democracy was Ditson's and always a busy place." Next there was Russell's, on Tremont Street, which dispensed "high-grade literature," mostly German. The atmosphere was quiet and dignified and seemed to attract musicians rarely seen at Ditson's. Last, there were the warerooms of Chickering Piano on Tremont Street, with the studio of B. J. Lang in the same building. This was the locus of the "musically inclined aristocracy" and the headquarters of the Cecilia Singing Society and the Apollo Club.[17]

Young Arthur Foote's Boston

After earning his M.A., Foote returned briefly to Salem. Foote was twenty-two years of age and had his mark to make as a musician and composer. He decided to reside in Boston because it afforded greater opportunity for musical employment. He felt accepted and comfortable in the city. After all, its old families shared the same heritage with Salem and his family. Besides, his brother Henry was here, the minister of King's Chapel. It was a city with a lengthy tradition and a growing partiality for the fine arts. It was a place where he could practice his art with peace of mind. It was also a place where he thought he might earn an income through teaching. He would possibly have concurred with Henry James, who worried about the ceaseless eradication of the past that was going on in America: "It takes an endless amount of history to make even a little tradition, and an endless amount of tradition to make even a little taste, and an endless amount of taste, by the same token, to make even a little tranquillity."[18]

Foote knew firsthand that the city led the United States in choral, oratorio, and instrumental performance and in musical instruction, though it lagged behind other cities in operatic presentations. He respected the area's eminent pianists (such as William Sherwood, Ernst Perabo, and Carlyle Petersilea) and enjoyed the lectures on musical history presented by authoritative figures (among them, Otto Dresel, B. J. Lang, and William Apthorp), which were continuously offered to the general public. Most of all, he was pleased with what he saw as the public's untiring involvement in all artistic matters and its reliable and sincere enthusiasm. One recalls the heated debate over the appropriateness of a bronze fountain in the courtyard of the new Boston Public Library. The architect Charles F. McKim and the sculptor Augustus Saint-Gaudens observed the "animated crowd assembled there, viewing the fountain from all points, discussing, praising, criticizing. . . . The assemblage made up of all ranks, including some 'great ones of the city.'" McKim's comment on the scene was:

> I don't care whether they take it or not. It is amazing to see in an American city so much genuine feeling upon an artistic problem! The fine thing about Boston is that when a

matter of this sort comes up, it proves always to be a burning question.[19]

Arthur Foote writes that Boston began its greatest musical growth soon after he started living there. He attributes much of this growth to the local women and their clubs. They eagerly joined forces with musicians and a lesser number of male music lovers to support concerts and encourage instruction in singing and instrumental playing. They made an effort to gain knowledge of the history and evolution of music. Thanks greatly to them, music was made "a dignified study."[20] He was undoubtedly also remembering the several prominent local women who befriended him, directed keyboard students to him, and helped his music get a hearing. These women took on more projects than just musical ones. During Foote's residency in Boston, he would see them push for, then prevail in, the building of the Boston Public Library, Trinity Church, and the old Museum of Fine Arts.

The preeminent example of a woman dedicated to the arts was the wealthy Isabella Stewart Gardner, Foote's kindly friend and patron. She gave moral and monetary support to musical performers, composers, painters, and sculptors. She backed Henry Lee Higginson when he launched the Boston Symphony Orchestra. She exerted herself in helping musicians to establish the Boston Composers' Manuscript Society. Its aim was to give local composers a hearing. Mrs. Gardner collected instruments, letters, and manuscripts of noted musicians. Countless concerts took place first in her Beacon Street home and then in the glorious Fenway Court, which was completed in January 1903. Morris Carter quotes the painter Whistler as saying that she spurned whatever she detected of "fossilized conventions" in Boston society. What is more pertinent to our discussion is Carter's remark:

> Whether a social renaissance was created or not may be a question, but 'the Brimmer set, which represents the old Puritan aristocracy,' and 'the Apthorp set, which represents the new Bohemianism,' did meet in her house on a common ground.[21]

Arthur Foote fitted in with both sets!

When he was seventy-two years of age, Foote read a paper

entitled "The Succulent Seventies" at a dinner meeting of the
Harvard Musical Association. Courtenay Guild, the presiding of-
ficer at the annual dinner had asked him to present it. Looking
back at the Boston of fifty years before, as he launched his career in music, Foote mentioned the sporadic chamber concerts.
Offsetting them were the more abundant song recitals where he
heard the songs of Schubert, Schumann, Franz Jensen, and Anton Rubinstein. Foote spoke of the thriving choral organiza-
tions: the Apollo Club, the Cecilia Society, and the Handel and
Haydn Society. Native composers, he noted, were still scarce at
that time. The notable ones in Boston were John Knowles Paine
and J. C. D. Parker. George Chadwick, Horatio Parker, and Edward MacDowell were still in the future. The orchestral concerts by the Harvard Music Association were given by local
instrumentalists "who happened to be here, never I think, as
large as fifty, and with the scantiness of rehearsal of which London, Paris, and Berlin complain nowadays." Volunteer pianists
rendered the harp parts on an upright piano. Other volunteers
might play cymbals ("I remember, for instance, Apthorp with
the tam-tam in Saint-Saëns 'Phaeton'"). Nevertheless, the conductor Zerrahn did his best, and "in the old Music Hall our audience of real music-lovers had hours as happy as those which
the listeners of today enjoy in more fortunate conditions." His
tone grows excited when he says: "Just imagine the first hearings of the Unfinished Symphony and that in C of Schubert, of
the 9th of Beethoven, later the first two of Brahms, the 'Tan-
nhäuser' overture in its youth, and that of the 'Meistersinger'—
at least such is the recollection of a junior at Harvard—in 1873,
who was to be seen Thursday afternoon at these concerts."
Within two years, after graduation from Harvard, he joined the
program committee of the Harvard Musical Association, and got
to know Dwight and Dresel. Among the respected names in music at the time were B. J. Lang, William Apthorp, Charles C. Perkins, S. Lothrop Thorndale, and William P. Blake.[22]

Both the less versed general music public and the cultivated
aficionados did have certain expectations of the musician and
composer that they shared. *Dwight's Journal of Music*, William
Apthorp's *Musicians and Music Lovers* (1894) and *By the Way*
(1898), Martin Green's study of *The Mount Vernon Street Warrens, 1869–1910* (1989), Arlo Bates's novel *The Pagans* (1888),

and T. R. Sullivan's *Boston, New and Old* (1912) concur on these expectations. To summarize, first, Bostonians wanted music to evidence feelings they could identify with and absorb. They wanted the composer to have creative insights into the profounder messages of life and to communicate them effectively to listeners. In addition, they wanted to experience delight and beauty through music that was melodious and expertly put together. However, they manifested no adventurous tastes, no desire to experiment with novelties for their own sake. As I will substantiate later, Foote was acutely aware of and often sympathized with these views. After all, the disposition of a group in which the composer feels he belongs does have an influence. It determines, at least in part, how he evolves and makes use of his inherent gifts. Moreover, Foote found it essential to win some public support because, without it, his career was certain to perish. Thus, even as Boston might encourage his creativity, it would also exert a check on his conduct. Moreover, it would limit the incidence of unfamiliar components in the music he would write.

But there were others who were even more unreceptive to novelty, such as influential New Yorker: George Templeton Strong. He genuinely enjoyed the music of Mozart. Yet, when he heard the newfangled prelude to *Lohengrin* of Wagner and the *Carnival* overture of Berlioz, he declared that Wagner wrote "like an intoxified pig" and Berlioz, "like a tipsy chimpanzee." Concerning Berlioz's *Le Carnival Romain*, he said: "I can compare it to nothing but the caperings and gibberings of a big baboon, over-excited by a dose of alcoholic stimulus." On Liszt's *Poème Symphonique—Lamento e Trionfo*, the comment was that the low strings sounded "dreary" and "cowlike," the brasses described "a hero triumphant with his hands in his pockets, jingling his pennies and his bunch of keys." Everything new that he heard was "rubbish."[23] Boston's John Sullivan Dwight and Otto Dresel would have agreed, but in less colorful terms.

Arthur Foote, As Bostonians Saw Him

When Arthur was a baby, his mother decided that he would not be handsome. At the same time, she thought he looked good-natured and lovable, and showed signs of good sense. His friends have confirmed this early assessment. They agree that he was short and somewhat stooped in stature, and had a rough, irregular face, a firm, resolute chin, and sharp, alert eyes. He seemed energetic and had a ready appreciation of anything that was humorous. Indeed, this faculty is on display in his scrapbooks, where I have often found humorous items, both related and unrelated to music, which he apparently relished. For example, around 1880, he saved a newspaper fragment that read: "Mr. Labouchere is informed by English dancers that the Liverpool Lurch and the Boston Swing are no longer in fashion, having been replaced by the Brighton Grip and the Southsea Cuddle."[24] Later, he saved a "certificate" issued to him, stating: "The Society in Dedham for Apprehending Horse Thieves, founded June 4, 1810. This is to certify that Mr. Arthur Foote is a member of this Society. December 11, 1901."[25]

Very rarely, a criticism of a fellow musician comes through. For example, sometime in the eighties, he saved the following limerick:

> There was a young lady from Rio,
> Who attempted a Beethoven trio,
> But her technic was scanty,
> So she played it andante
> Instead of allegro con brio.[26]

Perhaps ten years later, he saved a newspaper announcement of the performance of the Mass in E-flat by Amy Beach, which was to take place on 7 February 1892. The announcement concludes with "Mrs. Beach will <u>crown the eventful evening</u> [the underlining is Foote's, undoubtedly amused by the hyperbole] by playing the piano part in the Choral Fantasia [of Beethoven]." To accompany this announcement, Foote has rewritten the limerick as follows:

> There was a young lady of Rio,
> Who tried to play Hummel's grand Trio:
> But her technic was scanty,
> So she played it Andante!
> Instead of allegro con Brio —[27]

Censure, even when implied, is exceptional. Men and women who were familiar with him point to his kindliness, amiable disposition, loyalty to friends, and singular commitment to his students. Edith Lane, who knew him over a number of years, speaks of this loyalty to others and adds: "Throughout his life he always ended his correspondence—'Faithfully yours!'"[28] As a case in point, the as yet unknown composer Ethelbert Nevin once dropped in on him in January 1887, a few years after Foote had married. Nevin wrote to his father:

> I called on Arthur Foote, of whom I spoke some time ago. He was cordial as could be. I am going round soon to meet his wife and babe. He is the most promising of the rising musicians and I'm getting in with the best. My apartments on Mt. Vernon St. are in the swell part of the town—Beacon Hill—nicest sort of people there and altogether things look promising.[29]

The hospitality that Foote offered Nevin is in contrast to the suspiciously self-seeking reason behind Nevin's visit. Foote was always courteous, never pushy. When to his delight a musician performed one of his works, the performer always received a note of grateful appreciation for what Foote interpreted as the good turn done for him and his music. In an article remembering Foote one hundred years after his birth, an unnamed writer states: "Musicians, as a class, take great praise as merely something due them; not so Foote. He was not gracious or affable or helpful because he sought popularity—he was born that way."[30]

We also find in him a steadfast involvement in all of the fine arts and humanities, and with literary works.[31] His passion for locomotives, which his father mentioned in 1853, continued until his death.[32] The scrapbooks he put together also show him to have been an unwavering Republican in politics, as his father before him had been.

Foote never tried to take on the appearance of a romantic Bohemian artist, although he did associate with Boston's "Bohemians."[33] An undated item, which Foote clipped from a newspaper, contains an interview with a fellow composer, Clayton Johns. The reporter writes:

> As the listener looked at Johns leaning back in an easy chair in his music room in Boston, he [Johns] reflected upon the unmusicianly appearance of the American composers of this day—that is, unmusicianly from the erstwhile standard of esthetically flowing locks and general Bohemian air of abandon.
>
> There is Mr. Edward A. MacDowell, who looks like an intelligent, well-to-do American of any profession; and Mr. George Chadwick, who might be a jolly good-natured business man or recent college graduate; and Mr. Arthur Foote, whose clean-shaven face and closely cropped hair give no musical indications.[34]

Olin Downes spoke of Foote as "spare of build, of less than average height, with rough-hewn, energetic features," adding that "only with his intimates was he disposed to many words." Furthermore, says Downes, Foote might be deeply religious, but he also had a hot temper, and could express himself picturesquely. Foote's friend, Grace Stutsman, speaks of his keenly analytical mind and of observations "occasionally tinged with acid."[35] A much lengthier description comes from an unnamed writer in *Musical America*, who said that Foote was a small man with

> rugged countenance, a sturdy independence of character, modest in all his dealings with his fellow men, always absorbed in his work, happily living in and for music. Foote in more ways than one somehow recalls the figure of another New Englander who was also one of America's pioneer artists, but in a different field, Dr. Oliver Wendell Holmes— the beloved "Autocrat"—although to be sure, there was never anything even mildly autocratic about Arthur Foote. He was endowed with at least a modicum of originality; he remained always himself, refusing to be drawn out of his orbit by new musical comets that flashed across the sky; he went on creating music distinguished in its simplicity, sincerity, melodic freshness, and marked by good taste and good craftsmanship as well as independence.[36]

There is nothing distinguished about his handwriting, which became gradually more and more impenetrable through the years. With sympathy, I read a newspaper item from around the end of 1887, in which the unidentified writer complained: "If the talented Arthur Foote, of Boston, wrote music as illegibly as he does his letters he would have to employ an amanuensis to fit it for the publishers. He uses a blunt pen and writes in a straggling, uncertain way like one unused to much corresponding."[37]

Living in Boston

After Foote graduated with his M.A. in August 1875 he tried to begin his professional life in Salem by offering lessons in keyboard playing and music composition. He won hardly any pupils and in December moved to Boston.

Private teaching at first proved unpromising in Boston, too. Students were slow in coming. Aware of the problem Foote was having in earning a living, B. J. Lang used his influence in 1876 to get him the post of organist at the Church of the Disciples on Warren Avenue in Boston. The minister was Rev. James Freeman Clarke. This position was easy to fill, since there was no choir. Foote was asked to play preludes, postludes, and hymns. "Nevertheless, in this modest beginning," writes Everett E. Truette, "he laid the foundation for his future career as an organist, by paying careful attention to every minor detail of the simple but important parts of the service which were in his 'hands.'"[38] In October 1878, Foote went on to a much better position as organist and choirmaster at the First Unitarian Church, where he would stay until 1910. There he composed anthems and organ pieces for church use. His best-known anthem was "Still, Still With Thee" (1893). At the same time, he continued to offer keyboard and composition lessons.[39] Little by little he won a reputation as an outstanding pedagogue and had all the students he could handle.

He appeared as a pianist in concerts, some of which he had organized himself. The most famous of the latter would be his trio concerts, where he introduced the best music of the past and the present to Boston audiences. By 1881, Bostonians were acknowledging that he had extraordinary "artistic instincts and abilities" and were identifying him as "a progressive man and one of the best educators in his art we have among us."[40] Planning concerts demanded a great deal of time and effort, not only in rehearsing but also in the thousand and one small preparations that had to be overseen. Witness the postcard he sent to F. H. Jenks concerning an approaching concert, which reads: "I say Apollo Club Hall, in spite of the 2 flights, but am willing to assent to Wesleyan Hall, Thursdays—or the Hawthorne Room, though the latter I understand to be too expensive."[41]

A recognition that must have pleased him came from President Charles Eliot of Harvard, who wrote to him on 8 March 1889 and requested that Foote give a lecture to Harvard students "on music as a profession." Yet, his elation would have diminished when he came to the end of the letter: "I am sorry to say that we don't pay anything for such lectures, but if you wrote it out you could, doubtless, utilize the manuscript in a magazine."[42] Despite his growing fame money problems still troubled him. For example, on 31 December 1886, Foote wrote to Rev. William White, thanking him for his Christmas gift of salad forks and spoons but admitting that he had exchanged them "for a new watch and chain for me, which I really wanted much, but which . . . I should have had to go without." His old watch had stopped. "It seems a little selfish to have it [the gift] all to myself, but it was Kitty's idea, and I was mean enough to do it."[43]

Kitty was his wife, the former Kate Grant Knowlton, daughter of Charles Knowlton, a musician, whom he married on 7 July 1880. We do not know how long he knew her before marriage. Nor is there much information about her during the fifty-seven years they lived together. There is every reason to believe that their marriage was happy. The first reference to her that I have come across is in a letter dated 26 December 1879 from Henry to his brother Arthur. He says that he and his wife Fanny were rejoicing in the news that Arthur has found someone to love. They advised him to love her sincerely. He was now responsible for another's happiness. "We are impatient to see Miss Knowlton but shall wait before coming till she sends us word . . . that she is ready; but you must tell her that she will find much love awaiting her for your sake, and very soon her own sake, too."[44] M. A. DeWolfe Howe wrote about her shortly after she married Arthur. He gave some information about her mother, Mrs. Knowlton, landlady of a boardinghouse, and indicates that her daughter, Kate Grant Knowlton Foote, was very pretty. This leads us to conjecture that Arthur might have met his future wife while taking board with her mother:

> With my brother Wallis . . . I lodged for several years over Clough and Shackley's drugstore then on Charles Street just behind its present location. First to the "Hole-in-the-Ground" we resorted for sustenance, and then to a Holmsian boardinghouse on Chestnut Street. This was kept by a vivacious Mrs. Knowlton, whose daughter Mrs. Arthur Foote, the composer's wife, called forth from my friend Copeland [Charles Townsend Copeland] an early *mot* touching this lady, whom he admired, and "the beautiful Mrs. Inches," possibly known to him best through Sargent's portrait. "It takes twelve Mrs. Inches," he said, "to make a Mrs. Foote."[45]

Mrs. Knowlton was known to have quipped back at Copeland, who was from the state of Maine, by calling him "a bit of Machias delft."[46]

We gather from a letter that Isabella Stewart Gardner sent to Mrs. Foote from Benares, India, in March 1884 (three and a half years after the marriage), that she was a retiring type, chary of intruding herself on others. Isabella Gardner tells Mrs. Foote that a letter just received from her "gave me *very great pleasure*," and scolds her for not writing until she had heard from Mrs. Gardner. Isabella Gardner also mentions the daughter Katharine, for whom Mrs. Gardner had stood as godmother. She writes:

> Please always remember that when I say I want to hear from you, of you, and all about you, and yours that I really truly mean it. . . . Katherine [*sic*] must be growing, growing and that I shall hardly know in the big girl, the dear little baby of a year ago. . . . There is a native, a beautiful tall lithe Hindu strolling by—it is a night with the young moon. The native is singing to himself or his god such a weird soft strain. I wonder what Mr. Foote would think of it? Remember me to him.[47]

Mrs. Foote appears to have had a compassionate nature, judging from her daughter Katharine: "One of my first memories is of seeing Charles Loeffler (then a young violinist in the Boston Symphony Orchestra) lying on the divan in agony with earache. I felt sympathetic as I had earaches too. Mama comforted him, as she did so often for me, with hot sandbags under his ear."[48]

She was apparently not as given over to music as her husband was, as suggested in a letter sent to her by Clara Rogers:

> Tomorrow eve: (Tuesday) I am going to try over my Violin Sonata with Mr. Loeffler, & if you & Arthur have nothing better to do, will you come to take the quietest of quiet home dinners with us at half past six o'clock. There will be nobody but yourselves & Mr. Loeffler, unless Mr. Whiting [the composer Arthur Whiting] can come also; & so I would beg you to come—just as you are—do not put on any frills! I can lend you a large chair & screen, so that if you feel sleepy while Mr. Loeffler and I are practicing, you can take forty winks unobserved![49]

Clara Rogers was probably referring to her *Sonata Dramatico* in D Minor, op. 25, which was premiered on 19 January 1888 at the Gardner home as part of a program presented by the Boston Manuscript Club.[50] Eventually, Mrs. Foote died as quietly as she lived on 8 April 1943.[51]

Arthur Foote's daughter and only child, Katharine, was born 26 September 1881. Throughout her life, she loved Arthur Foote as a father and revered him as a composer. He, in turn, doted on his daughter. He insisted that she and her mother Kitty accompany him whenever he traveled to Europe. In the summer of 1883, they crossed the Atlantic and went on to Bayreuth to attend the Wagner festival. A letter from his friend George Henschel, singer, composer, and first conductor of the Boston Symphony, sent 13 July 1883, urged him to listen twice to *Parsifal*. He advised him on where he could locate a baby carriage. Apparently, the infant had taken sick, since Henschel also hoped "Katherine [*sic*] is all right again."[52] As she grew up, her father supervised her musical education. A newspaper item from December 1901 noted that Katharine was in New Orleans, visiting Arthur's nephew (the son of his brother Henry):

Rev. Henry Wilder Foote of New Orleans, LA, will preach
in the Unitarian church next Sunday and his niece, Miss
Foote, daughter of Mr. Arthur Foote, the well-known musician, will sing. . . . Miss Foote has a fine voice, thoroughly
trained and . . . [?] guidance of her father.[53]

The reporter had confused Rev. Henry the father and Rev.
Henry the son. Arthur's brother had died in 1889. That Katharine
had a voice of professional quality is verified by a song recital she
gave at Chickering Hall, Boston, on 17 November 1904. Her father proudly preserved the program.[54]

Very soon after their marriage in 1880, the Footes took up
residence at 2 (or possibly 3) West Cedar Street, Boston, next to
the original entrance of the Harvard Musical Association. Here
they remained until 1895. Years later, Katharine recalled the Cedar Street home:

The door was dark green and shiny with a brass name-
plate, Arthur Foote, over the letter slot. From the white
painted vestibule, through the lightly curtained glass of
the inner door, one could look into the music room. Sundays the door stood open, but most of the time it was
closed soon after breakfast and again after a short and often delayed luncheon hour. It was a lovely room. Two tall
windows, each in three sections, gave onto a balcony
where Papa often sat in the early summer evenings smok-
ing his after-dinner cigar, very likely "thinking music," as
he often answered when I asked him what he was thinking
about. There had been a mountain ash planted when the
house was bought; it flourished and was a joy to us all. I
was soon old enough to wait impatiently for the berries,
which delighted us all to see. The ash is a big tree now and
shades the whole yard. To return to the room: the piano
was against the outside wall, the keyboard being by the
lower left-hand window. The fireplace was on the left wall,
a yellow divan near it. Across the room the other wall was
lined with deep shelves, filled with music—bound and
unbound. A large bust of Bach crowned the whole. Papa's
desk was in the corner near the door. A gas fixture with a
green glass shade gave such a pleasant light. How well I

remember it all! Papa's dear head bent over his writing
and the friendly light over all.[55]

New Friendships

From the beginning of their residence in Boston, the Footes were
busy with the many musical at-homes, called parlor concerts, they
were invited to attend. Often dinner was provided. Foote himself
was frequently called on to perform, sometimes to present a new
work of his own. For example, on 6 January 1885, Mrs. F. W. Palfrey, 255 Beacon St., had the Beethoven Musical Club, with Foote
as pianist, play a program that included his Trio for Piano, Violin,
and Cello, op. 5. These parlor concerts were regular affairs at the
homes of the Gardners, Apthorps, Moultons, Montgomery Sears-
es, and others. Foote's Scrapbook I, in particular, contains the announcements and programs of many such invitations. Sometimes
the home offerings were quite ambitious. Thomas Sullivan relates
that he heard a song recital at the Apthorps on one night, and on
the next: "Music and more music!—this time at the house of Mrs.
Montgomery Sears, who had the better part of the Symphony Orchestra, with Nikisch to lead. Paderewski gave the host a pleasant
surprise by appearing suddenly and asking leave to play, which he
did in his best manner."[56]
   A great deal of music, of course, was heard at the Foote
home. Katharine writes about intimates of her parents, "who
came to our house in those early years" and "became our friends
for as long as they lived." [57] She names Breslau-born George Henschel, conductor of the Boston Symphony during its first three
concert seasons, and his wife, the former Lillian Bailey, an American soprano active in the Boston area. During his Boston residency, Henschel did what he could to advance the music of local
composers. He championed the music of Brahms, despite local
criticisms that it was too modern and afforded no valuable listening experience. The flashes of Brahms-like sound in Foote's music may be owing in part to Henschel's influence. This suggests
that Foote's style was contemporary, not reactionary, during his
own era. Henschel later moved on to England, but kept up his
friendship with Foote. Katharine also names the Scottish-born

Helen Hopekirk, noted pianist and composer, and her husband William Wilson, writer and landscape painter. When they visited Boston together in 1883, they first got to know the Footes. In 1897, Helen came to teach at the New England Conservatory and, with her husband, established permanent residence in Boston. Helen Hopekirk was a sensitive musician with whom Arthur could freely discuss his music. She persuaded him to recast four of the *Five Poems after Omar Khayyám* for piano into orchestral form, thereby helping him achieve his greatest orchestral success. Also "dear friends" were the famous Polish actress Helena Modjeska, who would introduce Arthur Foote to the plays of Ibsen,[58] and the American actress Julia Arthur, "who Papa felt was never really appreciated in this country."

Although he came from old Puritan stock, Foote felt at one with the "new Bohemianism" already mentioned—the unconventional circle that did not identify with the staid, business-oriented local people of high social standing. Among his acquaintances were men and women referred to as aesthetic and decadent, many of whom had homosexual leanings.[59] They traveled and showed an insatiable curiosity about what was going on in the international world of arts and literature. A few, like boyhood friend Ernest Fenollosa, had a special interest in the cultures of Asia. Certainly Foote knew about and often discussed their interests with them.

Not just musicians and composers but literary figures came to the West Cedar house. Louise Chandler Moulton authored mild, pleasing poetry with effortless ease and fluency. Born in Connecticut, she married a Boston editor and wrote reports from Boston for the New York papers. She took a great interest in the new poetry from England and France. Moulton undoubtedly called this poetry to Foote's attention. Perhaps she struck him, as she did Van Wyck Brooks, as a "good-hearted, sympathetic literary go-between, sincerely devoted to poetry."[60] Another poet friend, Louise Logan Guiney, was the daughter of an Irishman who was a Civil War brigadier general. A Catholic and a liberal, she strongly advocated women's rights. She supported herself by working as postmaster of the Boston suburb of Auburndale and later as a cataloguer at the Boston Public Library. She wrote essays and poems and has been recognized as an important link

between Emily Dickinson and Edna St. Vincent Millay.[61] Her poetry had a delicate elegance that often counterfeited the ambiance
of a bygone age. It was published in *Harper's*, the *Atlantic*, and
Scribner's magazines, and in books put out by Houghton Mifflin.
In 1901, Louise Guiney would depart Boston to live in England.
When Brooks writes that "she lived in a dream world of the seventeenth century with other Bostonians of her time,"[62] we cannot help but wonder if she aided and abetted Foote's affection
for the musical Baroque. Two other friends were the poets
Charles Flandrau and Annie Fields, who also was the biographer
of Whittier and Harriet Beecher Stowe. Annie Fields was celebrated for her Boston literary salon. Katharine Foote states:

> We went often to her Saturday afternoons. I was very
> young when I was first taken. Her friendship was most
> precious to us all. We often stayed with her at Manchester
> in the summer and to the end of her life she loved to have
> Papa come in and play to her, even when she no longer
> saw people. It was he who played at her simple funeral:
> parts of the Unfinished Symphony and other things that
> she was especially fond of.[63]

At her salons, the Footes met the foremost representatives of
the world of literature. Saturday afternoons, the Footes went
regularly to visit Annie Fields; Sunday evenings, to visit the William Foster Apthorps at Otis Place. Katharine says:

> There my parents met many more of the great figures of
> the world of music, art, literature and the stage, among
> them Ellen Terry and Henry Irving, Sara Bernhardt, the
> Kendals—a husband and wife team who were the Lunts of
> their day, Eleanora Duse, Melba, and many more that I
> have forgotten.[64]

Clayton Johns confirms what Katharine has to say about the
Apthorps. Their Sunday evenings, he says, were unique. Six to
eight people were usually present for dinner and some important musical guests like Paderewski, Melba, or Sarah Bernhardt.
Mrs. Gardner and the Boston Symphony conductor from 1884 to
1889, Wilhelm Gericke, were always there. "Later in the evening,

beer and cigars lent a Bohemian air to the occasions. Mrs. Apthorp appeared carrying a large pitcher of beer in one hand, beer mugs hanging from each finger of her other hand." Then they danced until midnight.[65]

Isabella Stewart Gardner was an intimate friend and Katharine's godmother, a role she took seriously. The Footes were frequently to be seen at the Gardner home. One year, "Mrs. Jack" insisted they go with her to the Copley Society's costume ball. She dressed Arthur and his wife Kate in elaborate Korean costumes, which greatly impressed Katharine "when they let me see them before they left. Mrs. Gardner was such a wonderful Godmother to me, and such a good friend to Papa and Mama."

Katharine mentions Ignacy Paderewski next. When Paderewski first came to America [1891–93][66] he knew hardly anyone. The Footes befriended him. The lonely Paderewski constantly visited the Footes when in Boston: "I remember the first time he came to dinner he was TWO hours late. He never acquired any sense of time. He was a delightful companion, played endlessly for us and even played Papa's duets with me! Later he had many friends and we saw little of him. But he always played Papa's Study in 3rds, which he liked very much, wherever he went." The piece was one of the *Nine Pianoforte Studies for Musical Expression and Technical Development*, op. 27, which Foote composed in the summer of 1891 and Arthur P. Schmidt published in 1892.

Two painters also called on the Footes, Theodor Langerfeldt and Ignaz Marcel Gaugengiegl. The latter is especially interesting because he was born in Passau, Bavaria, and son of a professor of oriental languages. Did he encourage Foote's fascination with the Omar Khayyam poetry? Foote would have found them extremely congenial to his own disposition. Gaugengiegl specialized in intimate genre scenes, studio interiors, and portraits, which he executed meticulously, highly finished small-scale works. Bostonians admired the paintings for their "skill of execution, their decorative qualities, and their spirited humor."[67] Katharine next names Mrs. Pratt and Mrs. Bell as good friends. The two women were daughters of Rufus Choate, lawyer and member of the U.S. House of Representatives and later of the U.S. Senate. Helen Choate Bell was a small, slender woman with bright golden brown hair and well-defined facial features. Widowed early, she lived with her sister on Chestnut Street, close by the Foote house. Famous for her wit and outspokenness, she loved books, music, and conversation. For Arthur to be accepted as her friend "was to be as far 'in' the Society of the day as it was possible to get."[68] She disliked nature and encouraged friends to "kick a tree" for her when they visited the countryside. A famous quip about Henry James started with: "I do not believe Henry James is so silly as to pompously announce that he is no longer an American [the news had just reached Boston that James had become a naturalized British subject]. He probably said it was a pleasant day in such a roundabout way that no one knew what he was driving at."[69] As for her father's composer friends, Katharine writes: "Until the BIG FOUR lost Parker to New Haven, and Whiting to New York, the families met often but after that only the Chadwicks remained close friends to the end. Ethelbert Nevin and MacDowell lived near us on the hill for a while and we saw much of them. But they too moved away and then Mac-Dowell had his breakdown and the musicians saw little of him ever again." Katharine closes her reminiscences, "2 West Cedar Street, 1882–1895," as follows:

> Before I close the book of memory I must not forget Henry M. Rogers and his wife Clara Kathleen. I was very small when I first knew them and they remained part of my world until I was more than grown up. What a grand pair they were! One more memory and I shall have done. I remember so well hearing Papa and Mama talking about the early days of the [Boston Symphony] orchestra, the simple gatherings after the concerts at the Henry Higginsons, when beer and pretzels, or crackers, would be served. Also I remember their saying that Gericke had played Strauss waltzes delightfully at Mrs. Gardner's after the concert one night. And later on, in Emil Paur's time, I remember many Saturday evenings when some of the Kneisel Quartette came for dinner and then had that pleasant walk across the Common to the old Music Hall.[70]

The catalog of Arthur Foote's acquaintances in literature, the arts, and the dramatic stage is extensive. Frederick Kopp claims that people were drawn to him by the sincere admiration and respect that they had for him as a person and a musician. No enemies attacked him during his lifetime, and most music reviewers praised his music. He never advocated any specific method for writing music, nor did he disparage the work of any other composer. Foote believed that people were usually well-meaning. He preferred to praise their strengths. Moreover, he was swift to admit to what he owed to the men and women whose advice and example furthered his own music making.[71]

Many of his friendships originated through, or were reinforced by, his membership in two clubs, the St. Botolph Club and the Tavern Club. He joined the former on 16 January 1887.[72] The St. Botolph members included prominent painters, sculptors, composers, musicians, journalists, lawyers, physicians, and patrons of the arts. A newspaper report on the club published in 1893 states that no cliques had influence. It goes on to say that evenings were informal, relaxed affairs with much free discussion of art, literature, and music. On Saturday night after the symphony concert until early morning the club was "at the height of its enjoyment. There almost any Saturday night one will meet such men as Arthur Foote, E. A. MacDowell, Ethelbert Nevin, Otto Roth, Kneisel. . . ." Longfellow, Apthorp, Philip Hale, and, when in town, the conductor Theodore Thomas, and the music critics Henry Krehbiel and William Henderson were found there. The novelist Arlo Bates surveyed the scene and "found much of the material and inspiration for both 'The Pagans' and 'The Philistines.'"[73]

In *The Pagans*, Bates calls it the "St. Filipe Club" and describes a typical evening, as follows:

> It was midnight, yet the group of men seated in easy attitudes before the fire in one of the sitting-rooms . . . showed no sign of breaking up. Indeed, the room was so pleasant and warm, with its artistically combined colors, its good pictures and glowing grates, and the storm outside raged so savagely beating its wind and sleet against the windows, that a reluctance to issue from the clubhouse door was only natural, and there would be little room for surprise should the men conclude to remain where they were until daylight. The conversation, carried

on amid clouds of fragrant tobacco smoke and with pota-
tions not excessive but comfortably frequent, was quiet
and unflagging, possessing, for the most part, that mellow
quality which is seldom attained before the small hours
and the third cigar.[74]

Further on in the novel, Bates writes:

At the St. Filipe Club, somewhere in the small hours . . .
half-a-dozen members were lingering. One was at the piano, recalling snatches from various composers, the air
being clouded alike with music and smoke wreaths.[75]

Foote, cooperating with other musician members, oftentimes helped plan the programs for the musicals that took place
at the St. Botolph Club.[76]

He joined the Tavern Club in 1890. He had been going to the
club prior to 1890, as a handwritten letter (dated 18 May 1889),
to Foote from G. H. Monks, secretary of the Tavern Club, testifies: "The pleasure of your company is requested at a farewell
dinner to Mr. Wilhelm Gericke to be given at the Tavern Club on
Friday evening, May 24th at 6.30 o'clock. Will you kindly let us
know if we may expect you?"[77] George Chadwick was already a
member, and Horatio Parker and Charles Loeffler joined later.
The Tavern Club was similar to the St. Botolph Club. Indeed several men, including Foote, were members of both. The Tavern
Club provided rooms for informal meeting, dining, reading, and
billiard playing. Banquets and frequent entertainments took
place on the third floor. One member, composer Clayton Johns,
reports:

In a lighter vein, Mr. Higginson [founder of the Boston
Symphony Orchestra] was for twenty years president of
the "Tavern Club," a little club formed for the enjoyment
of music and good-fellowship. Gericke, coming to Boston
at the time the club started [1884], took an active part in
the entertainments. Paderewski spent much time there,
playing billiards and the piano. The de Reszkes sang,
Salvini and Coquelin dined, wined, and recited, and a
host of other celebrities shared the club's hospitality. Even

> Lilli Lehman ("no ladies admitted"), having said, "I want
> to go to the Tavern Club," went, sang, and (if I remember
> rightly) danced, taking with her a few choice spirits."[78]

The fool's evening at the club was famous. Men dressed in amusing costumes as "inappropriate as the maddest fancy could imagine." The satirical "Salon" evening was put on to the astonishment and hilarity of spectators, including invited non-members, who witnessed scenes such as inartistic "artists" trying to paint pictures and unmusical "musicians" trying to perform on instruments. On the "Dime Show" evening, patterned after P.T. Barnum's Dime Museum, members were gotten up as "freaks, like 'the tattooed man,' [and] the India rubber man." At one time, Wilhelm Gericke, otherwise the dignified Boston Symphony conductor, appeared hilariously as "the bearded lady." Classical plays, musical comedies, and pantomimes were put on. Two events that members looked forward to were the baseball match with the St. Botolph Club and the Christmas Eve celebration, with pageants, a log ceremony, dinner, games, traditional dances, and music.[79]

Another club to which Foote belonged seems to have existed solely for music making, entertainment, and, socializing—The Clefs. It was formed on 31 October 1881 with sixty members, three-quarters of them professional musicians. It met once a month. For the 1882–83 season, Foote was the "Master" in charge of planning for the club's events.[80]

Trips Abroad

Spending his entire life in Boston, however many visits from friends of another country, might have led Foote to dwell in a rather circumscribed provincialism. Relying on Paine's teaching, his own studies in musical composition, and the few concerts available in Boston might have limited the range of his perceptions about, and actions in, musical composition. That neither outcome occurred is attributable to his travels to Europe. In England, France, and Germany he sought new music for listening and purchase. He made friends of contemporary musicians and composers with whom he conversed about musical matters. In

late spring of 1876, he went with his brother Henry to the Philadelphia Exposition and heard the music that Paine, Buck, and
Wagner wrote for the opening exercises. He was displeased with
Wagner's lackluster *Centennial March* and amazed at the $5,000
paid him for it.[81] On 24 June 1876 he embarked in New York on
the White Star Line steamship *Britannic* for Liverpool, which he
reached in eight days (he returned on the steamship *Celtic* on 7
September).[82] The main purpose of the trip for Arthur was to attend the first performance of Wagner's *Ring* at Bayreuth in August. Lang, who had conveyed to Foote his conviction of
Wagner's seminal importance in music, now accompanied him
abroad, as did several other Bostonians. Foote took special delight in rural England as he traveled to London. In London, he
met with musicians and purchased a great deal of music. Then
he proceeded to Paris, Bern, Nuremberg, and Bayreuth, where
he arrived two weeks early to attend rehearsals. Foote says that
the town was overcrowded and lodging was difficult to come by.
His rented room was nothing but "a large closet." Unfortunaely
illness prevented his attending a reception for Wagner, at which
Franz Liszt performed on the piano and Wagner spoke pridefully
about giving Germany "a new art."[83] Little of the Wagnerian manner rubbed off on the young American. Fifty years later, Foote
commented: "As today I look over these volumes bought in London fifty years ago, I see how little we then realized that Wagner
was the strongest musical influence of these fifty years, 1850–
1900, and now know that he was the greatest harmonic discover-
er since Bach (even granting that he owed much of this to
Liszt)."[84]

In 1878, his brother Henry wished to consult the English
throat specialist Morell McKenzie over a persistent ailment, and
Arthur decided to cross the Atlantic with him. They boarded the
Cunard liner *Parthia* in Boston on 15 June (Arthur would take another ship back from Liverpool on 29 August). (About this time
Foote began dispensing with his middle name, William, and sign-
ing himself "Arthur Foote."[85] His mother had given him this middle
name in honor of her younger half-brother, William Orne White.)
From London he went to the Paris Exposition, the Loire valley, and
back to London before returning to Boston. His scrapbook, now at
the New England Conservatory, contains the programs of the con-

certs, operas, operettas, vaudevilles, and even minstrel shows that he attended in London and Paris. "This year," Foote states, "I really began to feel at home in London and Paris, and not a tourist."[86] His perspective was getting less Boston centered.

The summer of 1879, he was back in London and Paris. Again, the scrapbook at the New England Conservatory shows the many concerts and theater performances that he attended. He met with musicians like George Henschel, men and women of the London stage like John Drew and Julia Arthur, and expatriate painters like Frank Chadwick of Paris. At that time, Henschel was teaching Lillian Bailey, his future wife. Foote writes of that summer, "I began . . . one of those friendships that are really anchors in one's life."[87]

In the summer of 1883, he was off again, but this time with his wife Kitty and two-year-old Katharine. I did not locate the "List of Saloon Passengers" sailing to Europe. The list of the return to Boston on the steamship, starting from Liverpool on 29 August 1883, cites: "Mr. Arthur Foote. Mrs. Foote, Infant, and Maid." At the top of the page of the scrapbook that contains the list, Foote has written "Paris—Strasburg—Nuremberg—Bayreuth and back." Below the list is a slip of paper that gives the "Freuden-Liste" of people attending the presentation of Wagner's *Parsifal* on 28 July. One is Foote.[88]

He and his family spent two months of the summer at Neuilly sur Seine, a suburb of Paris. Here, he wrote several piano pieces and revised the Piano Trio, op. 5. He had heard it performed in Boston on 8 April 1882 and decided that it needed rewriting. He went in to Paris to attend concerts and the theater. Additionally, he had some lessons "on his own compositions with Stephen Heller," whose charm and simplicity, "like his music," Foote admired. Foote says he picked up "valuable hints" but little "on the technical side." (In 1884, Foote heard that Heller was in financial need and collected money to send to him.)[89] His view had now become cosmopolitan: "It was a happy summer, and confirmed me definitely in my belief that this is the part of the world where one would most wish to live."[90]

The summer of 1888 found him and his family again in Europe and traveling the circuit of London–Paris–Bayreuth–London. When he arrived in England, he wrote to his brother that he had

visited the Henschels and then "had one very interesting experience at least, in a visit to Alma Tadema's studio."[91] Sir Lawrence
Alma-Tadema was an English painter known for his learned and
painstakingly precise paintings of scenes depicting ancient Greek
and Roman life. Later, on this trip, Foote tried but failed to per-
suade Theodor Leschetizky, the celebrated Austrian pianist and
pedagogue, to give him lessons. He also visited two American
composers, MacDowell in Wiesbaden and then Templeton
Strong. We wonder what Foote said to MacDowell about Boston
when we read a letter from MacDowell to Foote, sent 8 September 1888 from Wiesbaden, which reads: "You will probably think
me mad when you learn that I am, after all, going to give Boston a
trial. I sail on the 22nd this month."[92]

Before they left for home, the Foote family spent a few days
on the Isle of Jersey. There, tiny Katharine became ominously ill
with typhoid fever. Arthur recalled with horror how his brother
Henry had come down with the sickness and how it had then destroyed his mother. For a month, he spent every night, and his
wife Kitty every day, by their daughter's bedside, caring for her
until she was out of danger. Because he had commitments in
Boston, he returned home alone, with his family to follow when
the babe had regained her health.[93]

At thirty-five years of age in 1888, Arthur Foote had achieved a
reputation as a fine choral director, an excellent keyboard artist, a
respected teacher of piano, and an entrepreneur presenting
chamber music concerts of uncommon interest. He had composed several excellent and well-received works, and his creative
talents were continuing to develop. Moreover, he could point to
the many lasting friendships he had made at home and abroad.
His experiences as a person and a musician were rich and diverse. Many of them were pleasurable, but one or two, harrow-
ing. He had emerged from these experiences as a mature man
who had proven himself to be mentally sensible and socially
sound, and who showed promise of contributing in notable degree to his society.

Notes

1.   Theodore Thomas, "Musical Possibilities," in *Musical Autobiography*, ed. George P. Upton (Chicago: McClurg, 1905), 265–68.

2.   William T. Apthorp, *Musicians and Music Lovers* (New York: Scribner's Sons), 6.

3.   Oliver Wendell Holmes, *The Autocrat of the Breakfast Table*, in *Works*, 14 vols. (Boston: Houghton Mifflin, 1892), 1:111.

4.   Marlene Deahl Merrill, Introduction to *Growing Up in Boston's Gilded Age: The Journal of Alice Stone Blackwell, 1872–1874*, ed. Marlene Deahl Merrill (New Haven: Yale University Press, 1990), 12.

5.   Thomas Ryan, *Recollections of an Old Musician* (New York: Dutton, 1899), 20, 45.

6.   Martin Green, *The Mount Vernon Street Warrens* (New York: Scribner's Sons, 1989), 59.

7.   Ryan, *Recollections of an Old Musician*, 102.

8.   Arthur Foote, Scrapbook, 1869–76, Harvard University Archives, shelf no. 874.27F.

9.   Louis C. Elson, *The History of American Music*, rev. to 1925 by Arthur Elson (New York: Macmillan, 1925), 59.

10.   See Arthur Foote's Scrapbook, at the New England Conservatory of Music; pagination is not indicated here.

11.   William Foster Apthorp, *By the Way*, vol. 2 (Boston: Copeland & Day, 1898), 75–79.

12.   Arthur Foote, *An Autobiography* (Norwood, Mass.: Plimpton Press, 1946), 40.

13.   Arthur Foote, Scrapbook I, Boston Public Library, shelf no. **ML. 46.F65.

14.   Ryan, *Recollections of an Old Musician*, 92, 95–96.

15.   Arthur Foote, Scrapbook, New England Conservatory of Music, 6.

16.   Clara Kathleen Rogers, *Memories of a Musical Career* (Boston: Little, Brown, 1919), 403, 417.

17.   Henry Morton Dunham, *The Life of a Musician* (New York: Mrs. Henry M. Dunham, 1931), 74, 77.

18.   Quoted in Leon Edel's Introduction to Henry James, *The American Scene* (Bloomington: Indiana University Press, 1968), xii.

19.   T. R. Sullivan, *Boston, New and Old* (Boston: Houghton Mifflin, 1912), 101–02.

20.   Arthur Foote, "Then and Now, Thirty Years of Advance in Musical America," *Etude*, January 1913, 19.

21.   Morris Carter, *Isabella Stewart Gardner and Fenway Court* (Boston: Houghton Mifflin, 1925), 91.

22.   The paper may be found in the *Boston Evening Transcript*, 28 March 1925, pt. 3, p. 8.

23.   Allan Nevins and Milton Halsey Thomas, eds., *Diary of George Templeton Strong*, vol. 4 (New York: Macmillan, 1952), 116, 126.

24.   Arthur Foote, Scrapbook, New England Conservatory of Music. Foote did not number the page.

25.   Arthur Foote, Scrapbook III, Boston Public Library, shelf no. **ML. 46.F65.

26.   Arthur Foote, Scrapbook I, Boston Public Library, shelf no. **ML. 46.F65.

27.   Arthur Foote, Scrapbook II, Boston Public Library, shelf no. **ML. 46.F65.

28.   Edith Lane, "Arthur Foote, Massachusetts' Own Musician," typewritten MS at the Essex Institute, shelf no. E F688.3L 19–, p. 10.

29.   Vance Thompson, *The Life of Ethelbert Nevin* (Boston: Boston Music, 1913), 77–78.

30.   The article, source unknown, is entitled "Arthur Foote Born Hundred Years Ago; His Work Recalled," on which is written by hand the date "July 1, 1953."

31.   This, for example, is the way Nicolas Slonimsky describes him, in the *Dictionary of American Biography*, s.v. "Foote, Arthur William."

32.   "Arthur Foote and the Flowering of American Music" (sermon delivered by an unnamed minister, possibly Rev. Duncan Howard, at the First Church Unitarian, Boston, on 8 November 1953). Brahms and Stravinsky shared the same passion.

33.   For more information about Boston's nonconformists, see Douglas Shand-Tucci, *Boston Bohemia, 1881–1900* (Amherst: University of Massachusetts Press, 1995).

34.   Arthur Foote, Scrapbook II, Boston Public Library, shelf no. **ML. 46.F65.

35.   Olin Downes, "Works of Arthur Foote," *New York Times*, 18 April 1937, sec. 11, p. 5; Grace May Stutsman, "Bostonians Honor Memory of Foote," *Musical America*, 10 May 1937, 30.

36.   "Arthur Foote, Worthy Artist," *Musical America*, 25 April 1937, 32.

37.   Arthur Foote, Scrapbook I, Boston Public Library, shelf no. **ML. 46.F65.

38.   Everett E. Truette, "Two American Organists and Composers," *The Musician* 15 (1910): 348.

39.   Arthur Foote describes the beginning of his professional life in *An Autobiography* (Norwood, Mass.: Plimpton Press, 1946), 35–39.

40.   Arthur Foote, Scrapbook I, Boston Public Library, shelf no. **ML. 46.F65. This clipping is a review of a chamber concert that Foote gave on 5 March 1881. Above, Foote has written *Courier*.

41.   The postcard dated 19 November 1883 is numbered 194 in a folder, shelf no. ML28.B7 E9, Boston Public Library.

42.   Arthur Foote, Scrapbook II, Boston Public Library, shelf no. **ML. 46.F65.

43.   The letter is in the Arthur Foote Collection, Williams College, Williamstown, Massachusetts.

44.   The letter is in the Arthur Foote Collection.

45.   M. A. DeWolfe Howe, *A Venture in Remembrance* (Boston: Little, Brown, 1941), 140–41.

46.   Ibid., 155.

47.   I have read a copy of the letter, now in the archives of the Gardner Museum, Boston.

48.   Katharine Foote Raffy, "2 West Cedar Street, 1882–1885," a typewritten MS, whose photocopy I received from Arthur Foote II. I later read the original in the Arthur Foote Collection.

49.   Arthur Foote, "Letters Collected by Arthur Foote: Gift to the Library in Memory of Arthur Foote, 1940," Spaulding Library, New England Conservatory of Music, Letter no. 58.

50.   The program is in the archives of the Gardner Museum.

51.   *Polk's Newton City Directory for 1943* (Boston: Polk, 1943), 233; the entry reads, "Foote, Kate wid Arth died Apr 8, 1943."

52.   Foote, "Letters Collected by Arthur Foote," Letter no. 51.

53.   Arthur Foote, Scrapbook III, Boston Public Library, shelf no. **ML.46.F65. Handwritten above the clipping is the date "Dec. 1901." The question mark indicates a word or words that proved unreadable.

54.   Ibid.

55.   Katharine Foote Raffy, "2 West Cedar Street, 1882–1895," a three-page typewritten MS now in the Arthur Foote Collection.

56.   Thomas Russell Sullivan, *Passages from the Journal of Thomas Russell Sullivan, 1891–1903* (Boston: Houghton Mifflin, 1917), 58.

57.   Ibid.

58. For example, on 18 April 1894, we find Arthur Foote attending a presentation of *Ghosts* at the Tremont Theater; the program is in Arthur Foote, Scrapbook II, Boston Public Library.

59. A lengthy examination of these topics will be found in Douglas Shand-Tucci, *Boston Bohemia, 1881–1900* (Amherst: University of Massachusetts Press, 1995)

60. Van Wyck Brooks, *New England Indian Summer: 1865–1915* (New York: Dutton, 1940), 313–14.

61. Douglas Shand-Tucci, *Boston Bohemia, 1881–1900*, 36–37.

62. Van Wyck Brooks, *New England Summer*, 451.

63. Katharine Foote Raffy, "2 West Cedar Street, 1882–1895."

64. Ibid.

65. Clayton Johns, *Reminiscences of a Musician* (Cambridge, Mass: Washburn & Thomas, 1929), 69–70.

66. Paderewski's concert diary shows him to have first been in Boston during those years; see *Diariusz Koncertowy Ignacego Jana Paderewskiego* (Polskie Wydawnictivo Muzyczne: 1990), 46–49.

67. Trevor J. Fairbrother, *The Bostonians, Painters of an Elegant Age, 1870–1930* (Boston: Museum of Fine Arts, 1986), 208.

68. Cleveland Amory, *The Proper Bostonians* (New York: Dutton, 1947), 126.

69. Van Wyck Brooks, *New England Indian Summer: 1865–1915*, 417.

70. All of the information given by Katharine Foote Raffy is taken from her manuscript, "2 West Cedar Street, 1882–1895."

71. For more on this subject, see Frederick E. Kopp, "Arthur Foote: American Composer and Theorist" (Ph.D. diss., Eastman School of Music, University of Rochester, 1957), 132–33.

72. *Constitution and By-Laws of the St. Botolph Club* (Boston: St. Botolph, 1898), 31.

73. Clipping in Foote, Scrapbook II, Boston Public Library; there is no date on the clipping, but Foote has written "1893" above it.

74. Arlo Bates, *The Pagans* (Boston: Ticknor, 1888), 8.

75. Ibid., 209.

76. For example, Foote, Scrapbook II, Boston Public Library, contains a notice stating that Nikisch, Lamson, Foote, and Whiting were getting ready a special program for 24 March 1893.

77. Foote, Scrapbook I, Boston Public Library.

78. Johns, *Reminiscences of a Musician*, 68–69.

79. Foote, Scrapbook II, Boston Public Library. The unidentified article on the Tavern Club is placed next to the one on the St. Botolph Club; see note 64.

80. Foote, Scrapbook I, Boston Public Library.

81. Foote, *An Autobiography*, 60.

82. Foote, Scrapbook, New England Conservatory of Music, 43–43.

83. Foote, *An Autobiography*, 62–64.

84. Ibid., 62.

85. Katharine Foote Raffy informed Doric Alviani that Foote's middle name, William, was dropped from his name early in life; see the preface to Alviani's "The Choral Music of Arthur William Foote," (D.S.M. diss., Union Theological Seminary, 1962). Henry Foote II, in an unpublished MS on the Foote family, p. 17, says that Arthur dropped his middle name, William, soon after his graduation from Harvard in 1874.

86. Ibid., 66.

87. Ibid., 67.

88. Foote, Scrapbook I, Boston Public Library.

89. Foote, *An Autobiography*, 46.

90. Ibid., 67.

91. Letter from Arthur Foote to Henry Foote from Dinard, France, dated 20 August 1888; now in the Arthur Foote Collection.

92. Foote, "Letters Collected by Arthur Foote," Letter no.168.

93. *An Autobiography*, 48.

4

Attitudes and Activities

In a book published in 1900, Rupert Hughes commented that art music written by Americans was a recent phenomenon. Excluding a few men such as Lowell Mason, Louis Moreau Gottschalk, Stephen A. Emery, and George F. Bristow, virtually all American composers worthy of the name were still living.[1] Foote also acknowledged the youthfulness of American music. He believed that the major pioneering days in musical composition had taken place in the last quarter of the nineteenth century. He looked back longingly to this era in 1936, having witnessed the turmoil and controversy produced by music modernists over the past two decades:

> Those of us who lived in Boston from 1875 till 1905 look back with happiness to the days when we had there as composers Paine, Chadwick, J.C.D. Parker, MacDowell, Horatio Parker, Loeffler, Whiting, Nevin, Johns, among the men, and, among the women, Margaret Ruthven Lang, Mrs. Henry M. Rogers, and Mrs. Beach.[2]

The modernists spoke against tonality, consonance, and triadic chord construction. They scorned the general music public, belittling it as Philistine. Even though audiences rejected them, they determinedly diverged from tradition in favor of radically different forms of expression.

During the last quarter of the nineteenth century, for the first time in the cultural history of the United States, all the factors necessary to sustain art music and produce its composers in a steady stream had come together. Superior music education for fledgling musicians was available in America and abroad. Composers could make a living through teaching, performing, and directing musical groups. Capable professional instrumentalists and vocalists were on hand to perform what the native artists created. Some wealthy patrons and other influential people were coming forward to support various musical undertakings and advance the cause of art music. The growing audience for art music listened sympathetically to contemporary works. Composers felt no need to harangue the public or assail cultural leaders. They worked steadily at teaching, performing, and composing, in friendship with each other and with a tranquil everyday existence. Compared to the 1930s, everybody active in music in the 1880s seemed to have acted with one accord—hence, Foote's happiness.

Foote's personal life was similarly tranquil and unremarkable. He made several visits to Europe, one long visit to California, and a number of concert tours to other parts of the United States. Nevertheless, for his entire adult existence he remained mostly an educator, church musician, and keyboard performer who chose to reside in one locality, Boston. He filled what free time he had with composing, listening to music, studying scores, and carrying out the domestic duties that came with family living. He did not make himself conspicuous by consciously seeking out and hobnobbing with celebrated or modish people, or by engaging in flamboyant actions. Nor did he attempt to establish a "school" of composers to perpetuate his ideas and general style. How then did it happen that his music may suit the exigencies of an America that exists over a hundred years later?

The United States is fundamentally different from what it was a century ago. Earthshaking events have demolished the principles and verities of former times. Religious and moral beliefs have weakened. Any sort of authority is suspect. Such developments have contributed to the modernist outlook and have combined to make the twentieth-century arts, whatever their merits, less than inviting to many men and women. A communicator who expresses himself plainly through the time-tested certainties, endeavoring to maintain methods, ideas, and customs readily intelligible to others, can be an inspiriting personage. This is especially so to music-lovers who feel let down by the doctrines and practices of the modernists. Arthur Foote may well be seen as an authentic artist in the judgment of new devotees to his music. It is not the iconoclastic avant-gardists who are likely to command this sort of interest, nor their followers, who have expounded the modern cause with such persistence throughout the twentieth century. It is more likely to be the composer who convinces today's public of sincerity and soundness of mind, feeling, and moral character, while keeping faith with the cumulative wisdom from the past. It is more likely to be the creator searching into authentic humanness and expressing the desires and limits of the audience with conviction and awareness. Was Arthur Foote that person?

In order to ascertain if Foote is such a composer, my first step is to take a further look at his influences, his attitudes that at least in part were affected by these influences, and the musical activities that put his beliefs and values into practice.

Musical Influences

All nineteenth-century American composers faced the dilemma of having no tradition to grow in and build upon, says Daniel Gregory Mason. The first art music tradition to take hold in the United States was German Romanticism, which was dominant from 1850 to around 1890. The rival influence of French music did not begin until the 1890s.[3] Owing to the dearth of art music composers and institutions in American cultural history, a musical neophyte had to look to Europe for an education, either by studying abroad or with a local instructor well versed in European practices. Foote did not travel to Germany to complete his studies, as did most of his colleagues and teachers, Stephen Emery, John Knowles Paine, and B. J. Lang. Yet, through these three men, he acquired a style closely akin to that of Central Europe. He reinforced that style by associating with the many highly competent German musicians residing in Boston, especially Otto

Dresel, Franz Kneisel, George Henschel, and Wilhelm Gericke. Whatever his achievements, he could not help being subject to the state of affairs that prevailed in his age.

Foote himself acknowledges that he was under the rule of determining factors beyond his control. These influences and his inclinations from the beginning could not help but be mainly Germanic and conservative; the principal composers attracting him, Mendelssohn, Schumann, Chopin, and Brahms.[4] He did, however, remain abreast of his times in his tastes and thinking: "These were the days when St. Saëns' music came to us as a stunning novelty, when (1875) we had the first (MS) performance by Von Bülow of the Tschaikovsky Concerto with Lang conducting (what a sensation it was!); when the new Grieg Concerto fascinated every one, and when some of us went over to Bayreuth in 1876 to the first performances of the 'Nieblungen Ring.'"[5] As he matured as a composer, he also profited from the example of Liszt, Tchaikovsky, Dvořák, and Rimsky-Korsakov, all of them his contemporaries.

In a lecture delivered at the University of California in 1911 he said Mendelssohn's sanity offset the composer's reluctance to advance into less explored territory. He admired the perfect craftsmanship, the beauty of sound, and the elevated artistic aspiration of the music. All things considered, more could be said for his music than for the music of composers now preferred to him.[6] Henschel, who knew personally both Clara Schumann and Johannes Brahms, was the friend who deepened Foote's admiration of Schumann and encouraged him to extend his admiration to Brahms. Urged on by B. J. Lang, Foote traveled to Bayreuth to take in Wagner's operas. He was one of several musicians who invited Gustav Kolbe in 1883 to give lectures on the origins and development of Wagner's musical dramas. The next year, he was attending the six evenings devoted to scenes from Wagner's operas, presented by Theodore Thomas and a touring band of Wagnerian singers. In April 1891, he was an enthusiastic supporter of Lang, when this comrade produced *Parsifal* at the Music Hall.[7] Despite being fascinated by the music, Foote rarely appropriated anything of Wagner's style for his own use. Perhaps he was put off by Wagner's character. He certainly would have agreed with Amy Fay's assessment. She criticized Wagner's anti-Semitism, defiance of morality, and rejection of honor and gratitude. Germans, she said, forgave Wagner every moral lapse because of his genius, wryly adding: "I must say that if Germany can teach *us* Music, we can teach *her* Morals."[8] Even more pertinent, he found Wagner's approach completely at variance with his own predilections for clear-cut and highly melodious designs after the example of composers from the eighteenth and earlier nineteenth centuries. He tried his best to write nonprogrammatic music in unambiguous structures. The music was meant to express deep personal emotion or to capture moods aroused by poetry, nature, and common human existence. To dwell with gods, goddesses, and ultraheroic warriors was not his desire.

On the other hand, when Dresel and Dwight attacked Brahms, Wagner, and Liszt, he refused to go along. When they attempted to exclude contemporary works from the programs of the Harvard Musical Association, he sided with Lang and proposed their inclusion. Foote, who had joined the program committee of the association in 1875, just after receiving his M.A. degree, says that Dwight and Dresel were the conservatives on the committee, while "B. J. Lang, W. F. Apthorp, W. P. Blake, and I made what is today [1935] called the 'liberal' element on the committee."[9] In all of these circumstances, Foote was asserting his democratic right to decide for himself. During his adulthood and later, as a much older composer confronted by musical modernism, he would accept only suggestions that were appropriate to his own background, tastes, and proclivities. He would incorporate them into his own musical substance, attempting to make whatever was European fit for New England use by giving it a native shape. This process of domestication, of consuming and incorporating the sounds of another country, was far more a matter of assimilation and transformation than of imitation. To take his lead from the great composers of Europe was instructive, to be sure. Nevertheless, it was his duty to realize his own musical aptitude. Eventually, he knew he had the ability to join learning to craft and talent and produce finished musical compositions. This was behind his statement about forgoing law for music as a youth: "Fate stepped in, and the profession of the law has escaped one rather inefficient exponent. For I am confident that I was meant to do just what I have done."[10]

As we continue to examine Foote's musical preferences, we see that he favored a balance between traditional beliefs and practices and novelty and constant stylistic alteration. He heeded the bold forward thrust of contemporary musicians, especially in harmony and orchestration. He also safeguarded cultural properties from the past, remained skeptical of swift, revolutionary change, and approved musical evolution only by degrees. Yet, he never inclined to the pessimism of the cultural reactionaries. To him, continuity from past to present to future was essential for the integrity and soundness of musical culture. However, he did not oppose rapid stylistic modification in areas that cried for revitalization. If a new work puzzled him, he preferred to give it a chance to grow on him rather than condemn it out of hand. Therefore when in the 1930s he remembered the disagreements with Dwight and Dresel of fifty years before over programming new music, he commented: "Two or three of us used to fight like cats to get a performance of, say, a new symphony by Raff or Rubinstein (now gone with last year's snows); perhaps it is remembrance of this that makes me slower in reaching an opinion of the Hindemiths and Stravinskys of today."[11] This statement reveals the exemplary tolerance that was deeply embedded in his character.

His Temperament and Values

During my research into Foote's beliefs, I could find next to nothing about his religious convictions. In his autobiography, he praises Rev. James Freeman Clarke, who was minister at the Church of the Disciples when Foote worked there for a brief time, calling him "an unusual man" and adding, "His sermons . . . were well worth hearing. Largely through his influence the church was a place that meant much to its people, who, by the way, were kind and hospitable to me."[12] Other tantalizing scraps of information came my way. As an elderly man, he commented that during his boyhood in Salem he went with his father to the Unitarian North Church, to which he returned on one important occasion:

> In the spring of 1929 I sat again in my father's pew, and
> heard my dear brother's boy, the Rev. H[enry] W. Foote,

make the address at the Church's centenary. At the same
time, Mr. George J. Perry played two of my anthems.
Edmund B. Willson was the minister of the North Church
during my youth and until 1895. He was a dear man . . .
and his son Bob was a pal of mine.[13]

On 29 December 1994, I wrote to his grandnephew, Rev.
Arthur Foote II, saying that Unitarians spread themselves all over
the religious spectrum, but Arthur Foote had never revealed
where he stood. Bothered by my defeat, I added: "Yet, there must
have been some sort of exchange with his brother Henry and,
perhaps, with your father, Henry II. To know how your granduncle felt (and he certainly had firm religious beliefs) would give
further insights into his music, not just into the pieces intended
for church use, but also into the instrumental works." The Reverend Arthur Foote II replied in a letter dated 9 May 1995:

Uncle Arthur was a loyal, all-be-it conservative Unitarian,
what nowadays we call a Channing Unitarian. He grew up
in a devout and very conservative home. He adored his
brother, and if he differed with him theologically (as I
imagine he may have at certain points) he would have preferred to keep quiet rather than openly disagree. Theological debate had little interest for him. He was happy in
his thirty years at First Church, writing the many anthems
which were later published. You are quite right, music was
the consuming interest and focus of his life, and his so-
called secular compositions as surely as his music for his
church expressed his religious convictions, his devotion
to truth, his breadth of spirit.[14]

In a sermon delivered at the First Church on 8 November
1953 Rev. Duncan Howard declared Foote to have played an important part in the church's worship. During the years he was
the music director, he invariably chose to present anthems that
reinforced what the minister had to say:

He was always careful to tell the minister what he had in
mind for the quartet to sing, and then inquired solici-
tously whether or not his selections were suitable to the

theme the minister had in mind. He served under three
different ministers and treated all three alike. He was as
solicitous of Dr. Park's wishes, when Dr. Park came to this
church as a young man of thirty-three, as he had been of
Rufus Ellis, who was very much his senior. He had a sense
of the fitness of things, and that included the use of music
for worship on Sunday morning.[15]

It is not necessary to speculate about his many altruistic acts,
which assuredly went hand-in-hand with his religious views. He
was one of the "thoughtful persons [who] have for years realized
. . . the great disproportion in what is got out of life by the poorer
and richer groups," and hoped it "was bound to disappear by degrees."[16] He was constantly contributing money or volunteering
his services to some cause or other. On 10 February 1877, he was
one of four musicians assisting the young unknown vocalist Lillian Bailey in an early appearance before a public. This was not
his first offer of help. She had made her début at a Lang concert
in the spring of 1876, when sixteen years of age. She "on that occasion was assisted also by a pianist and composer rapidly rising
into prominence—Arthur Foote," writes her future husband,
George Henschel, the first conductor of the Boston Symphony
Orchestra. "These two men [Lang and Foote], natives both of historical Salem . . . had from that time on taken a most kindly interest in the young lady . . . and it was only natural that they should
have been the first of her many friends to whom my young wife
was anxious to introduce me. . . . These two men exercised a decided and most beneficent influence on the musical life of Boston
and the development of its taste. And their friendship and generous support from the very first, which former in the case of the
young man has, I am happy to say, survived to this day [1918]."[17]

Instances of his generous regard for the welfare of others
abound. For example, on 12 December 1883, he performed at
the organ for a "Meeting in the interest of Indian and Negro Education." On 14 November 1884, he gave a piano recital at the
Blind Asylum (now the Perkins Institute for the Blind). On 11
February 1889, after he had appeared at the Essex Institute in Salem, he wrote back to a Mrs. Hunt at the institute: "Thank you for
the check: it was a very great pleasure to me to play. I supposed

from the look of the bill that the concerts paid, and am glad at any rate that they nearly do. Another year I wish you would remember that I should be very glad to be a volunteer for anything that is up."[18] He was always ready to help collect money or assist in a benefit concert for an individual musician who found himself or herself impoverished. We also will find him heading the Oliver Ditson Society for the Relief of Needy Musicians. When not actively helping others with a performance, money, or personal effort, he was giving moral support. To cite one instance, Arthur Falkland-Bachman wrote to him on 16 February 1889: "Many thanks indeed for your kind note and kinder remarks about my efforts. It gave me great pleasure to see your faces in the stalls. With kindest regards in which Mary joins me."[19]

Foote's assistance to his fellow American composers was continuous and unstinting. We have already seen him paying attention to the young Ethelbert Nevin. We found him voting to include Chadwick's Overture to *Rip Van Winkle* and Symphony in C on the programs of the Harvard Musical Association. In 1880, he was helping solicit subscribers for Schmidt's proposed publication of the score to Paine's Second "Spring" Symphony. Concert after concert that he put on called young American composers to public attention. For example, writing of a concert he gave at Chickering Hall on 15 March 1887, a reviewer said: "It was a kindly idea of Mr. Foote's to devote so large a part of his programme to compositions by musicians either new resident in or near Boston, or who have been intimately associated with our city." Named were Paine, Johns, Whiting, Chadwick, Thayer, and MacDowell.[20] Most interesting of all is a letter that the then unknown Horatio Parker sent to Foote on 20 January 1886. He had returned the summer before from his musical studies in Germany. Parker writes:

> Dear Mr. Foote,
>
> Schmidt has just written that you would be good enough to finger my two pieces which he is going to publish. Thank you for it heartily. I send him by this mail three other pieces belonging to the same set. If you would kindly look at the fingering, such as it is, of them and correct blunders and supply deficiencies, you would increase

my obligation to you greatly. I know it is easy for you, and,
also that such work is so hard for me, in my blissful ignorance of everything pertaining to the piano, that I can't do
it properly."[21]

In addition, Parker asks Foote to give him what advice on
music that he can, "which I shall follow." Finally, he wants guidance in dealing with Schmidt, who is asking Parker what price he
wants for the music. Does he, as a green composer, dare ask for a
royalty?

The industrial age dawned during his youth, with its money-
centeredness, corruption and robber barons, and rampant nationalism. Belief in manifest destiny and the jingoism that
eventually brought on the Spanish-American war occurred during
Foote's maturity. These physical and social disturbances may explain some of the allure of European cultures and the idealistic
views, which came to be designated as "the genteel tradition,"
that Foote experienced. Regrettably, in the rough-and-tumble of
twentieth-century living, the word *genteel* acquired a bundle of
pejorative meanings: false delicacy, timid taste, boasting about
one's ancestry, excessive deference to an unimaginative and con-
formist morality and religion, and endeavoring to keep up a pre-
tense of superior standing. Foote and his intimates demonstrated
none of these characteristics.

He must have read with bemusement his friend Arlo Bates's
commentary on taste, morality, art, and religion in the novel *The
Pagans*. This view of taste and art might have corresponded to
his own. He presumably had reservations about Bates's relative
demotion of morality and religion. On the whole, Foote would
have found Bates's argument overdone but would have applauded the principle of the artist's obligation to engage in earnest
communication. Nevertheless, what follows is the kind of discussion that did go on at the St. Botolph Club. Here, whatever the
beliefs of Foote, Bates, and others, they were certain to be debated and tested. Bates writes:

> "You're right, Tom," he said, "in your view of taste. Taste is
> sublimated morality. It is the appreciation of the propor-
> tion and fitness of all things in the universe, and of course

it is above simple morality, for that is founded upon a partial view. Taste is the universal, where a system of morals is local."

"Can't you say that of art?" asked Rangely. "I should think art is the universal, where religion is the provincial. A religion expresses the needs and aspirations of a race or country, while art embodies the aspirations and attributes of humanity."

"Good!" Bentley responded. "That is better than I should have said it, but it's my belief, all the same. There are so few people who have imagination enough even to understand what one means by saying art is the only thing in the world worth living for. Why, art is the supreme expression of humanity; the apotheosis of all the best there is in the race."[22]

The above helps us to understand better what went on when Foote mentions that he, Parker, Whiting, and Chadwick used to meet at the St. Botolph Club after dinner:

We allowed ourselves frank discussion and the most outspoken criticism I have ever heard. I got no end of good from it. As an example of what a few words can do in the way of opening one's eyes, I remember Parker saying, after I had ended the playing through of a movement from my orchestra Suite, "All in D minor, isn't it?" And that was the trouble; easily remedied by the simple alteration of some authentic cadences to deceptive ones.[23]

Referring to her father M. A. DeWolfe Howe and his friends, including Foote, Helen Howe found them honest, sincere men trying their best to live up to the standards they set for themselves, reexamining and altering them when necessary. She rejected the charge of "shabby genteel" because to her ears "genteel" implied "a phony veneer, with emphasis on nonessential appearances." Her father's set, she insisted, honored the commitments they made and never dwelled on the achievements of dead ancestors nor measured others in terms of dollars and cents.[24]

Honesty occupied a prominent place in Foote's thinking. He admired it in his father's character and recalled with pride his father's crusade with "courage and honesty to oppose and expose" a corrupt but politically powerful Ben Butler.[25] In 1911, when he lectured about the history of music in the United States, he praised William Billings, the eighteenth-century singing-school teacher and composer, naming him one of

> the first of the native composers . . . self-taught, and though an eccentric, winning many friends through his honesty of purpose. . . . He later, when Boston was occupied by British troops in Revolutionary times, poured out his soul as follows —
> > "By the waters of Watertown, we sat down;
> > Yea, we wept as we rememb'red Boston."[26]

He applauded Billings for striving after the best that was available to him in his time. He may have perceived Billings as furnishing instruction in morality as well as music. Foote thought that people like Billings held the representation of the ideal through high-minded yet beautiful music as an important objective of art.[27] He also was trying to accomplish this. He acknowledged the example of his teacher, John Knowles Paine, whose "influence was always for what was strong and good in music." Then there was the example of Franz Kneisel, Hans Richter, and Theodore Thomas, musicians who remained "simple in methods, big musically, with the highest ideals."[28]

Foote's lectures delivered at the University of California in 1911, the side comments in his *Etude* articles, and the letters that refer to his music explain what he meant by the beautiful. To him, a perception of beauty resulted when a work of art gave pleasure to both the artist and the public. Of equal moment was the manner in which a composer went about realizing it. To achieve the beautiful, Foote believed that the composer first went about producing his work out of the tones available to him. Expertise came next. The composer put his training to work in forging the tones into an artistic expression. Taste now entered the equation, that is to say, personal preference and the discernment of what is aesthetically appropriate. However spontaneous and inspired the artist, however much his mind encompassed visions of perfection, this taste joined to expertise was indispensable for achieving artistic aims. The test of that achievement came when the work was presented to an audience, the final arbiter. His good composer-friend Horatio Parker spoke similarly, pointing out that composers of excellence had to first have a knowledge of various styles; next, a thorough command of the materials of music: melody, harmony, rhythm, and forms. Parker says: "Every good composer has inherited all previous music and must know much of it, exactly as the author must know literature." His task is through taste and talent to put imitation behind him and realize his own creative goal.[29]

Foote advocated giving pleasure to the public. Redfern Mason made this clear when he eulogized Foote, at the same time lauding "his strength of purpose, his unwavering pertinacity." Mason said that Foote never pushed himself forward and was ashamed of self-advertisement. Furthermore, "when he stood up in old Chickering Hall to direct his chamber music, or when he played the piano in his Piano Quintet with the Kneisels, then he was happy. The toys of ambition had no fascination for him. To create something beautiful; to write a song that would express what was in the minds of the people; to do that was more to Arthur Foote than to make a fortune."[30] The composer reveals his delight in successfully reaching his public when he writes a comment on the program of a New York concert of the Adamowski Quartet. After the listing of his Piano Quartet, he adds, "A great success!"[31]

Foote agreed with his friend Apthorp, who said the music public was always on the lookout, first, for melody it could enjoy and that it accepted and understood an artist's work on its own terms; not on the artist's.[32] The composer disclosed his attitude further in choosing to preserve a newspaper item from around 1880. It quotes from an eighteenth-century source, dated 19 March 1797, on the applause Haydn would welcome for his oratorio *The Creation*. The parentheses were inserted in pencil by Foote himself:

> Nothing can be more gratifying to Haydn than the applause of his audience. He has always tried to deserve it and has obtained it more frequently than he expected. (He hopes in the present instant to meet with the same

encouragement which he has hitherto experienced, much to his comfort; and he wishes on this occasion to look upon applause merely as a highly esteemed expression of satisfaction and not as a demand for the repetition of a number, as this would mar the continuity by which the work aims at effect as a whole, and thus diminish the pleasure which, perhaps, a too great reputation has led the public to expect.)[33]

Teacher, Performer, and Music Director, 1876–1889

At various periods in his career, Foote taught in his home, in a studio at the Chickering Building, 153 Tremont Street, Boston, and at 6 Newbury Street, Boston, "where Lang and a colony of his pupils occupied rooms at the Lang Studios." Many of his students later became teachers, thus perpetuating and spreading his thoughts about music in general along with his teaching methods. Foote instructed young learners even as he played as many as seventy-five concerts yearly.[34] His charge was $40 per quarter, for twenty lessons (one a week) or $50 a quarter (two a week). Eventually, he had all the students he could handle, a large number coming from outside Boston.[35] Foote, of course, advertised his availability, as in the following:

Mr. Arthur Foote,
will be at his room,
2 West Cedar Street, Boston,
on Wednesdays and Saturday's throughout
the summer,
from 12 to 1, to arrange for
Pianoforte and Organ Lessons.[36]

We are fortunate to have his daughter Katharine's account of his teaching at home at 2 West Cedar Street:

Papa taught at home until 1895. The pupils used the dining room as a waiting room. Fortunately, there was a bookcase of interesting books there, as Papa often got so ab-

sorbed in a pupil that lessons were prolonged beyond
their normal length. Luncheon was a very movable feast
and dinner often came late. It was a long day for Papa as
lessons began at nine and sometimes lasted until dinner
time. Once in a while Papa would leave the pupil at work
and go to see if there were any letters—even run upstairs
for a hanky or some such errand. The pupil, left alone, became over-confident and made a mistake. Quickly she
heard from somewhere, "A sharp" or "1-2-1-2" or some
other correction. Poor pupil![37]

To promote education, he prepared an edition of Charles
Buttschardt's *Method of Pianoforte Technique*, issued by Schmidt
in 1886, and an *Etude Album: A Collection of Etudes for the Pianoforte*, which Schmidt put out the following year. He also
translated Ernst Richter's *A Treatise on Fugue, Including the
Study of Imitation and Canon* and *A Treatise on Canon and
Fugue, Including the Study of Imitation and Canon, from the
Third German Edition*, that Oliver Ditson of Boston published in
1878 and 1888, respectively. A highly regarded reviewer, Eben-
ezer Prout, called the translation from the German "well done,"
and according to an unidentified writer, the Richter treatise on
fugue "was used for some time at Harvard."[38] In addition, he edited many individual pieces by Bach, Dvořák, Mendelssohn, Mosz-
kowski, Raff, Saint-Saëns, Scharwenka, Mozart, Schubert, and
Rheinberger for Schmidt to publish. Invariably, he kept in mind
his own and other keyboard teachers' needs.

Foote joined musical associations for the sake of education.
In July 1884, he accompanied B. J. Lang to a meeting of the Music
Teachers National Association in Cleveland. His friend wanted to
organize a teachers' interest group to standardize instruction.
However, Lang found himself opposed to the M.T.N.A.'s leadership and left. In a demonstration of independence, Foote remained. He joined the organization and was soon working
tirelessly to improve musical education and the advancement of
the cause of American music throughout the country. In 1886, the
annual meeting was held in Boston, and Foote acted as chairman
of the concert committee. Later, he became a member of its executive committee and remained active in the organization for
twenty years. This association's meetings, Foote says, allowed

him to meet musicians from all over the United States, thus broadening his ideas and making him less provincial. Another reward of membership was the performance of his works, thus allowing him to gain a wider recognition than otherwise would have been possible. One such occasion, of considerable importance to Foote, was the performance of his Overture *In the Mountains*. It was played at the annual meeting held in Indianapolis on 5 July 1887.[39] Nine years after this, he was a cofounder of the American Guild of Organists and served as its president from 1909 to 1912. He would also head the South End Music School.

Quite a few of his concert appearances had an educational aim. Sometimes he also spoke at schools where he performed. For example, in 1876 he was a guest at the Worcester County Music School, where he presented a piano program. The next year he was featured there on 21 June in B. D. Allen's "Evenings with the Musicians," one of the school's educational courses. By the next decade, he was traveling farther afield. For example, on 8 November 1888, he was at Miss Porter and Mrs. Dow's Young Ladies' School, Farmington, Connecticut, where he and the Kneisel Quartet presented "SOIRÉE (No. 170)." Among the works they played was Schumann's Piano Quartet in E-flat, op. 44.[40]

By the end of the 1880s, he was in demand as a lecturer on musical subjects. An enthusiastic comment appeared in Harvard's *The Daily Crimson*, of 25 April 1889: "Mr. Arthur Foote, one of the greatest American composers, lectured in Sever Hall last evening on the choice of music as a profession. He was introduced by President Eliot." Foote preserved this report and a letter he received from Charles Eliot, who wrote:

> I entirely agree with you that music is a part of general education, and is entitled to be counted among the humanities. . . . I should like to have it accepted as a subject to count for admission to Harvard College. Before this can be done, however, it will be necessary to have the teaching of music in the secondary schools reinforced.[41]

Charles Eliot looked with favor on his young kinsman by marriage and in 1879, he placed Foote on the Visiting Committee for Music at Harvard. In this position, Foote oversaw the music department and made suggestions for improvements. In

1889, he became a member of the Library Committee of the Harvard Musical Association.[42] Foote would do his best to improve the association's music holdings. Its collection at that time was considered "one of the three or four fullest and most valuable musical libraries in America."[43] A letter that Foote sent to John Sullivan Dwight from Neuilly, France, on 16 July 1883 indicates that Foote was already gathering scores for the association. He writes that he has received Dwight's two notes and the money and is now "getting a lot of music for P. F. and strings, here of Hamelle." (Jacques Hamelle was a French music publisher who issued works by Franck, Saint-Säens, Fauré, and d'Indy.) He says he tried to see Saint-Säens without success because the composer was beset with "nervous exhaustion." He had visited Stephen Heller, whose eyes were afflicted with cataracts.[44]

More evidence of his work for the association comes from an undated letter to Allan Brown. Foote writes from 153 Tremont Street, Boston: "Has Dannreuther sent you the list of his library with pieces? I thought it might be an opportunity for the Harvard Musical Association! Can't you come in a minute some morning, if on your way down town?"[45] Gustav Dannreuther was a Cincinnati-born violinist who lived in Boston for a time.

Foote's activities as a recitalist and organizer of the several chamber concert series in which he appeared at the keyboard were also educational. Foote's dedication—and he consistently demonstrated this dedication in solo recitals, chamber concerts, appearances with orchestra, and concert tours—was centered on bringing the finest music, old and contemporary, to the community. On this point he would not compromise. He was also aware that the highly honored John Knowles Paine was concentrating his energies on the Harvard campus and was not one for concertizing. Foote scheduled his own compositions for performance whenever possible. In due time, as his success grew, even in the Midwest and New York, Foote increasingly hoped that he would achieve notice as a significant composer.

As early as 1875, Foote assisted at the keyboard in concerts given by the Salem Oratorio Society and the Cecilia Society.[46] His first piano recital took place in 1876. He played with the score on the piano, "for I had not been forced to memorize." In the same year, he assisted Lang in two Boston concerts. For one of the Lang concerts, Foote arranged the orchestral part of the Saint-Säens

Second Piano Concerto in G Minor so that he could accompany Lang in it. On 10 March 1876, he appeared at the New England Conservatory of Music in Mendelssohn's Trio in D Minor. On 18 February 1878, he appeared with the young singer Lillian Bailey (the future wife of George Henschel) at a concert in Salem, where he was a soloist in Beethoven's Thirty-Two Variations in C Minor and Liszt's Hungarian Rhapsody no. 5. Foote has written the year "79" over a report that he played on one of three pianos in "Bach's Concerto in D-minor, for three pianos and strings," at a Harvard symphony concert. His hometown, Salem, did not neglect him. The two concerts he participated in, on 10 January and 18 December 1876, were the first of many that he would give at the Essex Institute.[47]

Other towns were easily reached from Boston by railroad. He began to visit them regularly in the early 1880s. Recorded in his Scrapbook I at the Boston Public Library is a recital at Abbott Academy Hall, Andover, on 21 January 1881. On 6 June 1883, he appeared with the baritone Clarence E. Hay at the Music Hall, Pittsfield. On 27 February 1884, he and the cellist Wulf Fries played at Academy Hall, Bradford; two days later, at the Town Hall, Andover. The demand for concerts remained high. In some towns, he returned several times during a season. Entertainments were few, and Foote's musical evenings were well attended.

During the years 1876–1883, his public appearances multiplied. In 1884 he began tours of a week or so to the Midwest and New York. These tours continued until 1909. Also in 1884 the Chickering Musical Bureau, managed by John E. Pinkham, enrolled him as a client and sought to find him engagements.[48] We do have newspaper reviews of the concert he gave in Cleveland on 27 October 1884. Perhaps his earlier travel to Cleveland (during the summer) to attend the M.T.N.A. meeting with Lang paved the way for the concert. The newspaper writers who listened to his performance said that he came to the city as an "unknown." They listened to him play Beethoven, Saint-Saëns, Liszt, and Schumann and, however skeptical, were won over. They found that he did not play with the superficial brilliance of a virtuoso. Instead, he was thoroughly a musician and played artistically. His phrasing was musical; his use of the pedals, skilled. Technique was solid; touch, refined and pure. They thought, to give one instance, that Schumann's *Etudes Symphoniques* had received an exceptional interpretation.[49]

Scrapbook I at the Boston Public Library contains Foote's own handwritten lists of solo recitals, joint concerts with other musicians, chamber music presentations, and other performances that he gave from 1884 to 1886:

1884–85 Season

1884: Buffalo 27 Oct., Cleveland 28 Oct, Wells College [at Aurora, New York], 29 Oct., Lang concert sessions 6 Nov., Blind Asylum, 14 Nov.

1885: Beethoven Club (Mrs. Palfrey's) 6 Jan., Cecilia (organ) 15 Jan., Campanari concert 26 Jan., Geise concert 5 Feb., Salem Schubert Club 9 Feb., Apollo Club (organ) 11 Feb., 2nd Church concert 9 March, Lang concert 12 March, Lavallée concert 10 March, Miss Hall concert 18 March, Lang (Bach) concert 21 March, "Indian" concert 27 March, Bradford 1 April, Louis Schmidt concert at New York 7 April, Salem Schubert Concert 9 April, Hartford 15 May.

1885–86 Season

1885: Lexington 16 Sept., Cohasset, 17 Sept., Wells College [at Aurora, New York], 29 Oct., Saratoga [New York], 30 Oct., A.F. Chickering Hall 20 Nov., Salem (Miss Putnam) 1 Dec., Art Club (Frau Reuter) 15 Dec., Bumstead Hall (this with Kneisel and Fries) 21 Dec.

1886: Buffalo (New York), 4 Jan., Beethoven Club (Mrs. Scull's) 18 Jan., Norton (Seminary) 5 Feb., Symphony (Bach Suite) 13 Feb., Apollo Club (accompanist) 10 & 15 Feb., Loeffler's (111 Beacon St.) 15 Feb., Schubert Club (Salem) 17 Feb., Loeffler's (111 Tremont St.) 23 Feb., Miss Edmundson (Me—[?]) 14 April, Worcester (Miss Rockwood) 26 Apr., Schubert Club ("Athalie") 28 April, MTNA 30 June, Nantasket Rink 18 Aug., Saratoga 24 Aug., Saratoga (Temple Grove Seminary) 23 Sept.

The record is an extraordinarily long one for someone who was also holding down a church job and giving private music lessons. It seems almost miraculous that he was able to compose the works that he did during those years. His energy must have been boundless.

Foote appeared three times as a piano soloist with the Boston Symphony Orchestra during the years 1883–1886. His initial appearance on 10 November 1883 attracted a great deal of attention. For his orchestral debut, he played Ferdinand Hiller's Piano Concerto in F-sharp Minor, op. 69, with the orchestra directed by George Henschel. In addition, he played Prelude in C Major and Gavotte in B Minor by Bach and Etude in D-flat Major by Liszt, as the orchestra remained silent. Reviewers described him as an intellectual player, yet one able to perform with intensity and power. They agreed that he had thoroughly studied the four works and mastered their structures and expressive details. What he needed was greater clarity of touch and, here and there, less dryness. They also agreed that Foote was extremely popular with the audience, his performance applauded enthusiastically.[50] Foote was always modest about his piano-playing abilities, especially during the 1870s and 1880s. Probably too critical of himself, he wrote, "On the intellectual side [the playing] was really good, but I was blind to the fact that I was wanting in the sensuous, beautiful element in piano playing, with little feeling for quality in tone and finesse in phrasing."[51]

I mentioned earlier that Foote was serious about his work as organist and music director at the First Church, trying to integrate the musical selections with the Sunday topic. When he took over his directorship, he found a three-manual organ, installed there in 1869 and built by E. F. Walcher & Son, Germany, probably to the specifications of the then organist Eugene Thayer. It was installed close to the altar. Foote gave a small number of organ recitals on this instrument. A new organ in the gallery replaced it in 1903.[52] Everett Truette says of the organ at Foote's church: "The specification was meagre, and the instrument soon became an antique. Notwithstanding the limits of the organ, Mr. Foote made a feature of the musical portions of the regular services."[53] Foote rehearsed a quartet-choir, not a bona fide chorus. These soloists, who had fine voices, supplied vocal music for morning and afternoon services.

A newspaper clipping on which Foote has written "1878" prints the music for his first morning Christmas service. He did one carol each by Arthur Sullivan and Dudley Buck, an anthem by Berthold Tours, a Te Deum by Grenville Wilson, and a Jubilate by Joseph Mosenthal. For vespers at 3:30 p.m. the organ prelude was the allegro from Mendelssohn's Second Sonata; the vocal music was by Charles Gounod, John Stainer, Buck, and Wilson. On another clipping, he has written "Easter '79." The music is by Buck, Edward Hopkins, and Mosenthal. Interestingly, on 17 April 1879 he and the quartet-choir gave a mostly secular concert at the church, which included works by Joseph Rheinberger, Giuseppe Verdi, and Bach.[54] Buck and Wilson were Americans. As more and more American composers came on the scene, their vocal works would be represented more liberally in his musical offerings.

His most important engagement as director of church music came on 18 November 1880, when a commemorative service was held to celebrate the First Church's 250th anniversary. The original church covenant of August 1630, signed by Governor John Winthrop was put on exhibit. Psalm 107, "China," was sung from the eighth Boston edition (1695) of *Psalms, Hymns and Spiritual Songs of the Old and New Testaments*. Charles Eliot, President of Harvard, and Noah Porter, President of Yale, gave addresses.[55]

Foote also directed vocal groups not connected with the First Church. For example, there was the Salem Schubert Club, organized on 3 May 1878 to do cantatas, part songs, and similar music. In the 1880s, it had around 60 singing members and 150 associate members. Chadwick had been the director in 1883 and 1884. Foote took over from him in 1885.[56] In 1878, Lang was scheduled to conduct a Cecilia concert, but broke his arm in an accident. Foote replaced him at the last minute and, among other things, conducted Mendelssohn's *Athalie*. He was a master of the situation, at ease with the music and the technical demands of conducting according to witnesses to the performance.[57] On 28 January 1889, he conducted the thirty male voices of the Arion Glee Club, of Chelsea, Massachusetts. Prior to his appearance with the group, the men had sung with a considerable lack of proficiency. There was notable improvement under Foote's skilled direction. Discipline was imposed, voice quality was bettered, and the renditions were pleasing.[58]

Probably his first organ recital at the First Church took place on 15 November 1879, when he played Bach's Prelude and Fugue in C Major, Handel's Second Organ Concerto in B-flat Major, and Mendelssohn's Organ Sonata in F Minor. The quartet-choir also performed that evening. Another concert of which we have a record was given jointly with the vocalist Louise Gage at the First Church on 20 November 1882. He played Handel's Concerto in F Major, Bach's Fantasie and Fugue in G Minor, and Gustav Merkel's Sonata in F Minor, op. 115. An unidentified newspaper reviewer said Foote was not a great organ player, but he was musical, artistic, and performed delightfully. The writer liked his clear understanding of the compositions and his refusal to constantly change his stops. Foote's polyphonic playing was even, steady, and transparent. He was content to abide by the natural limitations of his instrument and center his attention on developing its resources within those limitations. On 27 March 1884, Foote appeared at a Cecilia Club concert, playing the Mendelssohn Organ Sonata op. 65, no. 1. A reviewer loved the splendid playing by "a brilliant organist" but complained that the organ was annoyingly out of tune.[59]

During his early professional years Foote won his greatest fame as an organizer of and performer in chamber concerts. In March 1880, he inaugurated an ambitious and, for that time in Boston, daring succession of chamber music concerts, consisting mainly of piano-violin-cello trios but also of quartets and quintets normally involving the piano. He would give himself over to such presentations for more than a dozen years. Especially important was the concert he presented in Mechanics Hall, Boston, on 13 March 1880, assisted by Gustav Dannreuther on violin, Henry Heindl on viola, and Wulf Fries on cello. The featured numbers were the Brahms Piano Quartet in G Minor and the Mozart Piano Quartet in E-flat Major. A large and appreciative audience turned out. Critics admired his boldness in scheduling such a controversially contemporary piece as the Brahms quartet [!]. Regrettably, they voiced reservations about the work itself, which they found variously to be pedantic, vague, or without melody. The *Courier* reviewer, after observing the warm applause given to Foote, wrote: "Mr. Foote is rapidly making his way to the front rank of our resident pianists, a fact which it gives us great pleasure to record."[60]

Foote tested the performance waters several times that year, finding the experiments encouraging. The conviction strengthened in him that he might find success adventuring into a musical area that conventional wisdom insisted would appeal only to the specialized tastes of a small audience. I might add that having little to gain financially and facing exhausting exertion, Foote persisted in these activities. At the beginning of the year 1881 the following announcement appeared:

> On every Saturday evening in February and March, Mr. Arthur Foote will play Pianoforte Trios and Quartets with Messrs. Wulf Fries, Charles N. Allen, Gustav Dannreuther, and others, at Chickering's, 156 Tremont St. There will be two pieces of Chamber Music each time, with perhaps some Songs, to begin at a quarter to eight o'clock exactly. . . . Season tickets for the Eight Evenings will be Four Dollars, and Single Admission One Dollar.[61]

Subscriptions and single tickets were obtainable at Schmidt's music store and Foote's home, whose address he gives as "3 West Cedar Street." In Scrapbook I at the Boston Public Library he preserves the "Amusement License" issued to him by the Boston Police Department and a floor plan showing the availability of 458 seats in Chickering Hall.

I cannot overemphasize the importance of this venture into chamber music for its time and place. As well as the founding of the Boston Symphony about the same time, it would greatly advance the cause of art music in Boston and encourage its cultivation elsewhere. Not least were the chamber and orchestral works that other local composers would be encouraged to produce. The first concert, on 5 February, presented an older work, Beethoven's Trio in D, op. 70, no. 1, and a contemporary one, Rubinstein's Trio in F, op. 15, no. 1, plus four songs sung by Miss May Bryant. The reviewer in the *Home Journal*, 12 February 1881, praised him for not electing to do only agreeable works in selecting his programs and for always choosing music of the highest merit. He also congratulated Foote for not giving in to fashion: "It is not the stylish rhapsody of Liszt that one hears at such concerts, but to the reverse, a more transcendent and less sensuous order of music. . . .

The audience finely represented the élite and culture of the city."
The reviewer for the *Boston Evening Transcript*, possibly Apthorp,
commended Foote for providing the best musical literature
played by the finest talent and at the lowest prices: "This is indeed
an important consideration, and the artist in question merits the
success he is meeting with." For his third concert, on 12 February,
he presented the Mendelssohn Trio in D minor, op. 49, which everybody liked, and the Goldmark Trio in E minor, op. 33, which
sounded to Apthorp to be "rather cheap and school-boyish, and is
often terribly ugly." The listeners, however, were unanimous in
their praise of "the young concert-giver" and the "solid enjoyment" he had given them.[62] As with the Brahms, the Goldmark,
another contemporary piece, underlined the danger attending
the performance of anything new and unfamiliar.

Foote would not be deterred. For his fourth concert, on 26
February, he presented the Brahms quartet again, and added a
new work by his Boston colleague George Chadwick, the String
Quartet no. 2 in C Major. Other new works followed: the Raff
Trio in G Major, op. 112, the Dvorák Trio in B-flat Major, op. 21,
for a second time, the Rubinstein Trio in F Major, and for a third
time, the Brahms Quartet in G Minor. The public put a high value on the series despite the demands made on its attention. It
could relax when a captivating group of songs was introduced at
each concert. Presented in the middle of the performance, they
eased the mental pressure brought on by listening to two
lengthy instrumental works. The *Courier* critic summed up the
effect of the series:

> When one thinks of the number of difficult works of the
> highest character that are embraced in Mr. Foote's
> programmes for this series, and of the amount of labor
> necessary to present them in such an excellent manner
> . . . it must be acknowledged that he has shown a de-
> gree of ambition and nerve that reflects the greatest
> credit upon his artistic instincts and abilities. Mr. Foote
> is a progressive man and one of the best educators in
> his art we have among us.[63]

The next season, he offered another series that mixed the
old with the new, and included one premiere important to

Foote, his own Trio in C Minor, op. 5. In the words of an unidentified concertgoer, who presumed to speak for Bostonians, it was
refreshing in the midst of so much mediocrity in America to find
a musician of genuine worth. This person found that Foote possessed originality, talent, adaptability, grit, and intelligence. He
never failed "to assert his independence and his ability." Moreover, he was not one to prate "loudly of his travels abroad, or his
suppers with Liszt."[64]

In 1883, he offered his third series. Two striking novelties on
his programs were the Tchaikovsky Trio in A Minor, op. 50; and
Foote's own String Quartet in G Minor, op. 4. He was by now a
seasoned concert veteran, who had earned the respect of all who
heard him, both for his acumen in attracting an audience and his
dedication to the highest quality in music and in its presentation.

Supporters, Benefactors, and Advisers

A crucial number of native-born New Englanders, cultivated and
well educated, and before long other Americans, considered
Foote to be in accord with their values by birth, thought, and action. They were the most responsible for making Foote's ambi-
tions as musician and composer a reality. Musically, the kind of
art literature they were coming to cherish was one to which he
was trying to contribute. The fashion had not yet taken hold in
which the artist felt that he had to define himself as an individual
unsullied by a pervasive babbittry that infested every sector of
American society. He called valuable compositions to his audience's attention that it might otherwise have missed. He provided men and women with exquisite entertainment, which
frequently allowed for the transcendental experiences that they
believed had to go hand in hand with art. Not the least of his
abilities was his faculty for speaking to his constituency through
music of his own. In his creations, he demonstrated a consum-
mate instinct for inviting melody, richly appointed harmony, and
accomplished craftsmanship—properties the music public regarded highly. His society could feel proud of him because his
music making and his original compositions reflected the best of
its ideals and provided proof that it was civilized and worthy of
respect, in a way that Europe could appreciate. Finally, his in-

formed and edifying music helped provide an estimable counter-
poise to what they saw as the almost overpowering commonness
and aggressiveness of the new America.

Among Foote's supporters were several with more than a little musical training, like James Parker, others who passionately
loved music, like Celia Thaxter, and still others who had the
means to sponsor concerts in their homes, like Mr. and Mrs.
Montgomery Sears, or who had the wealth and dedication to
commence ambitious musical undertakings, like Henry Lee Higginson and the Boston Symphony Orchestra.[65] They were all part
of Foote's circle. His good friend George Henschel speaks in
praise of such enlightenment when he tells us of the wife of
Henry Lee Higginson:

> [She], a daughter of the great scientist, Louis Agazziz, was
> one of a small circle of ladies who held what in France
> they call a 'salon', at whose afternoon teas the representa-
> tives—resident or transitory—of art and science, music
> and literature, used to meet and discuss the events and
> questions of the day. These highly cultured women,
> among whom I recall with delight dear old Mrs. Julia Ward
> Howe . . . Mrs. George D. Howe, with Mrs. Bell and her
> sister Mrs. Pratt, Mrs. John L.—familiarly Mrs. Jack—
> Gardner, were the leaders of what certainly was society in
> the highest and best meaning of the word.[66]

These "leaders" have already been described as people the
Footes called upon socially or who called upon the Footes. They
were also among the staunch advocates he needed to gain respect for his music. Clara Rogers, a fine musician in her own
right, claims she was one of the first to hold weekly musical evenings at her home. One of her objectives was to bring together
fledgling instrumentalists and vocalists, established composers,
other noted musicians, music critics, and patrons. When not listening to music, they could enter into discussions and exchange
views. Those who attended included the composers Foote, Mac-
Dowell, and Chadwick, conductors of the Boston Symphony
Orchestra, B. J. Lang, the music writers Dwight and Apthorp, and
friends like Julia Ward Howe.[67]

An extremely important patron of Foote was Isabella Stewart Gardner. Throughout her life she remained a staunch and encouraging friend of his family. She introduced Foote to men and women who could benefit him, whether at her home or during travels in Europe. Her summer home in Beverly, Massachusetts, was at his disposal for vacations and peaceful seclusion so that he could compose music. Foote was asked to play at her musical evenings before distinguished gatherings. One letter, dated 2 December 1885, that Foote sent to her from 2 West Cedar Street reads:

> I must thank you for the greatest pleasure yesterday that a musician can have, and what he very seldom gets. It was also a peculiar pleasure to play upon your pianoforte, which I enjoyed more than the one which I used at my concert Monday.
>
> Mr. Geise and Mr. Kneisel will charge you $25 each, and, if you like, you can send me cheques for that amount to their order (Fritz Giese and Franz Kneisel) which I will see that they get.[68]

She helped Evelyn Ames launch the short-lived Manuscript Society in order to obtain informed hearings of his and other local composers' compositions in congenial surroundings. The concerts took place in her home. At the first concert, given 19 January 1888, Foote's Suite in E Major for string orchestra, op. 12, was performed.[69] He would dedicate his ambitious Symphonic Prologue, *Francesca da Rimini*, op. 24 to her after he completed it while vacationing at her summer place.

Unfortunately, there were other sorts of leaders that Foote could not really rely on—the well-to-do followers of fashion. As a writer in the *Home Journal* observed in April 1883, they at first flocked to his chamber concerts because it seemed fashionable to do so, not because of any love of music. Then they lost interest and fell away. They had no understanding of music, save for the name attached to a piece, and indulged in the most hypocritical expressions of admiration. They were incapable of appreciating "such excellent concerts as Mr. Foote is giving." The writer, however, does admit that in Boston "there is a wider sprinkling

of musical cultivation . . . than elsewhere."[70] For so-called music
lovers of the fashionable sort, Foote was "the artist to whom
[they] went . . . when no foreigner was for the moment in vogue
and on hand."[71]

These were the people the painter William Morris Hunt had
in mind when he complained one evening to Mrs. Annie Fields
that his art was entirely misunderstood. In reply, she urged him
"to stand firm" and assured him "that his efforts were neither
lost or in vain."[72] Without question, Annie Fields, and supporters
like her, played a similar function in Foote's life, strengthening
his resolve and assuring him of their understanding.

Then there were the knowledgeable writers on music. There
were many of them, and they had a fairly large readership. Most
of these writers spoke favorably of Foote's performances and
compositions. Their words often served as guides to Foote, directing his attention to what was right and wrong about his music making. The ever honest Foote preserved many of their
reviews, negative and positive, in his scrapbooks. William
Apthorp's writings appeared in the *Atlantic Monthly*, the *Sunday
Courier*, the *Boston Traveler*, and the *Boston Evening Transcript*.
Howard Ticknor wrote for the *Boston Advertiser*, *Boston Globe*,
and *Boston Herald*, and was assistant editor of the *Atlantic
Monthly*. Louis C. Elson edited the *Musical Herald*, and appeared in the *Boston Courier* and *Boston Advertiser*. Philip Hale
contributed to the *Boston Home Journal*, *Boston Post*, the *Boston Herald*, and *Musical Courier*, and edited the *Musical Record*
and *Musical World*. One writer on music, Benjamin Woolf, had
been born in England and exercised an extremely retrogressive
taste in his writings for the *Saturday Evening Gazette* and, later,
the *Herald*. He raged at contemporary composers like Wagner,
and was fond of attacking local American musicians, sometimes
including Foote, with ridicule and invective.[73]

Of them all, Apthorp (1848–1913) was the one that Foote
knew best and whose writings he took most seriously. His advice
was seriously considered. One cannot imagine them meeting frequently, as they did meet, without Foote discussing music with
this erudite man only five years his senior. It might have been
Foote speaking when Apthorp said that conventions in music
changed when they ceased to be authentic expressions of feel-

ings held in common. He continued by saying that when an exhausted convention was abolished, it had to be succeeded by another that genuinely addressed the needs of the age and more precisely expressed the sentiments of the artistic world. Newness by itself was ineffectual unless it became an acknowledged convention. If not so acknowledged, it took art in the direction of anarchy. There were radical innovators who cast aside not what was merely unserviceable, but what they personally found abhorrent. Someone was needed to probe the discards for some element that was still pertinent to his age.[74] As might be expected, Foote fitted this categorization.

Franz Kneisel arrived in Boston in the fall of 1885 to become concertmaster of the Boston Symphony under Gericke. He was immediately encouraged by Higginson to form a first-rate string quartet. To this musician's sponsorship, encouragement, and advice, Foote owed a great deal. He wrote:

> I played with [the Kneisel Quartet] a good many times, chiefly at first performances of my own compositions. Not only had I the honor and happiness of having a hearing of my Violin Sonata, Piano Trio in B-flat, Piano Quartet and Quintet, and String Quartet, but also learned much from Kneisel through his suggestions as to practical points in composition, and I became aware of a different and higher standard of performance through my work with him in rehearsal. . . . When Kneisel died, in 1925 [he actually died 26 March 1926], the grief was accompanied by the old feeling of thankfulness and a never-to-be-forgotten appreciation of his encouragement.[75]

Arthur P. Schmidt (1846–1921) was another man to whom Foote was thankful for his encouragement. He arrived in Boston from Germany in 1866 and began his own publishing house in 1877, just when Foote was coming on the scene as a composer. The Schmidt firm published the great majority of Foote's compositions, often in conjunction with European, normally German, publishers. When Schmidt died, in May 1921, Foote lauded him as one of the strongest influences in the development of American music, not letting a year go by when he did not publish at

least one or more American scores. He had high principles, definite opinions about music, and generosity in helping American
composers.[76] In his autobiography, Foote adds, "When it is remembered that before Schmidt there had been published in this
country no music other than such was of comparatively small
consequence, it is obvious that what he did was of far-reaching
importance."[77] Schmidt's imprints made Foote's name known
throughout the United States and Europe.

Among Foote's supporters were the several conductors of
the Boston Symphony who premiered work after work of his.
Noted concert singers like Louise Homer, John McCormack, and
Geraldine Farrar took up his songs, as did pianists his piano
pieces. The first was Annette Essipoff, on 12 May 1877, who
played his Gavotte in B Minor in Boston. This was one of three
pieces he had just completed (*Trois Morceaux*, op. 3) and dared
show Essipoff. She accepted it, and "I had the delight . . . of hearing it played at this concert spoken of. The sensation of hearing a
public performance of one's work, for the first time, can be
imagined."[78]

The helping hands were many. When George Henschel left
the Boston Symphony and relocated in London, he saw to several performances there of Foote's music. For example, on 29 January 1887 he wrote to Foote: "Your Trio was magnificently
performed and had a great success." Two years later, another
friend, Frank Van Der Stucken, wrote to him, "Please send score
& parts "In the Mountains" at once, as I leave for Paris *next
Wednesday*." One musician totally committed to Foote's music
was Jacob H. Hahn, who founded the Detroit Conservatory of
Music in 1875. In a letter he sent to the composer on 13 March
1889, he gives an extremely full and informative description of
how he was lending his support. He wrote to Foote from Detroit, saying:

> My dear Foote,
> You will no doubt be interested to know that the con-
> cert of your compositions proved a complete success. The
> arrangement of the program furnished plenty of contrast
> and every number was beautifully done. The singers and

players have looked upon the thing as a genuine labor of love and neither time nor labor has been spared to bring about the result stated. The audience was very enthusiastic and it has been the talk of the town ever since. Every prominent musician in the country has received the program and I have already received many letters of acknowledgment of the same. I will hereafter keep these things before the public in this section as I am determined that they shall become familiar and well known and which they so thoroughly deserve. The cello pieces went especially well, although it will be difficult to create a violent demand for them—but I am sure that Schmidt will see the effect of the Concert in calls for the songs and piano pieces. With cordial greetings, I am

Your friend,

J. H. Hahn[79]

Many other musicians could be named who were delighted to assist in advancing Foote's career as a composer. Among them were the conductors B. J. Lang in Boston and Theodore Thomas in Chicago, the pianist Helen Hopekirk, the string players Joseph and Timothée Adamowski, and the flutist Georges Laurent. They gave their assistance partly because of his amiability, but more because they perceived the excellence of his overall musicianship and creative abilities.

As a final comment, let me say that the adviser whom he loved and most trusted would no longer be able to counsel him after the 1880s. His older brother, Henry, died on 5 May 1889.

Notes

1. Rupert Hughes, *Contemporary American Composers* (Boston: Page, 1900), 16–17.

2. Arthur Foote, "A Bostonian Remembers," *Musical Quarterly* 23 (1937): 41.

3. Daniel Gregory Mason, *The Dilemma of American Music* (New York: Macmillan, 1928), 2–4.

4. Arthur Foote, *An Autobiography* (Norwood, Mass.: Plimpton Press,

1946), 57. See also Oscar G. Sonneck, *Suum Cuique* (New York: Schirmer, 1916), 139; Wilma Reid Cipolla, introduction to *A Catalog of the Works of Arthur Foote*, Bibliographies in American Music, no. 6 (Detroit: Information Coordinators, 1980), vi, xii.

5. Arthur Foote, *An Autobiography* (Norwood, Massachusetts: Privately printed at the Plimpton Press, 1946), 44.

6. Arthur Foote, MS of lectures delivered at the University of California, Berkeley, in 1911, now in the Boston Public Library, shelf no. **M.472.134; see p.19.

7. Arthur Foote, Scrapbook I and Scrapbook II, Boston Public Library, shelf no. **ML.46F65, contain these and other references to Wagner.

8. Amy Fay, *Music-Study in Germany* (New York: Macmillan, 1896), 122.

9. Bulletin no. 4 (December 1935) of the Harvard Musical Association contains Foote's reminiscences on the decade 1870–1880.

10. Foote, *An Autobiography*, 34.

11. Foote, "A Bostonian Remembers," 42.

12. Foote, *An Autobiography*, 35–36.

13. Ibid., 16.

14. The letter was sent from Arthur II's home in Southwest Harbor, Maine.

15. "Arthur Foote and the Flowering of American Music," sermon, First Church Unitarian, Boston, 8 November 1953.

16. Foote, *An Autobiography*, 13.

17. Sir George Henschel, *Musings & Memories of a Musician* (London: Macmillan, 1918), 268–69.

18. The letter is at the Essex Institute, in a folder without shelf number that contains items of the Foote family. The other references may be found in Scrapbook I at the Boston Public Library.

19. Arthur Foote, "Letters Collected by Arthur Foote: Gift to the Library in Memory of Arthur Foote, April 16, 1940," Spaulding Library, New England Conservatory of Music, letter no. 11.

20. The effort to publish the Paine score by subscription is contained in the Scrapbook at the New England Conservatory. The page is unnumbered. The review is entitled "Mr. Foote's Concert," *Boston Evening Transcript*, 16 March 1887, 1.

21. Foote, "Letters Collected by Arthur Foote," letter no. 88.

22. Arlo Bates, *The Pagans* (Boston: Ticknor, 1888), 253–54.

23. Foote, *An Autobiography*, 55.

24.   Helen Howe, *The Gentle Americans, 1864–1960* (New York: Harper & Row, 1965), 104–05.

25.   Foote, *An Autobiography*, 28.

26.   Foote, "Music in the United States," 7.

27.   These values of the time are discussed in Richard Guy Wilson, "The Great Civilization," in *The American Renaissance, 1876–1917* (New York: Brooklyn Museum, 1979), 28–30.

28.   Foote, *An Autobiography*, 33, 77.

29.   See, for example, the introduction in Horatio Parker, *Music and Public Entertainment* (Boston: Hall & Locke, 1911), xv.

30.   Redfern Mason, "The Passing of Arthur Foote," *Boston Evening Transcript*, 17 April 1937, an editorial that is preserved as a clipping in a scrapbook not kept by Foote, at the Boston Public Library, shelf no. **ML.46.B6F6.

31.   Foote, Scrapbook III, Boston Public Library, shelf no. **ML.46F65. The program is dated 30 January 1899.

32.   William Foster Apthorp, *Musicians and Music Lovers* (New York: Scribner's Sons, 1894), 34; *By the Way*, vol. 2 (Boston: Copeland & Day, 1898), 192.

33.   Arthur Foote, Scrapbook, New England Conservatory of Music, n.p.

34.   Foote, *An Autobiography*, 48–49.

35.   Ibid., 43.

36.   The undated and unidentified advertisement is found in Foote, Scrapbook I, Boston Public Library, shelf no. **ML.46F65, among other clippings dating from the late spring of 1885.

37.   Katharine Foote Raffy, "2 West Cedar Street, 1882–1885," typewritten MS, Arthur Foote Collection, Williams College, Williamstown, Massachusetts.

38.   Page 1 of the Foote, Scrapbook, New England Conservatory of Music, contains the Prout review. The comment on the treatise's use at Harvard is included in a clipping in the Arthur Foote Collection. Foote has written "1899" on the clipping.

39.   Foote, *An Autobiography*, 50–51; Scrapbook I, Boston Public Library.

40.   The Worcester program is in the Scrapbook, at the New England Conservatory of Music, p. 10; the Farmington one is in Scrapbook I, at the Boston Public Library.

41.   Foote, Scrapbooks I and III, respectively, Boston Public Library. The letter bears the date 5 November 1902.

42.   Kopp, "Arthur Foote: American Composer and Theorist," 64.

43.   John Sullivan Dwight, "Music in Boston," in *The Memorial History of Boston*, vol. 4, edited by Justin Winsor (Boston: Ticknor, 1881), 438.

44.   Letter, now in the Special Collections Room of the Boston Public Library, M. Cab.2.41 V2, p. 28.

45.   Letter, now in the Special Collections Room of the Boston Public Library, M. Cab.2.41 V2, p. 29.

46.   Frederick Edward Kopp, "Arthur Foote: American Composer and Theorist" (Ph.D. diss., Eastman School of Music, University of Rochester, 1957), 59.

47.   They are listed in the Scrapbook at the New England Conservatory.

48.   Foote, *An Autobiography*, 44; Scrapbook, New England Conservatory, 3, 14, 17, 57; Scrapbook I, Boston Public Library.

49.   Foote, Scrapbook I, Boston Public Library; the page number 114 is written above, on the outer corner of the page.

50.   Foote, Scrapbook I, Boston Public Library, contains the Boston Symphony Orchestra program. In addition, on page 89 of "Boston Symphony Orchestra. Clippings and Reviews," collected by Allan A. Brown, Boston Public Library, shelf no. **M.125.5, will be found the several newspaper reviews of the performance.

51.   Foote, *An Autobiography*, 43.

52.   Wayne Leupold, preface to *The Organ Works of Arthur Foote*, ed. Wayne Leupold (n.p.: McAfee Music, 1977), 3.

53.   Everett E. Truette, "Two American Organists and Composers," *The Musician* 15 (1910): 347-8.

54.   Foote, Scrapbook, New England Conservatory of Music, 1, 9.

55.   Ibid.; n.p.

56.   George N. Whipple, "A Sketch of the Musical Societies of Salem," in *Historical Collections of the Essex Institute*, vol. 23 (Salem: Essex Institute, 1886), 127. Foote in *An Autobiography* says he gave a concert with the club on 9 February 1885.

57.   Foote, Scrapbook, New England Conservatory of Music, 3,11.

58.   Ibid., n.p.

59.   Announcements, programs, and reviews are found in Scrapbook I, Boston Public Library.

60.   Both the scrapbook at the New England Conservatory of Music, and the scrapbook, shelf no. **ML.46.B6F6 at the Boston Public Library contain the program and clippings of the newspaper reviews.

61.　Foote, Scrapbook I, Boston Public Library; also in the Scrapbook, at the New England Conservatory of Music..

62.　The programs and reviews may be found in Foote, Scrapbook I, and in another scrapbook not compiled by Foote, shelf no. **ML.46.B6F6, both in the Boston Public Library.

63.　The review, dated 5 March 1881, is in Scrapbook I, Boston Public Library.

64.　Scrapbook, Boston Public Library, shelf no. **ML.46.B6F6.

65.　Foote's Scrapbook I at the Boston Public Library contains these and other names of Bostonians who were upholding art music. He was present at their musical afternoons and evenings, as a guest, a performer, and a composer whose music was to be performed.

66.　Sir George Henschel, *Musings & Memories of a Musician*, 67, 254–55.

67.　Clara Kathleen Rogers, *Memories of a Musical Career* (Boston: Little, Brown, 1919), 30.

68.　The letter is in the Archives of the Gardner Museum.

69.　Clara Kathleen Rogers, *The Story of Two Lives* (Boston: Plimpton Press, 1932), 187–88.

70.　A clipping of the report is found in Foote, Scrapbook I, Boston Public Library.

71.　Foote's friend, Arlo Bates, in *The Philistines* (Boston: Ticknor, 1889), 12, is writing not about Foote per se, but about the Boston artist in relation to the fashionable but artistically ignorant social set.

72.　M. A. DeWolfe Howe, *Memories of a Hostess* (Boston: Atlantic Monthly Press, 1922), 98.

73.　Louis C. Elson, *The History of American Music*, rev. to 1925 by Arthur Elson (New York: Macmillan, 1925), 322–26.

74.　William F. Apthorp, *By the Way*, vol. 2 (Boston: Copeland & Day, 1898), 108–9, 114.

75.　Foote, *An Autobiography*, 45–46.

76.　"A. P. Schmidt, Pioneer Publisher of American Music, Is Dead," *Musical America* (14 May 1921), 55. The writer of the article, who quotes Foote, is unidentified.

77.　Foote, *An Autobiography*, 51.

78.　Ibid., 52.

79.　"Letters Collected by Arthur Foote," letters 109, 13, and 14, respectively.

5

The Composer Speaks

The title of this chapter obviously refers back to "The Poet Speaks," a character piece from Schumann's *Scenes from Childhood*, op. 15, for the piano. It is most appropriate for describing Arthur Foote the composer. Like Schumann, Foote had a propensity for writing character pieces that are short, melodious, and full of romantic imagery and grouping them into suites. Needlessly long compositions irked him, as is evidenced by a program he saved of the Boston Symphony concert of 7 October 1882, which featured the Anton Rubinstein Symphony no. 5 (the "Russian"). The impatient Foote wrote "47 minutes long!"[1]

His artistry welcomed the discipline of the smaller forms, among them those of the eighteenth century. Individual compositions received abstract titles but romantic content. Some titles indicate specific moods—a happy recollection of blooming roses in the first light of morning, a projection of subdued sorrow over beauty destined to fade away, a sensitive invocation of unhurried older times, or a blithe portrayal of rain on a garret roof or a bagpipe player. In this regard he participated in the poetic imagery of his day, but never in excess. He invariably demonstrated a dedication to finished workmanship guided by finely honed aesthetic judgment. Every character piece appeared as an elegant small-scale portrayal of a distinctive atmosphere or feeling, a whole that lacked nothing essential to the portrayal. In composing it, Foote eschewed exaggerated sentiment and the strain of sustained dramatic argument. His character pieces remained restrained in expression, the outcome of concentrated artisanry. At the same time, they were distinct additions to musical literature.

From time to time, he resorted to the stylized Baroque structures inherited from Bach and Handel. This represented the effort of a polished gentleman, an endeavor to retrieve the courteous refinements of a former era that seemed lost to memory. Recalling an earlier style undoubtedly helped him avoid the frequently distorted, high-strung locution of several contemporary composers and allowed him to substitute a neatly designed style reminiscent of an age that valued grace and balance. He may also have been taking a stand against the vulgar and indiscriminate overindulgence that went hand in hand with nouveau-riche tastes in the United States.

What did the act of composing mean to Foote? What was in the back of his mind as he set music notes to paper? When Foote began composing with all seriousness in the second half of the seventies, he was more than aware that art music was a European venture of the few, listened to and sustained by a select group. Scarcely anyone in the United States had taken it up. Yet, he believed it to be a superb display of an ascendant human expression that was valuable to a democracy and realizable only through the agency of tonal sound. It was what he wanted to achieve in his own works. A dedicated democrat, he did not wish to restrict his music to performers, special listeners, and the musically erudite. His music addressed human aspirations that were everyone's patrimony and opened to every citizen the prospect of embracing them. He was, however, aware that art music had achieved no more than a toehold in American consciousness by the seventies and eighties. It required assiduous nurturing in order to acquire more than occasional significance.

During Foote's time, an immense growth in population was occurring and with it the numbers of the musically uneducated and half-educated. As regarded art music, Americans who made up the rank and file were unlike those who had gone before in that they represented an unprecedented mixture of races, religions, and ethnic groups, of native farm and industrial workers and European laborers, and of languages and ways of thinking in collision with each other. They were different also because large numbers of them were wage earners. People had the means, however modest, to choose to attend concerts, purchase scores, and make music in their homes. One result of this unprecedented growth and change was the weakening of old cultural ties. The question became: In what direction would cultural activities turn? If they desired and if they arrived at a consensus, Americans in general could exercise their strength to reject an art music that now, as formerly, more often than not failed to engage them.

After the Civil War the American populace gradually gained possession of a tremendous cultural authority. Regrettably for Foote, it did not employ its authority on behalf of listening to art music. Instead it opted not to listen, in any case not to listen to art music. Foote realized that popular music was what held people's attention. Art music in his era was hardly for all the people, any more than it is now. Although his own tastes were partial to art music, he had no desire to appear patronizing to the multitude. After all, he himself had enjoyed listening to and participating in the performance of the popular music it preferred.

As he wrote, he continued to trust that some would find value in his offerings, despite the obstacles impeding their acceptance. He never simply wrote off people who had no taste for his music. He knew that other activities could ennoble—religious, family-oriented, and work-connected activities, and even certain musics that did not aspire to the aesthetic heights.

He frequently seems to have held back from publication a composition that had not proven itself before a sufficiently large segment of the music public. In this regard, a letter dated 6 November 1990, which Arthur Foote II sent to Douglas Moore, is interesting. Reverend Foote said that he had found copies of two songs, one entitled "The Eden Rose" and another untitled song in manuscript, opening on the words, "Marjorie with the patient face." He asks, "Why was it never published? When was it composed? One guesses that A. F. decided it wasn't sufficiently successful." This surmise comes from a grandnephew who knew the composer well.[2]

Foote's steps to composition did not include the exceptional level of self-consciousness and the justifications of the music's difficulties that characterized so many twentieth-century approaches. He never felt that complexity and a consequent impermeability for the average listener were indispensable components of his music. Rather, his approach was to speak as simply and communicatively as possible, alert to the audience's prerequisites and listening capabilities. He could at least try to reach the thousands, if not the millions. He recognized no insurmountable cultural void in America, viewing the emptiness rather as an unoccupied cultural area awaiting the civilizing contributions of the arts. In later life, he was amused when atonal and other posttriadic composers insisted that theirs was an inevitable step in the evolution of music and that their musical complications were in fact a transmission of true perceptions and wisdom rather than a quest for them. He was even more amused when they admonished listeners that if a composition proved incomprehensible, there were compelling justifications for the impossibility of understanding it. It was altogether snobbish to insist that the fault lay with the music public, which needed to examine its own ineptitudes.

In regard to the relation of autonomy and freedom to the artist, he interpreted autonomy as the absence of constraints on the artist, and freedom as the absence of excessive constraints. Autonomy could leave the artist isolated; freedom would allow connection with the rest of the musical world. In artistic terms, then, a limitation to full autonomy was essential for a culturally enlightened composer. The composer then could exercise his freedom as circumscribed by common musical practices. In the 1920s, he saw the threat of anarchy that resulted when some composers took it upon themselves to insist on full autonomy.

Finally, as Foote put notes on paper, he was alive to the fact that what he was inking in could command continuing attention only if it disclosed a far-reaching knowledge of the available tonal materials. Much of this knowledge came from assimilating all prior arrangements of tones in their variety. This certainly was what Bach, Mozart, Beethoven, and Schubert had done in the past, and what Brahms was doing in the present.

Especially in his early works, he wished to grasp the important styles of other composers that paralleled his in expression and in technical realizations of that expression. He recognized the danger of imitation and when he employed an idiom and articulated a form, perhaps that of Schumann, he made sure there was no chance of the listener's mistaking the two. That his music does show an awareness of what was bequeathed him from the past, he was convinced, was to the good. It allowed him to transform what he had learned into shapes that heightened the consequence of what he wrote.

His was a cosmopolitan, international approach. It avoided what he saw as the limitations of national, regional, or racial expression. He would not consciously strive to be American, or Yankee, or pseudo-African American, or pseudo-Amerindian. He was also aware that a characteristic of one group could also be typical of others. For example, he once observed that the pentatonic scale, "an ancient scale in China," was also "found in old Irish and Scotch melodies, not to speak of other cases. It is curious how easily melodies can be made of the pentatonic scale."[3] He spoke of the use of old modes "to obtain distinctive effects. . . . The effect produced by them is to our ears something antique." But he added that no one should think that modes and their effects characterized any one people; they were endemic to many people— old Gaelic, English, Russian, Polish, and so forth.[4] Nevertheless, when it suited the occasion, he was not averse to writing melodies on gapped scales or in a modal system that had a kinship to Anglo-Celtic American song or New England psalmody. His relationship to the former is obvious in "An Irish Folk Song" (1891); to the latter, more subtle in the last movement of the Violin Sonata (1889). Still, almost all of his melodies are original ones and in a major or minor scale. Rarely does he employ an extant tune.

Yes, he felt empathy for the goals of those who introduced the American vernacular into their music. Especially when the American musical world was debating the issue of a national music in the nineties, he frequently talked over the subject with colleagues like Chadwick, Parker, and Whiting. However, he would travel only a path that he found congenial. Music for him evolved from an inner-directed, emotional drive to communicate with other humans. This came before any obligation to convey a sense of nation. Foote wanted to put himself forward as just a composer rather than a national composer or a fashionable composer. He left it to others to decide if what he contributed to music would become part of the lasting body of American musical literature. Foote did not have the ego to unilaterally assign his compositions a supreme valuation. On the other hand, he was gratified when a musician he respected had kind words to say about him, as did Thomas Ryan toward the end of the nineties:

As a composer [Arthur Foote] has presented us with a long list of fine works, including most charming songs; while his larger compositions have been played and sung in the best concerts throughout the country. And as he is still in the prime of life it is to be hoped that he will produce many more works from that fine musical vein which he so abundantly possesses,—a vein of warm, rare musical feeling, aptly controlled by musical science.[5]

The Musical Craft of Arthur Foote

About his early compositions, Foote says:

I formed myself, so to speak, on Mendelssohn (having none the less a love for Schumann and Chopin). Consecutive fifths, even cross-relations, were anathema to my teachers and to me. My harmony was correct but with little variety, the structure of my pieces conventional; and it was only much later that I absorbed harmonic finesse and became sensitive to it. Somehow, although deeply moved by Wagner, I did not have sense enough for a long time to learn from his music, and was late in appreciating early Debussy. The idea that certain things simply must not be had become too thoroughly ingrained.[6]

Foote is much too dismissive toward his early craftsmanship. His harmony, while not intruding into new territory, is varied enough and handled with adroitness. As the decade of the eighties went by, he made freer and freer use of dominant and non-dominant seventh chords, third relations, chromaticism, and flexible tonalities.[7] Chord constructions of the ninth, once in a great while of the thirteenth, are also heard. His arrangement of movements in a work whose keys are a third apart and modulations within a movement by thirds (C major to A major or minor, to A-flat major, to E major or minor, or to E-flat major) are common procedures. Of the "third relationship," which he is one of the first theorists to discuss in detail, Foote writes:

[It] is almost as strong as that by fifths [in modulation]. We find that the familiar statement as to keys nearly related to be a tonic major or minor shows this point conclusively; *e.g.* besides G (the 5th above) and F (the 5th below) we have, as nearly related to C, *a* (the 3d below C), *e* (the 3d below G), and *d* (the third below F); as nearest related to *a*, besides E and *e* (the 5th above) and *d* (the 5th below), we have C (the 3d above *a*), G (the 3d above *e*) and F the 3d above *d*).[8]

His music neither imitates nor paraphrases its models. In a question-and-answer session following a Composer's Forum laboratory concert of his music, which took place in the year before his death, he said it is the quality of his thought, experienced in his music, that concerns him, whatever the stylistic antecedents. When he composed, Foote said, he might or might not use the piano as a tool. To him, "inspiration" was "mostly perspiration." The composing of a piece was "hard work," although occasionally inspiration did take over and allow the quick writing of a work. As he started a piece he might frequently alter his ideas, but once he was convinced that he had arrived at the theme, it retained its identity even when elaborated on during the course of the composition. Asked to compare the importance of striking themes with stimulating and resourceful development, Foote replied: "I am an old-fashioned believer in things, and I can almost always find that if a composer writes a first-class theme, he generally can develop it and, of course, the idea of developing can be carried very little materially and that unfortunately is so in my own case."[9] What he says is that when he succeeded in inventing a melody of some quality, the piece might grow from it, but in itself it remained many times a closed-off theme, not open in any significant way to transformation in rhythm and phrase shape, nor freely amenable to contrapuntal treatment or melodic fragmentation, augmentation, and diminution. Since he did like writing a polished melody with beginning, middle, and end, it was the lyrical character piece and the suite format that in many instances suited his purpose rather than the sonata formats and their dramatic manipulations of short motifs.

He once made an illuminating comment that along with melody, the "lower bass" was "of the utmost importance, the remainder being generally 'filling-in.'"[10] He said this of music on the whole. Knowledgeable about counterpoint as he was, he preferred homophonic writing in his own music, with special attention given melody and bass and with not much of thematic importance going on in the middle parts. Whatever inner contrapuntal activity occurs, it inclines toward activated harmony rather than a real interweaving of independent lines.

In hardly any piece are innovative or even distinctive rhythms apparent. Syncopations remain mild. The skittish pulsations of minstrel dance, cakewalk, and ragtime are rarely encountered. Constructions in uneven phrase lengths (3, 5, or 7 measures) remain in the minority. He wanted his melody-centered music to roll on effortlessly and normally. For dances, he resorted to well established European formats: the gavotte, rigaudon, minuet, and sarabande of the eighteenth century, and the polonaise, mazurka, polka, and waltz of the nineteenth century. Foote imparted the characteristic mood of each piece by means of (1) melody, (2) harmony, and (3) an impression of natural motion. Naturalness was always in the foreground. Less evident is any urge to garnish the flow and framework of his musical content with academic cleverness. Every sound is balanced and unified to other sounds within an intelligible tonal ambit. A favorite directive for an entire section or movement is the word *comodo* (as in *allegro comodo*), which means to maintain a comfortable and relaxed tempo, without any suggestion of effort.

Foote said that the composer had to remain sensitive to the mechanical means by which instruments produced sound. To achieve expressiveness on the piano, for example, one had to take care that the percussive nature of the piano did not obtrude. While the difference between, say, an E-sharp and an F-natural might not be felt on a well-tempered instrument like the piano, the composer did sense that "the two notes do really differ (very slightly) in pitch, and often occur in such a way that they are *used* differently."[11] The awareness of such a distinction helps explain his effectiveness when writing for strings.

Finally, the controlling structures he favored were the ternary and variation forms. In multimovemented compositions based on the sonata idea, however, the sonata-allegro form appears, as in three early works: the String Quartet no. 1, the Piano Trio no. 1, and the Violin Sonata.

The Earliest CompositionśsThe First Six Years

We begin a survey of Foote's music, keeping in mind that Tchaikovsky was only thirteen years older than Foote; Dvořák, twelve; Grieg, ten. Chausson was born two years after Foote; Elgar, four years; Puccini, five years. This will enable us to avoid the error of classifying him as a reactionary because his style was less up to date than that of composers who were twenty or more years younger than he was. Indeed, in the ways that count, Foote was a composer very much of his own time. If he did not choose to adapt his method to the later ones of the twentieth century, it was because he wished not to venture into areas toward which he was fundamentally unsympathetic. This did not mean that he repudiated change, only that the change was not for him. Until his death, he remained fascinated by and did listen carefully to the innovative compositions of people like Schoenberg and Stravinsky.

During adolescence and youth, Foote had devoted what time he could to his keyboard practice, theoretical studies, and concerts that came his way. He began to practice what was to be his lifetime preoccupation by writing musical pieces that were little more than creative studies that prepared him for the later major endeavors: the *Trois Morceaux*, op. 3, for piano, dating from 1877 to 1880, and the *Drei Stücke* for Piano and Cello, op. 1, of 1881. He wanted from the beginning to achieve a telling lyricism and draw convincing mood pictures through a craftsmanship the cognoscenti would admire. The result was that the young composer, with opus 1 and opus 3, did establish himself as a fluent and skilled practitioner of his art, but before he had something really compelling to convey. Later in life, he said:

> It was not until 1877 that I attempted to write real music. I was late in this respect in comparison with Chadwick, Parker, and MacDowell; and of course I lacked their train-

> ing. My first published music was three pieces for 'cello
> (reminiscent and rather of a stencil pattern, but melodi-
> ous), which I played with Wulf Fries a good deal. This as
> well as the three piano pieces . . . was published by Cranz
> of Hamburg, for which Schmidt was agent, as he was for
> Litolff. These pieces are all commonplace, but their com-
> position gave me encouragement.[12]

Despite the opus 3 designation and the copyright date 1882 on the published music, the three pieces for piano are the earliest composed music that he had printed. The original publication assigned no opus number to the work.[13] The *Trois Morceaux* are an Impromptu in G minor, a Gavotte in B minor, and a Mazurka in G minor. Although we find a third relationship in their keys, the three movements share no thematic ideas. The opus was dedicated to the pianist Annette Essipoff-Leschetizky, who had given the Boston premiere of the Gavotte on 12 May 1877.[14] There is little doubt that Foote himself tried out one or more of the movements before an audience before this date, most probably in Salem.

All three are in ternary form and remarkably pianistic. Syncopation is not present. None is as harmonically conservative as Foote claims in his autobiography. Of all the music that he wrote, they most approximate salon music—music that is charming, of slight weight, having softly emotional inflections, and more appropriate for performance in the parlor than the concert hall. The Impromptu, whose style is reminiscent of Schumann, is the most interesting of the three. The tempo is a standard allegretto, but the time signature is written ⁹⁄₈ ⁶⁄₈, bold for a novice composer writing for an American public. The first section is in seven four-measure phrases—the first three measures in ⁹⁄₈ and the fourth, cadential measure in ⁶⁄₈. The result is a dynamism that tends to push the music forward even as it cadences. The first and last phrase are cast as prelude and postlude, featuring sixteenth-note roulades. The four s-curved phrases between elaborate a legato stepwise melody in a quarter-note plus eighth-note rhythm:

♩♪ ♩♪ ♩♪ ♩♪

over an eighth-note accompaniment. A rocking motion is set up. The effect is quite fetching. Each phrase swells to a gentle climax that subsides as it reaches the cadence. Mild appoggiatura dissonances give the tune a vaguely yearning quality. Most secondary key references are to the dominant and mediant major. The harmony boasts some skilled touches, as in the second phrase's close on I / N^6 of V - III^6_4 - V^7_5 of III / III. The middle section in G major changes harmonies more slowly than the first section and has a courtly nonlyrical melody that skips about over a flowing sixteenth-note arpeggiated figure that spreads itself over two octaves. This second idea, though a nice contrast, is rather pedestrian. The listener welcomes the return to the first melody, which is now moved down an octave into the rich midrange of the piano and provided with a fuller accompaniment.

The Gavotte, an *allegro comodo*, is in the expected ²⁄₂ time, with phrases starting in the middle of a bar. A polarity is set up between actively moving treble and bass lines. These are skillfully dovetailed with each other. Here, his proficiency in his craft is more than established. Yet, the ideas, however pleasant, are undistinguished and no individual expressive profile emerges. The non-Chopinesque Mazurka, in ³⁄₄ time, is slightly more attractive, but nevertheless conventional. Some harmonic interest is generated in the middle section, where Foote inserts some nondominant and dominant ninth chords.

Obviously, the fledgling musician exerted caution in his early work, knowing that the public would be forming an opinion on his qualifications as a composer. The consensus of the contemporary reviewers of the *Trois Morceaux* was that the ideas were uneven in their attractiveness and not especially original. But Foote had handled them judiciously and thus had established his competence. Opus 3 gives evidence of his assimilation of sonorous and formulaic principles from composers like Schumann, Mendelssohn, and Chopin. No specific compositions or musical passages of these earlier musicians can be singled out as models. Thus, the three pieces are to be taken more as the manifestation of an earnest individual artistry than as an aftereffect of imitated past styles. Louis Elson said that Foote charms the listener by his polish and naturalness and by his easy leading of voices. Furthermore, says Elson, he never has written anything that lacked merit.[15]

Drei Stücke for Piano and Cello, op. 1, also bears the published copyright date of 1882 and the names of the same publishers. The dedication is to Wulf Fries. The three pieces are only numbered, not titled. The tempo indications are Andante con moto, Andante, and Allegro con fuoco, respectively. Although Foote finished them in 1881, after he had completed the *Trois Morceaux*, he may have tried out at least one as early as 1877, since a program presented by him and the cellist Wulf Fries at the Essex Institute at Salem on 9 April lists one number as a duet for piano and cello, by Foote.[16] The two players gave the entire set its Boston premiere on 12 January 1882. The public received the music warmly, and the critics heard songs without words, each having interesting and effectively lyrical themes.[17]

The musical ideas are stronger and the melodies more attractive than those of opus 3. As a sign of his growing expertise, Foote achieves better effects by simpler means. Harmony is more controlled and, superficially, less adventurous. The cello monopolizes the melodic material; the piano usually provides the accompaniment. The first number, in an A B A¹ B¹ A² structure, opens in G minor on a tune stated in even, *non legato* eighth notes around the area of middle C. The bass line is strong; some inner contrapuntal movement occurs. Section 2 starts loudly in D major. It is based on a broader, more animated cello theme, which the piano imitates at some points. After eleven measures, the tune leaves the key of D, intensifies, and modulates constantly until it cadences in F major (the third above D minor). In the next section, the first theme returns, but is quieter and placed a fourth lower than before, in D minor. Again, tonality is destabilized. The second theme then enters in G major and very loudly. After four measures, modulation begins and the music grows more intense through twenty-one measures of development to close in B-flat major (the third above G minor). The first theme returns for a final time, back again in the home key of G minor (the symmetry in the sequence of keys becomes clear). However, it sounds very gently, an octave lower than the opening. The piano supplies the simplest of accompaniments. The entire piece manifests expressive planning with an eye for total effect, as the first theme becomes calmer and calmer, and the second more and more intense, with a close on utmost calmness.

We find in this piece a typical treatment of the material by Foote, an exploitation of two contrasting states, each impacting on the other. Usually in his pieces utilizing this contrast, a mild, pensive, or euphoric situation yields to a more anxious state of being that may encompass turmoil, grief, or some peril on the horizon. Next comes a reinstatement of the previous state, now permeated with remembrance of the more agitated theme. Here, this happens twice, only the contrast is even stronger in the second presentation. Yet, Foote's goal is not to surrender to confusion and disturbance. Instead, after each flare-up dies down, he acts to restore the initial, quiet state.

The second number, whose structure is A B C A^1, opens in F major and $\frac{3}{4}$ time. The first melody shows a new departure; it is a simple British-American folklike tune given a mostly diatonic, unobtrusive accompaniment. Innocent of any jarring sensation, a congenial and artlessly flowing section is the result both of Foote's selection of notes and his organization of them so that they roll on comfortably, one after another (example 2a). Notice the suggestion of the Lydian mode in measures 7–8, the lingering on the submediant tone in measure 13, and the descent to the tonic in measures 14–17. After a repetition of this melody, a second, contradictory section enters in C major. Chords in reiterated eighth-note triplets underlie a second, more animated tune. This is followed by a third section in A minor, fast and agitated, as the cello plays sixteenth-note scale passages and finally achieves a climax. The first tune closes off the number, at the very end played *con sordino* and with extreme quietness. The typical treatment mentioned in connection with the previous number also applies here.

Number 3 of opus 1, like the impromptu of opus 3, has a double time signature, $\frac{12}{8}$ $\frac{4}{4}$, and an A B A^1 B^1 structure. The fiery first section in D minor remains entirely in $\frac{12}{8}$ until measure 9, when the treble line alone changes to $\frac{4}{4}$ meter and a development begins that grows more and more excited. The tune presents the first evidence of rhythmic adventuring in a Foote piece, mild as it is, as each four-measure phrase starts on an anacrusis of two eighth notes on the first beat, leaping up an octave to a dotted half note on the second beat (example 2b). The next section is quieter, in longer notes, and shows a dual tonality of B-flat major and G minor, with incidental landings on E-flat major. For the first time, Foote foregoes his four-measure squared-off phrasing and begins the new tune with two five-measure phrases. The opening theme returns, only this time starting on F major then moving to D minor. This is followed by the return of the second theme, now very loud. For the first time, the piano participates in playing the tune, first in unison with the cello, second by itself as the cello accompanies with double-stop eighth-note triplets. Evidently, with this third number, the composer was attempting to treat his opening theme developmentally in preparation for a more ambitious project—the Trio in C Minor, for Piano, Violin, and Cello, op. 5.

By the end of 1881, Foote had established himself as adept in the briefer lyrical forms. To confirm further his credentials as a composer to his fellow Bostonians, he also had to write a multi-movemented work based on the sonata principle. Even here, he would be tuneful to an extreme. His entire musical thought in such a work centered on the melodic. Many musical subjects that he invented for works like the trio could, with little modification, have appeared with song texts and, in first movements, we will find even the development of his subjects to sing without exception. Curiously, he is often found at his lyrical best in the passages, such as those in sonata-allegro form that would seem least to require singing lines—as in the transition between the two important tonalities and the closing codetta in the exposition, the working out of the themes in the development section, and in the coda. For this reason, the opening movement of the trio, like those in other works based on the sonata principle, struck his contemporaries as having fullness, warmth, and strength. The elaboration of his first-movement subjects, of course, did call for a chain of shifting tonalities. Yet, these gave proportion and consequence to ideas that might have sounded only smooth and elegant in pieces without such a structural design. The sonata principle also called for the first movement to be followed by a more rhythmic and less substantial movement, usually of the dance type, whose contrariety magnified the distinctive attributes of the other movements and allowed some relaxation to the listener. This lighter, simpler movement was meant to glint and twinkle. In so doing, it relieved the weight of the sonata-allegro opening and of the serious slow movement by substituting a perceptibly less emotional manner of writing. With other composers the relief had come in the form of a minuet, scherzo, or waltz. For the Trio, Foote would provide a vivacious fast movement with more than a little cheerfulness to do just that. As for the slow movement, it seemed to him that a songfulness sufficient unto itself should be its outstanding feature, and an overflow of such songfulness its primary agency of communication with the music public. A movement of this sort could stand on its own. It is for this reason that we find Foote detaching many slow movements from their original moorings and giving them an independent life on the concert circuit.

In works like the trio, we confront his inborn melodic prodigality blended with the conventions of the sonata. Eventually, as the music continues from passage to passage and movement to movement, we find that while it impresses us with a substantial splendor. It also satisfies us owing to its musical richness, regardless of its expressive aim. Mendelssohn and Schumann have served as models for his compositional methods. Yet, his concepts are not as emotionally cautious as those of the former, nor as suffused with extramusical imagery as the latter's. His are more like singing voices forever wafting their very human sounds toward the listener and filling the ear with their song.

The first presentation of the trio took place on 8 April 1882, with Foote at the piano, Fries on cello, and Gustav Dannreuther on violin. Listeners found the work to be intensely melodious, full of fire and passion, and skillfully realized. The audience experienced real enjoyment as it listened, and applauded the composer heatedly and appreciatively.[18] Foote, however, was not satisfied. Because he was coming to apply stringent standards to the music he wrote and also because he wished to win recognition as a composer with the highest level of attainment, he wanted to be more certain of this first ambitious offering. Foote said later: "This performance showed the need of re-writing. I now look back at myself with amusement, the piano part being so ab-

surdly difficult. I was then in the state of mind when one wishes
to show all one can do."[19] He took the manuscript with him to
Europe and revised the music at Neuilly sur Seine in the summer
of 1883. The publication of the score, copyright date 1884, was
seen to by Schmidt in Boston and by B. Schott's Söhne in Mainz.
It was dedicated to his friend George Henschel. The title page
describes the trio as "Opus 5," while the first page of the score
designates it as "Opus 3."[20] The first concerts of the work also list
it as opus 3. Behind the confusion is possibly the fact that this
was his third work composed, though not the third published.

The first movement of the Trio in C Minor for Piano, Violin,
and Cello, op. 5, is in $^3/_4$ meter and starts off as an *allegro con
brio*. An orthodox sonata structure delineates its sections. The
violin presents a principal theme whose expression bespeaks the
composer's deeper nature. The sentiment is melancholic but not
morose. The thirty-two measure theme is lyrical and cadences on
the dominant. The great number of melodic syncopations is surprising in light of previous compositions (example 3a). Harmony
at the beginning is conservative and little varied, consisting of
tonic, dominant, dominant of the subdominant, and subdominant chords. The piano simply accompanies, and the cello enters
with a subordinate part after sixteen measures. The lengthy transitional section, which comes next, lights a small fire under the
music as it develops the opening motif of the theme, with piano
and cello interchanging important material with the violin. The
stately second subject, in E-flat major, is first presented by the piano in dotted-half notes. It seems to descend from the New
England psalmodic tradition that Foote was so well acquainted
with (example 3b). As the principal theme was inner-directed,
this one is outer-directed, its gestures prayerful and calming. No
codetta is appended to the close of this exposition of ideas. It is
as if the composer wanted the listener to grasp, without any possibility of doubt, the two predominant expressions of the entire
trio. The development devotes itself to enlarging on the two
themes simultaneously. This section goes beyond generating drama and excitement to focus on the subtly expressive alterations
that the juxtapositions make possible—the variations in emotion
prompted by the paradoxical fusion of inner sadness and the
bedrock of faith. The recapitulation presents a reorchestrated

version of the principal theme, after which a lengthy climax enters, not as drama but as an upwelling of feeling. The second theme, now in C major, has a calming effect. The coda ends emphatically on motifs from the first theme.

The second movement, *allegro vivace*, begins as a light-as-air scherzo, with technical precedents in Mendelssohn. In G minor and $\frac{2}{4}$ time, the quiet scurry of the violin, and then the cello, proves delightful (example 3c). A middle section in G major, less fast and in longer notes, is to be played legato and dolce. However, no Mendelssohnian sweetness enters its measures. The music is new but the expression harks back to the pacific prayerfulness of the hymn tune (example 3d). Note, too, the similarities, though admittedly faint, between the two themes. For example, the beginning of the theme outlines a stepwise move downward, b to a, and a skip upward of a perfect interval to e-flat′. After the reorchestrated return of the scherzo, there is a most effective sixteen-measure ending where pizzicato strings engage in an eighth-note scamper to close softly in the final measure.

Previously, in the *Morceaux* and the *Stücke*, we had seen the use of a double time signature. This is also true of the trio's third movement, an *adagio molto* in A-flat major and $\frac{9}{8}$ $\frac{6}{8}$ time. The design is ternary, A B A^1. No regular pattern of alternation between the two time signatures is discernible. Intriguingly, the principal melody utilizes rhythms and phrase layouts that derive from the first theme of the first movement. Yet, now the effect is consoling, as if inner melancholy has found surcease; the ear is captivated by the loveliness of sound (example 3e). The cello sings to piano accompaniment, then the violin joins with it in a duet. Suddenly, the music dashes into F minor. The sound has turned loud, animated, and stressful. The piano resounds with a forceful new tune. Before long the concurrent development of this tune with the principal one occurs, and the music mounts to a tumultuous, emotional climax. The return of the principal theme in A-flat but reorchestrated brings relief.

The finale is an *allegro comodo* in C minor and $\frac{2}{2}$ time. The cello bounds forth with a quirky and novel idea, a jump of a diminished fifth, from middle c^1 down to an f-sharp, over an augmented IV^{6}5$_3$ chord, sometimes known as the German sixth chord (example 3f). Soon, the violin takes it up, a fifth higher.

The tune is *non legato*, bold, modulatory, and, when the piano continues it, builds mainly on the figure of a dotted eighth note and a sixteenth note:

The passage soon achieves an extremely loud *fff*. The subsequent theme, in E-flat major, is broad, unruffled, and prayerful. The connection to prayer grows clearer when this section closes on an augmented version of the first theme, which in some ways reminds the listener of the hymn tune "St. Anne," better known by the text "O God, our help in ages past." The principal theme returns reorchestrated. The coda shifts to C major and begins with an animated *fugato* on the principal theme. However, the ending is *maestoso e sostenuto*, on repeatedly alternating subdominant-minor and tonic-major chords. The effect is a prolonged plagal cadence, frequently described as the "amen" cadence of Protestant hymns. This ending reinforces my notion that Foote had somewhere in his mind the elaboration of two expressions: inner-directed melancholy and outer-directed devotion, which contend with each other until the final resolution in a reverential "amen." On this aspect, I point to an 1882 *Transcript* review of the work: "One feels sure that the composer wrote [the music of the first three movements] from a purely musical necessity; not because either he or his friends had come to the conclusion it was time for him to produce something." The reviewer found more premeditation and deliberation in the last movement.[21] After the composer had revised the Trio, the newspaper reviewers found the music much improved. Frederic Gleason, a Chicago composer, wrote program annotations for a Chicago performance of the revised trio, on 25 September 1885. He said that a portion of the last movement had "a somewhat mystic swing" and is at the same time not wanting in tenderness.[22] The trio, by this year, was rapidly becoming an audience favorite wherever it was played.

Amazing for an accomplished pianist, Foote keeps his own instrument usually in the background. He wrote scarcely any brilliant passages for it and allowed the violin and cello to predominate. In addition, for a musician well versed in Baroque contrapuntal practices, he allowed few truly contrapuntal measures to interrupt the homophonic musical flow. Assuredly, it was the nature of his material, its essential lyricism, that determined this course of action.

The same year that Foote revised his trio (1883), he also completed two other compositions, the Quartet for Strings in G Minor, op. 4, and *Cinq Pièces* for Piano, op. 6. The former, dedicated to Theodore Thomas, was published by Litolff's Verlag of Braunschweig, and by Schmidt of Boston in 1885. What the *Transcript* reviewer wrote of the trio, describing it as written "from a purely musical necessity," is no less true of the quartet. Foote turned to composing chamber music because of this necessity, and also because he had great affection for the genre. This is more than adequately established in the trio and the quartet by their technical distinction and their thematic elegance and expressiveness. Nevertheless, Foote was a private person and seldom indicated what he thought. Nor did he often signify his own pleasure with a score that he knew he had executed particularly well. But he preserved whatever reviews he could find or were sent to him, and he commented in his autobiography that a work had been well received and had come by numerous performances.

When I speak of Foote's expressiveness, I never have in mind a sticky sentimentality. When I speak of his strong emotion, I never have in mind unbridled passion. The years of young adulthood did find Foote penning heated compositions, it is true. But they were in no way excessively agitated or fiercely impassioned, after the fashion of several prominent composers of his day like Wagner, Tchaikovsky, Liszt, and Strauss. Where these four and others like them were wringing out sounds of abandoned ecstasy, grandiosity, torment, and utter despair from their melodies, harmonies, and rhythms, Foote maintained emotional restraint. To hustle, to appear perturbed, to demonstrate excessive zeal, or to be heedless of all save self were to him simply ludicrous or reprehensible forms of conduct. He remained thoughtful, prudent, and orderly in expression when responding to the creative impulse. He refused to exhibit in music a frenzied power or a lean-and-mean brawny ardor. We find him cultivating his own special field as unruffled as an ordinary farmer cultivates his acre of grain. In short, to throw over all traces of civilized conduct in the production of art was not his style.

Keeping what was just said in mind, we find the first movement of the quartet beginning *allegro appassionato* in G minor
and ⁴⁄₄ time. The movement is, as expected, cast in a sonata-allegro form. The first strain of the theme in the first violin emerges
as a smooth, melodious, and fervent melody that is stated in two
upwardly sweeping waves. It initially rises an octave and a half,
from d′ to climax on b-flat″ (example 4a), against a background
of tremolo strings; next, it rises two octaves to a more vehement
climax on d‴. Continuing in G minor, the second segment of the
theme, which now becomes more modulatory, more staccato,
and more syncopated, rises to the largest climax, on g‴. Descending triplet eighth notes, which eventually end two octaves
below over a perfect cadence, provide release. However poignant the music, the delineation shows careful planning for total
effect, in a way not as clearly evident in the trio. The ensuing
subsidiary idea in B-flat major, *espressivo e poco marcato*, must
be played in the faster tempo that Foote specifies. It sounds with
a concentrated lyricism that tempts players to linger on portions
of the tune, especially on the upward moving *appoggiatura*,
from c-sharp′ to d′ (example 4b). To loiter thusly would add a
sentimental interpretation that Foote wishes to avoid. Unlike the
trio, this quartet adds a codetta, which utilizes a motif from the
first theme, to close the exposition of its ideas. It also helps
round off the first section of the movement to form a symmetry
of ideas that is absent from the trio. The developmental section
that follows grows quite agitated, yields to sudden dramatic
changes in dynamics, and enlarges on motifs from both themes,
usually simultaneously. The recapitulation is regular, and the
coda ends with an extremely rapid outburst of speed. This and
the movements that follow exhibit a structural integration not
nearly as evident in the trio.

The second movement is a spirited Scherzo in E-flat major,
triple time and ternary form. Interestingly, the middle section,
which traditionally sounds at a slower tempo, is here to be played
faster, *molto piu allegro*. As with the first movement's subsidiary
theme, the temptation is to sentimentalize an affecting tune, this
one in the unexpected key of A-flat minor. Foote wants no such
reading.

The following movement, an *andante con moto* in B-flat major and $\%$ time, is given a ternary shape. A lovely, chaste melody sings in the violin against a gently syncopated background (example 4c). The middle section in G minor accelerates to a much faster tempo, turns dramatic, and eventually develops a motif from the opening. The return to B-flat features a graceful figurative variation on the first melody. In this movement, as in the previous two movements, we note Foote's insistence on a faster tempo for the material succeeding the opening. As with the trio, the composer seems to want the listener to grasp, without any possibility of doubt, the two predominant expressions of the composition.

The finale is in G minor and rondo form (A B A^1 C A^2 B^1 A^3), and it has a very fast, energetic first theme. The two secondary themes provide effective contrasts. The second of these themes displays similar devotional properties to those mentioned in the trio. Throughout the quartet, the first violin is the reigning instrument. However, in all movements, and particularly when a developmental scheme is being carried out, the thematic material is shared with the other instruments.

Warmth of feeling, directness of expression, simplicity of means, and clarity of structure were found to be the quartet's outstanding merits by the audience and critics who heard its premiere on the night of 7 December 1883. The force of the ideas in the outer movements and the irresistible appeal of the slow movement found especial favor. The second movement was pleasing but lightweight. Some wished for more contrapuntal passages; others, for more extended developments of his themes. The several reviewers of the concert[23] concluded that Foote had successfully coped with the unflagging expressiveness required by the string quartet format. He might also have anticipated easier acceptance as a major composer after he proved himself in this chosen vehicle for so much classical music. Writing for full orchestra, especially the writing of symphonies, was less suited to his nature. Yet, it was a difficult task for him to write the quartet because his musical bent was lyrical rather than rhetorical, and his manner more comfortable with the limited space of the character piece than with the more spacious regions inhabited by compositions in sonata designs.

For this reason, the *Cinq Pièces* for Piano, op. 6, which he apparently composed while at Neuilly in the summer of 1883, must have come as a relief. They were published by Litolff's Verlag of Braunschweig and by Schmidt of Boston in 1885, and dedicated to Stephen Heller. A light-footed Prelude in F minor and $^9/_8$ time exploits a one-measure figure throughout, in the manner of an etude exploring the full piano range from FF to f'''. There is much warmth in the sound and some adventuring in the harmony. The Nocturne that follows, in F major, $^3/_4$ time, and moderate tempo, is sad and ruminative. A Sarabande in G major comes next. It exploits a one-measure figure, though not as consistently as in the Prelude. It is in triple time and generates a slow, stately motion of great dignity. Perhaps the most salonlike piece is the Petite Valse for left hand alone. Its middle section again relies on one figure, this time two measures long, thus continuing the etude manner. Finally, the Polonaise in D major is given a regal swing and all the rhythmic characteristics of the processional, as defined by Chopin. Nevertheless, the conduct of the melodies and harmonies are Foote's and do not derive from Chopin. It is the most difficult of the five numbers to perform. In these pleasurable compositions, Foote reveals himself as an out-and-out romanticist. At the same time, he was thinking in terms of writing some effective teaching pieces for his and other teachers' use. These characteristics came into view frequently in the keyboard works he composed.

The Compositions for Voice of the Late Eighties

Arthur Foote never issued a flood of compositions during any year of his creative life. His daughter Katharine wrote that his yearly output was limited "presumably because his teaching occupied a great part of his life—also, he never composed unless 'he had something to say'—also, he was a perfectionist, and worked a long time on his compositions before he was willing to publish them."[24] Of course, he also had his time tied up in teaching, performing, and church music activities.

Foote did not cultivate the field of vocal music during his first six years as a composer. Keeping in mind his reputation as a

church music director, an accompanist to vocalists, and a devo-
tee of lyricism, it is remarkable that he was satisfied to compose
for instruments only for so many years. It was not until 1884,
having explored the piano and chamber-music genres, that he
chose the category of vocal composition. This interest he would
retain throughout his life. Later, as a more seasoned and more
proficient artist, he turned out many fine songs and sacred vocal
compositions. However, no work of his maturity is superior to
several of his early more instinctive settings, when his feelings
were given their fullest rein.

The early songs clearly show an acute understanding of what
is feasible for the voice. They demonstrate his lyrical gift, and
make evident his resourcefulness in inventing sympathetic accompaniments for the singer. He would eventually write over
one hundred solo songs, over fifty part songs, and around thirty-
five sacred works. William Treat Upton says that Foote and Chadwick pioneered the field of American art song, and owing to
them, the "high German ideal of sincerity, of thoroughness, in
short 'the artistic conscience,' was . . . deeply implanted in our
native song at its beginning." Though not all their songs were of
equal merit, none was crude or insincere. All reveal an admirable
spirit and workmanship that marked them as the beginning of
real artistry in American song, Upton states.[25] This is not to say
that Foote went over completely to the style of the German *Lieder*. On the contrary, the antecedents of his songs are as easily
found in the traditional and composed ballads of the British Isles
and America that had been prevalent in the United States in the
previous century. American song with some pretension to artistry had its start in the mid-eighteenth century with Francis Hop-
kinson. Various late eighteenth century English emigrés to
America, beginning with the composers Benjamin Carr and Alexander Reinagle, had contributed to the genre. In the early nineteenth century there was Oliver Shaw of Providence, followed by
Louis Moreau Gottschalk, J. C. D. Parker, Alfred Pease, Homer
Bartlett, Dudley Buck, and John Knowles Paine, among others.
They shared with Foote a preference for the simple, directly
communicative, comfortable to perform, and highly lyrical representation of song.

Foote's texts came from past poetic masters like William

Shakespeare, John Marston, and Edmund Waller, from highly regarded nineteenth century English writers like Percy Shelley, Alfred Tennyson and Rudyard Kipling; the Anglo-Canadian Sir Gilbert Parker; and from Americans, most of them friends and acquaintances, like Henry Wadsworth Longfellow, Arlo Bates, and Louise Chandler Moulton. His musical emphasis tends to be on the melody as a complete entity, with a tuneful beginning, middle, and end. The melody is designed to encompass an entire stanza. Brief preludes of two to four measures and equally brief postludes are the norm. He may repeat the concluding line of text in order to provide a fitting conclusion for the singer. All the harmonic paraphernalia of his time is put to use—nondominant sevenths, lingering appoggiaturas, frequent secondary references to other tonalities. If in the major mode, the song swiftly alludes to the minor keys of the mediant and submediant, giving a plaintive tinge to the proceedings. Or, as often with Schumann, he introduces an unprepared tonal shift into the major key of the lowered submediant. If in the minor mode, the relative major key or the mediant major key lightens the heft of the music. Structure is ordinarily either strophic, involving two stanzas to the same music, or ternary when three or more stanzas are set (most often A B A or A A B A). The strophic form is preferred when the stanzas encompass the same thought and expression. Individual musical interpretations of specific words or phrases, which interrupt the melodic flow, are uncommon.[26] Moreover, Foote's songs, like those of Chadwick, MacDowell, and Beach, are close enough to the preferences of the general public that they oftentimes won a popular following.[27]

In 1884, Schmidt published Foote's song "Go, Lovely Rose," the text being a noted seventeenth-century poem by Edmund Waller. The dedication is to the vocalist Mrs. George Henschel, the former Lillian Bailey, for whom the song was written. She evidently premiered the song on 19 February 1884.[28] Foote's setting is pensive and imaginative. Its key is E-flat major; time signature, $^4/_4$; tempo, moderately fast; vocal range, an eleventh; and form, A A B A[1]. A glance at the music shows it brimful of memorable details (example 5). There is the hint of inquietude in the reiterated triplets of the accompaniment. The listener senses a wisp of melancholy when the vocal melody in its first two measures is heard simultaneously an octave below in the piano. There is the prolonged cadence in G minor on the words "to thee," as well as the subsequent soaring upward to g'' and then the dying away on "To thee, to thee, / How sweet and fair she seems to be," above chromatically shifting harmonies. We hear not just a pretty tune. Foote has succeeded in capturing the mood of the speaker. The B section goes more slowly, starts in D-flat major but modulates freely as the voice summons "beauty" to come forth. Shortly, the music turns to C minor for a lamentation centering on the words "then die!" which is "the common fate." At the close, the A returns, now truncated and sung very softly and more slowly than at the beginning as the singer contemplates the brief existence of all living things.

In the same year, Schmidt published Foote's "When Icicles Hang on the Wall," the text by William Shakespeare. D minor, $^6/_8$ time, and a fast tempo characterize it. The two stanzas are given a strophic setting. Again, the vocal range is an eleventh. The song is an excellent vehicle for a bass voice. Its tune corresponds to the Anglo-American ballad style given a bit of antique seasoning. Only once is there an attempt at word painting. On the owl's cry "To who! To whit!" an abrupt call sounds in the voice, plus a staccato piano leap and descent. A reviewer, in *Keynote* (February 1885) declared it "a vigorous and characteristic bass song. Mr. Foote has happily caught the rollicking spirit of the words, and wedded them to entirely appropriate music." A second reviewer praised the composer's "delicate ear for harmonic effects" and "lively fancy."[29]

Composed about the same time and published by Schmidt in 1885 were the *Three Songs*, op. 10: "It Was a Lover and His Lass," text by William Shakespeare; "The Pleasant Summer's Come," text by Robert Burns; and "The Milkmaid's Song," text by Alfred, Lord Tennyson. The enjoyable first song is almost entirely within the Anglo-American ballad tradition. It is in F minor. Its two stanzas are strophically set. The vocal range is limited to a ninth. The tune is diatonic, but with one surprise toward the end—a lowered supertonic note above a V^7 of VI to VI harmony. One early reviewer called the music "quaintly minor" and approximating "the old English vein," especially in the accompaniment.[30] The second number is a bit disappointing, the music appearing emotionally neutral and not sufficiently expressive of the text. On the other hand, "The Milkmaid's Song" is a gem. The coquettish, playful banter of the milkmaid is beautifully captured in the music. Foote is especially careful to follow the natural accentuation of the English words, as in:

♪♩   ♪♩
"kiss me, would you?"

At the end, as her request becomes more urgent, the tempo goes faster, and the accompaniment sounds more nervous. One reviewer found this song "the best of the set, having the *naïveté* and playful tenderness of the subject well set forth in the music."[31]

"Love's Philosophy," text from Percy Bysshe Shelley, was written in 1886 and published by Schmidt in the same year. The words are about love and the joining together of things in nature, so "why not I with thine." The two stanzas receive a strophic setting in C major. An engaging tune unfolds over a gently throbbing, mildly syncopated accompaniment.

Five Songs, op. 13, include "O My Luv's Like a Red, Red Rose," words by Robert Burns, "I'm Wearing Awa'," words by Carolina Nairne, "Love Took Me Softly by the Hand," words by an anonymous hand, "Ho! Pretty Page," words by William Thackeray, and "If You Become a Nun, Dear," words by Leigh Hunt. The first four were written in 1886 and published by Schmidt the next year; the last was apparently completed later and published in 1888. These compositions demonstrate Foote's growing awareness of the voice's capabilities, his translating of this awareness into inspired lyricism, and the abetting of the singer with resourceful accompaniments. The first piece, in two stanzas and strophic, receives a straightforward and fairly conventional musical framework. There is something rather stalwart about the song. One can easily imagine the amiable melody sung with relish by a man standing with the thumb of his left hand hooked into a coat lapel and the right hand pushing on the piano to thrust his body forward.

The second piece is an altogether different matter. It is one of Foote's best and achieved a popularity that endured over several decades. The subject focuses on a person exhausted of life and awaiting a welcome death. In a letter sent to Rosalie Housman, Foote states: "'I'm wearing awa' is an instance of what happens rarely, i. e. a composition coming into the mind complete in all detail,—for it was written one Sunday morning in an hour or so, before going to church to play the service."[32] Like its predecessor, it is a strophic, two-stanza piece in D-flat major and ⁹⁄₈ time. Most often, the dynamics are on the soft or very soft side. The prelude is a bare D-flat arpeggio. A very touching message is conveyed in melodic strains of the wave type, curving upward from d-flat' to f″, then back again. The simple chordal accompaniment adds delicate changes in harmony, especially touches of B-flat minor and F minor, in order to support the text's tone of sadness and weariness (example 6). No postlude closes the piece.

The third number boasts some prettiness, but remains clothed in conventionality with scarcely any interesting quirks to catch the attention. The fourth, "Ho! Pretty Page," is quite opposite. Satiric raillery is the tone as an older speaker derides the passions of youth and the manifestations of young love. Foote took pains to get the music right. The form differs from all that has gone before: A (in F major), B (starting in F but modulatory and sans tonal focus), A (in F major again), C (starting in F minor but modulatory and unstable), D (a complete change of pace, going from F major to C major), A (in F major again). Less lyricism is heard, especially in section B and C, but with one exception—section D, which is to be rendered with a counterfeit expressive sweetness. The melodic rhythms remain extremely flexible, responding to the natural stresses of the text. Foote makes certain the singer understands what interpretation he wants by adorning text phrases like "sighing and singing," with the direction "with mock sentiment."

The fifth song, "If You Become a Nun, Dear," is another fake-serious conceit. The work is given the usual strophic, two-stanza format. The accompaniment shows individuality with its combination of arpeggiated harmonies, which give way to nonarpeggiated chords and then to broken chords. Concerning this song and "Ho! Pretty Page," Rupert Hughes said they were interpretations of modern poetry of a half-archaic character, through music displaying a delicious and subtly ironic musical humor.[33]

Foote also turned to writing secular compositions intended for chorus that were also performable as part-songs by soloists. A list of them includes:

> "1874–1884" an occasional piece for 2-part men's chorus, composed for the 1884 reunion of the Harvard Class of 1874, unpublished.
>
> "If Doughty Deeds My Lady Please," for 4-part men's chorus, unaccompanied, text by Graham of Gartmore, composed 1885, published by Schmidt, 1885.
>
> "Into the Silent Land," for 4-part men's chorus, unaccompanied, text by Johann Gaudenz Salis, translated by Henry Wadsworth Longfellow, composed 1886, published by Schmidt, 1886; arranged for women's chorus and published 1889.
>
> "Song for the Clefs," an occasional piece, text by John Sullivan Dwight, composed for a dinner of the Clef Club in 1887.
>
> "To Daffodils," for mixed chorus, text by Robert Herrick, composed 1887, published by Schmidt, 1887.
>
> "Come Live with Me and Be My Love," for 2-part women's chorus, text by Christopher Marlowe, composed 1889, published Schmidt 1889; also published as a 2-part song for high or low voice, 1889.

Save for the occasional pieces, this is music written for singing clubs and choral societies, particularly those of Boston. Foote had already served a long apprenticeship as accompanist for or director of groups of this sort—the Harvard Glee Club, Salem Schubert Club, Apollo Club, Arion Glee Club, and Cecilia Society. Vocal ensembles were plentiful and wanted new music. Foote, like other local composers, acted to satisfy their needs. Thus, the above compositions may be regarded as quasi-functional. As with his other music, homophony is to the fore, rhythmic experimentation is negligible, and accompaniment is supportive only. In general, all parts sound together, with few rests introduced to relieve the prevailing texture. Passages for one or two voices only are not often heard. It is mostly easy going music, yet with moments of dryness and monotony. Little is truly remarkable. The distinctiveness evident in Foote's chamber music and songs is not found here.

"If Doughty Deeds My Lady Please" for TTBB chorus was by far the best received of these compositions, beginning with its initial presentation by the Apollo Club under Lang on 29 April 1885. As frequently was the case with the composer, an older text is used (Graham of Gartmore lived from 1735 to 1797). In E-flat major and a fast tempo, the full chorus sings to the end, except for a couple of brief passages for second bass only and for first tenor. Although tempo changes take place, dullness does threaten if the singing is unexceptional. Yet, the work is skillfully composed. On the occasion of its premiere, Lang's guidance and the Apollo's singing were excellent. One attendee wrote:

> Mr. Foote's "If Doughty Deeds" has a fine antique flavor, appealing to the fancy of the listener as an old portrait appeals to the eye and the mind's eye. In other words, Mr. Foote's music is well fitted to the antique verse of Graham of Gartmore, the effect produced being generally that of artistic propriety, while in the use of the refrain—and especially in the sudden change of key, by which the return of the thought is effected near the close of the composition—there is a genuine call to the sensibilities of the listener.[34]

"To Daffodils," which the Boylston Club performed on 4 May 1887, employs an old text by Robert Herrick (1591–1674). The music sounds slightly archaic, as in "If Doughty Deeds," but its rhythmic patterns, harmonic progressions, and textures are more varied. Some imitation is also introduced. However, this treatment is the exception rather than the rule for choral compositions.

Foote also wrote compositions for church use. The religious and serious bent of Boston's society in the second half of the nineteenth century, which Foote and his musical colleagues shared, prompted the creation of sacred music for local use at a time when less of it was being produced on the European continent. Soon after completing the *Three Songs*, op. 10, he finished

his first church work, the Te Deum and Jubilate in E-flat Major for
Chorus and Soloists, op. 7, which Schmidt published in 1886. He
completed two other works for SATB chorus and organ, "God Is
Our Refuge and Strength," which Gray published in New York
and Novello in London, in 1889; and a Te Deum in B-flat Minor,
completed in 1889 and published by Schmidt in 1890. This is
functional music in the truest sense, valuable and appropriate for
church services. Foote aims at usefulness, not originality. He tries
sincerely to project the message of the words. The keyboard accompaniment is unobtrusive. The chorus learns its music quickly
enough and without difficulty; each part is laid out so that it all
but sings itself. In this and other sacred works, the music takes little time to complete; no one work overstays its welcome. If the
choir director has the group follow directions and enunciate
clearly, these pieces have a lovely effect on a congregation.[35] The
style belongs to the British-American anthem tradition, as exemplified by the American Dudley Buck. Surely, Foote's singing with
the Salem Oratorio Society and directing of a church quartet-
choir served him well when writing sacred music for chorus.

The first venture into orchestral writing took place in 1885,
when Foote composed *The Farewell of Hiawatha* for baritone
solo, four-part men's chorus, and orchestra, op. 11, to a text by
Longfellow. Contemporary critics were delighted that an American composer had chosen to apply music to an American subject
in an American poem. Lang and the Apollo Club gave it a first
performance on 12 May 1886. Foote had sent the score to Dudley Buck and was trying to get him to perform it in Brooklyn.
Buck wrote to Foote on 1 June 1886:

> I am only too glad to produce an American work which
> has something to say. If I, as the elder man, may introduce
> a word of criticism, I would say—don't write too high *con-
> tinuously* for American tenors. It is not the compass *per
> se,—that* we have, but the sustaining of reiterated high
> tones as compared with German voices.[36]

Schmidt published the vocal score in 1886. The full score in
manuscript, dated May 1886, is in the library of the Harvard Musical Association. When Foote asked Houghton Mifflin, publish-

ers of the poem, for permission to use the text, he received the following reply, a letter dated 5 October 1885: "If the fragment of Hiawatha which you have set to music is to be published separately in sheet form, we would say that our usual conditions for the use of the words in such cases is that we shall receive a royalty of 5 per cent on the retail price of all copies sold."[37] Whether this condition was met or not is not known.

It is the close of the Longfellow poem, starting with "From his place rose Hiawatha," that was set. In order to cope with the verse, Foote had to overcome some specific problems. First, the poem's strongly registered, insistent meter promises to force itself upon the music. Moreover, the verse music and rhythm, plus a certain calculated monotony, are so completely identified with "Hiawatha" that any composer's endeavor to run counter to them might sound excessively artificial and strained. In short, Foote had to treat the text circumspectly, yet remain true to himself.

There are no references to Amerindian music, no use of modal or gapped scales. The tonality goes from the E minor of the opening to the E major of the close. Throughout, the poetry threatens to act as a hindrance to musical imagination. Nevertheless, the first part has appeal and feeling. The orchestra provides a brief prelude in moderately slow tempo and then the chorus enters quietly, in declamatory narrative fashion. This music goes before a warm-hearted baritone solo for Hiawatha ("I am going, O Nokomis"). Next, a supple cello passage introduces a short choral section and a recounting of Hiawatha's adieu to the Amerindian warriors ("I am going, O my People"), which sounds tuneful and even forceful. Yet it achieves a high degree of animation only once, with the words: "The Master of Life has sent them!" This first section ends gently and confidently. The chorus dominates the remainder of the work, as Hiawatha sails west, into "the fiery sunset." The "purple vapors" and "dusk of evening" receive a colorful accompaniment that gradually becomes softer, indicating his departure. The music then gets faster, louder, and more animated in order to present the good-bye of "the forests dark and lonely." The last measures for chorus rapidly go from very soft to very loud, closing with an elated flare-up of voices, on "Thus departed Hiawatha."[38] On the whole, the music is attractively though cautiously orchestrated. There are times, however, when

the words are made unintelligible, as with the unexpected erup-
tion of percussion on "Westward, westward, Hiawatha." There are
times, also, when monotony prevails and discourages the pathos
that Longfellow reached for. A tediousness develops that neither
Longfellow nor Foote intended. The treatment is lyric rather than
dramatic. For the most part, a unity of expression prevails, and
the quality of the themes remains high. Foote managed to per-
suade many listeners that here was something worth listening to.

In 1887, Foote completed the vocal score for another venture
combining voices with orchestra, *The Wreck of the Hesperus*, for
mixed chorus and orchestra, op. 17. The text again came from
Longfellow. The orchestration was finished in May 1888. His dependable friend Lang had the Cecilia Society perform it with piano accompaniment on 26 January 1888, and with orchestral
accompaniment on 27 March 1890. Just as dependable, Schmidt
published the vocal score in 1888, as did Curwen in London during the following year. The poem is far more dramatic than *Hiawatha*; the music, more contrapuntal. Foote does not hesitate to
repeat words in order to fill out his musical structures and produce a longer work. The musical imagination is fertile; the colorations are rich, dark, and diverse. The use of major tonalities
assuages a potential sentimentality in the text, as the music turns
either clamorous to depict panic or grief-stricken to depict the afflictions of the crew and passengers. The work begins in the key
of C with a turbulent prelude that becomes hushed for the two
measures before the chorus enters. The narration starts with the
full chorus threatening doom to the ship and its occupants. A description of the skipper's daughter is allotted mainly to a solo violin playing *allegretto grazioso* and the meter in $^{12}/_8$. When the
poem describes the growing gale—a northeaster—the menacing
billows, and the driving snow, the music mirrors the drama by entering F minor, constantly modulating and increasing the volume
of sound to *ff*. A shift to F major and *andante con moto* allows a
tenor soloist to describe the maiden's prayer to syncopated accompaniment. Compassionate and poetic is the music to "Blue
were her eyes." Discreet minor shadings of mediant, submediant,
and supertonic harmonies underline the girl's plea for the safety
of the ship. A delicate eloquence informs the lyrics: "O father, I

see a gleaming light. / O say, what may it be!" To no avail. Rescue is not possible. A final *allegro agitato* in E minor describes the wreck of the ship, and a coda in C major presents a lugubrious picture of the frozen body of the maiden lashed to a drifting mast.

Foote achieves the greatest expressiveness of all in the moments when the orchestra plays alone. There is a surfeit of four-part choral singing and too few contrasting solos. Yet, every measure is of interest, and the work is worthy of admiration. Even Gilbert Chase, normally unsympathetic to the music of the nineteenth-century New Englanders, admitted in 1987: "These [this composition and Foote's *Skeleton in Armor*, finished five years later] may be regarded as a culmination of the long, productive tradition of the dramatic cantata in America, of which *The Wreck of the Hesperus*, in particular, is exemplary. It deserves to be rescued from the sea of oblivion."[39]

The Compositions for Piano of the Late Eighties

The latter half of the eighties saw Foote veering more and more away from the Mendelssohn and Schumann influences and sounding more like himself. On occasion a dark somberness enters, not unlike Brahms. Four works for piano came after the *Cinq Pièces*:

> *Two Pianoforte Pedal Studies*, composed in 1884 and published by Schmidt in 1885.
>
> Gavotte in C Minor (no. II) and Eclogue, op. 8, composed in 1885–86 and published by Schmidt in 1886.
>
> Suite in D Minor, op. 15, composed in 1886 and published by Schmidt in 1887.
>
> *Serenade*, op. 18, no. 1, composed in 1887 and published by Brainard's Sons, Cleveland, in 1887; and *Humoresque*, op. 18, no. 2, composed in 1887 and published by Presser, Philadelphia, in 1887.

The two studies consist of A Pedal Study in F Major and an Etude in B Minor, which draws on one of Stephen Heller's op.

46 pieces. The music is pedagogically useful, acceptable to the ear, but not a major work. The other three offerings are more substantial.

Regarding the problems he faced writing for the piano, Foote remarked in 1931:

> It is without the interest of orchestral color, without the expressiveness of the string and wood instruments, without the help which the poem often gives. . . . Also, to write in an interesting technical way gets harder and harder. When the scale and arpeggio ruled supreme, things were indeed simple; but as they practically wore threadbare, and Chopin and Liszt, with their inventive minds, quite changed piano technique, it has become exceedingly difficult to make piano pieces interesting to the player. This may also be the reasoning for the great increase in difficulty seen in music of the last twenty-five years.[40]

This statement may also help explain why he wrote so few works and no sonatas for keyboard during his lifetime. What he did write (in the years under discussion) were fairly brief piano works skillfully crafted for piano. As Foote continued to write such pieces, his style did not greatly alter. It became more polished and increased in dexterity, effectiveness, and flexibility. These pieces were almost always simple and lucid in form, their measures plumped out with unintimidating rhythms, warm, enjoyable tunes, and romantic and chromatically inflected harmonies. Melody, as expected, is the central conveyer of the composer's thoughts. These thoughts become even more tangible through Foote's use of background rhythm and syncopation, appropriate harmonies, homophonic and contrapuntal textures, and the mechanical means available on the keyboard. His music sounds pianistically idiomatic, yet does not exploit every aspect of piano technique with brilliance and virtuosity. Rupert Hughes spoke rightly when he commented that Foote rarely swept the keyboard in his piano compositions, rarely hunted for any startling novelties of piano effect, and rarely showed a fondness for the cloudy upper-note regions. An enthusiastic Benjamin Lambord later spoke of the wide fame Foote had gained as a pianist and added that the "pianoforte pieces are written with an appreciation of pianistic effect which distinguishes them in the main from nearly all other pianoforte music produced in this country."[41]

Immediately after the pianist F. G. Ilsley performed the Gavotte in C Minor (no. II) and Eclogue, op. 8, at an evening musicale in Newark, New Jersey, he wrote a complimentary letter to the composer on 24 January 1886:

> They made an instant success. The musicians all said— "Who made that?"—The "Gavotte" is strongly written and while quaint & old fashioned in a way, leans decidedly to the modern advanced school—The "Eclogue" I particularly fancy—It is charmingly poetic and very original—The interpolated ⁵⁄₄ passage is extremely effective.[42]

The gavotte is indeed far superior to the one of *Trois Morceaux*. The melodic element is stronger; the rhythmic variety has increased; the more interesting harmonies unfold with a logic more firmly anchored to melody and rhythm. The piece is fast, in C minor, ²⁄₂ meter, and ternary form. The attractive outer sections no longer conduct themselves, as in previous works, only in two- and four-measure phrases. We find five-measure phrases, too. The less animated middle section changes to C major, sets up a reiterated bass rhythmic pattern on tonic and dominant, and weaves a delicate tune into the fabric above. Foote liked the piece sufficiently to transcribe it for strings as the third movement of the unpublished Suite in E, op. 12 (1886). It later found its way into the Serenade in E for Strings, op. 25 (1891).

An eclogue is supposed to take on a pastoral character, but instead the piece is a graceful allegretto, in G major and ³⁄₄ time. A brief six-measure middle section in ⁵⁄₄ time is inserted before the return of the principal theme. The theme adheres to a large extent to the tunes heard in American musical stage presentations of the day (example 7). The touch of B minor in measures 6 and 9, of A minor in measure 11, and the momentary shift into the major of the lowered submediant in measure 14 are typical. Of further interest are the instances of parallel fifths in the bass from measure 5 to 6 to 7, measure 8 to 9 to 10 to 11, and measure 13 to 14 to 15. They impart a hollow sound that could be interpreted as adding a little plein air pictorialism to the proceedings. Interesting in this regard is a letter that Foote sent to

The Musical Times of London shortly after he composed the *Eclogue*. It shows him working free of his conservative attitudes toward harmonic progressions and voice leading. The communication, published in the 1 December 1887 issue, read:

> May I add two more examples of consecutive fifths to those quoted in your October number? They are rather curious, as being perpetrated by Chopin, the most sensitive and refined of pianoforte writers. But I fear you will consider them so dangerous as examples for young writers that you will be unwilling to print them, for they certainly *sound* most beautifully.[43]

The Chopin examples are measures 19–20 of Etude, op. 35, no. 8, where the fifths are between inner voices, not nearly as exposed as Foote's, and measures 54–55 of Scherzo, op. 39, where the fifths are between the outer voices.

The Suite in D Minor, op. 15, consists of Prelude and Fugue, Romance, and Capriccio. The D-minor tonality is a favored one for suites. Foote would apply it to the orchestral Suite, op. 36 (1896) and the organ Suite, op. 54 (1904). In this piano suite, he advances from measure to measure, movement to movement, in a steady flow and without vehemence or florid virtuosity. Like the daily flow of his existence, the music spills forth imperturbably and euphoniously, achieving classical clarity and romantic feeling. A dignified homophonic but decidedly romantic introductory movement, in moderate tempo and ¾ time, gives way to a sturdy three-voiced fugue in D minor. This marvelous music starts with a virile energetic fugue subject (example 8) and is brought to completion effortlessly. Especially magnetizing is the return to the D-minor tonality at the end, when the subject is thundered out in octaves in the bass. The balladlike Romance in F major is an expressive slow movement in triple time. The tune is presented thrice, each time treated differently. The Capriccio in D major, ⁹⁄₈ time, and ternary form is the most difficult to play of the four pieces. Yet, it does not speed forward too rapidly and always appeals to the ear with its agile and flowing tones and buoyant spirit. The suite quickly became a favorite with pianists.

Last in the piano music, we reach the two movements of opus 18, the Serenade and Humoresque. Each movement is put together with the acumen expected from the composer. A serenade is traditionally night music sung or played outdoors, giving gallant or loving praise to a woman. In nineteenth-century Boston, amorous bachelors roamed the streets alone or with a few musical companions to offer evening serenades to admired young ladies—some of them delivered within earshot of West Cedar Street.[44] Similarly, Foote's Serenade caresses us with lovely tunes in smooth and elegant triple time, accompanied by what appears to be an imitation of a guitar. The music begins in F-sharp minor, the melody kept within the treble staff, then goes to A major with a second theme that sounds like a continuation of the first. F-sharp minor and the first melody return, only now everything is placed an octave higher. A slight variant of the second tune, again in A major, is heard next. Its final measures are set off by six cascading cadenzas that start very high on the keyboard and then plunge down in sparkling fashion. F-sharp minor makes its final appearance and then the first theme, with the tune placed an octave lower than its first appearance. Eight measures before the piece closes, we hear "strumming" arpeggiated chords in the right hand that further reinforce the notion of a guitarlike accompaniment.

A humoresque is usually thought of as a playful, whimsical, even capricious work. Part of the whimsy in Foote's Humoresque is the absence of a tempo indication. A certain eccentric wandering feature reveals itself in the music. Triple meter is again heard, only the key now is E minor. The middle section goes from F major to A minor to C major before making a transition back to E minor and a recapitulation of the opening material. Most unusual for Foote, there is a great deal of inner contrapuntal motion. Save for the first sixteen measures of the middle section, a constant eighth-note rhythmic stream rolls on in Baroque fashion to the end. Neither of the opus 18 pieces makes great emotional demands on the listener. Each remains mostly on the quiet side of the dynamic range. Both are refreshing. They are civil tonal musings from a civilized artist and have a definite place in the musical literature of a literate society.

Chamber and Orchestral Music
of the Late Eighties

By the mid-eighties, Foote's standing as an instrumental composer of importance had been established in much of the United
States. This recognition encouraged him to continue along this
road. The *Drei Charakterstücke* for Violin and Piano, op. 9, dates
from 1885 and was published the next year by Litolff's Verlag in
Braunschweig and by Schmidt in Boston. The first performance
of the opus, with Charles Allen on the violin and Foote at the piano, occurred on 30 November 1885.[45] The three character pieces are *Morning Song, Menuetto Serioso*, and *Romanza*. No
evident connection exists between them. Melodiousness in the
violin with an acute sensitivity to its idiom and a ternary design
of A B A^1 prevail in all three. Well-drawn and promising themes
are discerningly and euphoniously elaborated on. Though the
piano seldom presents anything of thematic importance, it does
add engagingly rich harmonies in rhythmic configurations sympathetic to the violin line. The first piece is moderately slow, in G
major and $^9/_8$ time. Its expression, mostly insouciant and sometimes gloomy, remains within the fairly relaxed parameters of a
morning serenade. The second, in $^3/_4$ time and G minor, starts
quasi recitative, but soon changes to a *moderato grazioso* tempo. An overall melancholy and several uneasy moments present
themselves in the violin part, whose emotionalism is made even
more persuasive by an adroit accompaniment. More than a suggestion of drama is present. The third is also in triple time but
slow and in E major. The sentiment is stronger than usual for
this type of piece, but effective nonetheless. Brahms's influence
on Foote is clear. It continued in Foote's next multimovemented
composition.

In 1889, Foote completed one of his finest chamber works,
the Sonata in G Minor for Piano and Violin, op. 20. Schmidt published it the next year. With it, Foote won over large numbers of
Americans to the cause of native composers, convincing listeners
of the viability of the local product. By so doing, he displayed a
patience and capacity to endure that deserves praise. The sonata
is not remarkable simply for the technical knowledge that informs it, but for manifesting so well the guiding aesthetic ideals
that girded his Boston community at its best and of which he was

so much a part. The excellence of his results merely bears out his faith in what he hoped to accomplish. He had accepted the attendant circumstances of a free society and now proved that he had also preserved an inborn soundness that stood him in good stead when working as a creative artist within that society. So much of what he was given by his countrymen had been straw; yet, miraculously, the bricks he managed to fashion were solid and golden.

Although the style of his sonata reveals nothing radical or even exceptional for its time, it has a bracing energy, an absence of hackneyed sounds, a rejection of maudlin public display, and the stamp of a pungent New England character that sets it apart from similar works of its era, whether American or European. To Foote, a chamber work of the sonata type was the topmost musical form. He intended the composition for his valued friend and Boston's leading violinist, Franz Kneisel, and wanted it to be impeccable. The exacting attentiveness he must have sustained while writing the music has given us the finest of his early works. Whether conveying charm, imaginativeness, delicate feeling, lyrical loveliness, or extreme ardor, the musical ideas struck contemporary music lovers as having considerable potency. After hearing the violin sonata's performance on 2 December 1889, a newspaper critic wrote a typical appraisal of its reception: "It was extremely well received and all its good points immediately felt and appreciated, the charming Siciliano being applauded with special heartiness."[46] The sonata appeared again and again on concert programs over the next quarter-century after its premiere, and was heard from the Atlantic coast to the Pacific.

The first movement is in ⁹⁄₈ time and opens on a dynamic, impassioned, and freewheeling subject presented by the violin above an animated accompaniment (Example 9a). Syncopations occur with some frequency. After establishing the tonality, Foote navigates the harmonic stream with virtuosity and some assertiveness. In measures 7–8, for example, the unexpected move into V⁷ of VI is followed by a delayed resolution via an appoggiatura chord in the right hand. The piano after measure 8 becomes an equal partner with the violin, sharing in motivic give-and-take, playing important countermelodies and frequently assuming a dominant role. This partnership holds true in all movements. The transition, based on the same material, arrives imperceptibly and takes us smoothly to the second subject in B-flat major. Here, the

expressive contrast continues with the first theme, already encountered in the first movement of the quartet for strings. A similar lyricism might tempt players to linger on the notes and
produce a sweetness that the composer wishes to avoid. Therefore, as before, he instructs them to render the music at a livelier
tempo. The expression is meditative and inward. From the beginning, the phrasing of the melody shows a desire to alleviate the
squareness of two-, four-, and eight-measure units. The grouping
starts off as 3, 3, 2, and 2 (example 9b). The development capital-
izes on the passionate nature of the first and the tranquil nature
of the second subject, opposing them, having one take on the expressive characteristics of the other, or combining them. The recapitulation is reasonably regular, with the second idea now in G
major. The coda returns to G minor and sounds more animated
as the violin excitedly dashes to the conclusion.

The second movement is titled *Alla Siciliano* and is in D major. Like the instrumental movement of the same name from the
high Baroque, it is in slow triple time (^{6}/$_8$), begins on an upbeat,
employs a dotted figure, and establishes a reassuring pastoral atmosphere (Example 9c). The piano leads off. As it is about to
close on a perfect cadence, the music suddenly switches to an *allegretto grazioso* and the key of B-flat major. The violin dashes
about, rather in a gypsy mode, before restating the first theme to
complete the ternary design. Like the second movement of the
quartet, the middle section is faster than the outer ones.

The third movement is an adagio in E-flat major and ^{4}/$_4$ time.
Again the piano leads off, but the violin takes over and mounts to
a very loud climax. An abrupt change to C minor, which is a third
below the first tonality, takes place and the stately tread of a solemn march starts up.   (Brahms's influence is perceptible, as it
was in the gypsylike center of the previous movement.) This
brings the listener to a third idea, lyrical but unsettled, going
from the key of B, to A, to C, to A-flat. The music grows louder
and becomes agitated. Then suddenly the march returns, now in
A-flat minor, a third below its earlier C minor. This time, it takes
us to a return of the initial theme in the home tonality. Yet again
the march returns, only its tonality lingers in C minor; at the
end, the movement returns once more to the first theme, inton-
ing it very quietly to the final measure (Example 9d).

The very fast final movement is in $^4/_4$ time and G minor. There is a fiery urgency about the first subject, which proceeds directly to a spirited transition. The second subject is in E-flat and assumes the devotional, hymnlike expression already mentioned in the trio. Especially when the piano takes over the lead does the music sound psalmodic indeed, as if Foote were acknowledging his own antecedents (Example 9f). Both themes are then developed. A recapitulation comes next. And the composition closes on the "hymn," followed by a restatement of the opening melody of the third music, which enters out of the blue and continues for the final thirty-two measures. He has united the grave and rising intonations of hymnody to the heartfelt meditative inflections of the aspiring human. The expressive links to both the trio and quartet are obvious.

Foote has traversed an extensive expanse of feeling, electing for drama and strong contrast in this sonata. The composer has graduated from the position in which a Cleveland writer had placed him twelve months before, "a young man who has begun a most promising career and gives every promise of making that career an enviable one."[47] He has begun his maturity, every promise to be fulfilled.

In the latter part of the eighties Foote began composing for orchestra. Since 1881, he had had before him the possibility that the qualitatively excellent Boston Symphony Orchestra might perform what he offered it. He noted criticisms that had been made—the orchestral programs included too much Beethoven, Mozart, and Haydn; a lesser amount of Berlioz, Liszt, and other contemporary Europeans; and no Americans.[48] Matters grew more propitious for Americans after the middle of the decade, when the leaders of the symphony became sensitive to the criticisms. It was then that Foote composed three works for instrumental ensemble that the orchestra took up. The Suite in E Major for String Orchestra, op. 12, was completed early in 1886 and premiered by the orchestra, under Wilhelm Gericke, on 15 May 1886.[49] The Overture *In the Mountains* for Full Orchestra, op. 14, was completed September 1886 and premiered by the orchestra, under Gericke, on 4 February 1887. Suite no. 2 in D Major for String Orchestra, op. 21, was completed in the summer of 1889 and premiered by the orchestra, under Arthur Nikisch, on 22 November 1889. In 1890, Theodore Thomas would conduct it twice in Chicago and at the national convention of the Music Teachers National Association in Detroit on 2 July 1990.

The Suite in E Major consists of three movements: Allegro comodo, Andante con moto, and Gavotte. The second movement may have been heard as early as 3 June 1885, when Adolf Neuendorff conducted Foote's Andante for String Orchestra at a Popular Concert in the Boston Music Hall. The third movement was a re-write of the Gavotte for Piano, op. 8 no. 1. Although the suite was never published and the composer retired the work, the Gavotte later found a new home in Serenade, op. 25. The consensus of opinion in the first year of its appearance was that the work was carefully constructed, perhaps too carefully, possibly because Foote wanted to write only what seemed right. Most of its melodic phrases are brief but elaborated with skill. Logic, fancy, taste, fine feeling, and some eloquence are present, but, as the reviewer in the *Advertiser* said, he sometimes kept "too much within himself." The first movement flowed easily but with insufficient contrast. The second movement was softer in character though not melancholic. The charming final movement was stronger and more rhythmic. It contained a fine contrasting trio with a somewhat prolonged melody in the violas. All the reviewers commented on how warmly the audience received the music.[50]

The Overture *In the Mountains*, op. 14, for orchestra, was also never published, although it proved popular and was performed many times in the United States, as well as in Paris, Berlin, and London. John Philip Sousa played a version of it for band in 1902. Foote revised the score in 1910. The score-manuscript that I examined is in the Boston Public Library, shelf no. **M.451.77. On the bottom of the first page is found "Written in 1886"; and on the last page, "Copied Dec. 1918."

It would be difficult to relate the music to any mountainous region. Perhaps the modest heights of the Blue Hills nearby to Boston were what he had in mind. More arguably, the feeling that mountains conjured up within him might have been what he wished to express. Serenity, thoughtfulness, and elegance rather than power and grandeur sound in the music. At any rate, Foote never once tried to explain its programmatic content.

This concert overture is in a regular sonata-allegro form. The conservative orchestration calls for flutes, oboes, clarinets, and bassoons in pairs, four horns, two trumpets, three trombones, tuba, and two tympani. The ³⁄₄ time signature continues throughout. The music begins with a slow introduction in E minor, on a theme that will recur throughout the piece (example 10). Just before the introduction ends, four French horns play a brief passage in C major that gives an open-air impression—one of the rare moments that recall the outdoors. The ensuing allegro in E major sports an ebullient first subject in the first violins. The second subject makes important allusions to the opening theme of the introduction. When the expected development arrives, it treats both themes at length. The recapitulation and coda follow with scarcely any surprises. Melodic lines are agreeable but contain inconsiderable substance. Harmony never goes beyond the precedents set by Mendelssohn. No strong rhythmic interest holds the attention. No innovative orchestral colors are heard, though the orchestration is effective. The technical and expressive boldness of the sonata finds no counterpart here. Obviously, Foote takes no chances. Nevertheless, there is a confident management of the musical material and an attractiveness about the results that listeners, including newspaper critics, found appealing. About forty years after it was completed, Foote said of his work:

> Though I knew little about orchestration, the Overture is effective, if old-fashioned; and it is singular that, in spite of my not playing any stringed instrument, nor indeed knowing in detail about the technique of even the violin, everything for strings has been practical and grateful. Much of my early reputation came from the Overture and from . . . [the] Trio, which forty years afterwards is still sometimes on programs.[51]

The important sonata for violin was still a few years in the future when the overture was heard, and the composer did not regard it as an "early" work.

The Suite no. 2 in D Major, op. 21, contains a Prelude, Minuetto, Air, and Gavotte. It was composed during the summer of 1889 on the island of Nantucket off the southern Massachusetts coast, but was never published. A couple of years later, the second and third movements were redeployed in Serenade, op. 25. The use of the old Baroque dance forms generated a great deal of debate at its premiere. The first movement is simple, based on one subject, and contains some pleasant contrapuntal activity. The second movement's main attraction is the featuring of a solo cello, next a solo violin, next the two solo instruments dueting amongst muted strings. The lovely Air, mostly a prolonged melody for first violin and not too far removed from Bach's style, was thought the best of the four movements. The finale alludes to the theme of the first movement, and it achieves some charming ancient bagpipe effects in its trio.

At the end of the eighties, Foote had not yet arrived at an orchestral style that felt comfortable to him. Some critics had already commented about some of the music sounding like exercises in composition.[52] Despite the overture's favorable reception, he held it back, choosing to revise it well after the turn of the century. As for the two suites, much of their music would be reworked and later find a new home in Serenade, op. 25. It was not until the nineties that he would allow a composition, whether for string or full orchestra, to be published.

Notes

1. Arthur Foote, Scrapbook I, Boston Public Library, shelf no. **ML.46F65.

2. The letter is in the Arthur Foote Collection, Williams College, Williamstown, Massachusetts.

3. Arthur Foote, "A Summary of the Principles of Harmony," MS written for the instruction of Arthur Foote II in 1932.

4. Arthur Foote and Walter R. Spalding, *Modern Harmony in Its Theory and Practice* (Boston: Schmidt, 1905), 249.

5. Thomas Ryan, *Recollections of an Old Musician* (New York: Dutton, 1899), 261–62.

6. Arthur Foote, *An Autobiography* (Norwood, Mass.: Plimpton Press, 1946), 57–58.

7. See Douglas Bryant Moore, "The Cello Music of Arthur Foote" (D.M.A. diss., Catholic University, 1976), 2.

8. Arthur Foote, *Modulation and Related Harmonic Questions* (Boston: Schmidt, 1919), 12.

9. "As a Composer Regards His Craft," *Boston Evening Transcript*, 8 October 1936; clipping in the Arthur Foote Collection. The newspaper reprinted a report on the proceedings that had been prepared by the W.P.A. publicity department.

10. Una L. Allen, "The Composer's Corner. No. 18 – Arthur Foote," *The Musician*, March 1931, 31.

11. Foote, "A Summary of the Principles of Harmony," 3. See also "Mr. Foote on Piano Touch," *Music* (1894), 96; Arthur Foote, "Some Unconsidered Details Often Neglected," *Etude* 44 (1926), 811–12.

12. Foote, *An Autobiography*, 55–56.

13. The publishers are described on the title page as "Boston, Arthur P. Schmidt" and "Hamburg, Aug. Cranz."

14. Arthur Foote, Scrapbook, at the New England Conservatory of Music, p. 10, contains the program of her concert.

15. Louis C. Elson, *The History of American Music*, rev. to 1925 by Arthur Elson (New York: Macmillan, 1925), 188, 190.

16. The program is found in Foote, Scrapbook, at the New England Conservatory of Music.

17. The program plus the reviews in the *Transcript*, *Courier*, and *Gazette* are in Foote, Scrapbook I, Boston Public Library. The number 43 is written at the top of the page.

18. The program and clippings of the newspaper reviews of the concert are contained in a scrapbook at the Boston Public Library, shelf no. **ML.46.B6F6.

19. Foote, *An Autobiography*, 67.

20. Foote's own copy of the published score at the Harvard Musical Association, shelf no. MC F738, vol. 1, has handwritten in the front "Neuilly, Summer of 1883." He also refers to a 1926 edition, which I have been unable to confirm.

21. *Boston Evening Transcript*, 10 April 1882, 1.

22. Reviews of the original and revised versions of the trio and the Gleason annotations are found in Foote, Scrapbook I, Boston Public Library, shelf no. **ML.46F65.

23. The many reviews of performances of this quartet may be found in Scrapbook I, and two other scrapbooks in the Boston Public Library, shelf nos. **ML.46.B6F6 and **ML.371.4.

24. Letter dated 29 October 1958 sent to Doric Alviani; see Doric Alviani, "The Choral Music of Arthur William Foote" (S.M.D. diss., Union Theological Seminary, 1962), 25.

25.   William Treat Upton, "Some Recent Representative American Song Composers," *Musical Quarterly* 11 (1925): 383; *Art-Song in America* (Boston: Ditson, 1930), 112–13.

26.   For a definition of ballad and a discussion of British and American types of ballad, see Nicholas E. Tawa, *Sweet Songs for Gentle Americans, 1790–1860* (Bowling Green, Ohio: Bowling Green University Popular Press, 1980), 7–13, 158–92.

27.   See Nicholas E. Tawa, *The Way to Tin Pan Alley* (New York: Schirmer, 1990), 172–75.

28.   Scrapbook I at the Boston Public Library contains a concert program dated 19 February but without the year in which she sang "Go, Lovely Rose." The program, however, is inserted with material from 1884.

29.   The clipping may be found in Scrapbook I, Boston Public Library.

30.   Clipping from the *Musical Herald* (January 1886), in Scrapbook I.

31.   Ibid.

32.   Arthur Foote, "Letters. Undated from the Second [Rosalie] Houseman Gift," Library of Congress, shelf no. ML 95.F77.

33.   Hughes, *Contemporary American Composers*, 228.

34.   Unidentified clipping in Scrapbook I, Boston Public Library.

35.   When I was music director at the Foster Memorial Church in Springfield, Massachusetts, I conducted opus 7 at several Sunday services, always to the gratification of the minister and the delight of the congregation.

36.   Arthur Foote, "Letters collected by Arthur Foote. Gift to the library in memory of Arthur Foote, April 16, 1940" (Boston: Spaulding Library, New England Conservatory of Music).

37.   The letter is in Scrapbook I, Boston Public Library.

38.   For an analysis of the work, see George P. Upton, *The Standard Concert Guide* (Chicago: McClurg, 1912), 163–64.

39.   Gilbert Chase, *America's Music*, 3d ed. (Urbana: University of Illinois Press, 1987), 383.

40.   Una L. Allen, "The Composer's Corner," *The Musician*, March 1931, 31.

41.   Hughes, *Contemporary American Composers*, 225; Benjamin Lambord, "The Classic Period of American Composition," in *Music in America*, vol. 4 of *The Art of Music*, ed. Arthur Farwell and W. Dermot Darby (New York: National Society of Music, 1919), 339–40.

42.   Foote, Letters, (Spaulding Library, New England Conservatory of Music), letter no. 83.

43. Arthur Foote, "Letter to the Editor," *The Musical Times* 28 (1887): 749.

44. The practice had been quite common before the Civil War and gradually died afterward; see Tawa, *Sweet Songs for Gentle Americans*, 28.

45. The program of the concert at Chickering Hall is found in Scrapbook I, Boston Public Library.

46. *Boston Evening Transcript*, 3 December 1889, 4.

47. Unidentified writer in the *Cleveland Musical Art Journal*, 1 January 1889, 1.

48. See, for example, the editorial in Boston's *Musical Herald* 7 (1886): 134. The editors at that time were Louis Elson, Stephen Emery, William Sherwin, and George Whiting.

49. A clipping in the Arthur Foote Collection of a report in the *Boston Music Bulletin* (4 February 1886), which reads: "Of Mr. Foote's compositions the Suite for strings, Op. 12, was played by the Symphony Orchestra, at a popular concert in May, 1886. This Suite was recently brought out by Mr. Henschel in the London Symphony Concerts."

50. Clippings of the newspaper reviews are found in "Scrapbook V," Boston Public Library, shelf no. **M.125.5; Foote, Scrapbook I, Boston Public Library, shelf no. **ML.46.F65.

51. Foote, *An Autobiography*, 56.

52. This comment was made especially about the Suite no. 2; see the reviews in Foote, Scrapbook I.

Part III

The Mature Composer
(1890-1901)

6

Grown Man and Musical Practitioner

The Boston area, including the artists living within it, were beneficiaries of the "City Beautiful" activities of the nineties. These actions were driven by the era's reform movements and international expositions, part of whose aim was to bring order out of what was perceived as chaos. Businesspeople united with municipal art leagues and art commissions in order to bring about an artistic atmosphere. They also wished to encourage American arts that had excellence and represented democratic ideals. Equal in importance was the implanting of a "missionary spirit" in American artists.

Concurrent with the City Beautiful movement was a musical reawakening that took place at the end of the nineteenth century, a momentous occasion in American cultural history whose complete significance is still to be acknowledged. All of a sudden, a host of people appeared who were directly involved with art music—composers, instrumentalists, singers, academics, historians, journalists, applied-music instructors, and music directors of vocal and instrumental ensembles. By 1892, the Czech nationalist composer Antonín Dvořák was in New York, demonstrating in his music the bracing strength of compositions that came from a national awareness. Whether or not American composers followed the Dvořák example and turned to the vernacular as a source for their music, they had to confront and debate the issues he raised about what constituted an American music.

In addition, they became acutely aware of the responsibilities of their pioneering position in the United States.

In Boston, the building of McKim, Mead and White's magnificent public library (1887–95) was one outcome of the City Beautiful movement. The structure was considered the equivalent of any grand Renaissance palace of former times. Today it stands across the broad plaza of Copley Square, facing the majestically Romanesque Trinity Church, designed by Henry Hobson Richardson and completed in winter 1877. The noted artist John LaFarge was responsible for the church's decorations. The library's murals, statues, and various memorials were the work of Augustus Saint-Gaudens, Frederick MacMonnies, Puvis de Chavannes, Edwin Austin Abbey, and John Singer Sargent. Daniel Chester French executed magnificent bronze doors for it. According to Richard Wilson, these, as well as the noble stairhall, courtyard, and great reading room, were meant to proclaim the edifice to be a center of civilization.[1] It was a decade when Boston's cultural leaders were intensely aware of the delicate balancing act between artist and public. Every art was subject to some give-and-take with its audience as part of an automatically regenerating scheme within a democratic society.

In 1893, Foote attested to the musical consequences of this artistic "atmosphere, of which so much is said [and which] is certainly not wanting here in Boston." Referring to Americans who crossed the Atlantic to Europe for music, he added that "in all but a very few of the places frequented by Americans, the number of concerts is absurdly small in comparison to what we have in Boston and New York."[2] The nineties were a part of a period that "was a fruitful and important one" in the creation of music by Americans, "when Chadwick, Horatio Parker, Paine, MacDowell, Mrs. Beach, Nevin and others were composing music, much of which will live; for instance Paine's 'Oedipus' choruses [1881, rev. 1895], Chadwick's 'Melpomene' overture [1887], Parker's 'Hora Novissima' [1893]—I was lucky to be in that group."[3] Foote surely read and concurred with the editorial "Nothing Musical in Narrowness" that appeared in the *Boston Musical Herald* in June 1890. Eben Tourjée managed the publication, and its editors were Louis Elson, George Wilson, and Benjamin Cutter. It lambasted the narrow, bigoted views of Europeans who pronounced judgment on the United States. It called out the pianist Anton Rubinstein for saying that Americans were among the most unmusical people in the world, though he was willing to play for us so long as he was bountifully paid for his appearances. Another pianist, D'Albert, had spoken scornfully and sarcastically about Americans and had laughed at our musical efforts, all the while pocketing our dollars. The painter Herbert Herkomer toured America and announced that it was impossible to produce any art there. These remarks demonstrated the relentless European prejudice against Americans. "We can claim to be musical," the editorial insisted.[4]

A reference to him in the English edition of Hugo Riemann's *Musik-Lexikon*, first published in Leipzig in 1882, must have irked Foote. At any rate, he cut out and preserved an 1897 interview of Franz Kneisel, who spoke up for and praised the compositions of Chadwick and Foote, "who by a curious ignorance is classed in the English edition of Riemann's dictionary as a 'composer of light pieces.'"[5] Light pieces indeed! Was this all the credit he could gain for his efforts to bring about a greater openness to all art music and to write music that tried for distinction and the affirmation of democratic principles?

Nevertheless, he did not turn a blind eye to problems in America. Several items in the scrapbooks and in the Arthur Foote Collection at Williams College testify to his ongoing interest in the political, economic, and social issues facing Boston and the country. During the nineties political power in Boston was shifting decisively to the Irish, and immigrants from southern Italy were coming to make up a higher and higher percentage of the population. Foote had no part of the Anglo-Saxon and Nordic mystique that claimed a natural superiority over other ethnic groups and races, and he rejected completely the anti-Semitism rampant in America. However, he had to accept the reality that most of the new arrivals had little education and no time for the high culture treasured by him and his acquaintances.[6] Their energies went into finding jobs and earning sufficient money to keep themselves and their families in food, clothing, and shelter. At the same time, New York City was gaining a decided ascendan-

cy over Boston in finance and commerce. Foote felt saddened
when eventually MacDowell, with the promise of a steady and
respectable income, left to teach at New York's Columbia University, and Franz Kneisel also left for the greater earning opportunities afforded by that city. This was also the decade known as
the "Gay Nineties," which displayed a mien of pleasure seeking,
dissipation, and boorish materialism. It was also the decade
when jingoism, imperialism, and a my-country-right-or-wrong attitude permeated the United States that culminated in the Spanish-American War of 1898. Foote had no part of any of this.

The group with whom Foote affiliated himself feared that the
contrariness of the period would wilt art's bloom. The few enlightened men and women were everywhere outnumbered by
hordes of "Philistines," whom Arlo Bates had been pillorying as
early as 1888: "There is no art in this country. New York is the
home of barbarism and Boston of Philistinism; while Cincinnati
is a chromo imitation of both." Those "prominent Philistines"
who "patronize art," do so by snubbing artists.[7]   A clipping
(found, with material dating from December 1898 through January 1899), on a fictitious family known as "the Philistines," that
Foote preserved in his third scrapbook is interesting in this regard. The article states that "the Philistines" include "the newly
rich and the newly educated, the Would-Bes and the Know-It-
Alls, the Prigs and the Pedants." This family had been growing
swiftly in size. Its members read Mrs. Humphrey Ward, enjoyed
Quo Vadis, Bouguereau's paintings, and popular reproductions
of "Breaking Home Ties" and "The Doctor." Those lower in the
taste scale gave Christmas presents of gilded rolling pins, hand-
painted griddles, clay statuary "immortalizing such appealing
subjects as 'The Soldier's Farewell' and 'Let Me Kiss Him for His
Mother.'" On the lips of Philistines were "new smart sounding"
phrases that they liked to pick up. Cant was their stock-in-trade.[8]

Yet Foote, like Emerson before him, did not disapprove of
the freshness, vibrancy, and rough strength that also characterize
popular culture. After all, he frequently attended the lighter offerings of the music stage, enjoyed the frivolities of the clubs to
which he belonged, and himself was the producer of a few songs
in the popular manner. What upset him was the sentimentality,

the triteness, and the thoughtless fashionable thinking that characterized many lives and directed the taste of men and women in
America and Europe. It concerned him that the City Beautiful
and other movements that intended to improve the quality of
democratic life might well founder on accusations of snobbery,
effetism, and affectation, and fall to the power wielded by an un-
reflective American majority.

Meanwhile, he continued to cultivate his own special acre as
best he could. He cherished his friends, who shared his views,
befriended him and his family, and strengthened his resolve to
keep on composing. Foote measured success in terms of his
achievements in association with family, friends, and the discern-
ing music public, not money. He was content with an income
sufficient to procure some of the comforts of life. More valuable
to him was an existence filled with enriching encounters. He
welcomed people in their variety and yielded to the joys of physical and mental activity, and to a life animated by feeling. Foote
made himself one with the people he knew, the places he enjoyed, and the natural settings in which he found himself.

Friendships

His circle of friends increased during the nineties to include
people throughout the United States and Europe. In November
1894, the editors of *The Song Journal* stated: "Arthur Foote is
one of the American composers whose name, attached to a composition, is a sure guarantee of its worth. And besides being one
of the foremost musicians of the land, he is so companionable a
gentleman that his personal friends are precisely as numerous as
his acquaintances."[9]

He met many new people through the agency of old friends:
"This [the nineties] was the era when Mrs. Bell, Mrs. Pratt, Mrs.
Whitman reigned supreme in Boston. The first two were . . .
sharp and witty, they had been everywhere and remained Boston
to the core."[10] At the Charles Street home of Mrs. Fields he encountered old acquaintances and found new ones: Louise Imo-
gen Guiney and Sarah Orne Jewett, M. A. DeWolfe Howe and

Thomas Bailey Aldrich, Mrs. Bell and Julia Ward Howe and Henry James. Henry James, along with his brother William, he would also see at the Tavern Club.[11] He continued in friendship with musical colleagues like William Apthorp and met younger ones like Philip Hale, who arrived in Boston in 1889 to write for several journals and newspapers and later prepared the program notes for the concerts of the Boston Symphony Orchestra. Foote was glad when fellow composer Horatio Parker returned to Boston in 1893 to accept the post of organist and choirmaster of Trinity Church. Parker's daughter says her father was delighted to rejoin friends like Chadwick and Foote and again spend "many happily contentious hours" with them, candidly discussing music and musical matters. "Boston had begun to reach out of its essential Puritanism to acknowledge and encourage the arts of music and painting; Father and Mother both enjoyed their life there."[12]

When he could, he repaid the debt he owed others. For example, on 9 May 1901, as president of the Cecilia Society, he was responsible for a commemoration that celebrated B. F. Lang's twenty-fifth anniversary as conductor of the Cecilia. Foote made the presentation speech and gave the veteran musician, to whom he owed so much, a silver bowl. In October of the same year, there was a celebration of the twenty-fifth anniversary of Arthur P. Schmidt's music publishing firm, and Foote was among those who honored the publisher who had "steadily pursued the policy of taking up compositions by the best American composers and publishing them."[13]

Isabella Stewart Gardner remained a staunch supporter, frequently inviting the Footes to her Boston home for social evenings, dinners, and concerts. She insisted that they summer at her oceanside vacation place at Pride's Crossing, Beverly, Massachusetts, and did all she could to encourage the composer to further creativity. A letter that he sent to her from the St. Botolph Club, dated only "Friday evening," reads:

> It was like you to leave that nice note to cheer me up after
> the exuberant reception of my piece this afternoon: I al-
> most felt that it ought not to have been written and that
> something must be wrong, but you honestly made me feel

much happier—It will be nice for me tomorrow to be able
to take Kitty to hear it, too, as she and Katharine got home
a day ago.

> Again thank you ever so much,
> Faithfully yours,
>   A. Foote[14]

Another encourager was a recent arrival to Boston, the pianist and composer Helen Hopekirk. She came from Scotland to
teach at the New England Conservatory in the fall of 1897 in order to earn money to send her invalid husband, William Wilson,
to Switzerland for the coming summer. She never really left Boston after that. Hopekirk took up Foote's piano pieces, performing them in Boston and Edinburgh. At one point, she returned to
Edinburgh to stay. Finding no musical renaissance in Scotland,
she returned to Boston.[15] It was Helen Hopekirk who persuaded
Foote to produce one of his best received orchestral works, the
orchestrated version of four of his *Omar Khayyám* piano pieces.

He won the goodwill of other musicians by being sensitive
to their feelings and helping them in their needs. When Lang
needed an organist for the Easter 1897 performance of Horatio
Parker's *Hora Novissima* with members of the Boston Symphony, Foote agreed to play the keyboard part, winning both Lang's
and Parker's gratitude. Probably at the end of the nineties, he
wrote a note to a Mr. Silgory [? Siegory?]: "I shall be very pleased
to accompany the songs—and thank you much for the singing of
them. Only please don't let it seem to interfere with the accompanist of the concert—in fact pray see that it is understood. I
hope you'll let me see you when you come to Boston—so that I
may put you up at the club."[16] About the same time, 1899, the pianist Leopold Godowsky played Schumann's *Carnival* in Boston, and local critics called his playing "inferior to Rosenthal's
brilliant interpretation." Knowing full well how unhappy
Godowsky must have felt, Foote sent him a note saying "his interpretation was the most beautiful he had ever heard."[17]

Other musicians reciprocated Foote's goodwill. Edward Mac-
Dowell sent Foote a note on 29 January 1896 from his 38 Chestnut Street, Boston, residence, which was close by Foote's home
on West Cedar Street, saying: "I am to play your Trio op. 5 (or 3?)

in Chicago with—[?] next month—and would you mind giving me your idea of it Sunday—If you care to stop here on your way anywhere."[18]

Foote and the Emergence of the Nineties

Foote maintained a full schedule of teaching throughout the nineties. On 26 March 1890, Foote's Overture *In the Mountains* was part of a "Concert of American Compositions" heard at Lincoln Music Hall in Washington, D. C.,[19] an event that should have satisfied him greatly. On the other hand, it must have occasioned unhappiness and unease for him in the same month to join Lang, Whiting, Paine, MacDowell, and about seventy others in a petition to the Massachusetts legislature: "The undersigned, interested in teaching music, languages or oratory in the city of Boston, respectfully and earnestly protest against granting to the New England Conservatory of Music in said city any funds or State aid, as has been requested by petition to the Legislature of the Commonwealth of Massachusetts for two successive years."[20] Indubitably, they feared the school's further encroachment into their territory. Conspicuously absent from the petition was the name of Chadwick, who had been on the conservatory faculty since 1882 and would be the conservatory's director in 1897. That summer Foote vacationed at Isabella Gardner's oceanside retreat, The Alhambra, at Pride's Crossing, Beverly, Massachusetts, where he completed the substantial Symphonic Prologue *Francesca da Rimini*, op. 24, for large orchestra. He dedicated it to his benefactor, Mrs. Gardner. In 1890, he would also finish the Quartet in C for Piano and Strings, op. 23. In addition, he and his sister, Mary W. Tileston got their deceased brother Henry's *Hymns of the Church Universal* into final shape and had J. Wilson and Son of Boston publish it.

The Boston Symphony Orchestra, Foote conducting, premiered his orchestral work on 23 January 1891; the Kneisel Quartet, Foote at the piano, premiered his chamber work on 16 February. On 1 February he appeared at a "Benefit Concert" for Fritz Giese, to play the solo part of Ferdinand Hiller's Piano Concerto in F-sharp Minor, op. 69, with Bernhard Listemann conducting the Boston Philharmonic Orchestra. As might be expected, the Salem Oratorio Society on 22 April sponsored a concert that Foote conducted. For this occasion, he played solo piano pieces and heard his choral piece "To Daffodils" sung. To encourage attendance, the sponsors advertised "special street cars and regular trains for surrounding towns at the close of the Tuesday and Wednesday evening concerts."[21]

It was this year that Harvard added to his growing professional stature. A communication from President Charles Eliot, dated 15 June 1891, went: "I beg to inform you that the Faculty of Arts and Sciences of Harvard University respectfully invites you to serve as a member of the Committee which recommends to the Faculty candidates for honors or higher degrees in Music. The Chairman of this Committee is Professor J. K. Paine, who will inform you more particularly about the services for which we hope to be indebted to you."[22] During July and August he spent his seaside vacation at Hull, Massachusetts. Here, he completed *The Skeleton in Armor*, op. 28, for chorus and orchestra, an ambitious setting of a poem by Henry Wadsworth Longfellow, and the *Nine Pianoforte Studies*, op. 27, which was of lesser consequence. In this same year, one of his most popular works appeared, "An Irish Folk Song," text by Sir Gilbert Parker. He would also put together his Serenade in E Major for String Orchestra, op. 25, reemploying a great deal of the music from his two previous suites for strings.

His music was now being performed frequently by various musicians in cities distant from Boston. For example, Frederic Root, of popular-song fame, sponsored a song recital in Chicago on 23 April 1892 that featured Foote's songs. On 28 April, Emilio Agramonte and the American Composers Choral Association presented *The Skeleton in Armor* in New York City. In this same month Franz Xavier Arens presented in Leipzig the Gavotte, which had first appeared as the last movement in the Suite in E Major for String Orchestra, op. 12, and next as the fifth movement of the Serenade in E major for String Orchestra. Three months later, Arens conducted it in Vienna. On 6 July, his Piano Quartet, op. 23, was done at the annual conference of the M.T.N.A. Finally, he received a letter (dated 15 November 1892) from the Trinity Historical Society of Dallas, Texas, which had been "organized February 24, 1887, for Historical and Scientific Study and Research, and the Promotion of Literature and the

Fine Arts in Texas." The secretary of the society, Ben Austin, wrote: "The members of this society, desiring to convey to you in some manner an expression of their esteem, have unanimously elected you an honorary member."[23]

The year 1892 was not all joy over performances and excitement over recognition. Three years before, he had lost his dear brother Henry and now his father was fading fast. A letter he sent to a Mrs. Hollister, 24 May 1892, is valuable for revealing his inner feelings, which he usually preferred to conceal. It reads:

> I was shocked to hear of your mother's death, and am very sorry for the grief that it must have been to you—But though a violent death is to us a greater shock, it often seems to me the easiest of all—Perhaps I feel so much strongly now, for my father, in his 90th year, is for the first time distinctly more feeble, and I dread his living to lose anything of his alertness and quickness of the mental faculties, which he has preserved so well 'till now. It would be the greatest pain to have him outlive *himself*. But after all, when it does come to one we love, nothing seems to be any good.[24]

He continued in close relationship with Isabella Gardner, as is evident in a letter he sent to her on 15 August 1892 from her summer home in Beverly, where he and his family were again vacationing:

> It is such a pleasure to get your note, with the magic Venice postmark.
>
> The song is by a man Strelezki, who had had a curious sort of life here in Detroit and other places, and is now living in Europe somewhere. It has been wonderfully popular, but not the sort of thing you care for.
>
> I'll have it left at 22 Congress Street to be forwarded as you may direct.
>
> We have a very happy summer—and I am doing a little writing. The "Francesca" (the first copy) has come, and the others will also directly, but I shall keep your copy until you come back, which will be a pleasant day.[25]

The "little writing" he did that year included mainly choral pieces but no large compositions.

His close relationship with Harvard also continued. On 16 November, he received a communication from Harvard: "In accordance with the Rules and By-Laws of the Board of Overseers of Harvard University, I have to notify you of your appointment as a member of the Committee on Music for the year 1893."[26] This would have been the third year he served on this committee, according to Elliot Forbes. Foote would eventually act as chairman of the committee.[27] Assuredly, Charles Eliot, the brother of his widowed sister-in-law, had something to do with these appointments.

The musical public of New York City took further notice of Foote's capabilities as a performer and composer when he and the Kneisels played the Piano Quartet in that city on 14 January 1893. An unidentified newspaper clipping testifies to the respect shown him and to a dry sense of humor that he possessed:

> It is a pleasure as well as an honor to take a genius by the hand, and so I was happy when Henry Holden Huss introduced me to Arthur Foote, of Boston. . . . Mr. Foote had just finished playing the piano part in his new quartet in C, with strings—a most delightful and musicianly work. I found him modest, unassuming, witty and affable; and I felt at home in the presence of the great man at once. . . . Mr. Colell congratulated the Boston man and told him he hoped to hear him in New York soon again. "Any time you will pay my expenses and $1,000 I shall be happy to run on," replied Mr. Foote, and all within hearing laughed a good laugh at Mr. Colell's expense.[28]

Clearly, by 1893, musicians recognized Foote's exceptional musical capabilities, which were generating not just uncommonly fine performances but also creative works. The music public saw him as radiating a sanity in his conduct and as having an approach to creativity that showed an admirable balance of intellect and intuition.

The most notable event in 1893 was the opening of the World's Columbian Exposition in Chicago. The secretary of the exposition wrote to Foote (and others, like Chadwick, Paine, Whiting, and MacDowell) from Chicago, on 7 November 1892, stating: "It is the desire of the Musical Director [Theodore Thomas] to perform representative works of yours, both choral and instrumental, at Exposition concerts. I write to ask you to name two or more compositions which you would like to have performed in this connection."[29] An announcement released to newspapers (dated 2 March 1893) stated that Foote's "Overture 'Francesca da Rimini,'" "Serenade for String Orchestra," and "Quartet for Pianoforte and Strings" would be performed at the exposition. *Francesca da Rimini*, however, was never presented at the fair.

Just before Foote left for Chicago and the fair, on 13 May he and the Harvard Musical Association gave a party, attended by Oliver Wendell Holmes and a large number of people to celebrate John Sullivan Dwight's eightieth birthday: "The party was entirely social with just enough music, chiefly furnished by Mr. Arthur Foote and Mr. Wulf Fries, to make it a most fitting occasion."[30] By this time, the musical world had passed Dwight by. He was a part of Boston's cultural past. However, Foote had never forgotten Dwight's vital contributions to that past.

Meanwhile, Theodore Thomas had come in for severe condemnation from local politicians and businesspeople, aided and abetted by a hostile press. They found it unpardonable that Thomas had allowed some piano soloists appearing at the fair, among them Paderewski, to use pianos from Steinway, who was not an exhibitor. Thomas was accused of deceitful and dishonest practices and was asked to resign as music director of the fair. On 12 May 1893, Foote received a telegram from W. C. B. Mathews, Chicago editor and writer on music: "Eddy and I preparing card of confidence in Theodore Thomas. Attacks wholly unjustifiable. Please wire today all good names, possibly Chadwick, MacDowell, etc." Foote complied. The music community rallied around Thomas and encouraged him to defy his detractors. Because Thomas refused to resign, the funding for music was trimmed in revenge.

On 22 May, Foote was staying at 88 Astor Street, Chicago, when he received a telegram from his wife Kitty: "Thomas wants you to conduct your suit [*sic*] at three tomorrow. All well. Send love." The next day, Foote conducted his new Serenade in E for String Orchestra. The day after, he and the Kneisels put on the Piano Quartet in C. Later in the year, various organ players performed one or another of his three *Opus 29* pieces for organ. Neally Stevens played the *Etude Mignone*, op. 34, no. 3, for piano, and the romanza and gavotte from the Serenade were done again. Heard twice at the fair, was his composition for voice or voices and piano, "Land to the Leeward."[31]

The same day that he received the telegram from Kitty, he was sent a letter from the Manuscript Society of New York, which had performed his String Quartet in G Minor, op. 4, on 5 May: "You are hereby notified that, at a regular meeting of the Board of Directors of the Manuscript Society held on Friday, May 19th, 1893, you were, by a unanimous vote, elected as one of the Honorary Vice-Presidents of the above Society for the ensuing year. Trusting that the Society may be encouraged by your acceptance, I beg to remain yours very respectfully, Harry W. Lindsley, Cor. Sec'y."[32]

By summer, Foote was back on the eastern seaboard, vacationing at Mrs. Gardner's summer place. There, he worked on his Quartet for Strings in E Major, op. 32, and Concerto for Cello and Orchestra in G Minor, op. 33. The quartet was premiered by the Kneisel Quartet in February of the following year; the concerto by the cellist Bruno Steindel and the Chicago Orchestra under Thomas in November. Neither work won much of a following or was published, although some of the music found its way into other compositions. In 1893, Foote subscribed the sum of $100 toward the building of Boston's new Symphony Hall. This was a handsome amount, given the value of the dollar at that time and the fact that Foote was not a wealthy man. His contribution may have been inspired by his friendship with the orchestra's founder, Henry Lee Higginson, his gratefulness for past and hopefulness for future performances of his orchestral music, and, not least, his genuine desire to further the cause of art music in Boston.[33]

Foote started the year 1894 by helping Julia Ward Howe present an "Authors' Matinee for the benefit of the suffering poor, given under the auspices of the New England Women's Press Association" on 25 January. He played the piano accompaniments in a presentation of four songs, one of them his "Irish Folk-Song," the other three by Ethelbert Nevin. This year 1894 was notable for his failure to produce a single major number. He attended the performances of Wagnerian opera given by Walter Damrosch, the New York Symphony Orchestra, and a German cast in Boston during April. Such an event and the premiering of two new works, however lukewarm their reception, would normally have led to the production of more works during the summer, when teaching and performing obligations were suspended. But this year, tragedy struck right before his vacation period—his father, Caleb Foote, died on 17 June. Foote was badly shaken, but kept his grief private. Aside for the preserving of one article on his father in Scrapbook II, he left no record of his reaction to his father's death.

The year finally ended on a cheerful note. Foote's Piano Quartet in C Major, op. 23, was played in Paris. An unidentified clipping entitled "Triumph for an American Composer in Paris," which Foote dated "Dec. 1994," is an account of the occasion:

> Every Wednesday evening at the house of M. Felix Darcy a select company of the best musicians in Paris, violinists, 'cellists, pianists, composers, many of them professors of the Conservatoire, meet and play over the latest and best music. Last evening the gem of the performance was a quartet in C for violin, viola, violoncello, and piano by Mr. Arthur Foote, of Boston.
>
> It was superbly played by master musicians and most enthusiastically received by these severest of all critics.
>
> "Bravo! Bravo! Bravo pour le jeune Américain!" &c., were the exclamations after each number and after the finale.
>
> Mr. G. Waring Stebbins, organist of the Emanuel Baptist Church, in Brooklyn, who is here studying with Guilmant, and who is a favored member of this circle, became the centre of interested attention because of being a friend of Mr. Foote.[34]

In 1895, Arthur Foote began three annual summer odysseys to Europe. In June, he left with wife Kitty and daughter Katharine for London. This year he was interested in meeting Europeans, and his reputation had grown sufficient that Europeans wanted to meet him. For a while, the Footes found lodgings at Notting Hill near the Baileys, the parents of Lillian Bailey Henschel. The Henschels, now resident in London, were delighted with the arrival of the Footes and took them to meet "the Felix Moscheles, the Blumenthals, the Tademas, etc." The actress Julia Arthur, then in London, visited with them. Social calls during the day and entertainments during the evening marked their stay. The Footes were thrilled by their reception.

The warm hospitality, splendid social evenings, opulent life, and lack of hurry impressed the composer. Through Clayton Johns, he met the vocalist David Bispham, who immediately invited him to "a big men's dinner." Shortly thereafter, Henschel gave a feast in Foote's honor, where the composer made friends with Hubert Parry, Villiers Stanford, and Joseph Barnby. Even in London, he was ever ready to do favors for Mrs. Gardner, to whom he owed a great deal. He wrote to her on 25 June, saying he would be glad to get her bag now in Paris, where he was going later, and bring it to her in Beverly. As for London: "What with receptions, dinners, and so on, London is a Kaleidoscope just now to my Boston eyes."[35]

Anxious to get a seaside place for the summer, Foote took Bispham's advice and went to Hythe, where he first became acquainted with the game of golf. He rented a piano and finished his Suite in D Minor for Orchestra, op. 36. Emil Paur and the Boston Symphony premiered it in Boston on 6 March of the following year. Its reception was not what Foote had hoped for. Possibly the interpretation and playing were not great. Foote thought Paur was "not a conductor of much refinement." The orchestra underestimated his abilities and disrespected his musicianship.[36]

The heat was unbearable when they made a ten-day visit to Paris. At any rate, he had to return to Boston and his church job. He had his wife and daughter go on to stay in Meran, a town with a beautiful countryside, then in the Austrian Alps, now renamed Merano and a part of Italy. Alone and lonely, he boarded a ship for America. On his arrival in Boston, he obtained lodgings at 96 Mount Vernon Street, where he remained until 1897, and took his meals at the St. Botolph Club. He taught privately in a studio located in the Chickering Building, which Lang also inhabited.[37]

Aspects of the Late Nineties

During 1896, he did not do very much composing. Indeed, he himself admits that though he continued to compose after 1895, it was mostly "on a smaller scale." Moreover, the end of 1895 closed off the period when he engaged in regular and extensive concert playing.[38] He listened to the Paur and Boston Symphony presentation of his suite, on 6 March, worried over its public reception, then waited impatiently to leave Boston and reunite himself with his family. He found, to his discouragement, "Its fortune has been the usual one of American compositions of its sort. It had a few first performances by orchestras here (and one in England by Henry J. Wood), and afterward little chance. The movement in variation form really satisfied me."[39]

When May came and his duties ended, he rushed back to Europe. In his autobiography, he called the two summers in Europe (1896-97) some of the happiest of his entire life.[40] He stopped for two weeks in London, where he visited with the Henschels and a fellow sojourner in Europe, Franz Kneisel, and for one week in Paris. Next, he went on to Meran, joyously greeted wife and daughter, and hired a piano. Soon, he had completed his *Three Piano Pieces for the Left Hand Alone*, op. 37: "What especially pleased me was some pieces for the left hand (one of which, a Prelude, is practical and effective; the other two, as I find now, horribly awkward to play)."[41] While in Meran, he met several women from Vienna and Graz, who were excellent musicians and knowledgeable about music literature. Through conversation with them he discovered that "we in Boston were much ahead of them, for when I showed them the score of the Tschaikovsky 'Pathetic' Symphony, with the remark that we had already heard it in Boston several times in successive years, they could hardly believe me, since they had not yet had that opportunity. It was the same with some of Brahms' pieces from his Op. 117 and 118."[42]

The summer ended much too quickly for him. When September arrived, he was again required in Boston and had to separate from his wife and daughter. Why he alone returned is not made clear, and, as he traveled away, he yearned to ignore his obligations and return. However, he had to provide for his family, regardless of how much he would have loved to remain to enjoy the mountain scenery, relax with Kitty and Katharine, and turn to composing music when he felt like it. But he conscientiously fulfilled his responsibility to give music lessons, to play organ and direct choirs for church services, and to give concerts. These obligations must have been annoying to him, for they absorbed precious time that might otherwise have been given to thinking out and conceiving new compositions.

This same year, he and his sister, Mary Tileston, had published their *Hymns for Church and Home* under the auspices of the American Unitarian Association. One final action of his in 1896 was to help found the American Guild of Organists, one of whose goals was to boost the quality of church music. He was elected honorary president of the guild in 1909 and occupied the position until 1912.

At the beginning of 1897, the Suite in D Minor brought him further disappointment. The Manuscript Society of New York had planned to present it at a February concert. Unfortunately, the ship transporting the parts from Boston to New York sank and the concert committee of the society had to announce: "In consequence of the sinking of the vessel containing the orchestral parts of Mr. Foote's work, and their non-arrival in response to a cablegram, in time for rehearsal, the committee have decided to [reserve] . . . Mr. Foote's suite for the last concert of the season." William Gilchrist's First Symphony was substituted for the missing composition.[43] New parts were sent and the suite was heard in New York on 22 April.

He was again with his family in Europe when summer arrived. Helen Hopekirk gave him the idea of vacationing on the Seine riverside near Paris, and his wife Kitty located a suite of rooms at Bas-Meudon, with a superb view of the river and convenient transportation to Paris. It was a serendipitous choice. He preferred spending his vacations near water, which he found favorable for relaxation and reflection. He relished the poetic attributes of river and sea. A gentle river endlessly flowing set up like rhythms within him. Mountain and country views provided a peace not afforded in his professional life. It was the seascape at Pride's Crossing, Gloucester, Hull,[44] and Hythe, the river view at Bas-Meudon and Dedham, the mountains at Meran and later the landscape at Rest Harrow that contributed to the pensive pacing of his slow melodies, especially. Lodgings amid serene surroundings stimulated some of his most touching music. Although this lyrical composer usually felt uncomfortable writing music of a scenic or programmatic character, he had a musical mind given over to the influence of the harmoniousness and unforced rhythms found in nature.

At Bas-Meudon, he was able to compose sufficient songs and piano pieces to regard the stay as fruitful. His housekeeper had been a model of Jean Léon Gérôme when she was young and told tales about the French artist. Perhaps under the spell of this historical and genre painter, he was influenced to turn to Edward Fitzgerald's translation of Omar Khayyám and set the "Song from the Rubáiyát of Omar Khayyám" ("Wake! For the sun") in Bas-Meudon. The next year he wrote *Five Poems after Omar Khayyám* for piano. Through the agency of Paul Verdot, he gained admission to quite a few musical evenings in Paris and even got to present his piano quartet and violin sonata. In Paris, too, he met with the Gardners and the Nevins. Come September, he left for Boston, this time with his family in tow. He did not realize it then, but his trips to Europe had ended. At the end of the 1920s, he would fondly recall his days in Bas-Meudon with "Monsieur Hallopé, our host, and his courageous struggle against diabetes; the Fraîches, housekeeper and cook—she the once sought-for model, with her painters still coming to her restaurant; the picturesque daily life of the river craft and their workers; the charming restaurant life; the carefree and colorful existence, animated by the gaiety and abounding life of Paris itself; dear friends, some gone, VALE."[45]

By the end of 1897, Foote had composed one of his most impressive works, the Quintet in A Minor for Piano and Strings, op. 38. Also by the end of 1897, he had taken a major step toward relocating his family in a more rural setting. A document dated 19 July 1897 in the Norfolk Registry of Deeds shows that A. W. Nickerson has deeded to "Kate Knowlton Foote, wife of Arthur Foote of Boston," land in Dedham, Massachusetts, at the corner of Bridge and Common Street: "Southeasterly by Bridge street, there measuring three hundred and forty feet; southwesterly by Common street, one hundred and fifty one and $^{81}/_{100}$ feet; northwesterly by land of the heirs or devises of said Albert W. Nickerson, three hundred and twenty one and $^{90}/_{100}$ feet, and northeasterly by same land one hundred and forty five and $^{92}/_{100}$ feet, each of the four corners of said parcel is marked by a stone

monument."[46] The Footes forthwith built a home on the property, which they would occupy from 1898 to 1912, and landscaped
their acreage with spruce and other trees.[47] Frederick Kopp as-
serts that Foote was extremely proud of his house, having built it
with the royalties he had earned from his compositions.[48] While
the house was being built, Foote composed the *Five Poems after
Omar Khayyám*, op. 41, for piano. Foote's copy of the published
work, now at the Harvard Musical Association,[49] has written in it:
"While house was building, Aug. 1898."

Foote says that in Dedham bicycling and golf became two of
his favorite indulgences. On 28 April 1898, the Dedham Golf
Club elected him a member. On 10 September 1901, the newly
formed Norfolk Country Club of Dedham and Westwood asked
him both for his initiation fee and annual dues.[50] During the
week, he would catch the 8:30 A.M.. train to his studio in Boston
and get back to Dedham around 6 P.M. He also gave instruction
in his Dedham home. A student, Edith Lane, who started her music studies with him in Dedham, writes: "After their return home,
they built their house in Dedham and it was here that they were
living when I studied with him. He loved the life of the country
and the games of golf with his friends."[51] Nonetheless, one big
disappointment marred the end of 1898. He, Chadwick, and
Parker, through the auspices of the Twentieth Century Club, had
been giving free concerts on organ in various churches over the
past two years, in order to overcome the lack of public appreciation of the instrument and such concerts. This laudable effort
failed. The public remained uninterested.[52] The failure was offset
by a singular honor—his election to the National Institute of Arts
and Letters.

Perhaps it was just as well that his mind was preoccupied with
building his house and life in the country, for the U.S. battleship
Maine had been sunk in Havana harbor on 15 February. By 24
April, the United States, urged on by the Hearst newspapers, su-
perpatriots, and business interests, was at war with Spain over
Cuba. Concerned Bostonians had formed an Anti-Imperialist
League and held protest meetings at Faneuil Hall because, "as a
matter of sternest principle" they wanted no empire for the United
States.[53] By July, with the American victories in the Philippines, the
war, to all purposes, was over. Peace officially was reestablished in
1899. The fears of the antiimperialists were realized when the

United States acquired Puerto Rico, Guam, and the Philippines. Dedham was a welcome relief from all of this, a peaceful place to return to daily, away from the agitated city.

In the summer of 1899, he had the pleasure of playing the piano part of his Piano Quintet in A Minor at the annual convention of the Music Teachers National Association in Cincinnati. The only work of real consequence that he completed over the years 1899–1901 was the *Four Character Pieces after the Rubáiyát of Omar Khayyám,* op. 48, for orchestra. The set was an arrangement of four of his *Khayyám* piano pieces, which he made around 1900. A matter of pride for Arthur Foote was the graduation of his nephew Henry Jr. from Harvard in 1899. The uncle has carefully snipped a picture of him from an unidentified publication and placed it into a scrapbook. Henry wears shorts and a turtle-neck sweater with an "H" on the front. The caption describes him as a Harvard divinity student who had been a long-distance runner for Harvard. Foote has written a "99" beneath the picture.[54]

In 1899 Foote had been following the Dreyfus affair in France, concerned over the rampant anti-Semitism it revealed. Then Theodore Thomas was invited to take his Chicago orchestra to the Paris Exposition the next year. Upset over the Dreyfus trial, Thomas refused the French invitation. It gave Foote some satisfaction to carefully preserve the report of Thomas's refusal in a scrapbook.[55] The Dreyfus situation may have stimulated Foote's music for a Jewish religious service. Foote became interested in the Jewish musical rites early in the year 1900 through his friend Benjamin Guckenberger, organist at a synagogue in Birmingham, Alabama. This friend and several local rabbis sorted out the meaning of the texts for him and indicated how the words were accented. After study, Foote found the entire ceremony striking and developed enthusiasm for the project. While summering in Gloucester, he set about composing the music. As he explained it, years later:

> While my conscious object was to fit the music to the feeling of the words by the use of a quasi-modal system, I was unconsciously led to a wholly different sort of writing from ever before, because of the words used—an example

of the fact that (as a rule) a composer will write different types of music to English, French, or Italian words. The reason is probably that accents and rhythms differ in the different languages. I always associate Gloucester with this service, for it was written there. I have heard it a few times at Jewish temples, and I have always been glad of the experiment of writing it.[56]

The result of the summer's creative activity was *Music for the Synagogue*, op. 53, for cantor, soloists, chorus, and organ. The composition marked certain changes in Foote's musical labors: increased use of the old modes, subtle though it remained, decreased subjective romantic expression, more writing for organ, and the end of writing for full orchestra.

Notes

1. Richard Guy Wilson, "The Great Civilization," in *The American Renaissance, 1876–1917* (New York: Brooklyn Museum, 1979), 21, 25; See also Wayne Andrews, *Architecture, Ambition and Americans* (New York: Free Press, 1966), 158–60, 189–90.

2. Arthur Foote, Scrapbook II, Boston Public Library, shelf no. **ML.46.F65. The unidentified clipping quotes Foote and underneath it is written in Foote's hand, "Arthur Foote, Boston, Jan. 25." It is with early 1893 material.

3. Arthur Foote, "Letters. Undated from the Second [Rosalie] Housman Gift," Library of Congress, shelf no. ML 95.F77.

4. *Boston Musical Herald* 11 (1890): 128.

5. The interview is contained in Arthur Foote, Scrapbook III, Boston Public Library, shelf no. **ML.46.F65.

6. Nicholas E. Tawa, *A Sound of Strangers* (Metuchen, N. J.: Scarecrow, 1982) examines the economic, social, and cultural backgrounds of immigrants arriving in the United States in the latter nineteenth and early twentieth centuries, including Italians and East-European Jews.

7. Arlo Bates, *The Pagans* (Boston: Ticknor, 1888), 11, 129.

8. Arthur Foote, Scrapbook III, Boston Public Library, shelf no. **ML.46.F65.

9. Ibid. Though the clipping bears no date, a letter to the editor that follows the statement about Foote is dated "November 20, 1894."

10.   Catherine Drinker Bowen, *Yankee from Olympus* (New York: Bantam Books, 1960), 301.

11.   M. A. DeWolfe Howe, *A Venture in Remembrance* (Boston: Little, Brown, 1941), 155–57, 224–25.

12.   Isabel Parker Semler, *Horatio Parker* (New York: Putnam's Sons, 1942), 83.

13.   The newspaper clippings on the two events may be found in Foote, Scrapbook III, Boston Public Library.

14.   The letter is in the archives of the Gardner Museum. I could not determine what the composition was. Apparently it was presented at the Friday afternoon concert of the Boston Symphony and was to be repeated on Saturday evening. Was it the Suite in D Minor for Orchestra, op.36 which Foote heard the orchestra play under Emil Paur on 6 and 7 March 1896? It did not receive an enthusiastic reception. He was living at the St. Botolph Club at that time, while his family remained in Europe.

15.   Constance Huntington Hall, in *Helen Hopekirk, 1856–1945*, ed. Constance Huntington Hall and Helen Ingersoll Tetlow (Cambridge, Mass.: privately printed, 1954), 8,10, 12.

16.   The letter is one of the "Family Mss." at the Essex Institute, Salem, Massachusetts.

17.   The report on Godowsky's playing and Foote's reaction is in Scrapbook III, Boston Public Library.

18.   Letter no. 47, in "Letters Collected by Arthur Foote. Gift to the library in memory of Arthur Foote, April 16, 1940," Spaulding Library, New England Conservatory of Music. Before MacDowell moved to 38 Chestnut Street he had been living at 13 West Cedar St., just a few doors up from the Footes. The question about the opus number has to do with some erroneous references to the trio as opus 3.

19.   Foote, Scrapbook II, Boston Public Library.

20.   See the clipping in Foote, Scrapbook I. The number 210 has been handwritten at the top of the page and the date "March 1890" beneath the clipping.

21.   The programs for all of the concerts may be seen in Scrapbook II, Boston Public Library. In April, the Salem Oratorio Society was sponsoring three Popular Concerts. The one in which Foote participated took place on a Wednesday and featured "The Ladies' Vocal Club, of Salem." See the clippings in Scrapbook II.

22.   The letter is contained in Scrapbook II, Boston Public Library.

23.   Foote, Scrapbook II, Boston Public Library, contains the notices or

programs of these concerts, as well as the letter from Dallas, Texas. The American Composers' Concert at Leipzig and Vienna also exhibited works by Chadwick, MacDowell, and others. Arens was born in Neef, Rhenish Prussia in 1856 and came to the United States at the age of twelve. He returned to Germany for his music studies. Later, he was the conductor of the Cleveland Philharmonic and Gesangverein, then went as president to the College of Music in Indianapolis. In 1900, he founded the New York People's Symphony Concerts. He died in Los Angeles in 1932.

24.   The letter is one of the "Family Mss." at the Essex Institute.

25.   The letter is in the archives of the Gardner Museum. Anton Strelezki, born in Croydon, England, in 1859, studied with Clara Schumann and eventually settled in London. His songs and piano pieces won a large following. He died around 1907.

26.   The letter is in Scrapbook II.

27.   Elliot Forbes, *A History of Music at Harvard to 1972* (Cambridge, Mass.: Department of Music, Harvard University, 1988), 17; see also, Walter Raymond Spalding, *Music at Harvard* (New York: Coward-McCann, 1935), 275.

28.   The clipping is in Scrapbook II, Boston Public Library.

29.   The letter is in Scrapbook II.

30.   George Willis Cooke, *John Sullivan Dwight* (Boston: Small, Maynard, 1898), 294.

31.   The programs for the several concerts are in Scrapbook II. See also Arthur Foote, *An Autobiography* (Norwood, Mass.: Plimpton Press, 1946), 53.

32.   The letter is in Scrapbook II.

33.   In Scrapbook II, Boston Public Library, is a letter sent 6 November 1893 by Higginson: "We hereby acknowledge that we have received from Arthur Foote the sum of Fifty Dollars as the first installment of his subscription of a 100.– towards a new Music Hall in the City of Boston."

34.   Foote, Scrapbook II. The page number 17 is included in the clipping.

35.   The letter, sent from 35 Clarendon Road, Notting Hill, is now in the archives, at the Gardner Museum.

36.   Foote, *An Autobiography*, 78.

37.   Ibid., 60–76, narrates all of the events of 1895 as described here. Isabella Gardner's guest book, now in the archives of the Gardner Museum, contains his signature for a visit on 7 October, when he was already

in his Mount Vernon quarters, only the address he gives is 94, not 96, Mount Vernon Street.

38. Ibid., 92.

39. Ibid., 82–83.

40. Edith Lane, "Arthur Foote, Massachusetts' Own Musician," typed MS dated 1937 in the Essex Institute, Salem, Massachusetts, shelf no. F688.3L

41. Ibid., 81.

42. Ibid., 81.

43. Foote, Scrapbook II, Boston Public Library, contains the announcement of the sinking and the substitution of the Gilchrist work.

44. For a year and a half, the author lived in Beverly (a town just north of Salem) near Pride's Crossing and can testify to the beauty of the ocean view seen from the elevation of the road curving around the estates located there. Another magnificent spot is Bass Rocks in Gloucester, a few miles north of Beverly, where the Footes also liked to summer. Here the height, where the road is located, is slighter, but the view of the surf crashing on the blackened rocks is most impressive. There is no rise to speak of in Hull, south of Boston, but Nantasket Beach in Foote's day afforded refreshing bathing and swimming and an unobstructed view of the open ocean.

45. Foote, *An Autobiography*, 89.

46. Library no. 789, folio no. 177, Norfolk Registry of Deeds, Dedham, Massachusetts.

47. When I was a little boy, I lived in West Roxbury, very close to the Dedham line. In the 1930s, I used to go fishing for horned pout and perch or tried to spear pickerel in the portion of the Charles River adjacent to the property. I was unaware that this was once Foote's land until I read the deed in November 1994.

48. Frederick Edward Kopp, "Arthur Foote: American Composer and Theorist" (Ph.D. diss., Eastman School of Music, University of Rochester, 1957), 95.

49. Shelf no. MC F738.

50. These communications are in Foote, Scrapbook III, Boston Public Library.

51. Lane, "Arthur Foote, Massachusetts' Own Musician."

52. Louis C. Elson, *The History of American Music*, rev. to 1925 by Arthur Elson (New York: Macmillan, 1925), 274–75.

53. Martin Green, *The Mount Vernon Street Warrens, A Boston Story, 1860–1910* (New York: Scribner's Sons, 1989), 154.

54. See Scrapbook III, Boston Public Library.

55. Ibid.

56. Foote, *An Autobiography*, 92–93.

7

Advancing through Middle Age

This chapter emphasizes historical criticism, viewing and appraising the music in relation to the necessary social and historical circumstances under which it was created and in relation to the particulars of Foote's life. Such an approach is the best way to begin a discussion of Foote's music of the nineties. A major aim is to communicate the significance and the merits that the music possessed for contemporary listeners, not today's audience. The intention is to inform the present-day listener about the wellsprings of the music so that the listener may respond appropriately and sympathetically, mindful of Foote's role and the signification of his music beginning with the year 1890. What are the personal, communal, and general connotations of the music? In contrast to a scientist, who endeavors to use words specifically, precisely, and literally, Foote depends on the implied meanings of his music to convey his most profound themes.

Foote spent most of his waking hours teaching, mostly the keyboard and sometimes theory and composition, curtailing concert performances and creative work. Therefore, this chapter begins by looking at his commitment to education.

As a musician, Foote retained attributes that might be considered ordinary when come upon singly but most effective when combined. Among these attributes were consciousness of the emotional needs of his audience and regard for the well-being of people he knew, including his students. There was also his faculty for explanation and elimination of superfluous detail when clarifying complex subjects for students. The advice in his articles and books on piano playing and on theory demonstrate how readily Foote conveys information to the reader.

He had an unwavering desire to pass on what he had learned through his own experiences, and he had an aptitude for producing excitement in others through the force of his personality. His books meant to educate the young, his many articles in magazines like *Etude*, and the statements of students like Edith Lane testify to these qualities. His scrapbooks show that, from the nineties on, he was constantly keeping up with the latest ideas on keyboard methods and answering inquiries about teaching problems that he received from musicians seeking authoritative answers. We find him carefully taking note of new training manuals that were coming on the market, recent developments in teaching techniques that were achieving prominence, and articles that were examining the efficacy of this or that instructional program. We observe him giving pragmatic answers to queries about teaching, keeping what seemed to work in his experience and discarding nonproductive procedures, no matter how logically argued the theory behind them or how glowingly they were advocated.

Typical of his self-effacement as a teacher was a declaration he made at the opening of a pamphlet on piano playing: "Originality is not claimed for what follows, nor are all the points discussed with thoroughness. An attempt has simply been made to express certain views clearly."[1] In January of 1893, he wrote that over the past twenty years, the number of good music teachers had increased along with the number of music students. There was no longer any need to go abroad for a music education. Besides, the cost of lessons was much too high in Europe, and as often as not the American student was overcharged. He concluded: "The American student is best understood and helped by an American, and will usually get more sympathy and help from his teacher for that reason."[2]

Foote himself did understand, help, and give sympathy, according to Edith Lane:

> As a teacher he was a man of great understanding and sympathy—he never counted the minutes. I am sure that he showed me more of the spiritual values derived from an Art that is made one's own by hard work, sometimes

even drudgery, than any other individual. He also showed me—a young girl of 17—how the arts were correlated, giving me tickets to the Boston Art Club and concerts, advising me about reading and once, when I was feeling tired and rather discouraged, taking me to the Symphony with his daughter. There was no reason why he should interest himself with an obscure harmony student but he had an understanding heart and was always ready to advise and help. It was all done so naturally and simply.[3]

In the last chapter, I suggested that there were times when Foote might have wished he did not have to teach. However, his customary attitude toward teaching was positive. Intelligent musical instruction for the young was a mission, however time-consuming and onerous, that he felt needed to be carried out.

From Teacher to Composer

On 20 January 1890, Foote wrote the following letter:

> Dear Jenks,
>   It was awfully kind of you to send me the clipping about my Trio—I had not seen it and was glad to. Of course your article in the M. E. Mag. was mighty interesting reading—and seemed to me full of things well-put—I mean that you ____? [took notice] of the question of American music as it should be—and did not make a 'slogan' of it. Harroo for Boston and the American musician, and yet made it show that something was coming of the ferment.[4]

Something indeed was coming of the ferment. Twenty-one years later Foote said that American composers had by that time achieved great success in their symphonic and chamber compositions, referring to the quality of what they had composed, not to the number of performances their music had received. The preponderance of European music teachers, instrumentalists, vocalists, and music directors in the United States meant that European compositions would come first. The bias of the affluent American music public also weighed against American music. In

1875, the condition of American music was grim, because native art composers were scarce and not always thoroughly trained. Yet, the situation brightened rapidly after 1875: "In '90, after fifteen years of remarkable growth, there were in Boston alone the veteran J. C. D. Parker, John K. Paine, Mrs. Beach, Miss Lang, MacDowell, Nevin, Chadwick, Horatio Parker and Arthur Whiting (besides others whom I do not mention), all but two of whom had begun their career after that date of '75," says Foote.[5] Obviously, one person he did not mention was himself.

Foote could have added that highly regarded American singers and instrumentalists were at last coming along, several of whom took up the cause of the American composer. The singer David Bispham, for example, had met Foote in London in 1895. They had immediately taken to each other, with Bispham quickly inviting him to "a big men's dinner" and later advising him to take his family to Hythe for the summer. While in London, Bispham never failed to introduce selections by Foote, Chadwick, and Parker into his recitals. He continued to do so on returning to America. To cite one instance, in January 1897, he gave the first of his Carnegie Hall concerts in New York and included songs by living American composers, one of them Foote. Bispham writes in 1920:

> Ever since that time I have endeavored to keep before the American public the work of its own gifted men. I was and am still well aware of the all but universal tendency to consider the work of any foreigner superior to that of our own people, but I have never held with that view . . . . Yet many are the mistakes which have been made in the concert room and at the Metropolitan Opera House in bringing forward compositions by foreigners, while well considered and carefully prepared material by our own native musicians has been deliberately put aside, or when performed has met with scant courtesy at the hands of press and public.
>
> This attitude on the part of Americans is one that has puzzled me considerably. In the intimate social circles which supported imported art there were few with the courage to proclaim America and Americanism as Walt Whitman proclaimed it two generations ago, and the

grand substratum of Europeanism remained. Most American men of leisure wanted to take their holiday in Europe, and American women knew that when they died they would go to Paris.[6]

Yet American composers, during the nineties, hewed to their rocky pathways despite the lack of road maps and the obstructions they had to surmount one after the other. They stoutly maintained their positions as artists, no matter what the temptations, though they were not fanatics about their beliefs. Foote and his composer friends refused to write principally for pay. Yet, they were not moonstruck. As a rule they happily accepted reimbursement for their labors in music and willingly accepted commissions when offered. Nor were they uneasy about gaining popularity. It meant they were communicating successfully, and this they valued. The good-sized following he won during the nineties was a delight for Foote.

Nevertheless, his techniques remained his own and did not cater to popular taste. The music of Wagner, Brahms, Dvořák, and others helped to polish his speech, but he never went overboard in emulating their writing, as evidenced in the works he wrote after the eighties. Full development of his talents and constant practice were now delivering greater richness of language and elegance of expression to his music (see chapter 8). Still and all, the fundamental nature of what he wrote did not alter. His musical manner kept its warm and immediate attractiveness, expert and scholarly craftsmanship, and predilection for disarming musical thoughts uttered plainly and agreeably. The manner of planning, shaping, and reshaping a work would always entail complex methodology, however easily the resultant music might capture the ear. No matter how large his audience was said to be, he knew that his true listeners represented principally the privileged few. Not many of those men and women who welcomed his music could actually discuss a composition. At best, they could describe how it made them feel, how they enjoyed it, or how it engaged their attention subjectively.[7]

Wisely, he understood that inspiration for him was not a lightning stroke from Zeus. It was not only the inner impulse that urged him on to compose but also the dedication that held him to his task. He was not one of those Romantics who separated tal-

ent from genius and claimed that the latter was more momentous, mysterious, and godlike. Nor did he try to claim his gifts
represented genius, even in the nineties, when praise for his ability and music was reaching a peak. On the contrary, he continued
to be glad if he simply had the capacity to get something right,
win the respect of connoisseurs, and please the general audience.
Whether what he accomplished represented talent or genius was
never an issue with him. Of course, he was sagacious enough to
understand that he was ahead of most of the American music
world as concerned art music. For this reason he had to remain in
the forefront of those trying to change and amend public ideas
about music. He recommended new principles for his art and
tried to demonstrate these principles through his compositions,
from the Piano Quartet and *Francesca da Rimini* of 1890 to the
Piano Quintet of 1897 and the *Four Character Pieces after the
Rubáiyát of Omar Khayyám* of 1900. That people listened to him
and his music was a tribute not only to the composer but also to
the man. He had hopefully suggested himself and offered his music to Americans as the manifestation of respected values that
lived within them, too, though they might forget they were there.
As Foote once wrote: "The object of the artist should be to tell us
in music . . . the truths of life and the beauty and sublimity of life
which we, with lack of genius, fail to grasp."[8]

If humanism is defined as devotion to human welfare and an
interest in man, and if it includes the idea of the humane, which
means civility, courteousness, considerateness, and sympathy for
the needs of others, Foote was ever more the humanist. This quality is exemplified in his compassionate, kind, and generous behavior, as well as in music showing his affirmation of New England
and American ideals. He deemed it arrogant and out of the question to consider himself the final authority on what he composed,
and in this regard also revealed his humanism. He regulated his
spontaneous inclinations by the methods and guidance offered by
the musical masters whom he respected and by the degree of support granted him by capable reviewers of what he wrote and had
performed. This did not mean debilitating compromise. On the
contrary, it was a check that caused him to ferret out imperfections
in craft or communication, to reconsider what he had noted on
the page, and to reexamine his convictions before going on. He
was never so egotistical as to consider himself perfect. Perhaps

failure to win support or a perception of some imperfections caused him to delay or hold back some works from publication. So long as he held them back, they remained works in progress. I can cite several substantial compositions of this sort: the Suite no. 1 in E Major for string orchestra, op. 12 (1886); Overture, *In the Mountains*, op. 14, for orchestra, (1886; rev. 1910); Suite no. 2 in D Major for String Orchestra, op. 21 (1889); Quartet in E Major for Strings, op. 32 (1893); Concerto in G Minor for Cello and Orchestra, op. 33 (1893); *Four Character Pieces After The Rubáiyát of Omar Khayyám*, opus 48, for orchestra (completed 1900 but not published until 1912); Sonata in E Minor for Cello or Viola and Piano, op. 78 (c. 1918–1919); *Nocturne and Scherzo* for flute and string quartet (1918); and *A Night Piece* for flute and strings (arranged in 1922 but not published until 1934).

A goal of considerable moment to him was to improve national culture, which, from his humanist standpoint, provided the ideal gauge for measuring America's intellectual, moral, and artistic civilization. As an enlightened individual of his day, he accepted Matthew Arnold's celebrated statement in the preface of the 1873 edition of *Literature and Dogma* that culture consisted of "the acquainting ourselves with the best that has been known and said in the world, and thus the history of the human spirit." He would also have concurred with Alfred North Whitehead's comment in *The Aims of Education* (1929) that "culture is activity of thought, and receptiveness to beauty and humane feeling. Scraps of information have nothing to do with it. A merely well-informed man is the most useless bore on God's earth." In addition, Foote would have heeded his friend Apthorp's warning not to approach culture by way of an intellectual art-formula that produced a narrow intellectual conviction, but stood between a person and the perception of the true quality and character of a work of art.[9]

The Mature Composer

By the nineties, Foote was perfectly aware that modifications and transformations in recognized musical standards arise as much from bias and shifts in taste as from alterations in music theory. Historically, most standards amount to systematizations of current musical practices. The last decade of the nineteenth century was rapidly approaching the era when musical vanguardism would decree iconoclastic standards. These standards were individual, not communal, systematizations and had scarcely any connection with current practices. These maverick trends puzzled Foote, although he followed them and tried to understand them.

When Foote had started off as a composer, Boston was in the process of assimilating the prevalent art music of Europe—from Bach to Schumann and Mendelssohn. Boston's cultural leaders were, if anything, die-hard conservatives. To offer a work of Berlioz, Liszt, Wagner, or Brahms was to defy local preferences, and presentation of such a work was exceptional. Learning about, let alone flirting with, advanced ideas was close to an impossibility under the circumstances. This state of affairs formed a part of Foote's background as he grew up. He was by his own admission a cautious young artist, careful not to break the precepts he thought of as obligatory rules. But surely by the nineties, he had discussed the so-called rules of music with his friend William Apthorp and had heard Apthorp say that no firm rules or laws existed in art, that composers broke them all the time.[10] He himself now stood ready to break a few. At the same time, he retained most of the conventions that Bostonians well-versed in music agreed upon in the nineties, knowing, as Apthorp said, that they should not be "rashly undervalued." Apthorp pointed out that the English language, in order that people could understand each other, was "nothing more than a long-inherited convention." Therefore, for music to be viable and understood, there had to be something customary in its procedures.[11] The following may be Apthorp's words, but they mirrored Foote's own convictions:

> I am a man of my own time; I was born into it, I live in it— and in it alone. My time may be a hideous time for aught I know—or care; but it is mine. The men of my time speak the language I best understand; they speak it fluently, and I catch their slightest innuendoes without effort. Do I regret other times and ages? How can I ? If I did, I should regret being myself.[12]

Because he was sincerely what he was, a highly endowed New England artist of the late nineteenth century, Foote kept on employing a fluent idiom to which concertgoers could relate, whatever the adjustments taking place in his approach to composition during the nineties. He was, in turn, honored for doing so. At the end of the decade, Rupert Hughes remarked that over the past few years, Foote had attained an elevated place in people's affections by his unswerving attachment to his own earnest, unclouded principles and by his bona fide culture and serious-mindedness. With pride, Hughes added that Foote was "thoroughly American by birth and training."[13]

Without the urge to be an absolute oddity, the composer had the good judgment not to chase after the newest modes, certain that the greatest composers of the past could furnish practical and beneficial footings for the erection of a countrywide American art-music edifice. European sources notwithstanding, native composers eventually would create a distinctive national art. Driven by these beliefs, he produced a substantial amount of music that found merit in the eyes of his contemporaries. It was vital music because it countenanced some novel ideas, had a perceptive awareness of effective music symbolism, and accepted the mental and emotional necessity for delving into what people had personally and collectively lived through. His compositions written after 1890 were heard as fresh and unique in years when most American music was regarded as mere emulation of European sources. Benjamin Lambord, in a book published in 1915, summarizes the opinions of many members of the music public, when he writes about Foote:

> Of his compositions as a whole it may be said that they are astonishingly original in an age which has found it all but impossible to escape imitation. He is, like most of the great composers, largely self-taught, and yet there is scarcely a trace of mannerisms; nor what is even more remarkable, of the mannerisms of others. His music is the pure and perfectly formed expression of a nature at once refined and imaginative. In these days of startling innovations, the sincerity of which may not be unhesitatingly trusted, it sounds none the less spirited because it is unquestionably genuine and relatively simple. It stands forth as a substantial proof that delicate poetry and clear-cut workmanship have not failed to charm.[14]

Sincerity and genuineness were two hallmarks that contemporary writers accorded his music, confirming the compatibility between the compositions Foote created and his thoughts and convictions. Foote's music was in accord with his life history. For this, he was respected. His music was honest in that it complied with its own needs, premises, and viewpoint. Foote was credited with looking carefully at the emotions his music called forth and managing the sound so as to avoid false hyperbole.

Foote's was a stabilizing achievement that accommodated two contrary conditions, constancy and transformation, respecting the past and progressing into the new. Listeners wanted both safeness and the allusion of adventure; he, the artist, wanted to retain what was indispensable from the past and exert some autonomy over what he chose to write. He was all for fidelity to a shared standard, provided there was flexibility in its application. It would provide sufficient stability for him to identify what adjustments he might make in a score, and to distinguish between a right and a wrong action, between giving a life breath or a deathblow to a composition. To obtain an equilibrium while enhancing development and to encourage development without disturbing equilibrium were the seemingly paradoxical guides that steered his writing.

Foote once stated that a person tried to understand the world within him, to discriminate between what was permanent and essential and what was accidental and vanishing. "The very foundation of all art lay in man's dissatisfaction with the material and imperfect. . . . All art is but an outward expression of the inner man" and "a reflection of the thoughts and emotions of the creator."[15] To surmount the distraction of material things, to reach for excellence, to express what was fundamental, to plumb the reflections and feelings of the composer, to uncover what was immutable in him and others was what he aspired to achieve.

Concerning the Music Making of His Maturity

Two sides of Foote the musician were revealed in 1899. On the one hand, there was the entertainer-composer who helped put together a *Minstrel Show* at the Massachusetts Institute of Technology and contributed the song "Scared Up," which he composed "expressly for this occasion."[16] On the other hand, there was the high-principled composer and his conclusions about church music. During an interview, he said:

> I disapprove of any adaptation to sacred words for use in church of secular music which is itself unfitted and which is familiarly identified with opera. For instance, we know that there is no such thing as sacred music as distinguished from secular music in character—only bad and good music; fit and unfit music. So far as a style goes, you could put new words to it, and palm off Bach's "Coffee Cantata" as one of his church works, so that to my mind the point is that music which is distinctly associated with surroundings that make it incongruous for church (e.g. "Faust," "Romeo and Juliet," etc.) should be discountenanced.[17]

What he says is that nobody can distinguish between sacred and secular musical styles, only between mediocre quality and good quality music, a badly crafted and a finely crafted work. His disapproval here involves the connotations attached to a specific music owing to its operatic text, whose secular verbal meaning would carry over into the church service, despite the substitution of a sacred text.

Foote himself never wrote an opera. Yet, he had no objection to, indeed greatly enjoyed, the genre, whether grand, comic, or so extremely "light" that it merged with operetta and the Broadway musical. He realized that this dramatic form called for music that made public a wide range of private human emotions—which he was not ready to do. Opera did not suit his personality; he had no flair for depicting searing conflict or unbuttoned jollity, and he knew it. He was not given to bold exaggeration or extravagant statement in order to express the strong emotion of outsized stage figures. Besides, there was the awareness, founded on a great deal of truth, that an American wasted time and effort writing a serious composition for the musical stage. No opera company stood ready to produce it and, if produced, it lingered for a short while before the audience, then entered the dustbin forever. It was difficult enough to get an orchestral work, even a chamber work, performed, let alone an opera. As Henry Finck once

ironically commented about John Knowles Paine, the many years
devoted to writing his opera *Azara*, and the failed efforts to have
the Metropolitan Opera mount it: "Undoubtedly, Harvard's professor of music had no end of fun composing his opera. But that
was all he ever did get out of it—that's about all most composers
of music usually get out of their works. . . ."[18]

Even as Foote wrote no opera, he employed no Amerindian
or African-American idioms in the music he did write. On his arrival in New York in the fall of 1892, Antonín Dvořák challenged
American composers to introduce vernacular idioms, especially
the two just named, and also melodies after the example of
Stephen Foster into their serious compositions. By so doing, he
said, an American national music might be achieved. On 24 May
1893, Fred Bacon, an editor of the *Boston Herald*, wrote to the
composer, as did several other people, curious to know what
Foote thought about Dvořák's views. Shortly thereafter, on 10
June 1893, Daniel Spillane, editor of New York's *The Keystone*,
asked Foote's opinion about Dvořák's assertion: "It is my opinion that I find a sure foundation in the negro melodies for a new
National school of music."[19]

First, Foote thought highly of Dvořák's abilities as a composer. When the Czech musician visited Boston to conduct his *Requiem* with the Cecilia Society, Foote and the Harvard Musical
Association put themselves out to give him a reception. Second,
Foote had a strong interest in the musical vernacular. He constantly attended lectures and concerts featuring British-American
folk music, African-American spirituals, and Amerindian song and
dance. He attended Henry Krehbiel's lectures on African-American songs. Krehbiel was a New York music critic and writer on
music. Foote, Chadwick, and Lang were among the people who
sponsored an evening at the home of Miss Susan Wainwright to
hear F. R. Burton's talk about Amerindian music and to listen to
members of the Ojibway tribe perform. He would note with interest the founding of the Wa-Wan Press by Arthur Farwell in
1903. It was devoted to music by American composers, and issued works delineating the Amerindians in particular. In July
1911, while lecturing in California, he met with Charles Wakefield Cadman and went over the whole Amerindian music question with him. Interested as he was in these musical matters,

however, Foote knew he was neither an African-American nor an Amerindian. He was a New Englander of Yankee stock and British descent and would define himself no other way.

As for Dvořák and his involvement with musical Americanisms, Foote turned skeptical. The Dvořák Symphony *From the New World* had received its New York premiere in December 1893. In 1895, Foote attended an evening of the Folk Lore Society and listened to the songs of the Hampton Singers ("young colored men"). He was asked after the performance about the Czech composer's use of this African-American idiom in the symphony. As a Boston newspaper writer reported: "There was some discussion at the meeting last night, and it was interesting, though perhaps not altogether cheering, to be told by an authority like Mr. Arthur Foote that there is not a trace of the real negro music discoverable in Dvořák's American symphony." Foote's verdict was justified. The symphony would eventually be considered a work with a Czech accent and some American overtones. Sixteen years later, at the height of the Americanist mania, Foote was still convinced that a conscious effort at nationalism would fail because no composer could "will it" into being. An American school of composers would only come about, he said, after America had produced "one great composer."[20]

Several important contemporary composers and music writers weighed in on Foote's side. MacDowell also admired Dvořák's music, including the Symphony *From the New World*. At the same time, he observed that "masquerading in the so-called nationalism of Negro clothes cut in Bohemia will not help us." He insisted that no composer could manufacture a distinctive national style merely by introducing traditional American song and dance into a work. Anyone, American or not, who took a fancy to doing so could duplicate the effort. A true reflection of America would come only from a composer born and raised in the United States, who, because he lived within the American civilization and experienced it wholly and constantly, could not help but unconsciously put what he had experienced into his music.[21] The respected New York writer Henry Krehbiel, who had a great interest in African-American music, agreed.[22]

Whatever Foote, MacDowell, Krehbiel, or others of the time said, the consensus was that the United States had to build a national individuality on the basis of European music, although its influence would gradually be shed as Americans continued to compose and build on the example of their American predecessors. Furthermore, the United States did not include just one or two races or ethnic groups, but a myriad of them. How could anyone justify the idea that one or two segments of the population could stand for the whole?[23] Foote showed in his music what he had absorbed by living in America and what he as an individual and according to the best of his ability could express through sound. Elements of New England psalmody and traditional American music that emerged out of a British-Celtic matrix, hints of popular music, representations of his Central-European oriented training, and precepts acquired after listening to and studying admired works from composers resident in every country of Europe are mixed in the pages of his music. All of these elements are strained through his critical faculties, purified according to his ideals, and given magnitude through his emotions and intellect. Whatever else critics thought he might sound like, he assuredly sounded like himself.

More Inquiries into Style

Foote's compositional style of the nineties was an aggregation of the full-grown principles already mentioned. His code and ideals, more than breakthroughs in technique, gave the music its actual character. Style was not just the musical constructions in a score, which could be inspected note by note and critiqued technically. These configurations on the music page were shaped by a fantasy on the inner life—a depiction of inwardness through subtle inflections and deflections of tones in measures, phrases, and sections. Admittedly, this description holds true for most sincere artists. However, his style also is a manifestation of the unique weight of shared memory regarding the New England past: its ethical self-examination, its persistent inner struggles, and its arrival at a strenuous peace. The manner of composing, whatever its progressive alterations, continued a recognition of his Puritan antecedents and was grounded in the community, religion, law, due process, and the potency of custom. The impact on his music of personal and commonly shared principles was regularly recognized by the composers of Foote's time. Witness Arthur Farwell's statement: "Too many persons are ready to suppose that the issues of music in America lie wholly within the scope of purely musical consideration, and that they do not depend, as is actually the case in certain important respects, upon the nature of the national ideals and tendencies."[24]

In his style, too, we discover an artist who was quickened not only by the past that he recalled but also by the age that he lived in and by the future that he mined for its promises and his expectations. He might delve into his own or other recent history or into the more distant record of musical and human culture for his inspiration. He did not accept the imperative always to look ahead. Foote felt free to return to ideas he had thought up some years before, as he would in the Serenade, op. 25. Or he set out on an entirely contrary path, as he would in the *Khayyám* music. His return to yesterday for prototypes or stimulation might be to a keyboard piece by Bach, a symphonic work by Mendelssohn, a New England hymn tune, or a folksong he had heard in New England. In the present, he would use the resources of the new music he was performing or hearing—the chromaticism of Wagner, the somber logicality of Brahms, the deceptively naive tunefulness of Dvořák, the vivid colorations of Tchaikovsky and Rimsky-Korsakov. He would receive stimulation from poets past and present for his songs; Dante for his only symphonic poem; Khayyám-Fitzgerald for his foray into exotica.

Foote's understanding of the old church modes, for example, enhanced his musical language, turning it pliable by releasing it from the limitations of major and minor keys. This did not mean that he surrounded the listener with archaic sounds. Usually avoiding the use of the modes for quaint purposes, he discovered how to introduce them appropriately, with fine sensitivity, and in especially elusive fashion. They enter to weave together a section, giving it an extraordinary and carefully spun texture. No academicism enters Foote's compositions; he does not resort to craftsmanship in order to make up for a paucity of musical stimuli. Expression and feeling come first. We hear in his music a fierce clash or two, some rhetorical complaints, now and again a declaration of power. But just as often there is buoyant and affectionate diversion, occasional unfeigned jubilance, and usually prayerfulness. The clashes and complaints may pass on to a music of withdrawal. Devastating tragedy is not his forte; serenity or quiet melancholy is. The divertissement commonly is blended with a wistful pensiveness. The jubilance does not always settle the strife that has come before but states that life goes on, in defiance of the strife. And always there is faith. As for prayerfulness, it is always a grave and respectful addressing of Divinity through music that embraces forms of entreaty, acclamation, and thanksgiving, as well as the unbosoming of personal failings.

The expressive findings of Arthur Foote have an entirely special quality in the music compositions written after 1889. This quality differentiates them from those of his innovating contemporaries. With him, a new usage—in melody, rhythm, harmony, or instrumentation—is in no way breathtakingly obvious. It enters uncontrivedly during the operation of a passage. It belongs where it is, situated there through a reasoning guided by inmost compulsion. It augments the musical dialogue so smoothly that we are unconscious of its appearance. For this reason, the existence of such usage was not noticed during the course of the twentieth century, a century when some form of bold innovation was the dominant style and thrust itself into the listener's ear like an invasive foreign body. Foote was rarely intent on delineating a program, and thus his most impressive harmonic transformations are not meant to heighten any particular of a scene. Instead, they generate a musical state, underscoring either an emotion or the physical beauty of a melody. This kind of tonal concord saturates his essential melodiousness with an enduring aroma, atmosphere, and radiance that arises out of the music itself, not out of a nonmusical gloss that the listener reads about in a concert program note.

A close listening of his music, especially the works beginning with the Violin Sonata, discloses many singular touches and a stream of feeling that surely indicates an American, not a European, fountainhead. Through an inexplicable emotional and intellectual but fundamentally unconscious compliance, Foote emerged as a living bearer of the typical musical style extant in his New England. He had a personal style and a varying quota of liberty that he exercised within the more extensive background of the Germanic and late-Romantic styles of his period. Nevertheless, the identification of this personal style is contingent on the ideological viewpoint of the commentators and chroniclers of musical history, as well as the depth of both their examination of and their sympathy for the music. In his own day, astute writers on music, like Waldo Selden Pratt, had no doubt that he had a distinctive style. Pratt was born in Philadelphia and was four years younger than Foote. Admiring Foote's work, Pratt said: "His writing has marked individuality and strength of construction."[25]

Foote is unequivocally a *musical* composer. He deploys a tonal poetry of unusual vibrancy as if by instinct. He prudently drops in his dissonances, always careful to integrate them into the measures. Foote is engaged in a rhetoric proceeding from the established style of his training years, which discouraged any discordant or imprudent obstructions to the free flow of musical speech without a compelling musical reason. During the nineties, he goes beyond what he was taught, except that the changes he makes are always discreet. If called for, absolute diatonicism and consonance is maintained. Also if called for, a chromatic stream full of dissonances flows forth.

As an example of his discretion, after 1889, he ameliorated his scores with many contemporary innovations in harmony and orchestration while retaining the contours of classical form. Again, I turn to Foote's friend Apthorp for explanation. Apthorp writes:

> Certain musical forms, from their essential stoutness, symmetry, and perfection, are worthy of undying admiration; doubly worthy of admiration till the time when other equally stout, symmetrical, and perfect forms shall have been developed to supplant them.
>
> To my mind, there are two forms in music which come under this head: the Fugue and the Sonata. . . . Unquestionably it may in time produce their worthy successors; but it has not done so yet.[26]

Foote utilizes Baroque forms, including the praeludium, air, gavotte, toccata, invention, and fugue. He looks to the Classical era for his sonata-allegro, dance-plus-trio, and rondo models. His usually ternary constructions, given fanciful titles like "Pierrot," "Valse peu dansante," and "Remembrance," are character pieces embedded wholly in his own Romantic era. Whatever the form, his aim is lucidity and balance. As for his titles, Foote knew listeners were tied to what they saw, touched, heard, and smelled. Their feelings were inseparably tied up with their daily encounters and environment, as well as the longings, anxieties, and aspirations of existence. Nonetheless, since music was awash in matters unknowable, it pushed the inexperienced American listeners in particular into bestowing names on its diverse revelations. This is a poetic operation, hence the insertion of an evocative poetic signifier contained in the title. Foote wanted people to bear in mind that the sole link between the music itself and any mental representations it invokes is found in listeners' imagination. The actual essence of music cannot be rendered verbally, especially not what is most fundamental and distinguishing in its expression. In short, music is not a representational art.[27]

A variation form is almost always set up as a series of alterations of a stated theme, each given its own distinct character—a treatment of variation form also characteristic of Schumann and Brahms. This form would prove one of Foote's most successful. In 1901, Foote sent the just published *Tema Con Variazioni in A Minor* to the composer-pianist Amy Beach. This was the only movement of the String Quartet in E Major, op. 32, completed in 1893, ever to be published. She pored over it and wrote to him on 20 December 1901, giving her address as 28 Commonwealth Avenue. Beach attests to the extraordinary attractiveness his music held even for his knowledgeable contemporaries:

> My dear Mr. Foote:
>   Many thanks for the Variations for Quartet, which I have studied with great pleasure. The theme haunts me persistently, and the various versions of its beauty are all full of charm, though differing widely in style, one from the other.
>   I should like very much to hear the entire composition, for it is so beautifully written for quartet that it cannot fail to be immensely effective, especially in the pathetic portions. The end is most beautiful.
>   I would like to tell you again how much enjoyment we have *all* had in your three left-hand pieces [for piano]. For the past two summers I have played them *daily*, sometimes several times, owing to the incessant demands

of my husband and friends. We never tire of them, and their beauty is quite independent of the clever way in which you have provided for their execution, though this constitutes an added charm especially to the performance![28]

His predilections in vocal music were for close harmony and adhering mostly to the middle range. His writing for piano does not often indulge in wide swings from one end of the keyboard to the other or in stunning new effects introduced for positively pianistic reasons. Says Hughes: "He is not fond of the cloudy regions of the upper notes, and though he may dart brilliantly skyward now and then just to show that his wings are good for lighter air, he is soon back again, drifting along the middle ether."[29]

Foreign to his thinking is any resort to a *coup de théâtre*, an unmotivated twist in the music that is intended to startle. Perhaps this is the reason why W. S. B. Mathews said, in 1892, that Foote's music was "sound" but "a trifle too intellectual." With the same breath, he admitted that Foote was an "American composer of the first rank," whose overture *In the Mountains* was heard often, and whose First String Quartet was "played with marked success" in Chicago.[30]

His inclination toward musical third-organization, already identified in his early music, increases in the nineties. He often makes secondary key references to the third above and below the tonic, say from C to A or A-flat and E or E-flat. In other compositions, the third-organization may involve the triad, say C - E or E-flat - G or, less often, C - A or A-flat - F. He also likes making lengthy modulations into these areas and arranging the tonalities of separate movements of a composition in a third-order.

Textures remain transparent. Chords are rarely thickened. Two- and three-part harmony is heard with some frequency. Homophony prevails. A contrast between simple, even folklike, melody and the underlying warm harmonic progressions is regularly encountered. The shifting, often sudden, between thematic components within a movement increases. Rhythmic variety and syncopation multiply. In this regard, a work like the Quartet in E Major for Strings, op. 32, with its persistent and sometimes surprising syncopated rhythms, goes indisputably beyond anything that he had attempted in the earlier works. As for orchestration, the brilliant colorations of *Four Character Pieces after The Rubáiyát of Omar Khayyám*, op. 48, for orchestra show a sophistication in the handling of the orchestra that is light years distant from the cautiously scored overture, *In the Mountains*, op. 14, for orchestra.

Before the decade was over, Foote composed twenty-one choral pieces, forty-two songs, two vocal duets, and two vocal-orchestral works; nine piano works, some multimovemented, and his first two forays into organ composition; and six chamber and four orchestral works. It was his most industrious decade yet as a composer.

Notes

1. Arthur Foote, *Some Practical Things in Piano Playing* (Boston: Schmidt, 1909), verso of the title page.

2. Clipping in Arthur Foote, Scrapbook II, Boston Public Library, shelf no. **ML. 46.F65. Underneath the clipping, he has written "Arthur Foote" and "Boston, Jan. 25."

3. Edith Lane, "Arthur Foote, Massachusetts' Own Musician," typewritten MS at the Essex Institute, Salem, Massachusetts, shelf no. E F688.3L. The MS shows a penciled "1937" on it.

4. The letter is in the Boston Public Library, shelf no. Ms. Acc. 2740 (33).

5. Arthur Foote, "Music in the United States," MS of lectures delivered at the University of California, Berkeley, in 1911, now in the Boston Public Library, shelf no. **M. 472.134, #1042, p. 22.

6. David Bispham, *A Quaker Singer's Recollections* (New York: Macmillan, 1920), 119, 197–98.

7. On this subject, see William Foster Apthorp, *Musicians and Music Lovers* (New York: Scribner's Sons, 1894), 7.

8. Arthur Foote, ed., *Theory of Music* (London: Squire, 1908), 237.

9. William Foster Apthorp, *By the Way*, vol. 2 (Boston: Copeland & Day, 1898), 118–19.

10. Ibid., 107.

11. Ibid., 108.

12. Ibid., 184–85.

13. Rupert Hughes, *Contemporary American Composers* (Boston: Page, 1900), 225–26.

14. Benjamin Lambord, "The Classic Period of American Composition," in *Music in America*, vol. 4 of *The Art of Music*, ed. Arthur Farwell and W. Dermot Derby (New York: National Society of Music, 1915), 340.

15. Foote, ed., *Theory of Music*, 230–31.

16. The program, on which is written by hand "Tech. *Minstrel Show* 1899," is in Foote, Scrapbook III, Boston Public Library.

17. Foote, Scrapbook III, Boston Public Library. On the clipping is handwritten "San Francisco 1899."

18. Henry T. Finck, *My Adventures in the Golden Age of Music* (New York: Funk & Wagnalls, 1926), 79.

19. The requests are contained in Foote, Scrapbook II, Boston Public Library.

20. Scrapbooks II and III contain letters, notices, and programs that testify to his interest. The quotation about the evening with the Folk Lore Society is in a clipping in Scrapbook II; the Amerindian evening with Burton is in Scrapbook III; the California items are from the *San Francisco Examiner*, 7 July 1911, 5; and 11 July 1911, 7. A few years ago, the same issue came up in the *Sonneck Society Newsletter*, of which I was then editor. Elie Siegmeister and I, in response to the question of a national identity, reached a conclusion similar to that of Foote. Later, Siegmeister wrote a brief article on these conclusions, which the *New York Times* published.

21. Lawrence Gilman, *Edward MacDowell* (New York: Lane, 1908), 83–85.

22. Henry E. Krehbiel, *Review of the New York Music Season* (New York: Novello, 1890), 172–73.

23. Hughes, *Contemporary American Composers*, 12–13.

24. Arthur Farwell, Introduction, *Music in America*, viii.

25. Waldo Selden Pratt, ed., *The New Encyclopedia of Music and Musicians* (New York: Carl Fischer, 1924), s.v. "Foote, Arthur William."

26. William Apthorp, *By the Way*, vol. 1 (Boston: Copeland & Day, 1898), 13.

27. Ibid., 4–5.

28. Arthur Foote, "Letters collected by Arthur Foote: Gift to the library in memory of Arthur Foote, April 16, 1940" (Boston: Spaulding Library, New England Conservatory of Music), letter no. 32.

29. Hughes, *Contemporary American Composers*, 225.

30. W. S. B. Mathews, "American Composers of the First Rank," *Music* (1892): 502.

8

The Music of the Nineties

Foote created several superb works during the nineties, as usual writing music during the summer, whether in New England or in Europe. When his wife and child were nearby his creative juices flowed freely; the flow shrank to a trickle in their absence. His greatest achievements were the orchestral and chamber works and some of the songs. The keyboard pieces were less notable. Least consequential were the part songs and compositions for chorus. Yet, nothing he wrote sounds insincere, mechanical, carelessly written, or trivial in content. His seriousness of purpose is never in doubt. Every piece contains something to engage the listener's interest—a lovely melodic phrase, an ingratiating rhythm, a felicitous turn of harmony. An explanation for the different levels of accomplishment among the genres may lie in his intentions for the music: the first group was intended for concert performance by professional musicians before the public; the second for students' study and practice; the third, much of it to sacred texts, for functional use. His songs, anthems, and piano pieces sold—something he, a practical man and head of a family, would not overlook when deciding what content such pieces would receive. He meant them to please a wide public.

His early music had sometimes succumbed to overly solid and unyielding sound, had observed excessively strict principles of voice leading, or had remained with the same safe harmonies. Occasionally it had demonstrated too faithful an adherence to what his conservative mentors thought to be the proper sphere of expression. Now, much of this was behind him. His sound became more flexible; his voice leading, freer; his harmonies considerably bolder; his expression, much more varied. Foote no longer seems preoccupied with looking over his shoulder at the composers of yesterday. He dared to be his own man, looking forward to what can be rather than back to what was. If he introduced anything from the past into his musical pages, he did so with full confidence in his own artistic endowments, in his own ability to bend an older format to his purposes. He now had the wherewithal to compose music that unquestionably was of his own day.

Vocal Compositions

Foote remains a song writer of his own century, contrary to what one might expect of a composer well versed in the music of the Baroque and Classical periods. He hardly ever looks back to the eighteenth century in his songs. He creates such works to capture a feeling or evoke a mood. The sentiment expressed does not result merely from a command of his craft; it proceeds from a fine-tuned imagination that captures sincerely felt emotions through sound. Poems condense subjective experience and suggest particular feelings to an experienced composer. Their words reproduce the impulsive responses of an otherwise reticent man to, say, nightfall ("The Night Has a Thousand Eyes," of 1891), winter ("When Icicles Hang on the Wall," of 1894), bird song ("The Nightingale Has a Lyre of Gold," of 1899), and roses at the end of summer ("The Roses are Dead," of 1899).

Subject matter of this sort suited Foote's moods, and he employed these references to connote devotion or desire, faith or disbelief, confidence or despondency. Natural phenomena ("When Winds are Raging o'er the Upper Ocean," of 1896) and places ("In Picardie," of 1896), enthusiastic lovers ("Sweetheart," of 1899), cast down elders ("Roumanian Song," of 1899) loom large in the poems he selected for setting. Such images stimulated Foote's musical imagination.

Foote composed a song *with a melody*, not fitting tones carefully to words in order to embody the verbal rhythms of the verse. He did not forfeit melodiousness for a musical diction that attempted to painstakingly represent each isolated notion of the poet. On the contrary, Foote felt that poetry had to become subservient to the music as the composer fashioned his melody and accompaniment. Nowhere was this more true than in the compositions from this period that most pleased him, music lovers, and serious critics of his day:

1. "Elaine's Song" (1890)
2. "A Ditty," op. 26 no. 8 (1891)
3. "An Irish Folk Song" (1891)
4. "On the Way to Kew" (1894)
5. "In Picardie" (1896)
6. "Song from the Rubáiyát of Omar Khayyám," op. 40 (1897)
7. "Memnon" (1898)
8. "Roumanian Song," op. 43, no. 2 (1899)

His songs from the nineties are seldom strictly strophic (that is, the same music repeated exactly for every stanza). Yet, one such was his most popular song, "An Irish Folk Song," which has two stanzas rendered in two identical musical strains. More usually in two-stanza song settings, the second strain begins with the same music as the first, but completes the strain with new music, as in "The Hawthorne Wins the Damask Rose" (1894). He wrote some songs in ternary form, such as "O Love, Stay By and Sing," op. 43, no. 6 (1899). Some receive a special structure, as does "A Roumanian Song," whose form is A B C A^1. Others are through-composed, that is to say with no musical repetition, or scarcely any. The words to "Song from the Rubáiyát of Omar Khayyám," for example, receive different music throughout, save for an extremely brief return to the music of the prelude just before the last section of the piece. However, whether ternary or special or through-composed, songs do not always change their music because of changing events in a narrative or to accommodate a dramatic situation. Foote prefers to set lyric verses with a subjective agenda. He uses the nonstrophic approach to provide further commentary on messages that are warmly personal. The "Roumanian" piece is a lament over personal loss and emptiness owing to love that has fled, a beloved who is absent, remembered woes of the past, and the death of loved ones. In the "Rubáiyát" work, we find an overriding preoccupation with human mortality

—that life on earth is brief, that nobody knows what will happen next, that each one must enjoy today because death comes at any moment and without warning, and that once dead nobody returns.

Not all songs are depressive. Some are lighthearted, as in the *Vier Gesänge aus Lieder eines Fahrenden Gesellen*, op. 39 (1897). The poetry, written by Rudolf Baumbach and translated by Frederick Bancroft, is ostensibly about a wandering youth, forever happy and carefree, who makes merry with friends or makes love to a maiden today and tomorrow is gone. Not one of the four songs is strophic.

Many poems that he chose to set were not always of the first rank. Perhaps he realized that a celebrated poem might distract from the music. The composer's efforts notwithstanding, the public might very well continue to cherish the poem but find the song wanting once music had been put to the verse. Foote knew that a song could be excellent despite weakness in the poetry and wrote music that frequently displaced the textual euphony. In almost all of his songs, Foote reacts musically not so much to the text's rhythmic and sound patterns as he does to the poetic circumstance and to particular verbal expressions. In "Bin ein fahrender Gesell," op. 39, no. 1, the word *amen*, which ends each stanza, catches his attention. Though the composition is otherwise through-composed, the *amen* is set to a musical refrain that returns at the end of each stanza. In "A Roumanian Song," it is a sigh of resignation, "Ah" that grips him. It is heard twice at the beginning and twice at the end as a prolonged cry, against a pianistic commentary in the right hand. The name "Ojalá" in "Ojalá! Would She Carry Me Away!" (1889) so captures his attention that at the beginning, he makes it carry the burden of the protagonist's feelings by having the singer vocalize melismatically on the word. At the end of the piece, he calls attention to it through syncopation and augmentation of the note values.

Because Foote remains constantly aware of the text's overall subject, he finds it at times more comfortable to relate the piano accompaniment to the general theme, a treatment that can be telling if the artist acts with discernment. For example, in "Sleep, Baby, Sleep," op. 26, no. 1 (1891), a lulling rocking motion is heard in the piano; in "Ojalá! Would She Carry Me Away!" the text coming from George Eliot's *Spanish Gypsy*, a lovely grace-noted

figure returns repeatedly to hint at a fascinatingly strange and picturesque atmosphere.

Foote realizes that, given his personal direct style, it is prudent for him to try for convincing tunefulness that leads to psychological perception. To affect this, the composer (1) identifies
the song's overall musical character; (2) shapes the melody to
embody the general mood of the piece; and (3) welds the vocal
line to an accompaniment and to harmonies that sustain and tie
together the expression throughout all the measures. This is exemplified in two outstanding compositions, "On the Way to
Kew" (1894) and "In Picardie" (1896). In the former piece, the
vocal melody always stands out and immediately establishes a
homespun mood akin to that of many an Anglo-American folk
song. The completely subordinate accompaniment supports the
voice but adds nothing of melodic importance. The harmony remains diatonic and gives emphasis to tonic and dominant
chords, with an appropriate but fleeting reference to the submediant minor on the word "gray," until the bucolic verbal description is brought up short with the words "I met a ghost," at which
point a dissonant dominant ninth with its fifth raised disturbs
the ear and the music briefly touches on the mediant minor key
(example 11). However, the melody goes on to fulfill its own
destiny, and harmonic equilibrium is eventually restored by a return to tonic and dominant chords.

He did not need to apply the entire technical paraphernalia
at his command to invoke torment owing to rejection by a sweetheart. He can project doleful intonation through a melodic approach, with some judicious harmonic implementation, as in
"Elaine's Song" (1890) from Tennyson's *Lancelot and Elaine*. It
is *her* song. Elaine serenades herself with a threnody on the agony of unrequited love and the expectancy of death (example 12).
The pianist strums a few guitarlike chords, thus abetting the serenade character of the piece. The first dissonance occurs on the
word "vain," underlining the futility of her love, and the next on
the word "sweet," lending irony if not bitterness to the expression, since it is death that is sweet. Meanwhile, the tune goes on,
melancholic, inwardly turned, and graceful.

In most of Foote's songs, attention to the vocal melody
comes before all else. Normally he sets the text syllabically, one
note to a syllable, and respects the accents of English speech.

But he puts aside accurate verbal accentuation when it threatens
the steady progression of the tune. The intelligent conduct of
the harmonic stream is impressive and kept in order by a logical
bass line. With the authority of the artist who is versed in Baroque practices and in the sensible yet subtle management of
harmony, he writes accompaniments that bolster and give varied
shadings to the vocal line, and also inject additional animation
to the whole.

Nowhere does the piano dominate the voice. Only an
occasional song doubles the voice in the piano throughout the
composition. Hardly ever does Foote resort to illustrative
pianistic figuration to depict things like galloping horses, blowing
winds, or rushing streams. Nor does he usually write a prelude or
postlude of any significance. Quite a few songs of the nineties
have neither prelude nor postlude. Most preludes that he does
write serve only as "vamps" for introducing the singer. In this
regard, he is more in line with the practices of the American
popular-song writers of his day and less with one pianist-
composer whose songs he admired, Robert Schumann.

The entire composition reveals a finely tuned technical cohesion. For example, "Memnon" (1898) describes a statue that
bursts out with a song of love for the day-god that arrives at
dawn, as the protagonist does at the appearance of his beloved.
The unity in the first strain, quoted in example 13, is provided by
the four-times recurring triplet figure first heard in measure 2,
the syncopated accompaniment that begins at measure 9, and
the steady chromatic march upward of the bass line from the low
G to F sharp, before the perfect-cadence close of tonic$^6_4$ to dominant to tonic chord. The voice melody quickly moves twice from
e′ up to b′ and back to e′, then slowly and windingly makes the
same ascent from e′ to b′, returns to e′, but then balances the
three ascents of a fifth to b′ with a descent of a fifth to a drawn
out a. Note, too, the closed expression of the melody, sad and
given a trace of the exotic, until arrival at the phrase "sounds of
love and rapture born" with its flare up of A major. The unity of
the entire composition is aided by the return of some of the prelude material in a brief interlude before the second and final
strain, by the second strain itself, which is a variant of the first,
with the postlude, which again resorts to the material of the pre-

lude, and altogether by the ruling tonality of A major-minor. The sum of these several factors is a well-proportioned, persuasively realized, and homogeneous configuration.

"Ojalá! Would She Carry Me Away!" was actually composed in 1889, though published by Schmidt in 1890. It tells of how all things are borne away; spring comes and goes; roses bud, flower, and wither. The speaker wants to be borne away by the stream Ojalá, or by summer light and soft winds. At the end, he hears birds sing over silent graves and then take wing into the distance. The song's meter is $^3/_4$, tonality C, tempo non troppo allegro, and structure A B B^1 A (with the A in the minor and B in the major). Surprisingly, there is a six-measure prelude, a five-measure interlude before the final A, and a six-measure postlude. The pleasing vocal melody captures the listener's attention from its opening on a dissonant appoggiatura descending from the fifth to the fourth tone over a subdominant minor chord.

"Elaine's Song" was composed and published in 1889. With a heading of *Andante espressivo* and in $^9/_8$ time, the song is in ternary form, A (in E minor) B (in E major) A^1 (in E minor, with only the first part like the opening A). A nonconsequential prelude lasting four measures comes first.

The year 1891 saw the completion of "An Irish Folk Song," to a poem by Gilbert Parker. It was written for Boston's reception of Parker in that year. The song achieved such widespread renown that it was also published in German and French, arranged for men's, women's and mixed chorus, and recast as a piano solo and as a piece for string orchestra. Schmidt, who published the song in 1894, sold around seventy-five thousand copies of the music in the first twenty years of the piece's existence. Thirty-five years after its first appearance, this "most successful" of Foote's songs was still selling well.[1] Typical of its reception is a report of how "an overflowing audience" acclaimed it at a song recital given in London's Queen's Hall on 1 April 1899:

> One of the most attractive individual performances was that by Miss Louise Dale of a very charming "Irish Folk Song" by Mr. Arthur Foote, an American song-writer [!], whose works are not nearly so well-known here as they fully deserve to be. Miss Dale, too, earned credit by repeat-

ing this song in response to an irresistible appeal for an
encore, instead of substituting another song.[2]

Because of its importance in Foote's total song output, the
setting of the entire first stanza of "An Irish Folk Song" appears in
example 14. First to be noted is that the text does not use a dialect, nor is the tune strikingly Irish. Thus a superficially old-fashioned tone is avoided in favor of more universal characteristics.
The twice heard strain is in two parts, a G-minor section that sets
most of the text in each stanza, and a G-major section on the
word "Ah." No unusual harmonies, rhythms, or piano figurations
assert themselves. No unusual melodic scheme emerges. The
close of the first part of the strain with an eighth-note downward
skip of leading tone to the fifth, on the word "darlin'!" (a nebu-
lous allusion to dialectalism), the somewhat surprising vocaliza-
tion in the major mode, and the modal conclusion to the entire
song are the only atypical features. The piece stands, and stands
triumphantly, on its melody—simple, expressive, and catching.

The eleven compositions in *Songs*, op. 26, were composed
mostly in 1891 and published by Schmidt in 1892: no. 1, "Sleep,
Baby, Sleep," text from the German and translated by Elizabeth
Prentiss; no. 2, "Love Me, If I Live!," text by Barry Cornwall; no. 3,
"The Night Has a Thousand Eyes," text by Francis W. Bourillon; no.
4, "The Eden Rose," text by Rudyard Kipling; no. 5, "Summer Longings," text by Denis Florence McCarthy; no. 6, "To Blossoms," text
by Robert Herrick; no. 7, "I Arise from Dreams of Thee," text by
Percy Bysshe Shelley; no. 8, "A Ditty," text by Sir Philip Sidney; no.
9, "In a Bower," text by Louise Chandler Moulton; no. 10, "The
Water-lily," text by Emanuel Geibel, translated by L. C.; no. 11,
"How Long, Dear Love?" text by Louise Chandler Moulton. The
third song, on how life ceases when love is gone, is one of his
shortest and most unassuming, only nine measures long. Yet it
boasts an elegant melody. The fourth is one of his longer songs, far
more complex in realization than number three, but not nearly as
attractive. A comparison of the two works underlines the fact that
Foote's best songs are usually his most unpretentious ones.

Certainly "A Ditty" is one of his finest pieces and is without
question plainly stated. Precedent may be found among the
brief and modest songs descended from folk song, the "ditties,"
that were written especially for English and American pleasure

gardens and inhabited the ballad operas staged in England and America during the latter half of the eighteenth century. No prelude and no postlude are found. The tune is completely diatonic and has an outdoors quality to it (example 15).

In 1894, the tender and nostalgic "On the Way to Kew," text by William E. Henley, and the sonorously accompanied "The Hawthorne Wins the Damask Rose," text by J. H. S., appeared. The next year it was the openly tuneful "Song of the Forge," text by Gilbert Parker, and the next year, the endearing "In Picardie," text by Graham R. Tomson. The last song beautifully illustrates one of Foote's musical thumbprints, a culmination of a strain achieved by an unexpected shift in tonality, here a dominant seventh chord in B-flat followed abruptly by the A-major triad (Example 16).

The year 1897 (published 1898) was notable for the cheerful *Vier Gesänge aus Lieder eines Fahrenden Gesellen*, op. 39, completed while summering in Bas Meudon. In no way do they resemble Gustav Mahler's four songs given the identical title. The Mahler songs, composed between 1884 and 1891 to his own poetry, are extremely intimate in nature, searing in expression, and possibly reflect the composer's despairing love for the singer Johanna Richter. The Foote songs are to insouciant poems of Rudolph Baumbach, translated by F. W. Bancroft. Foote may have become acquainted with Baumbach's work in 1891, when the Boston bookseller Schoenhof published selections from his *Märchen und Erzählungen*. All four are grateful to sing, refreshing to hear, and make no pretensions to depth of feeling.

Also completed that summer was "Song from the Rubáiyát of Omar Khayyám" (also known as the "Persian Song"), which Schmidt published the next year as opus 40. Foote furnished it with an orchestration in 1906. Eight quatrains in the translation by Edward Fitzgerald constitute the text. The interest in the *Rubáiyát* would continue. While busy with his new home in Dedham during the summer of 1898 he finished the *Five Poems after Omar Khayyám*, op. 41, for piano solo. Around 1900, he arranged four of these piano pieces for full orchestra, *Four Character Pieces after the Rubáiyát of Omar Khayyám*, op. 48. The song, one of Foote's longest and most complex, is quite successfully realized despite his usual propensity for brevity and plainness. The main tonality is G minor, and the meter is usually, though not always, $^3/_4$ time. No prominent exoticisms appear in the music, save for a little discreet back-and-forth half-step sliding in the voice, occasional use of the Neapolitan chord, and the feeling of languor that emerges from some measures. This through-composed composition is organized into three long sections. Modulations tend toward the flat side. The raised second to third tone, and the raised fourth to fifth tone appear several times, sometimes over an augmented triad. Perfect cadences are avoided. Even at the close, instead of the expected V⁷ - I minor progression, we hear III minor - V of III - III minor - VI minor - II minor - I major, all in root position.

Schmidt published two admirable songs in 1898, "Through the Long Days and Years," text by John Hay, and "Memnon," text by Arlo Bates. The structure of both is A A¹, the second strain, as expected in a song by Foote, duplicating the first only in its first half. "Memnon," like "In Picardie," discloses a Foote thumbprint, a culmination of a strain achieved by an unexpected shift in tonality, here a dominant seventh chord of G minor superseded without preparation by the C-major triad.

In 1899, *Six Songs*, op. 43, appeared: no. 1, "The Nightingale Has a Lyre of Gold," text by William E. Henley; no. 2, "Roumanian Song," text by "The Bard of the Dimbovitza" and translated by Carmen Sylva and Alma Strettell; no. 3, "Sweetheart," text by Richard W. Gilder; no. 4, "The Roses Are Dead," text by Graham R. Tomson (Rosamund Marriott Watson³); no. 5, "Up to Her Chamber Window," text by Thomas Bailey Aldrich; no. 6, "O Love, Stay By and Sing," text by Thomas Russell Sullivan.

Each of the six pieces has its own attractions. The first song allows an affirmative outburst of C major, similar to that in "Memnon." The second, one of his most affecting compositions, often achieves a modal effect by way of a lowered seventh tone in the minor. The fervent third song makes interesting use of a II $^6_5$ triad as a substitute dominant. The fifth song represents quite a change in style. Large portions of it, but especially the first eight measures, have a strong resemblance to the semi-artistic American popular songs of the nineties.⁴ I cannot help but wonder if the text of the sixth song had a special meaning for the composer. He was forty-nine years of age, well into middle age, and the century was ending. He perhaps now found: "Fame a field hard-fought, / And gained a thing of naught to have and

hold! / . . . And I am old! / . . . I leave the work unwrought, / I
leave the field unfought, / For thee and thine."

On the other hand, his renown was still spreading. More and
more singers found that his songs were written sympathetically
for the voice and were constantly received with enthusiasm by
their audiences. Among the vocalists of the time who began to
take up the Foote songs were John McCormick, Johanna Gadski,
Marcella Sembrich, Ernestine Schumann-Hienk, Grace Leslie,
Stephen Townsend, and Max Heinrich.[5]

Other published songs of the nineties are "Love from o'er the
Sea," text by Ernest Flower (1894); "O Swallow, Swallow Flying
South," text by Alfred Tennyson (1896); "When Winds Are Raging
o'er the Upper Ocean," text by Harriet Beecher Stowe (1896);
"And, If Thou Wilt, Remember," text by Christina Rossetti (1897);
"Loch Lomond," an Old Scotch Song (1897); "Love in Her Cold
Grave Lies," text by Sir Gilbert Parker (1897); "Through the Long
Days and Years," text by John Hay (1898); and *Two Old Scotch
Songs*: "My Boy Tammy" and "Wilt Thou Be My Dearie?" (1900).

Foote wrote vocal compositions other than solo songs: part
songs and choral numbers, secular and sacred, for male, female,
and mixed voices. Most of these were written for the many
greater-Boston ensembles, societies, and church choirs that stood
in need of a fresh supply of music. In these works, Foote predict-
ably gives greater attention to homophony than to polyphony,
and to vertical harmony than to the movement of independent
voices. Normally, one part alone has melodic content; the rest follow along. None is as interesting as his several outstanding solo
songs. Foote describes the "Bedouin Song," text by Bayard Taylor
(1891, published 1892), for men's voices and later arranged for
mixed voices, as "probably the most successful piece of the sort
written by an American."[6] Also intended for men's voices were the
"Bugle Song," text by Alfred Tennyson, published in 1895, and
"Crossing the Bar," text again by Tennyson, out in 1897. The second work contains an abundance of eloquent passages. A reviewer for the *Courier*, 4 December 1898, reports on the performance
of this last number at an Apollo Club concert:

> Mr. Foote always writes like a thoughtful scholar and a
> skillful musician; but his vocal composition does not usu-
> ally come home so closely to the listener as his instrumen-

tal. It is apt to smell of the lamp and speak intellectually
rather than from heart to heart; and then its phrases are
not always easily singable. But again his feelings and his
sympathy impel his pen, and then true emotion warms
and beautifies his pages. We remember some beautifully
expressive passages in his "Hiawatha" chorus, and various
single songs might be cited. But we cannot recall nothing
[*sic*] which so touched us with a true and tender pathos
and a poetry accordant with that of the words, as this chorus rising and falling as the pulse of the aged poet swelled
and sank through the stanzas, as the great yet gentle
thought of death and its mighty outgoing tide grew in his
soul.[7]

Benjamin Lambord was not especially taken by the merits of
Foote's sacred music. He said: "Foote and Chadwick have both
done much in church music; there is, however, a neutral quality
about their anthems and they possess neither the distinctive
qualities of the purely ecclesiastical style nor that of the popular
anthem."[8] Doric Alviani, who has made a study of Foote's
church music, found that the composer adapted Dudley Buck's
style to his own use—homophony, basic chords in close harmony and common progressions, regular meters and routine
rhythms, and employment of octave and unison singing. Occasionally there is a whiff of barbershop harmony. The choral pieces were kept short in order to fit into the service and kept easy to
sing in order to comply with the limited rehearsal time that was
ordinarily available to the director.[9]

Several church works are very good indeed. As one writer observed: "Naturally his church connection has resulted in the production of a large quantity of church music. As he puts it, this
music had to pass the ordeal of criticism from a frank choir and
was afterward published."[10] Very well received in his lifetime and
still occasionally sung in church are the "Magnificat in B Flat" and
"Benedictus in E Flat" (1892), "Still, Still with Thee" (1893), "And
There Were in the Same Country, Shepherds" (1893), the "Jubilate in E Flat" (1894), "The Lord's Prayer" (1896), the *Responses
for Church Use* (1896), and "Awake! Thou that Sleepest" (1897).

One sacred work that was most out of the ordinary for Foote
was the *Music for the Synagogue*, op. 53, for cantor, soloists,

chorus, and organ. The composer states that he became interested in sacred Jewish music during the spring of 1900. His friend Benjamin Guckenberger, organist for a temple in Birmingham, Alabama, discussed the music and the nature of the service with Foote, encouraging him to try writing something suitable for Jewish worship. Some rabbis that Foote knew explained the meaning of the words and indicated the correct accentuation. The undertaking fascinated him and he began to compose, endeavoring to fit the music to the feeling in the words by employing modal procedures:

> I was unconsciously led to a wholly different sort of writing from ever before, because of the words used—an example of the fact that (as a rule) a composer will write different types of music to English, French, or Italian words. The reason is probably that accents and rhythms differ in the different languages. I always associate Gloucester [Massachusetts] with the service, for it was written there. I have heard it a few times at Jewish temples and I have always been glad of the experience of writing it.[11]

The actual results are uneven, with only some music of telling quality. An important consequence of this exercise in sacred composition was the greater use of the old church modes in his everyday writing.

A final vocal work remains to be considered, the cantata *The Skeleton in Armor*, op. 28, for mixed chorus and orchestra, the text by Henry Wadsworth Longfellow. As an unnamed writer in the *Boston Evening Transcript* wrote: "Mr. Foote's 'Skeleton in Armor' . . . is a work to be spoken of both with respect and admiration. Mr. Foote's affection for Longfellow's ballads is apparently unquenchable; so, in spite of our conviction that they are not the best material in the world for extended musical setting, we will say no more on this head."[12] Foote completed it during the summer of 1891 at Hull, Massachusetts, where he was vacationing. Schmidt published it in 1892, and the premiere was given by the American Composers Choral Association, under Emilio Agramonte, in New York on 28 April 1892. The Choral Association also conferred a special honor on it. On the program is the legend: "This composition has obtained the Gold Medal offered by the American Composers' Choral Association, for the best Cantata, in its first yearly competition."[13]

Foote conducted the Boston Symphony in a performance on 3 February 1893. Foote wrote on his copy of the score:

> Hull, July August 1891
> BSO0 —1893 —Feb.[14]

On the whole, the piece does have a bardic, archaic character, mostly owing to the modal minor writing and the somewhat declamatory nature of many of the sections. Unfortunately, the chorus is almost always treated as one unit, with no exploitation of different compasses in its vocal range, and with the negligible relief of only a few short orchestral interruptions and vocal quartet passages. Four measures of counterpoint in $^4/_4$ time are heard on the words "so the loud laugh of scorn," and another fifteen measures of counterpoint in $^3/_4$ time on the words "there, from the flowing bow"; otherwise homophonic four-part treatment is the norm.

A brief, somber twenty-measure orchestral prelude, in $^3/_4$ time and modal C minor sounds in a loud *allegro deciso*. When the first interlude is heard, the modal archaic effect returns. It does so again when the chorus takes up the Viking's story, "I was a Viking old," beginning in C major but evoking old times with a plagal cadence in E minor. For the most part, the writing is an unrelieved series of firm lockstep SATB progressions. Those rare moments when the music veers away from this treatment are most welcome, as on the words "And as to catch the gale," where the modal motive from the first four measures of the prelude returns, followed by an animated section featuring voice imitation. This last, in turn, introduces the most dramatic portion of the piece, as the chorus describes the sinking of the Viking ship through the sinking of the voices on the word "down." The soprano descends from g" to g' to d', a drop of an eleventh. However, drama is absent from the rest of the score. The loveliest portion follows, an *andantino grazioso* in $^9/_8$ time, which describes the protagonist's beloved.

Despite its lack of musical histrionics and its uniform character, the cantata, according to most reviewers of the time, revealed superior craftsmanship and imaginative invention. Perfect clarity and a commendably competent execution of the composer's ideas prevailed from beginning to end. Concerning the Boston performance of 1893, a critic wrote: "It was very enthusiastically received, the composer being frequently called out after it. Mr. Foote has scored one more success."[15]

A verification of this conclusion is supplied by a music lover, John Cunnie, whose diary has an entry describing his attendance at a Boston Symphony rehearsal for the February 1893 performance. Of the Foote work, he writes:

> I enjoyed it immensely, as I had not heard any good music for a long time. Foote's "Skeleton in Armor" was very good although I could not understand all of it. He used a quartet in what would have been the solo parts, which sounded very well from where I sat. I liked the finale especially well.[16]

Keyboard Pieces

Foote's piano pieces of the nineties continue the melodious attributes that entered keyboard music with Schubert, Mendelssohn, Schumann, and Chopin. They are almost always small-scale pieces with warm, expressive themes that address the listener from completely realized small structures. They rarely call for performers whose technique is firm and interpretation is profound, since most of the music was intended to advance keyboard technique and develop interpretation. Contemporary piano teachers assigned Foote's piano pieces to students, as they also did the many keyboard classics that he edited for Schmidt. As one writer explained:

> His piano pieces, without being quite as spontaneous as those of MacDowell, are well made and thoroughly useful for purposes of instruction. In fact, if one charge might be made against Mr. Foote's tone poetry more easily than another, it would be that it is perhaps a trifle too intellectual. But it is always sound music, which any one is better for

> hearing or playing. Personally, Mr. Foote is one of the most
> charming of men, cultivated, quiet, and capable. He is an
> able teacher of the pianoforte and a good organist.[17]

More than ever, he was capably expressing his own impulsive feelings in short character pieces for piano, yet editing out any passage that was flimsy or mawkish. The elaborate development of a primary motif was of lesser moment to him. Consequently, he avoided writing ambitious, large-scale piano movements that demanded a logical elaboration of musical ideas such as those encountered in the sonata-allegro form.

Owing to his pianistic expertise, Foote was versed in writing what was comfortable for the hand. Because he fashioned the note patterns to accommodate his own fingers, these compositions invariably feel physically right to pianists. He treats the sustaining pedal knowledgeably. The sonorities are carefully calibrated and diversified; they are never muddy. He continued to refrain from capitalizing on elements of technique that would dazzle the listener. A reliable pianist but not a virtuosic performer, Foote did not subscribe to ostentatious display in his pieces. He possessed a boundless resourcefulness that allowed him to invest his music with much diversity in sound while rarely exploiting the more extreme ranges of the piano. He would not in any way renounce his creative principles merely to excite audience.

The summer in which he composed *The Skeleton in Armor* also saw the completion of his *Neun Klavier-Studien für den Musikalishen Vortrag und zur Technischen Entwickelung* (Nine Pianoforte Studies for Musical Expression and Technical Development), op. 27, published by Schmidt in 1892. Numbers 5 and 9 of the studies were published separately in the same year as *Zwei Kleine Capricen aus den Op. 27* (Two Little Caprices from op. 27). They are well thought out and pedagogically valuable exercises. At the same time they permit the player a challenging venture into poetic expression. The second number develops a lyrical touch. The first, fourth, fifth, sixth, and eighth studies concentrate mostly on technical development. The third and seventh blend the two approaches. The Chicago music writer W. S. B. Mathews reviewed the nine studies in 1892, saying they had been quite successful with the public. He commented:

This work is the first of many others in the same department which we may expect to get from our younger writers as soon as the utilitarian consideration weans them off
from the national hallucination that the first duty of man
is to write a grand opera—which under existing circumstances he cannot hope to hear performed.[18]

The *Five Bagatelles*, op. 34: "Pierrot," "Pierrette," "Without
Haste, without Rest" (Étude Mignonne), "Idyl," and "Valse peu
Dansante" were probably finished in 1892-93. The first two came
out in 1893, the third in 1895, and the remainder in 1898. They
are technically undemanding works of little weight. The first resembles a light-footed gavotte. The second sings with a plaintive
tunefulness. The third, a more difficult exercise in double-note
execution, can give pleasure when properly played. "Idyl" goes
from being mild spoken and charming to being more fervent,
then back to mild spoken and charming. Its outer sections meet
the aim of the title by evoking a pastoral, innocent, and peaceful
atmosphere. More than the other eight pieces, the waltz has a direct attractiveness.

The *Zweite Suite in C Moll* (Second Suite in C Minor), op. 30,
for piano, received a performance from the composer on 15 April
1993, but waited another year for its publication by Schmidt. It
consists of three movements labeled "Appassionato," "Romanze,"
and "Toccata." All of them have a ternary structure. When Foote
presented the suite in Chickering Hall, the critic for the *Boston
Evening Transcript* found "much that is striking even at first hearing; we like especially the Romanza [*sic*] and the Toccata. He
played the suite with great fire and musicianly clearness."[19]

This second suite is a more significant work than the very
popular First Suite in D Minor, op. 15, for piano. It has a higher
intensity of feeling and a larger amplitude of effect. Every measure establishes a more fully developed craftsmanship. The music
demands greater concentration from the listener and has less surface appeal, which helps explain the smaller interest accorded it
as compared to the first suite. The first movement, in $\frac{4}{4}$ time, is
dark, brooding and fast in its opening (example 17a). It presents
a C-minor first subject mostly in the piano's lower range, with
dense chords in the left hand and a melody plus a triplet eighth-
note accompaniment in the right. Twice the music rises to a fiery

climax before modulating to the key of A-flat major. The second subject is chordal, stately, and, in some spots, bold. It moves from A-flat to F minor, A major, and D minor before returning to A-flat. The first subject then returns with the melody an octave higher than it was in the opening and with its accompaniment changed. There is also an abbreviated return to the second subject, in C minor, before the close on the C-major triad. This turbulent movement at times seems somewhat Brahmsian, but nowhere is the resemblance explicit.

The second movement is a decided contrast—an *andante espressivo con moto* in ³/₄ time and A-flat major. It begins with a distinctly pleasing melody, whose initial measures are not unlike an American folk song of Anglo-Celtic origin (example 17b). The middle section, in F minor, is livelier and characterized by downward runs of sixteenth notes against a new theme in the right hand. Again, the music gives a hint of Brahms. The recapitulation of the opening finds the melody in the bass, set against upward sweeps of sixteenth notes in the treble.

The last movement is the most virtuosic of the three, with its feel of improvisation, brilliant octave sixteenth-note passage work in the C-minor outer sections, and broken-chord figuration in the C-major and *più moderato* middle section—three characteristics of the toccata style.

The Prélude-Etude, Polka, and Romanze of *Drei Clavierstücke für Die Linke Hand Allein*, op. 37 (1896), the Scherzino and Etude Arabesque of *Opus 42* (1899), and the Invention, Air, A Dance, and Finale of *Serenade in F Major*, opus 45 (1900) are all slight but agreeable pieces, instructive to study, comfortable to play, and entertaining to hear. The *Serenade* was reissued in a revised edition, in 1914, and had as movements an Aubade, Air, A Dance, and Finale and Toccatina.

The most important piano composition of these years, besides the second suite, was *Five Poems After Omar Khayyám*, op. 41, with the movements bearing the titles: 1. Iram Indeed Is Gone; 2. They Say the Lion and the Lizard; Yet Ah, That Spring; 3. Think, In This Battered Caravanserai; 4. A Book of Verses; and 5. Yon Rising Moon. Foote did most of the work in 1898, finishing and publishing in 1899. In the Arthur Foote Collection at Williams College is a small, thin book, the *Rubâiyât of Omar Khayyâm*, "rendered into English Verse by Edward Fitzgerald. Authorized Edition." (Boston: Privately printed by Nathan Haskell Dole, 1898). Following the cover and on the first blank page, the composer has written:

Arthur Foote
Dedham, July 1898
Bas Meudon June 16
        } 1897
Sept. 4

Twelve of the quatrains, including the six attached to the piano composition, are marked with a pencil slash in the right margin. Foote states:

> In 1897, I happened to read the Omar Khayyam quatrains for the first time, and quickly soaked myself in them, with the result of *Five Poems, Op. 41.* They were the outcome of a *love for the verses*, for which reason they are probably the best of all my piano work and the most played.[20]

There is a discrepancy between the book's date of publication and the year Foote said he first read the verses. Possibly he had read an earlier publication of the poetry while he was in Europe, or the book might have appeared a year prior to the cited publication date. At any rate, exoticism was in the air at the end of the nineteenth century. Bayard Taylor had already issued his popular travel books on the East, and responsive Americans, including Foote, had enjoyed his two volumes of poetry—*Ximena* (1844) and *Poems of the Orient* (1854). Indeed, Foote had used one of his poems for "Bedouin Song," published in 1892. His former Salem playmate and Harvard roommate, Ernest Fenollosa, had won a reputation as a "Boston orientalist" and had become the first curator of Japanese art at the Museum of Fine Arts.[21] His good friend Arlo Bates had written poetry redolent of the East, which Foote's colleague George Chadwick had set to music in 1897, *Lyrics from "Told in the Gate."* Foote shared this romanticized interest in faraway and unfamiliar lands beyond the Mediterranean and wished to write music reflective of these foreign settings. He had no desire to research the music of the Middle East for his own use, but wanted to incorporate certain extrinsic elements not essentially exotic into his music. In the past, these elements had not formed a part of his own practices. He felt comfortable using them now because they were not completely extraneous to his own experience.

Consequently, he introduced more unusual harmonies and more unique phrase constructions within a lucid overall framework. He also showed a greater willingness to capitalize on the piano's resources. Each piece sounds like a colorful, mood-delineating bit of musical shorthand rather than a thoroughly realized tone poem. At no time does he resort to motivic development after the German fashion. He retains chromaticism and fluctuating tonalities, but he tones down the clichés of musical orientalism —the ceaseless minor modes, augmented seconds, and harmonies sliding in and out of Neapolitan formations. I discuss four of the five in their arranged orchestral form, *Four Character Pieces after the Rubáiyát of Omar Khayyám*. Movement 3, Think, In This Battered Caravanserai, exists only in its keyboard version. It is captioned with the quatrain:

> Think, in this batter'd Caravanserai
> Whose Portals are alternate Night and Day,
> How Sultán after Sultán with his pomp
> Abode his destined Hour, and went his way."

Foote writes a curt processional to show the coming and the going of the sultans' camel trains. It begins softly, grows louder and louder as the sound advances toward us, reaches a maximum volume, and then fades away as if receding into the distance. A persistent rhythmic pulsation in the bass and shifting major and minor modes enhance the impression of a strange cavalcade, now here for a fleeting moment, now gone.[22] Why it was omitted from the orchestral version is not clear.

His unmistakable involvement with organ playing and literature notwithstanding, Foote waited until 1893 before he permitted Schmidt to publish his first contribution to the medium, the *Three Compositions*, op. 29, for organ: Festival March, Allegretto, and Pastorale. They were shortly taken up by American organists and proved attractive to listeners. Foote has preserved a copy of the program of Samuel P. Warren's organ recital of 26 August 1893 in Great Barrington, Massachusetts, where the Festival March and Pastorale were presented. The organist had mailed the program to him on August 29. At the top of the program, Warren has written: "The pieces are charming and gave great pleasure. SPW Aug. 29."[23] Soon leading organists of the Western world were playing them. For example, Alexandre Guilmant, a French organist of the first rank, played the Allegretto in September 1904 during a concert at the World's Fair in St. Louis.

As usual Foote chooses ternary forms and prefers not to write in a contrapuntal style. The middle and lower registers of the organ are emphasized and chords in close position characterize the sound. The music is always effective and oftentimes powerful; nothing is feeble and maudlin. The Festival March, in $^4/_4$ time and F major, is to be played *maestoso, ma con moto*. The direction asks that the piece be presented in a dignified (*maestoso*) and unsentimentalized (*con moto*) manner. The third-relationships that identify his style are here represented by a move from F major to D-flat and later to A-flat. Surprises are found in the swift in-and-out references to distant keys and in the unanticipated turns of phrase (example 18). The second (in D minor) and third (in B-flat major) numbers are both in a graceful triple time and not as individual as the march. Yet the Pastorale has an engaging middle section in a freewheeling G minor, with the tune hovering around middle C and staccato eighth-note chordal passages rapped out above it.

Two other less significant organ compositions were published about the time of the *Three Compositions*: the Prelude in A-flat (1893) and the Postlude in C Major (1896).[24] Other than these (and curious for an organist), there was nothing issued for organ during the nineties.

Chamber Music

The first chamber work to be mentioned is the unpublished Romance and Scherzo for Cello and Piano, opus 22, which Foote worked on between 1887 and 1890. Romance is actually from the second movement of the Concerto for Cello, op. 33, and also unpublished. It is discussed with that work. Schmidt issued the Romance by itself and transposed into D major as opus 33 (the same number as the unpublished concerto) in 1908. The Romance was first performed in 1889; the Scherzo in 1890; and the entire composition at the end of 1890. The Scherzo in D minor goes along at an amiable pace but is by no means a major chamber composition. The smooth and melodious trio-section in B-flat has one unique feature; a variant of the Scherzo theme returns for a while as a countermelody to the trio's tune.

The Quartet in C Major for Piano and Strings, op. 23, is a major work dedicated to John Knowles Paine. Foote composed much of it during the summer of 1890 while Foote summered in Beverly, though he tinkered with it during the following months. He and the Kneisels gave it a first performance early the next year,[25] and Schmidt published it in 1892. Its movements are *Allegro comodo, Scherzo, Adagio, ma con moto,* and *Allegro non troppo.*

The piece makes a statement that is benevolent and compassionate rather than passionate. Foote makes no attempt to achieve the heroism of Beethoven, the sensuousness of Wagner, the nostalgic sadness of Brahms, or the hysteria of Tchaikovsky. Like Schubert, he is a melodist first, but of quite a different sort. Schubert's edge of bittersweetness, ingenuous yearning, and moments of vehement excitement are absent. In contrast, Foote feels there is room in humankind's experience for a long stretch of quietude and repose that is relatively free from high turbulence, mental agitation, and emotional pressure. The quartet inhabits an expressive domain that is strictly the composer's own. Some critics have had reservations about Foote's music precisely because they have difficulty in assaying the work in terms of the composers and music that they know. Given the aesthetic attitudes that they hold, the quartet is not easy for them to accept. Louis Elson admitted the quartet was "held by some musicians to be the best example of his chamber music," but he himself interpreted it as "a scholarly rather than an impassioned work." John Sullivan Dwight listened to the first movement and decided that "the musical matter . . . did not interest us very deeply, pleasant as the cheerful humor of it was." The Scherzo was "perverse, cantankerous, peevish, will-o'-the-wisp in its jerky and irregular rhythm." The quartet, he said, did not come up to the quality of the Piano Trio, op. 5. Dwight was magnanimous enough to add, "The quartet as a whole was warmly received and evidently gave much pleasure; and we may well mistrust our own impression from a single hearing. . . ."[26] Several more recent critics who claim to an advanced taste cannot abide what is interpreted as its genteelness and a fear of grappling with the "real" world and "real" issues.

Foote never hesitated to include clippings of adverse criticisms in his scrapbooks. He often showed amusement at the misinterpretation of his music and the falsification of his playing abilities. On one such item, part of a review of either this quartet or the String Quartet in E Major, op. 32 (1893) by an unidentified writer, Foote has written, "Criticism in Boston: 1895!" and also "95 Dec." It reads:

> Mr. Foote's quartet has been played here before. As a whole it is one of the most interesting works of this *industrious* [the underlining is Foote's] composer. I hope, however, that in the future the Boston String Quartet will not go out of its way to coddle parochial talent or kowtow to it. The returns for such devotion are generally disappointing socially, musically and pecuniarily. Gentlemen, let us hear some of the new chamber music of the fierce Russians and the immoral Frenchmen. They will furnish stronger contrast to the works of Mozart, Haydn and Beethoven.

Placed close to the above is an even briefer item commenting probably on the same event: "Mr. Foote's performance was without sense of rhythm, and his touch was dry and hard throughout."[27]

The first movement of the piano quartet is lucidly written, tuneful, and animated. It projects a celebratory frame of mind, and it is excellently designed for the instruments. The first movement in ¾ time bears the caption "allegro comodo," and there is indeed something comfortable and easygoing about its liveliness. The opening subject is mellifluous and relaxed and does not conform to the usual Germanic expressiveness. The treble line receives gentle, soft shadings by means of minor submediant and mediant chords (example 19a). Fauré comes to mind for comparison. Foote lays out the first subject somewhat unconventionally. After the first violin's initial say, the piano enters prominently with an extension of the first subject. Quickly, the music moves away from C major in what looks like a transition. Ignoring listeners' expectations, the opening theme in the home key returns in the piano only to supply another surprise—the return is cut short and the music moves on to the second thematic area in the dominant. The change in key does not bring about a strong contrast in expression. The music continues to sing in an unruffled manner through the codetta and to the end of the exposition section. The working out is not lengthy and eschews genuine conflict, and the recapitulation follows in the line of the exposition. To use an analogy, it is as if the music is limning a sunny afternoon in summer—relaxed, meditative, without bustle or commotion, but nevertheless as honest a human encounter as one depicting a scene larger than life and abrim with passion and strife. Foote is not a swashbuckling Wagner or Strauss.

The Scherzo offers a divergence. It is a vivacious, sprightly triple-time movement in G minor, interesting for its opening phrases of 5 + 5 + 6 measures, which may account for its "jerky" impression on Dwight. The music has quirky moments. Foote again reveals a disposition to proceed in a less conventional manner than usual. The theme unfurls in two short repeated sections, then goes on a lengthier excursion into other keys before returning to the earlier material and ending in the home key. Presumably, Dwight liked better the sustained lyricism and *hemiola* rhythms of the less speedy Trio in E-flat major.

The cap of the work, as often is the case with Foote's multi-movemented compositions, is the slow movement, an *adagio, ma con moto* in ⁴/₄ time and A-flat major. Even Dwight liked its "finer feeling and a sweeter melody, with more to say well worth the hearing."[28] For the first twenty-six measures the first violin intones in honeyed accents an ingratiating melody of the sort that contemporary audiences had come to admire and expect of the composer (example 19b). A contrasting idea enters, the piano playing an upward scale passage of sixteenth notes in thirds and the strings answering with a downward movement of dotted eighth and sixteenth notes

It begins in C minor, departs for other keys and returns to C minor in the middle and close. Foote's inspiration is to have the transition that links up with the recapitulation of the principal subject begin with the piano silent and the three strings playing high up in their range and legato. They foreshadow the return by sounding a phrase of the initial melody. The transition continues with the piano playing alone. Soon the other instruments join the piano to continue the transition and further elaborate on the phrase. The transition culminates on an intense *ff*, after which the return proper begins. When the coda commences, one hears the secondary idea transposed into the home key, but the movement closes on a portion of the main melody with the strings *con sordino* and the piano greatly subdued in volume.

Some connection exists between the phrasing in the last movement's opening theme and the phrasing of the slow movement. Yet, the impact of the new sound on the listener is forcefully different. The music moves in $^2/_2$ time and C minor, rather than the expected C major. The tune (example 19c), which keeps up a moderately fast pace, strides across the measures with more abandon than has heretofore been the case in this composition. The climax incorporates unexpected tension. A parallel to the treatment of the first movement's opening subject is seen in the modulations that soon take place away from C minor—a hymn-like idea intervenes at this point (example 19d); then there is an abbreviated return to the opening in C minor. The piano intones an expansive second subject in E flat. The development section becomes most interesting when the composer elaborates on the hymn idea, starting with a *fugato* passage. The listener then hears the return of the first subject in C minor, the second in C major, and finally the hymn as the main argument of the coda. Dwight liked it best of all the movements: "The last movement (*Allegro non troppo*) seemed to us to contain more musical good sense than any part of the quartet. Clear, spontaneous, consistent, well wrought, especially in the contrapuntal passages near the end, it satisfied the musical sense."[29]

It was inevitable that at some point in the nineties, Foote would engage in an activity he enjoyed, the composition of a set of character pieces. *Trois Pièces* for oboe or flute and piano, op. 31, was presented to the Boston public in 1893. On 15 January, Foote and the oboist August Sautet did the last two movements at the St. Botolph Club, and on 13 April, they did the entire opus at Chickering Hall. Publication waited until 1896 and B. Schött's Söhne of Mainz, Germany, to issue them. The set consists of an Aubade villageoise, a Mélodie, and a Pastorale. As the *Transcript* reviewer of the April concert said, Bostonians found the music "delightful and admirably adapted to the character of the instrument, especially the last of the set, Allegretto in F major."[30] Foote's expertise is here sufficiently complete to hide an immense amount of harmonic subtlety beneath the music's surface simplicity. Nancy E. Miller writes that opus 31 harbors "complex progressions, deceptive cadences and sudden enharmonic shifts . . . couched in a serenely orderly flow." For example, a great deal of the first number's coda sounds in the mediant key, then is made to arrive adroitly at the tonic minor at the very close. In the third number, she writes, "what sounds like a return midway through . . . actually happens a half-step too low (and what an intricate course he charted to get us there!)."[31] I would also like to mention the middle of Mélodie, (no. 2), where Foote slips away from a diatonic rendition of the tune in A major into a series of intricate modulations, to the mediant minor, the dominant major, the dominant minor, the lowered mediant major, the submediant minor, the mediant minor, until he finally returns to A major. All the while, the tune continues its unruffled flow, as if the proceedings were elementary, modest, and as artless as can be.

Yet nothing of what has just been said indicates, nor can there be indicated, the real virtues of these three pieces to contemporary audiences: the melodies themselves and their insouciant appeal for listeners. Moreover, there was an additional virtue in the eyes of the amateur wind player, their easy playability.

The second major chamber work of the nineties was the Quartet in E Major for Strings, op. 32. Three copies of the manuscript exist, one by Foote at the Harvard Musical Association, a second and later copy by Foote, in a bound volume dated April 1921, at the New England Conservatory, and a third copy, apparently done by Allen A. Brown, at the Boston Public Library. Comparing the copies, the greatest differences are found in the outer movements, especially with the treatment of the first thematic group, the least in the inner movements. For example, in the third movement, which consists of a theme and variations, the only really important difference is that the third and fourth variations are switched around. The discussion that follows is based mainly on the manuscript at the conservatory, which designates the movements as Allegro giocoso, Scherzo, Andante con moto —Tema con variazioni, and Allegro assai. Although the composition in its entirety was never published, the second movement was reworked for use in the also unpublished Nocturne and Scherzo for Flute and String Quartet (1918). The third movement alone, of all the movements, was published by Schmidt in 1901 as Tema con Variazioni, op. 32.

Foote completed the score in 1893 while summering in Beverly. The quartet's earliest performances, given by the Kneisel Quartet, came on 12 February 1894 at Boston's Chickering Hall and on 25 February 1894 at the St. Botolph Club. The program and the reviews of the Chickering Hall concert designate the movements with almost identical terms as those in the manuscript: "Allegro comodo," "Scherzo," "Andante un poco con moto," and "Allegro con fuoco." The reviewer in the *Boston Evening Transcript* said that the work showed more individuality than heretofore had been the case with Foote and "something which is recognizable as his own style." The writer praised the first movement's expertly deployed harmony and coherent development section. He found the last movement to lack the feel of a finale. He especially liked the two middle movements. The variations had "unmistakable beauty and force." All in all the composition "made a fine impression" on the audience.[32] The reviewer for the *Boston Globe* liked the third movement best, but admitted that the music held the audience's attention throughout and the applause at the conclusion was "persistent."[33]

There was always a practical side to Foote's nature. He probably noted that the inner movements, especially the Andante,

had met with the greatest approval. It was therefore these movements he would redeploy in other guises. An element of self-
criticism was certainly involved—why else the revisions? At any
rate, the first movement is unusual for Foote. The music, in ⁶⁄₈
time, is highly rhythmic and syncopated, reminiscent of the first
movement of Schubert's Quartet in G Major, op. 161. Except for
wisps of lyricism in the second subject, the music does not sing
in the Foote manner and comes across as more dissonant than
anything he had previously composed, and more "impetuoso"
than "giocoso."

The second movement, a vivace in E minor, is likable for its
pixielike playfulness. As already seen in earlier works, the trio of
this movement is meant to go faster, here indicated by *più vivace*. It is more individual in sound than the outer sections. A
declamatory subject in the first violin sounds in a modal A minor
(example 20a) but moves on to F major; then starts up again,
played by the viola, in a modal D minor to close firmly in D major. In the example, one may recognize the special color added
to the harmony by the F-sharp in the viola and the D-sharp in the
second violin.

The theme and six variations of the slow movement is the
main event in the quartet. When first stated by the first violin, the
melody is as plain as can be (example 20b). It emerges as the
brainchild of a meditative artist—a spread-out and solemnly developing line in ²⁄₄ time, with not a superfluous note. It eventually
arrives at a solemn close, on a plagal cadence, submediant minor
to tonic major chord. The subsequent modifications represent
different facets of the expressive idea. The composer does not indulge in pretentious or banal actions, nor the trite, simperingly
sweet lyricism that characterized pieces of this kind during an earlier era. He keeps to a tempered graveness, whether in the atmosphere he evokes or in the emotion he captures. The sureness of
his ideas come from a technical wisdom that is never ostenta-
tiously displayed. The closest equivalence that I could find was to
the slow movement of the Schubert String Quartet in D Minor,
(Posthumous), also an andante con moto whose unembellished
theme comes from the Schubert song "Death and the Maiden."

The first variation has the melody in the middle instruments,
with a countermelody in the first violin, consisting mainly of flu-

ent sixteenth-note ornamentation. The plagal close is absent. The second variation is a brisk tarantella in ¹²/₈ time. This nimble, triple-time dance, originating in southern Italy, had already been adopted for concert use by several nineteenth-century composers. The last movement of Mendelssohn's *Italian Symphony* (1833), for one, could have set a precedent for Foote. However, Foote's craggy and brusque rendition of the dance has nothing Mendelssohnian about it. Next comes a majestic slow march, the tune given first to the cello and next to the first violin. Interestingly, there are similarities between the start of the cello melody and the start of the first movement of the Cello Concerto, opus 33, which was finished at the same time as the quartet. The fourth variation, *tranquillo: ma con moto*, is in A major and is assuredly one of the most effective sections in the movement. (The composer has made an inadvertent error by adding an extra sharp in the second violin's key signature.) The variation features the four instruments playing quietly and with mutes on (example 20c). The motive on which the variation is based, heard from the first measure on, stems from an idea that had already appeared in the previous two movements. It was first heard played by the second violin in measure 5 and by the viola in measure 6 of the first movement. The fifth variation is a swift, will-o'-the-wisp section set forth in sixteenth notes and based on the same motive. The minor mode returns with the sixth variation, which leads directly to a reprise of the main tune and its plagal ending.

The finale, as expected, is fast and, in the New England Conservatory manuscript, announces its first subject by means of a *fugato*. The motive reoccurs as an accompaniment to the second subject. Otherwise the movement is in a regular sonata-allegro form until the coda is reached. At this point, without warning, Foote calls for a *tempo del I° movimento*, and the opening subject of the first movement returns in augmentation. Seven measures from the close, the motive is heard for the last time in the first violin and the quartet ends decisively in E major.

Especially as we advance on to the next work, the Quintet in A Minor for Piano and Strings, op. 38, we want to remind the reader that Foote's style was quite alive to its time. By the century's end, he was reaching the highest point in his professional career. More than ever, audiences found his music consequential and intelligible. In addition to the music public, accomplished musicians throughout the country considered his works to be substantial and stimulating. Although Foote's style in the piano quintet is neither newly minted or absolutely unique in the twentieth-century sense, his contemporaries found it to be fresh and valuable. For one thing, they recognized its firm artistic base. Moreover, musicians admired his ceaseless attempts to identify additional possibilities in those expressive modes meaningful to his time. When he decided to compose the quintet, he assumed that the nineteenth-century musical practices remained undepleted and acted accordingly. Although this belief was later tested by the polemics and radically different music of modernism, he never found any compelling reason to change it.

The piano quintet was finished in 1897 and received its initial performance on 31 January 1898 in a Boston concert given by Foote and the Kneisel Quartet. Schmidt published the work in 1898. The four movements are an Allegro guisto, Intermezzo, Scherzo, and Allegro giusto. Written in the fullness of his creative maturity, critics and audiences unanimously found it to be the finest work he had yet composed.

The composition immediately made a strong impression on a Boston audience that had felt discomfited by the more audacious contemporary sounds coming from "the 'new men,'" from "Richard Strauss and the neo-Russians." Foote was proving that his more traditional style "was not yet quite worked out." A minute or two of listening to the first movement revealed its patterns to be "fresh and full of life and vigor." Bostonians heard no *Kapellmeistermusik*, no "machine-made article," but a work that "had come straight from a living man's heart." The *Transcript* reviewer who made these comments then went on to add:

> We should say that this quintet was one of the strongest pieces of work, if not the strongest, that Mr. Foote has yet given out. The form is so clear, the development so natural, so inevitable-seeming, the writing so brilliant and vivacious; then the fertility of melodic invention and resource the composer shows, the warm glow and charm of his second themes, all these elements combine to make the work a continuous inspiration to the listener.[34]

The other Boston reviewers agreed with this assessment of the piano quintet, saying that while the audience loved the entire composition, it especially cherished the two middle movements (a comment also made about the second string quartet). When it was performed in New York on 7 March 1899, the *Tribune* reviewer spoke about an admirable performance before a delighted audience and about round after round of applause that followed the completion of the third movement. He decided that "the quintet is a most worthy contribution to American music and, better still, is distinctly worthy of performance regardless of origin."[35]

In June 1899, the piano quintet was heard at the annual convention of the Music Teachers National Association, held in Cincinnati. A witness to the event wrote:

> Mr. Arthur Foote's quintet in A minor, for piano and strings, brought every musician to his place, and their enthusiasm grew as the work proceeded.
>
> Here at last there is solid ground. The quintet is after the true classic mold, respecting the limitations of chamber music, appreciating its privilege in a composition of easy flowing melody admirably developed throughout and played under the guiding hand of the master with an enthusiasm and verve simply delightful to the jaded spirits of the audience. With the thermometer [at the] stifling point, the audience shouted bravos and expanded its last available remnant of strength on pounding with canes and umbrellas. Mr. Foote was rather warm, too, but radiant as he mopped his fevered brow, the center of an admiring throng of musicians and critics. Any one that has doubts about American music should hear that quintet, by Mr. Arthur Foote of Boston.[36]

Finally, after the Spiering Quartet performed it in St. Louis on 17 January 1900, along with Schubert's String Quartet in A Minor, op. 29, and Wilhelm Stenhammar's String Quartet in C Minor, op. 14, an approving local critic wrote: "The Foote number was the most pleasing one on the programme, and was received with intense enthusiasm."[37]

From the beginning to the end of the composition, all instruments share in important thematic material—far more than had been true in any earlier chamber work of Foote. Textures are varied constantly and contrasts are emphasized to an extent not evident in the earlier piano quartet. Foote picks up where he left off in the Second String Quartet and often constructs sections with a rhythmic and syncopated emphasis. The entire piece is distinguished by sprightliness and imagination.

It is possible that the piano quintet was to some degree intended as homage to Brahms, who had died on 3 April 1897. The first movement, in particular, reveals some ramifications from the Brahms style. It opens passionately with a big dramatic gesture, followed by the agitated quasi-*fugato* entry of each string instrument on the main subject. (example 21a). Twenty-four measures before the second subject is heard, Foote introduces a transitional idea whose tune has a similarity to the "Irish Folk Song" of six years before and whose milieu is faintly gypsyish à la Brahms. The second subject, in G major, also somewhat Brahmsian, starts off in the piano alone. The mood changes from agitated to elegiac. A grand, expansive melody advances at an unhurried pace. Later, the first subject and the transitional idea provide the material for an animated and exhilarating development section. An abbreviated recapitulation rounds off the movement.

Moving at a moderate allegretto tempo, the Intermezzo in F major starts off on a touching melody whose ancestry is Anglo-Celtic American folk song (example 21b). In the first eight measures, all chords remain in first position, the submediant minor chord provides an essential coloring to the whole, the melody only once barely touches on the leading tone, and the submediant tone is a significant factor in the line's structure. A faster moving trio, made up of a wide-spaced arpeggiated accompaniment in the piano supporting nervous, contrapuntal, and at times fugal lines in the strings, provides the requisite middle-section contrast. The piece then returns to a reorchestrated statement of the folklike tune. Especially affecting are the last sixteen measures, when the song is heard in the piano, while the string instruments weave an eloquent contrapuntal web around it.

The Scherzo, in ⁶⁄₈ and D minor, is full of little rhythmic surprises, unexpected accents, and mercurial shifts in the progression of themes from one measure to the next and from one phrase to the next. The listener's attention is caught at the beginning by a spirited staccato theme and never let go (example 21c). After a few measures of sheer fancy, the music becomes more animated and the melody, in the strings, more legato. Then the whimsical theme returns. The D-major trio, in contrast, presents a *perpetuum mobile* in the piano that skillfully builds up momentum in the listener's mind for a return to the "Scherzo." The reprise, however, is brief. The Coda that cuts off the return substitutes an even briefer allusion to the *perpetuum mobile*. The movement ends by leaving the listener up in the air but delightedly so.

The last movement, in D major, is cast in a simple rondo form, A B A C A. The dancelike main subject has a whiff of the gypsy about it, but is interrupted by a sudden interjection of a beautiful ruminative idea in a modal C-sharp minor, played by the strings alone before being allowed to continue with the piano (example 21d). The first contrasting theme, in F-sharp minor, focuses mainly on a running sixteenth-note figure in the piano. The second contrasting theme, in E major, consists of a broad melody whose expression replicates that of the first movement's second subject.

One final chamber work came from Foote before the century's end, the Melody for violin and piano, op. 44, which dates from 1899. Schmidt published it the next year. The piece is straightforwardly laid out in the style we have come to anticipate from the composer. Nothing about it suggests the *Five Poems after Omar Khayyám*, which Foote was also writing that year. Here there is no allusion to distant places and exotic sounds. The heading confidently announces what the piece is all about. It is indeed a silver-tongued melody, an affecting song without words in ternary form. The violin sounds a lulling tune at first, then swells with feeling for the middle section, and, lastly, reestablishes the atmosphere of quietude.

Music for String Ensemble and for Full Orchestra

In some respects, the Serenade in E Major, op. 25 (1886–91), is a collection of dances beholden to the Baroque style of Bach and seemingly contrived to make a deliciously old-fashioned impression on the audience. However, Foote was not accommodating himself to the conservative-nostalgic views of his era when he looked to the first half of the eighteenth century for a stimulus. Neither was he trying to exhibit the fruits of his learnedness, solid as they might be. Far from functioning as anachronisms, these older procedures provided him with the means for a wider range of expressive inflections.

Consequently, the composition may be taken as a succession of modest instrumental vignettes that follow an expressive agenda. In them, he harbors the sensibility of the Romantic composer and reveals an older time to us as if the outcome of a sincerely felt personal fantasy. The melodies he creates are inviting and delectable in ways no Baroque composer could have contemplated. The harmonies are of his own day, fully realized and rich. They engage in modulatory schemes pertinent to his own era and not to an earlier one. It should be evident that, whatever his engagements with the past, Foote has conducted a series of limited poetic transactions with an earlier style. What he garners is matter suitable for further development and is marshaled differently in aid of contemporary expression. What he offers us are musical images expressing insights that he hopes we will consider beautiful.

The Serenade contains five numbers: Praeludium, Allegro comodo, Air, Intermezzo, Romance, and Gavotte. They are reconstituted movements taken from the earlier Suite no. 1 in E Major for String Orchestra, op. 12 (1886), and the Suite no. 2 in D Major for String Orchestra, op. 21, (1889). The tonalities of the movements outline the E-minor triad:

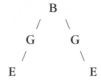

Foote prepared the new score in the summer of 1891, and Schmidt published it in 1892. At the bottom of the first page of the published score is a statement that the second (Air) and fourth movement (Romance) can be omitted if necessary. The first represents the closest approximation to a Baroque style and the second, the most purely Romantic segment of the composition. For much of the serenade, the cello is doubled by the bass. Yet, there is much use of divided strings, and there are several exquisite moments where the bass rests and the remaining strings soar into their higher regions.

Ross Jungnickel and the Baltimore Symphony gave the premiere of the serenade on 5 January 1893. It waited until April 1893 for Nikisch and the Boston Symphony to present it to the home audience. From then on, it was played in various cities of the United States and Europe, certainly a sign of its wide acceptance.

Of the first movement, Foote has written:

> The first movement (PRAELUDIUM) is built on a flowing melody, which by its cross-accents in syncopation produces at first the effect of a motion much slower; but in a few measures the rhythm (¾) is restored, so that the effect of a true *allegro* is obtained. The *trio* of this movement is of simple structure, and serves chiefly as contrast to the main theme, and is for the most part a melody by the first violins with accompaniment—with a contrasting middle movement of a more dramatic cast.[38]

The prelude, in ternary form, is ostensibly in ¾ time, but for the first thirty-two measures the constant syncopations cause it to sound actually in 3⁄2 time. The serene tune (*allegro comodo*) is by this means given a gentle lilt (example 22a). Leisurely excursions into other keys ensue. The close is a reprise of the opening. The middle portion is in C-sharp minor and much faster. Nevertheless, no strong expressive contrast is attempted. The Air that follows (example 22b) is obviously modeled after the second movement from Bach's Suite no. 3 in D Major for Orchestra (BWV 1068). Its affecting lyricism is the composer's; its sentiment is that of the Romantic period. The Intermezzo, far more than the previous two movements, veers away from the Baroque. Observe, for instance, the main harmonies of the first repeated section: I / II^6_5 / II^6_5 / II / V^6_5 - $VII^{6\#}_5$ of V / V; also, the sudden decision to add a *stretto* to the second point of imitation, not saving the effect for the climax (example 22c). The least Baroque part is the middle section, which begins with a plaintive cello solo cast in a veiled modal G-sharp minor (example 22d).

The Romance departs altogether from the Baroque. The same way that so many of Foote's allegro movements are modified with the word *comodo*, his slow movements have a tendency to be andante movements modified with the direction *con moto*, as it is here. Foote has written a Romantic serenade, always tender and full of polished sentiment (example 22e). Abruptly, the Gavotte lands the listener in the Baroque again. Foote describes the movements as follows:

> In the Gavotte, a return to the old style is found. It cannot differ from other Gavottes, except in the time, for the form is cast-iron; in the contrasting part (the so-called Musette), as should be the case, there is a hint of the old bagpipe effect—of open fifths through the whole of this, the most perfect instances are the familiar Bach D minor and G minor Gavottes, where the old Museau is imitated remarkably.[39]

The serenade makes no pretensions to grand emotion or searing dramatic conflict. It is much less bold than the piano quartet, composed in 1890. Nonetheless, it must be remembered that much of the music in the serenade had been composed in the four years before the piano quartet. Foote's writing for strings customarily demonstrates a strong affinity for the idiom. Amiable tunes extremely suited to the strings, well-ordered rhythms, and telling harmonies are meant to ingratiate their way into the contemporary listener's affections, and this they did. What he said about the Gavotte informs us that he knew of the juxtaposition of the "old style" with that of his time in the music. He must also have known that despite the tonal relationships between the movements, the composition did not coalesce into the sort of stylistic whole that some music critics considered all-important. Yet, the work is a serenade and not to be judged as a symphony. In the early part of the eighteenth century to which Foote refers in this work, the serenade was light, elegant, and homophonic night music of an amorous nature, as opposed to the graver fugal modes. It was designed to entertain and not deliver a lecture. If it intimated profounder depths of expression (and Foote's serenade does do so), so much the better—but this was not its main function. From this perspective, Foote's serenade succeeds eminently well.

Neither a revision of earlier music nor a reference back to an old style, the Symphonic Prologue *Francesca da Rimini*, op. 24, for full orchestra was a novel departure for Foote. He was trying his hand at writing program music in a city where John Sullivan Dwight and his conservative acquaintances had railed against program music for years. Despite the efforts of forward-looking musicians, program music was still not entirely accepted. Foote has written on his own copy of the published score, bound with opus 25 and opus 28, first the date that Schmidt published it and then the time period when he composed it: "June 1892 (The Alhambra, Pride's Crossing, June-October 1890)." The dedication is to his good friend and patron, Mrs. John L. Gardner. On the verso of the front cover of the bound volume that contains this score, Foote has written, "Bound December 1892. 2 West Cedar Street." He has also proudly inserted on the first blank page a clipping, entitled "Calendar of Famous Musicians," from an unnamed periodical, which gives the picture of and brief biographical information on six composers, with Foote at the head of the list and *Francesca da Rimini* cited as his best known work. Those named are Foote, Brahms, Sarasate, Guilmant, Bach, and Haydn.[40] From the evidence of all the items in the bound volume, this calendar antedates the publication of his Suite in D Minor for Full Orchestra, op. 36, which came out in 1896. Perhaps it was his newfound fame that emboldened him to try something out of the ordinary. His Overture *In the Mountains* does not count, since Foote mentioned no program whatsoever to go with it, and the music does not make "mountainous" gestures.

By the early nineties, Dante Alighieri and the *Divine Comedy* were the talk of educated and well-informed Bostonians. Longfellow had issued a poetic translation of the *Divine Comedy* in 1867. Charles Eliot Norton started to give Dante readings in the spring of 1885, which Mrs. Gardner and possibly Foote attended. Norton prepared a three-volume prose translation of the Italian text, which came out in 1891–92. May Alden Wood's biography of Dante was published in Boston in 1887. James Russell Lowell's

Dante studies and lectures on Dante were still in progress. The Dante Society of Cambridge, which had been meeting informally in the seventies, was formally organized in 1880. In 1881, Marion Crawford had introduced Dante's writing to Mrs. Gardner, and she quickly joined the society, remaining a member until her death. Crawford's novel *An American Politician* furnishes a picture of Mrs. Gardner's home in the eighties and says that long discussions of Dante took place there. Given Foote's friendship with Mrs. Gardner, he was conceivably present at some of these discussions. In the late eighties, she sponsored the compilation of a *Concordance of the "Divina Comedia"*, which was published by Edward Allen Fay.[41]

His own interest awakened, and especially aware of Mrs. Gardner's and other friends' preoccupation with the Italian poet, Foote introduced his own morsel into the Dante ferment. It was fitting that he should compose the music at Mrs. Gardner's The Alhambra and dedicate the composition to her. When he stood before the Boston Symphony Orchestra and conducted the premiere on 23 January 1891, he was confirming his familiar relationship to her and to Boston's literary and artistic circles. He also pleased listeners, as the piece became familiar to them. When the Boston Symphony conducted by Emil Paur did the work again on 2 March 1895: "The prologue . . . produced an exceedingly strong impression, Mr. Foote having to bow his acknowledgments of the applause from his hiding place in the corner of the first balcony."[42]

Francesca da Rimini was a tragic Italian historical figure. She and her brother-in-law, Paolo Malatesta, had fallen in love with each other as they read together the story of Lancelot. Her husband discovered their attachment and had them both killed around the year 1289. Dante, in the *Divine Comedy*, situates them in the second circle of the Inferno, where tempestuous winds coercively drive sexual transgressors about, as passions had driven them during life. Foote has very little to say about the connection between the story and his music. On the title page of the score, Foote quotes from Dante the motto:

> Nessun maggior dolore
> Che ricordarsi del tempo felice
> Nella miseria.

It translates: "There is no greater sorrow than to recall a time of happiness in misery."

The composition is in sonata form, the usual form for a concert overture. Its orchestration consists of woodwinds by twos, four French horns, two trumpets, three trombones and tuba, two timpani, and strings. In the program notes for the first concert,[43] he mentions the second theme, in E-flat major, as the theme of the two lovers, and the return of the recitative toward the completion of the recapitulation, which was first heard in the introduction played by trombones, cellos, and basses at the premiere, as indicating the catastrophe of the story. Foote revised the instrumentation and gave this recitative to the strings before publication,. He says that at the very end, the music recalls the motto from Dante. No other programmatic details are given. Obviously, he avoids talking about the chronological aspects of the work.

It would be strange if he had not discussed the limitations of program music with his friend William Apthorp. One suspects that Apthorp was speaking for both of them when he later wrote:

> When Berlioz claimed that the *Adagio* in his *Romeo and Juliet* symphony was a musical reproduction of the balcony-scene . . . and expressed the varying emotions of the two lovers, there was, to be sure, nothing in his claim to shock our ordinary notions of artistic dignity; but his claim was nevertheless no more tenable . . . than that of the Russian lady who thought to recognize in another movement of the same symphony "Romeo driving up to Capulet's door in his cabriolet."[44]

Francesca should not be confused with a symphonic poem. The motto is not a narrative text that the audience must read before hearing the music. No true program of events is attached to the work. The various sections of the piece are not shaped into an individual structure. Foote is trying to reach into the central being of the tragic lovers, not present a picture of them replete with an Italianate clash of personalities, rage, and the exaction of revenge. In a broader sense, he is portraying the contrariety that exists between the force of love and the coercive strength of society and religion, an incompatibility that causes discord within

Francesca. After the piece was done in Cincinnati with Frank Van der Stucken conducting on 18 January 1895, a reviewer said:

> The work can not be called descriptive. It reflects, perhaps, the impression created upon the composer's mind after reading the tragic story; it does not attempt to analyze or describe it musically. The gloomy introduction might suggest the composer brooding over the fate of Francesca. . . . The second theme [is] unquestionably a love motive. There is no theme in the aria, however, that can be associated with the personality of Francesca.[45]

The succinct and poignant fifteen-and-a-half-minute piece reveals an intelligible structure, clearly stated and vital themes, and a fine orchestration. The opposition of rhapsodic string passages to sonorously declaiming brass is especially attractive. The colors are somber. The music continuously refers to the ideas and feelings generated by the story. Foote provides striking contrasts in passages exemplifying torment and rapture, the vulnerability and desperation that come with ungovernable feeling and the ecstasy of loving. The work opens with an introduction in C minor, played *andante sostenuto* and in triple time. A low four-measure phrase heard in the lower strings, bassoons, and a French horn, against a held C-tone, sets the ambience of the piece. A brief, more ardent motive then sounds in the oboe (example 23a), which will later be heard as the first theme of the Allegro. Agitation and tempo increases; syncopation is introduced; the music reaches a climax. Shortly thereafter, the introduction ends on a recitative played by strings in unison, which presages the catastrophe to come.

The main body of the work starts in a fast tempo with an excited theme and nervous rhythms that receive extensive treatment. An episode in the French horns and trumpets in E-flat heralds the second theme, also in E-flat. This is a sustained song, tender to fervid, which continues to develop over many measures (example 23b). In the middle of this song and just before a major climax, a second episode featuring the quiet sound of the flute is heard (example 23c). Given the already lengthy handling of the material, the development section is brief. The agitated first theme then returns and is interrupted by a third episode in the brasses and winds, which is paced like a stern hymn. After an immense climax is reached, the recitative returns to announce the "catastrophe." The second theme softly reenters and briefly crescendos. Finally, tremolo strings slowly rise higher and higher in $^{12}/_8$ time while various instruments bring back the music of the second episode, as if giving a resigned farewell to happiness.

By 1900, several orchestras had successfully produced the prologue. The Aeolian Piano Company took notice of its effect on the music public, and C. B. Chilton, representing the company, wrote to Foote, care of the St. Botolph Club, on 20 October 1900:

> Dear Mr. Foote: —
> We are arranging your "Francesca da Rimini" overture, and we find that owing to the length it is impossible to run it through on one roll without a break as there is no break indicated in the score. We write to ask if you will kindly advise us as to a point, preferably near the middle, at which a rupture would do the least injury to the spirit of the performance. . . . I am going to send you the rolls of your Suite (2nd) for your judgment. It delights everyone here.[46]

As Foote was working on *Francesca*, a second major work remained half-completed. On 25 July 1887, Henry Holden Huss had sent Foote a letter from New York City mentioning Frank Van der Stucken's performance of the Overture *In the Mountains* and giving him Horatio Parker's New York address. Then he writes: "I wish you all success with the cello concerto."[47] The outstanding cellist-scholar Douglas Moore, director of the Arthur Foote Collection at Williams College, has championed the concerto in performance. He describes the composition's convoluted history, as follows:

> The story of the *Concerto* is intertwined with that of his published *Romanza* for cello and piano, since they share the same opus number. The *Concerto* was begun in Salem, Massachusetts in 1887. In 1889 [26 March], the slow movement was performed with piano at the Boston Manuscript Club under the title "Andante from the Con-

certo, Opus 16." Meanwhile, another work for cello and piano, the "Capriccio," was performed in Cleveland, in November, 1890. In December of that same year, the two works were played together, now titled "Scherzo [a new work not related to the Concerto] and Romance" and with a new number, Opus 22. Only one month later, in January 1891, the title was again changed to "Romanza in D Major and Scherzo," with no opus number.[48]

The entire concerto was completed in Beverly in 1893 and designated as opus 33. Apparently, Foote tried to get Victor Herbert to introduce the work, but Herbert wrote to Foote on 6 March, probably in 1894: "I had hoped to be able to play your Concerto at the H.S.S. concert but I go on a Concert Tour next week and don't return until May. I'll be very glad to play it next year, however, if that isn't too late."[49] At any rate, Theodore Thomas decided to do it in Chicago in May 1894, with Bruno Steindel, the principal cellist, as soloist, but the performance was postponed until 30 November. On 1 December 1894, Thomas sent Foote, at 2 West Cedar Street, a Western Union Night Message, which read: "Concerto great success, both matinee and evening. Steindel played superb. Congratulate you."[50] Unfortunately, one Chicago reviewer did not think the concerto itself was a great success:

> Of this new concerto, Mr. Steindel gave a first performance from the manuscript. In it there is evidence of ingenuity rather than inspiration. To the latter quality there is a nearer approach through the sympathy evidenced in the slow movement than Mr. Foote has generally obtained in the past. Not strikingly original, this melody, which mainly constitutes the andante, is genuine and even fluent. The first movement is full of difficulties not thankful in proportion to their demand upon the technical resources nor written as a cello player would have expressed them. This evidence of perversion through misapplied inventiveness is fortunately confined in the main to the first movement. There is ample evidence of diversity and resource, and there is restraint though a tendency to diffuseness in the andante. The final movement

> is stirring in rhythm and characteristic. In this movement
> and in the allegro the management of the orchestra in re-
> lation to the solo instrument is masterly and striking. Mr.
> Steindel . . . gave even the most awkward and exacting
> passages with ease and fluency.[51]

In part, perhaps, because of this negative review, Foote never had the work published and appears never to have pushed for
another performance. The concerto was given a second performance with Douglas Moore as soloist in 1981, after Foote had
been dead forty-four years. (In 1908, Schmidt published the Romanza in D Major, for cello and piano, op. 33) Like the Saint-
Saëns Cello Concerto in A Minor (1873), which Foote probably
did hear at a Boston Symphony concert, the three movements of
this concerto are played without a pause. Moore also has pointed out the similarities of figuration and passage work between
the two compositions.[52]

The orchestration of the Cello Concerto in G Minor is identical to that of the Overture *In the Mountains*, except that the
trumpets are omitted.[53] The first movement, an *allegro ma non
troppo* in $^4/_4$, is in the normal sonata-allegro form. A stately introduction is heard in the full orchestra twice (example 24a), followed by a cadenza in the cello, the second one much longer
than the first. The urbane first theme in G minor (example 24b) is
in a configuration that is easily remembered when it returns in
the development section and recapitulation. The second theme,
in the relative major and a little slower, makes a lyrical and expressive statement. The usual expansion on the two ideas takes
place. The second movement, an *andante con moto* in $^9/_8$ time,
opens on a graceful singing cello solo in E-flat major (example
24c). It goes on almost seamlessly to a second theme in B-flat and
makes a leisurely return to the first theme. The second theme in
E-flat appears briefly before the end. The finale, a sonata-allegro
movement, begins in a sprightly rhythmic *allegro comodo* in $^3/_4$
time (example 24d). The second portion of the main theme
changes gears and becomes *marcato*, somewhat modal, and
sounds *à la Russe* (example 24e). A secondary, rather springy
theme in the relative major supplies the needed contrast. Just before the beginning of the coda, the cello plays a cadenza and ends
the work with rapid animated sixteenth-note figurations.

Several close hearings of the work[54] lead me to queston the conclusions of the Chicago reviewer. I am surprised that Foote did not see his way to publishing and gaining additional performances for the entire work. It may well be that he intended, but never got around to making, a thorough revision of the piece. The concerto would have benefited from bolder chord construction, less predictable harmonic progressions, a stronger rhythmic profile, and a less cautious use of orchestra. As it stands, the cello's role is too dominant, and the musical style and orchestration belongs more to the conservative eighties than the more forward-looking nineties. Nevertheless, the music is well worth listening to. The concerto, as we now have it, is a sad, somberly colored, yet agreeable composition that now and again gives way to stabs of anguish. The middle movement is especially attractive. Thread after thread of achingly melancholic melody builds to a peak of poignancy.

Foote completed his third work for full orchestra in the summer of 1895 while in Hythe, England—the Suite in D Minor, op. 36. On his return to Boston in the fall, he showed one movement of the suite to his composer-friends Chadwick, Parker, and Whiting. As he tells it:

> One evening I brought a movement of an orchestral suite, which next year had its first performance, Paur conducting. As most composers in such circumstances, I played it through quite badly, and hopefully waited for criticism. Parker's was, "It is all in D minor." This happened to be exactly what was the matter, and the few words resulted in changes that obviated the monotony, which I myself had not felt.[55]

Paur and the Boston Symphony gave the first performance on 6 March 1896, and Schmidt published it the same year. Foote says that the winter was uneventful save for the first performance of the suite ("practically a symphony"), which showed a substantial advance in his treatment of the orchestra. Like many other American works for orchestra, it received several first performances and then was forgotten. He makes the observation: "It was only fairly successful, but with two really good movements. . . .The movement in variation form really satisfied me."[56] In recognizing its kinship to the symphony, Foote was signaling that he considered the suite to be one of the most ambitious creative efforts of his entire career as a composer.

Regrettably, the *Boston Evening Transcript* reviewer of the premiere was not pleased with the work, although he conceded that Foote received loud applause from the audience. He complained about its lack of unity and cohesion. The two middle movements, both slow, made him impatient. There were faults in the development section of the first movement. The second movement was weak. The third movement did not hold together. Only the finale pleased him, with its "ingenious development especially in the clever and distinctly humorous treatment of fugal forms."[57]

By the next spring, the critics' assessment had become positive. Henry E. Krehbiel heard the New York Manuscript Society perform the suite on 22 April 1897 and wrote in the *Tribune* that the society was not noted for the quality of the new music it sponsored. Hence his surprise and pleasure in listening to the Suite in D Minor, a work worth hearing, because it contained superb ideas that were executed with resourcefulness. Regrettably, however, the orchestra was inadequately rehearsed and the performance was substandard, thus diminishing the real beauty of the piece. In contrast to the *Transcript* reviewer of a year before, Krehbiel said the middle movements charmed him. The finale, which opened in a fugal manner, was engagingly "spirited and fresh."

Other New York reviewers praised the strong thematic substance, the command of form, and the skill in orchestration. The writer in the New York *Organist's Journal* reported, "The composition was received with marked enthusiasm and warmed the souls even of the severest critics."[58] Informing his readership about the same concert, the music critic of the *New York Times* heaped praise on the composer and composition ("the best thing the society has produced of late"), then lamented that Foote was a Bostonian rather than a New Yorker:

> Mr. Foote is a gifted young man, who has studied his art seriously, and who has a firm mastery of form and musical material. Furthermore, he has a bright and buoyant fancy. His themes are always dignified, yet graceful, and they are full of possibilities. I have not heard of late anything

fresher and more fluently melodious than the second and
last movements of his suite. I have already spoken of the
variations. They impressed me by the excellence of their
workmanship. The scoring was clear, well balanced, certain, and lovely in its solo effects. . . . Why do all our best
composers live in Boston? To be sure, Columbia College
succeeded in luring Mr. MacDowell away from the Hub of
the world, but Foote and Chadwick remain there. There
must be something especially invigorating in the nectar
which is brewed at the St. Botolph Club.[59]

Thomas performed the suite in Chicago in 1899, and so also
did Van der Stucken in Cincinnati in 1900. In both cities, music
reviewers and audiences acclaimed the work. The writers were
unanimous in the opinion that Foote "always has something to
say and says it effectively."[60] Whatever misgivings he might have
felt after the Boston premiere in 1896, Foote must have realized
that he had accomplished a great deal with this major work.

The orchestra was the largest that Foote had yet employed:
woodwinds by twos (one flute interchangeable with piccolo and
one oboe interchangeable with English horn), four horns, two
trumpets, three trombones, tuba, kettledrums, harp, and strings.
Although he has come abreast of his time in the use of the orchestra and has advanced his style beyond the seventies and
eighties, he is by no means on the cutting edge of musical exploration. Indeed, compared to the overripeness of Strauss, the per-
fumed eccentricities of Scriabin, and the fastidious delicateness
of Debussy, his is a stable and established style, a meat-and-pota-
toes music that keeps faith with tradition.

The first movement is an *allegro energico con brio* in 6/4
time. The forcefully robust first subject opens with an upward
sweep (example 25a) and is elaborated on in some detail as it
switches back and forth with two secondary ideas that derive
from the subject. A less spirited but lyrical second subject in the
relative-major key follows (example 25b). After a fairly extended
development of the two subjects, there comes the usual recapitulation and a lively coda.

The highly expressive *non troppo adagio* second movement
is in B-flat major, 2/4 time, and ternary form. This music is deeply
and sincerely felt. The quiet and richly melodic opening theme is

played first by the strings (example 25c). Other instruments join in as the composer elaborates on the subject, sometimes with great eloquence and resonance, and always with a variety of sensitive harmonic and instrumental colorings. A very welcome passage in the full brass enters *staccato* (example 25d) to usher in the second theme.

The third movement is slower and of a different form than might be expected after the previous adagio movement. It is a capricious variation movement, *andante espressivo, con moto*, in G minor and $^2/_4$ time. Changes in tempo occur frequently. The strings present the mildly syncopated theme unadorned, supported by uncomplicated harmony. Seven variations appear, each a small character piece vividly and distinctly contrasted with the other variations. One of the most striking divergences from the initial idea occurs in the seventh variation, which bursts forth loudly and modally (Example 25e).

The finale is in very fast $^3/_4$ time and D major. The treatment of the two contrasting themes in sonata-allegro form frequently resorts to counterpoint, a procedure we do not usually associate with Foote. The entire movement sounds festive and buoyant. The opening subject, which has a boisterous, dancelike quality to it (example 25f), becomes undeniably merry when shortly it turns into a fugue. The second subject (example 25g) is equally carefree and has a keenly American character in its syncopations.[61]

The composition might easily have been designated a symphony, the effervescence of the finale notwithstanding. But Foote's characteristic diffidence showed through when he opted for the less ambitious designation of suite. I cannot help but agree with critics and audiences who found the ideas impressive, new sprung, inviting, and skillfully handled. The music commands interest throughout and gives constant pleasure—surely, a masterly production.

Foote would complete one last work for full orchestra, the *Four Character Pieces after the Rubáiyát of Omar Khayyám*, op. 48. After finishing the five *Omar Khayyám* piano pieces, op. 41, in the summer of 1898, he continued to be fascinated by this poet who sang about humankind's limited stay on earth, questioned the possibility of life after death, and therefore advocated an attitude of carpe diem toward mortal existence. Every now and again, his attention was redirected to the Middle East. For example, Foote was aware that one of his songs was done alongside Liza Lehmann's very popular "In a Persian Garden" at Pittsburgh in October 1898.[62] On 31 March 1899, an Omar Khayyám Club of America was organized and held its first meeting in Boston, with Foote present. It met to discuss Eastern astronomy, algebra and mathematics, oriental languages, and, of course, the Fitzgerald translation of the poems.[63] Then Helen Hopekirk appeared to advocate orchestration of the piano pieces. Thinking he needed some exercise in orchestration, Foote went to work on what came to be entitled *Four Character Pieces after the Rubáiyát of Omar Khayyám*.

The Boston Symphony Orchestra performed the work on 19 April 1912, and Philip Hale states in the program notes that Foote told him the orchestration was done in 1900.[64] In Foote's autobiography, the composer says that Helen Hopekirk suggested orchestrating the piano pieces around 1905, at which point he took up the task. For some time he did nothing about what he regarded as practice work. Finally, he got around to sending them to Frederick Stock, the conductor of the Chicago Symphony. Stock liked the score and gave the music its premiere on 20 December 1907. Its success was immediate. Soon it was being "played practically everywhere."[65] Schmidt published the score in 1912. Foote sent one copy of it to Helen Hopekirk, writing on the title page: "To my dear friend, Helen Hopekirk Wilson, at whose suggestion these pieces were made. Arthur Foote, February 1913."[66]

The work comprises brief, uncomplicated impressions of four of the quatrains. The composer makes no attempt to explain the connection between the poetry and the music. Because the movements are only musical sketches, no development of the material is attempted. The orchestra is large: woodwinds by twos, four horns, two trumpets, three trombones, tuba, timpani, bass drum, cymbals, tambourine, harp, and strings. The composition shows the composer's style in its most individual guise in its expressiveness, artless yet persuasive exoticism, bold use of harmony, constant attention to the shaping of rhythm, and colorful exploitation of the orchestra. Above all, he knows how to get a maximum effect out of the simplest of means.[67]

The first movement is Foote's imaginative and haunting response to the verse:

Iram indeed is gone with all his Rose,
And Jamshyd's Sev'n-ring'd Cup where no one knows;
But still a Ruby kindles in the Vine,
And many a Garden by the Water blows.

An *andante comodo* in B major and ¾ time, the movement
is based on the theme heard from the beginning played by a clarinet. This lengthy clarinet solo foreshadows the extraordinarily
effective flute solo of *A Night Piece* (1922). The melody continues to the end, sometimes with an opposing countermelody. An
insistent but gentle rhythm, faintly like the thrum of an *oud* is
heard throughout. No onerous orientalisms are introduced, although some augmented seconds sound in the melody (example
26a). An exotic effect is achieved by the sudden shift in harmony
from tonic major to V⁷ of the lowered mediant and back to the
tonic. Yet, every sound is set forth subtly. The mood of elegiac
resignation is convincingly created.

The second movement is in ternary form. The outer sections
are on the verse:

They say the Lion and the Lizard keep
The Courts where Jamshyd gloried and drank deep:
And Bahrám, that great Hunter —the Wild Ass
Stamps o'er his Head, but cannot break his Sleep.

The music is an *allegro deciso* in B minor and ¾ time. The
languorousness of the previous piece is supplanted by an aggres-
sive, thrusting sound. Much of the movement is given over to
the full orchestra playing of a brawny, heavily stressed theme (example 26b).

The middle section meditates on the following:

Yet ah, that Spring should vanish with the Rose!
That Youth's sweet-scented manuscript should close!
The Nightingale that in the branches sang,
Ah whence, and whither flown again, who knows!

The tempo is slower; the key changes to E-flat minor. Harp
and strings quietly support a solo clarinet (example 26c), a solo
flute, and finally a violin solo.

The third movement is a lyrical reflection on the lines:

> A Book of Verses underneath the Bough,
> A Jug of Wine, a Loaf of Bread—and Thou
>   Beside me singing in the Wilderness—
> Oh, Wilderness were Paradise enow!

It is a muted pastorale. A moderate tempo in A major prevails. The melody, marked dolce, begins in the violins and violas (example 26d). Later it is heard in the woodwinds and brass before the theme dwindles to nothing in the high strings. An upward octave skipping figure of accompaniment on the tone E is the constant companion of the melody.

The fourth part contemplates first the verse:

> Yon rising Moon that looks for us again—
> How oft hereafter will she wax and wane;
>   How oft hereafter rising look for us
> Through this same Garden—and for *one* in vain!

The Tempo is an *andantino ben marcato* in ⁶/₈ time. A vamp on the E-minor chord in harp and pizzicato strings introduces a soothing theme played by solo cello and French horn. The music swells louder and louder to *ff*, then returns to quietness and the E-minor chord.

The next section of the movement is on the verse:

> Waste not your Hour, nor in the vain pursuit
> Of This and That endeavor and dispute;
>   Better be jocund with the fruitful Grape
> Than sadden after none, or bitter, Fruit.

Very fast, in ¾ time and B major, a sprightly diversion emerges (example 26e). Near its close appears a recollection of the melody of the first movement, played very loudly. Now the piece restores the initial mood and replays the andantino theme to the shimmering accompaniment of divided strings playing tremolo (example 26f). A very soft horn intonation of the tone E, then a chord in the flutes and clarinets, next high string harmonics on the tone E, a final pizzicato on a low E, and the entire composition reaches its expressive completion.

Wherever it was played, the composition met an enthusiastic audience response. This was especially so in Boston, as on the occasion of its performance by Max Fiedler and the Boston Symphony, in April 1912:

> When the applause swelled after each movement . . . Mr. Fiedler indicated the composer with a gesture and a smile, and when all four were done the audience called him twice or thrice to his feet. For the second time within two months, at the concert of the Cecilia and now at this Symphony Concert, Mr. Foote has deservedly received such reward from his audience.[68]

Ossip Gabrilovitch did the work with the Detroit Symphony in March 1919. He wrote to Foote that "they made a great hit with the audience as well as with the press and with the orchestra, to say nothing of the conductor. It is really most poetic and distinguished music, such as is seldom created in these days."[69] So popular was the piece that John Philip Sousa, who was a friend of Foote, arranged two of the movements for band and played them frequently in a "strikingly effective" arrangement.[70]

Through this composition, Foote had become as popular as any American composer could have hoped to be with local audiences.

Notes

1. See Frederick Edward Kopp, "Arthur Foote: American Composer and Theorist" (Ph.D. diss., Eastman School of Music, University of Rochester, 1957), 82; Arthur Foote, *An Autobiography* (Norwood, Mass.: Plimpton Press, 1946), 57.

2. Arthur Foote, Scrapbook III, Boston Public Library, shelf no. **ML. 46. F65.

3. See Wilma Reid Cipolla, *A Catalog of the Works of Arthur Foote*, Bibliographies in American Music 6 (Detroit: Information Coordinators, 1980),

4. See Nicholas E. Tawa, *The Way to Tin Pan Alley* (New York: Schirmer, 1990), 172-75.

5.   Doric Alviani, "The Choral Church Music of Arthur William Foote" (S.M.D. diss., Union Theological Seminary, 1962), 25.

6.   Foote, *An Autobiography*, 56.

7.   Allen A. Brown, Scrapbook VI, Boston Public Library, shelf no. **M. 304.1.

8.   Benjamin Lambord, in *Music in America*, ed. Arthur Farwell and W. Dermot Darby, The Art of Music 4 (New York: National Society of Music, 1915), 357.

9.   Alviani, "The Choral Church Music of Arthur William Foote," 66–67, 77.

10.   A clipping, on which Foote has written the date "1899," now in the Arthur Foote Collection, Williams College, Williamstown, Massachusetts.

11.   Foote, *An Autobiography*, 92-93.

12.   "Music Hall: Boston Symphony Orchestra," *Boston Evening Transcript*, 6 February 1893, 5.

13.   The program of 28 April 1892 is found in Arthur Foote, Scrapbook II, Boston Public Library, shelf no. **ML. 46.F65.

14.   On the verso of the cover, Foote wrote: "Bound December 1892, 2 West Cedar Street." The score is part of the bound volume *Foote. Op. 24, 25, 28*, at the Harvard Musical Association, shelf no. 05.1 F738.1.

15.   "Music Hall: Boston Symphony Orchestra," 5.

16.   Katharine Foote Raffy dated the diary excerpt "Feb. 1893" and sent it to Arthur Foote II on 25 May 1953. It is now in the Arthur Foote Collection.

17.   "American Composers of the First Rank," *Music* 2 (1892): 502. The article was probably written by the editor, W. S. B. Mathews.

18.   W. S. B. Mathews, "Reviews and Notices," *Music* 2 (1892): 525.

19.   "Chickering Hall: Mr. Foote's Concert," *Boston Evening Transcript*,15 April 1893, 7.

20.   Una L. Allen, "The Composer's Corner, No. 18 – Arthur Foote" *The Musician*, March 1931, 31.

21.   Douglas Shand-Tucci, *Boston Bohemia, 1881–1900* (Amherst: University of Massachusetts Press), 261, 340.

22.   In the spring of 1994, a few other Americans and I were in western Turkey, standing on a dirt road before a caravansary – a massive unornamented edifice surrounding a dilapidated inner court that was unpromisingly situated in a barren, waterless, unpopulated region. From the west, a dilapidated automobile and two battered, open-backed trucks filled with peasants dressed in native attire came up in a cloud of dust,

stopped for a moment to allow assorted country people to look us over, then proceeded east. Somehow Foote's music came to mind and seemed to fit the scene, despite the fact that the composer had never been further east than central Europe.

23. Arthur Foote, Scrapbook II, Boston Public Library, shelf no. **ML. 46.F65.

24. The first was published in *The Church Organist*, ed. C. H. Morse (Boston: White-Smith, 1893), 15–16; the second in *Vox Organi* , ed. Dudley Buck, vol. 4 (New York: Millet, 1896), 495.

25. Kopp in "Arthur Foote: American Composer and Theorist," 82, and Cipolla in *A Catalog of the Works of Arthur Foote*, 74, say the first performance was given by Foote and the Kneisels in Boston on 16 February 1891; and a second took place in Cambridge on 21 April 1892. Scrapbook II includes the program for a concert that took place at 8 P.M. on 21 April 1891 at Harvard's Brattle Hall. In the program there is the information "Manuscript. First Public Performance." Nevertheless, John Sullivan Dwight reviewed a public performance, possibly on 16 February, on page 7 of the *Boston Evening Transcript*, 21 February 1891.

26. Louis C. Elson, *The History of American Music*, rev. to 1925 by Arthur Elson (New York: Macmillan, 1925), 189; John Sullivan Dwight, "The Kneisel Quartet," *Boston Evening Transcript* (21 February 1891), 7.

27. Foote, Scrapbook II.

28. Dwight, "The Kneisel Quartet," 7.

29. Ibid.

30. "Chickering Hall: Mr. Foote's Concert," *Boston Evening Transcript*, 15 April 1893, 7.

31. Nancy E. Miller, notes to the recording *Aaron Copland and Arthur Foote: Chamber Music with Flute*, Northeastern NR 227-CD.

32. "Chickering Hall: The Kneisel Quartet," *Boston Evening Transcript*, 13 February 1894, 5.

33. In Allen A. Brown, Scrapbook, Boston Public Library, shelf no. **M. Cab. 1.38.

34. "Association Hall: The Kneisel Quartet," *Boston Evening Transcript*,1 February 1898, 5.

35. Clippings of the reviews are in Arthur Foote, Scrapbook III, Boston Public Library, shelf no. **ML. 46.F65.

36. Ibid.; Foote has written at the top of the clipping "Cincinnati June 99–."

37. A clipping of the review is in Scrapbook III.

38.   This is taken from a program for a concert given on 4 January 1901 in Pittsburgh, which omitted the Air and Intermezzo. The notes printed with the program and prepared by Foote are in the Foote Scrapbook III.

39.   Ibid.

40.   *Foote. Op. 24, 25, 28*, Harvard Musical Association, shelf no. 05.1 F738.1.

41.   Van Wyck Brooks, *New England Indian Summer: 1865–1915* (New York: Dutton, 1940), 25, 303, 435; Morris Carter, *Isabella Steward Gardner and Fenway Court* (Boston: Houghton Mifflin, 1925), 93–94.

42.   "Music Hall: Boston Symphony Orchestra," *Boston Evening Transcript*,4 March 1895, 5.

43.   *Boston Symphony Orchestra Programme* no. 10 (23–24 January 1891), 389, 391-92.

44.   William Foster Apthorp, *By the Way*, vol. 1 (Boston: Copeland & Day, 1898), 20.

45.   Clipping on which Foote has written "Cincinnati. Jan. 1895," in Foote, Scrapbook II.

46.   The letter may be found in Foote, Scrapbook III.

47.   Arthur Foote, *Letters Collected by Arthur Foote: Gift to the library in memory of Arthur Foote, April 16, 1940*, Spaulding Library, New England Conservatory of Music, letter no. 113.

48.   This quotation is from notes on the work, "Cello Concerto in G Minor, Opus 33 (1887/1893) by Arthur Foote," dated May 1986, sent to me by Douglas Moore on 2 December 1994.

49.   Foote, *Letters Collected by Arthur Foote*, letter no. 179. The letter is actually dated "March 6" without the year given.

50.   The telegraph is in Foote, Scrapbook II.

51.   The quoted review is reproduced from Moore, "Cello Concerto in G Minor, Opus 33."

52.   Ibid.

53.   For my comments, I have referred to the copy of the manuscript that Douglas Moore has kindly supplied me with. It shows some corrections and additions entered by the composer. Summy-Birchard, which took over the Schmidt firm, deposited this manuscript in the Fleisher Collection in Philadelphia. Moore has edited the score, comparing this manuscript with one in the New York Public Library at Lincoln Center.

54.   Douglas Moore kindly provided me with a tape of the concerto. He is the soloist with the Rochester (Minnesota) Symphony Orchestra in a concert given in 1983.

55. Arthur Foote, "A Bostonian Remembers," *Musical Quarterly* 23 (1937): 41.

56. Foote, *An Autobiography*, 82–83.

57. "Music Hall: Boston Symphony Orchestra," *Boston Evening Transcript*, 9 March 1896, 7.

58. All of these reviews are in Foote, Scrapbook II.

59. "Music," *New York Times Sunday Magazine Supplement*, 2 May 1897, 15.

60. These reviews are found in Foote, Scrapbook III. The quotation is from a Cincinnati review, the writer and newspaper unknown, but identified in Foote's handwriting with "Cincinnati, Jan. 1900."

61. It is a subject that Chadwick might have thought up for his Symphony No. 2 (1883-85) or *Symphonic Sketches* (1895–1904).

62. The program is in Foote, Scrapbook III, close to a report on a November 1898 blizzard that prevented him from getting to his church and an announcement that some quatrains from the *Rubáiyát* had been issued by Town Talk Printers.

63. This information comes from Foote, Scrapbook III.

64. *Boston Symphony Programme* no.31, 19–20 April 1912, 1436.

65. Foote, *An Autobiography*, 54.

66. Ms Mus 24 (1-3), no. 3, in the Boston Public Library.

67. This comment on effect and means may be found in the review of an all-Foote concert conducted by Fabien Sevitzky, in the *Boston Evening Transcript*, 9 December 1935, 4. The *Four Character Pieces* was featured.

68. "The Symphony Concert," *Boston Evening Transcript*, 20 April 1912, pt. 2, 14.

69. Letter to Arthur Foote, 81 Green Street, Brookline, from Ossip Gabrilovitch, 1065 Cass Ave., Detroit, 25 March 1919, in *A.F. 1913*, Harvard Musical Association, shelf no. F738 Vol. 2.

70. Foote, *An Autobiography*, 59, 110–11. See also, "News of Music and Plays," *Boston Evening Transcript* (13 April 1912), 2.

Part IV

The Modern Era
(1901-1937)

9

Living in the Twentieth Century

For most of the first two decades of the new century, Arthur Foote remained one of America's best known and most admired art composers. He received a letter from Chicago on 17 February 1910 addressed to:

> Mr. Arthur Foote
> Celebrated Composer of Music
> 2 W. Cedar Street
> Boston, Mass.

Foote, of course, had moved to Dedham over a decade before. The letter was finally forwarded to his studio on Newbury St.[1]

His prominence was also attested by the Guild of Organists, "on the happy termination of my pneumonia in 1915, by causing my Festival March to be played in churches throughout the country on Thanksgiving of that year."[2] In addition, there is the plaster cast of one of Foote's hands that Isabella Stewart Gardner acquired, now at Fenway Court (the Gardner Museum), and the bas-relief of Foote "that Bashka Paeva, a young Russian sculptress," made "of the eminent composer," in 1917.[3]

Audiences also esteemed him for admirable personal qualities that he disclosed during concerts. One incident, which occurred during a concert in Peoria, Illinois, on 7 June 1905 caused considerable favorable comment:

Mr. Foote earned the thanks of everyone present by the superb manner in which he kept his head and his audience in a most trying position. For without warning and with the suddenness of a cyclone, the electric light failed and the church was wrapped in total darkness, just as Mr. Foote had played his third measure in the Handel fugue. Evidently not a whit disturbed, Mr. Foote continued calmly with his work, never missing one note and finished his group of three numbers all the time in the most intense blackness. His reward amounted to an ovation, and while nothing was said, yet everyone knew that a serious incident had been averted by his superb presence of mind.[4]

Affiliations and Relationships

He continued his membership in the St. Botolph Club, the Tavern Club, and the Harvard Club and joined the Brae-Burn Country Club. He was still involved with the bohemian people who took up a freethinking, broadminded, and off-centered way of living. At the same time, he maintained his links with the more staid and traditional circles of Boston. He kept on making himself available for service to the world of music. Among the posts he held were those of president of the American Guild of Organists, the Cecilia Society, the South End Music School, and the Oliver Ditson Society for the Relief of Needy Musicians. In recognition of his celebrity as a composer and his tireless efforts on behalf of music in America, Trinity College (1919) and Dartmouth College (1925) gave him an honorary doctor of music degree. Moreover, he was made a member of the National Institute of Arts and Letters, and a fellow of the American Academy of Arts and Sciences.[5]

His dedication to expanding the audience for art music remained firm. While a member and president of the Cecilia Society, he cooperated with others to bring music to Bostonians with modest incomes. Wage-Earners' Concerts were started in 1891, which charged fifteen to twenty cents a ticket. The concept was appropriated from Chicago. These concerts repeated programs already presented at regular concerts. Tickets were made available through employers. Thousands of men and women, who would have been otherwise unable to attend, took advantage of this opportunity to hear art music. On 9 May 1901, after holding the office of president for three years, Foote reported at the annual meeting of the Society:

> It is a good thing that no change has been made as regards the Wage Earners' concerts. These have continued to be as much desired as ever by the audience for which they were intended. The listeners have been highly appreciative, and would have been greater in number if the hall could have been made elastic. No one can doubt that in these concerts the Cecilia is doing a good work, one in which it helps itself by helping others.[6]

As in previous years, Foote stood ready to aid or honor the composers that he valued. He helped young American composers like Henry Hadley and Frederick Shepherd Converse to get ahead in their profession. In the spring of 1901, he, Lang, Chadwick, and Charles Eliot Norton were members of the executive committee that guided the Giuseppe Verdi International Monument Fund. Its goal was to raise money for a Verdi memorial. J. Montgomery Sears was the treasurer.[7]

Needy musicians, the memory of respected composers, boys and girls from poor families in search of music lessons, and aid to destitute Poland were all causes he championed. On 14 February 1915, the noted opera singer Marcella Sembrich wrote to him from New York: "Though we were very sorry not to see you at my recital in Boston, I wish to tell you how much we appreciate the help you are giving our poor country by your lectures." On 23 April 1918, Mme. Szumowska Adamowska wrote from Cambridge thanking Foote for his generous donations to the "Friends of Poland," on behalf of "Polish sufferers."[8]

His affiliations with Harvard continued as strong as ever. Serving on the committee that acted as overseer to the department of music, he had urged throughout the nineties that a better physical space be provided for the music programs. In 1903 and 1904, he joined John Knowles Paine, Walter Spalding, and the Pierian Sodality in supporting the construction of a new music building. Foote was elected president of the newly formed Harvard Musical Union in 1906. The union was a federation of Har-

vard's music students, alumni, and societies, whose aim was to
support the music department and promote the proposed new
building. Success came in 1910, when James Loeb donated
$85,000 to the cause.[9] In 1903 President Charles Eliot of Harvard
became concerned over budgetary shortages and was urged to
economize by cutting funds for the music department, in particular, dismissing composer Frederick Shepherd Converse, who was
an instructor in music composition. Foote steadfastly opposed
the dismissal. On 7 January 1904, Eliot sent him a letter stating:

> We shall keep Mr. Converse if we possibly can, and I think
> we can. The promotion and the new appointment in the
> Department of Music were two of the causes of our defi-
> cits for the last year and this current year; but the Depart-
> ment is growing and improving, and Professor Paine is
> getting feeble.[10]

Foote and Walter Spalding of the Harvard music faculty col-
laborated on books of musical theory. Their highly successful
Modern Harmony in Its Theory and Practice was published by
Schmidt in 1905, revised in 1924, and revised again in 1936. *A
Key to the 510 Exercises in Modern Harmony and Its Theory
and Practice* came out in 1907 and in a revised edition in 1936,
both editions issued by Schmidt.

Foote was still busy at his church job in 1903 when the organ he had been playing, (which he had always considered an in-
adequate instrument) was finally replaced with a new
three-manual organ built by the Hutchings-Votey Organ Company. It was located at the opposite end of the church from the old
organ. The old instrument was kept where it was. A plan to connect the two instruments was never carried out.[11] Though he was
delighted to have the new instrument, he was at the same time
debating whether he should give up his church position. Attending the many choir rehearsals and church services may have begun to prove irksome, and in April 1910, he decided to retire
from church work:

> The organ was perhaps secondary to composition and pi-
> anoforte teaching when activities came to be lessened. . . .
> I can see that the sacrifice had to be made. When I left

> them the church people were generous to me in their
> kind words, and gave me besides a handsome sum of
> money. A year or two later I gave the money to Courtenay
> Pollock for one of his beautiful portrait busts of myself.[12]

His old friendships continued strong. Isabella Gardner had
stood as godmother for his daughter Katharine and through gifts
and invitations to her home maintained her friendship with the
Footes. When her new home, Fenway Court, was finished in
1902, the Footes were among the first to be invited there. Fenway
Court was very much like an Italian Renaissance palace, abrim
with precious paintings, sculptures, tapestries, and furnishings.
In his Scrapbook III, at the Boston Public Library, we find the
printed program of a special holiday concert given at Fenway
Court on New Year's Day, 1903, which he had attended. Typical of
his feelings about the music-making in the New World palazzo are
the sentiments contained in a note that he sent to Mrs. Gardner
on 12 March 1906, saying, "I really can't help it—I must write this
to tell you that I think I never heard a string quartet before last
Saturday. The marvelous beauty of the sound in your music hall
was hard to believe. I am very grateful that I was there."[13] When
he completed his Trio no. 2 in B major, for Piano, Violin, and Cello, op. 65, in 1908, Foote was pleased to give it its initial performance with the Kneisels at Fenway Court on 8 December 1908.[14]

As wholeheartedly as Foote acknowledged kindnesses done
him by others, he also extended the same courtesy to them.
When the Metropolitan planned a grand farewell celebration in
honor of Marcella Sembrich, a friend who was a famous singer at
the Metropolitan Opera, on 6 February 1909, he was one of the
first to volunteer his services for the occasion. In the Boston
Public Library are two letters that he sent to Allan A. Brown concerning this event. One says: "There is to be a Boston Committee
(of a dozen or so) to cooperate with the New York Committee in
regard to a testimonial to Marcella Sembrich. May we have your
name?" The second one reads: "I thank you for the N. Y. Committee for your kindness in sending the check. It was quite enough
for you to give us support of your name, but I thank you also for
your [?]ness in this."[15]

His warm professional connections with conductors and
performers are established by two letters that he received from

conductors of the Boston Symphony. One was from Max Fiedler, sent to him on 4 December 1910:

> How good of you to write me that card. It is true: I miss it when you don't peep in and have a talk with me. I was sad to feel that Tschaikowsky's orchestration is beginning to fade a little—sometimes it does not seem clever. (Saint Peter Ilyitsch forgive me, because you know I love you!) The slow movement suffered a bit by the uncertain and timid Hess-horn; I hope he will get up his courage for N. York. The Valse was perhaps finer than formerly . . . I think the Brigg-Fair had poetic spots; I fear the orchestra found it tiresome; funny: the musicians are *always against* a new piece!
>
> Hoping that the Trio went well and that you felt happy, with cordial greetings, yours, Max Fiedler.[16]

The second letter was sent to Foote by Serge Koussevitzky on 29 December 1936. In December, Koussevitzky and the Boston Symphony were in New York, where they performed his Suite in E Major, op. 63. The conductor writes to say he is sorry that Foote could not come to New York to hear his work performed but understood how much the trip would have been a strain on his health (Foote was 83 years of age and frail):

> I am deeply touched by your letter and thank you for your kind words. I should be honored to have a work dedicated to me by an American composer for whom I have a professional regard and admiration.[17]

It is not clear to what work Koussevitzky is referring.

California

A special distinction came to Foote when Julius R. Weber, a person with whom he was not acquainted, invited him to give a series of summer lectures at the University of California at Berkeley in 1911. He accepted, prepared himself to give twenty-four talks on the history of music, and left for California at the end of May. The talks, written out in longhand, are held by the Boston Public Library.[18] An account of his trip to California is found in his auto-biography.[19] His activities in California tell us a great deal about the man and his contemporary status.

Weber, two former pupils, and an old friend, H. J. Stewart, met Foote and installed him at the comfortable Cloyne Court in Berkeley, where he stayed for two months. He was to teach two courses at the university: Music 10, on the history of music; Music 11, on harmony, counterpoint, and composition. He was also to give a few talks about playing and teaching the piano. As soon as he arrived, he was asked for his opinion about the state of music in the Western world. Foote called it a period of transition and experimentation and, identified Strauss and Debussy as the chief influences. Even the most conservative musicians had to "admit that Debussy has made us all turn to and think whether every convention in music that we've been used to is worth while. And I might add, thinking is not a bad exercise." As for America and American music, "there has been a remarkable advance in the last twenty-five years in the composing of music," and the works com-posed "will stand with those of any other nation."[20]

Although he delivered his lectures in Berkeley, he visited San Francisco, especially the Loring Club, for concerts that included his compositions and for various entertainments. At his first Lor-ing Club concert, he was given a stirring welcome: "He made his appearance in the second part of the programme and when he stepped into view he was greeted with sincere and prolonged applause, for the big audience of cultured music-lovers had long known him from his works and his reputation."[21] Foote was also pleased to visit the Bohemian Club, whose members performed some of his compositions at their yearly forgathering at Bohemi-an Grove. California life was almost too exhausting for Foote, and when he got back to Boston, he was "pretty tired out."

A summer meeting of the California Music Teachers' Associa-tion featured his music. Thomas Nunan says that when he went to the event, he noticed the attendance was huge. To his surprise, he saw the "famous Foote . . . contentedly occupying some of the 'standing room only' that was left for late arrivals at the session." The composer refused to take advantage of the special privileges accorded him.[22] A special service of his church music was given on a Sunday at the Unitarian Church, with Foote at the organ. He spent a few days in Los Angeles with the Guild of Organists, helping examine candidates for associate and fellowship in the guild. Immediately thereafter, he assisted in founding a California chapter of the Guild of Organists.

The lecture series attracted around five-hundred people, all of whom were friendly, interested, and eager to learn. Foote's classes were "larger than those listening to any of the other departments." In these lectures he spoke up strongly for American composers:

> It is some time since people asked "who reads an American book?" and now we are showing that in painting, sculpture and music we have an art that can hold its own with any: but this in spite of drawbacks; without being Chauvinistic, one may feel strongly that we have convictions that make it more difficult for the composer here than in countries which give more encouragement. Leaving out the matter of official aid, the general public in Russia, France and other European countries does not look with mistrust upon its own musicians, as for a long while was the case here (though things are fairer today).[23]

He also spoke about two influential contemporaries—Strauss and Debussy. Strauss, he observed, had enormous ability; his music was powerful and effective. However, at times he forced his musical ideas to conform to some nonmusical scheme he had concocted, as in *Zarathustra* and *Sinfonia Domestica*, thus pushing beyond musical and artistic limits. With *Salome* and *Electra*, Strauss's music had reached a point "beyond which no one could pass, in complexity, demand on one's endurance, and indifference to beauty." Debussy's influence had been "in some respects for the good," although Foote questioned the free use of consecutive fifths, augmented triads, and whole-tone effects, which seemed to him pushed to extremes. Some of the impressionistic pictures Debussy tried to paint in his piano music "seems silly to many of us, with the bravado of the small boy who is naughty, but there are piano pieces and songs that are singularly beautiful."[24]

Whenever Foote had served on program committees, he had always struggled against other committee members' inclination to put the American composer on a level below that of Europeans. "Our composers must conquer their position by good work, and they are doing it, but they should not be held back because they are our own; we should not give their music, however, because it is by Americans, but if it is worthy, and then put it in programmes along with Beethoven, or Schumann, or Strauss, and let it take its chance."[25]

At the end of July, Thomas Nunan interviewed Foote about the relation of American to European music. He said that it would be parasitic for us to continue depending on the music of other nations, although it was unavoidable at first. "Natural or not, it is the fact and we cannot get away from it. Thirty years ago we had little music of our own and we had to get everything from Europe. Now we have a great deal of music of good quality. We have a small band of good composers and the future is full of promise."[26]

Nunan said that Californians found Foote to be "one of America's foremost authorities on harmony." A class of students grounded in music received his instruction on the techniques of musical composition. He presented his ideas intelligibly and without fuss, all in his eastern manner of speaking. Foote made "even the most prosaic subject entertaining." Auditors were fascinated by his criticism of harmony books for their rigid, incorrect and childish definitions, and for the "perfect mass of rubbish" that they contained, which had been "passed along from one to another."[27] Asked if music students should go to Europe for further study, he replied: "The romance of life and study abroad is the principal advantage in going to Europe, but the real education can be obtained just as well in this country."[28]

He was supposed to return to California in 1914, but appendicitis prevented his return and he sent David Stanley Smith instead. He was even asked to remain permanently in California and become head of the music department at the university:

> I had so fallen in love with California and the life there, everything I felt about me was so sympathetic and hopeful, and the opportunity for constructive work was so great and inviting that it was hard to decline. But the work

ahead in that case would have been tremendous, demanding a younger man than I, and the roots had gone too deep during the more than fifty years to make transplanting best, while the day was soon coming when work ought to be lessened and not increased, if one were able to bring that about. I have therefore never regretted the decision to remain in Boston, although I had really a strong desire to go to Berkeley for the remaining years of a professional life.[29]

Thomas Nunan reports in the *San Francisco Examiner* that the university tried to prevail on Foote to remain in California in order to build "a great department of music," but Foote refused, though the "ideal man" for the position and an eminent educator who had generated enthusiasm for musical study through his lectures. Wistfully, Mr. Nunan leaves off by saying: "He is the first man I have known to display the ability of getting all the local musical factions together in harmonious relationship"—an aptitude that tells us a great deal about the man.[30]

One of his last acts that season was to endorse Henry Hadley as the conductor for the newly formed San Francisco orchestra. In a letter sent to the *Examiner*, he writes: "We must also be glad that the directors have found the right man in an American."[31] At last, he was able to return to his Dedham home, which "looked more lovely than ever in midsummer."[32]

Resuming His Life in Greater Boston

However much he loved his house in Dedham, while in California he learned of a house for sale at 81 Green Street, Coolidge Corner, Brookline, and told his wife to buy it. On 7 December 1911, the Footes sold the Dedham property, with the Boston Safe Deposit and Trust Company named as purchaser.[33] Early in 1912, the Footes moved to Green Street. He claims several reasons for the move, but gives only one—the house was much closer to Boston and only a half-hour's walk brought him into the city. A few months later, he bought a farm in South Hampton, New Hampshire ("twelve acres of varied southern upland . . . three miles from Amesbury, Massachusetts"). Called Rest Harrow, the proper-

ty was adjacent to the Massachusetts state line. Owing to his serious bout with appendicitis, however, he did not actually get to
the farm until 1914. That was the year of the great Salem fire
("which we watched from where we were, twenty-five miles
away") and the start of World War I. He had no respite from ill
health. The next year, he came down with pneumonia, which almost ended his life and forced him to limit his future activities.
He gave up piano performances and restricted his teaching work
to mornings. He gave up his studio at 6 Newbury Street to teach
at home.[34] He did not recover his health until the end of 1916.
An article dated 19 January 1917 in *Musical America*, states:

> Mr. Foote has completely recovered from the critical op-
> eration and illness which he went through last spring and
> is now busily teaching at his home in Greene [sic] Street,
> Brookline, and doing that composing for which he finds
> time. He is still keenly interested in public musical affairs
> in this city and is a familiar figure at many concerts.[35]

In 1916, his much loved daughter Katharine, left for France
as member of the Voluntary Aid Detachment, and worked in hospitals caring for wounded soldiers. While at Tours, France, she
met a patient, Henri Raffy, who would eventually become her
husband. Her father experienced overwhelming joy when she returned safely home in 1918.[36]

Katharine had grown into young womanhood and was still
the apple of her father's eye. Proudly, he had saved a brief newspaper item written by Katharine in 1904, which extolled a virtue
that he believed in. Captioned "Faithfulness to Duty," her piece
describes "a most lovable and affectionate" St. Bernard named
Fanny, who was watchdog for the "Country Club near Dedham."
She had had nine puppies, but knowing the trust placed on her,
she divided her time between her duties and mothering, "going
up and down four or five times during the night."[37]

In 1910, Katharine was described as a "soprano in one of the
Dedham churches."[38] Arthur Foote's friendship with Isabella
Stewart Gardner was immensely strengthened by his daughter's
affection for her "Marraine," the French word for godmother. In
August 1913, when Katharine was at Rest Harrow, she wrote to
Isabella Gardner, inviting her to visit. Mrs. Gardner wrote back,

the envelope postmarked "Aug. 12, 1913," and addressed to "Miss Katharine Foote, South Hampton, N.H. Near the line between Mass. and N.H." She looked forward to visiting Rest Harrow and thanked Katharine for offering to fetch her from Newburyport if she went by train. She finishes with: "I think some Newburyport train leaving Boston about 10 a.m. would be rather nice."[39] After Katharine's return from France, she saw through to publication, in 1919, her *Letters from Two Hospitals by an American V.A.D.* and sent Mrs. Gardner a copy. After her godmother wrote to say that she enjoyed the book, a delighted Katharine thanked her for reading it and said that the family would be staying in South Hampton until mid-October. If Mrs. Gardner wanted to reach them, "our post office, telephone and telegraph is Amesbury, Mass." One of the warmest letters Katharine ever wrote to her godmother confesses her newfound love for and expectation of marriage to Henri Raffy, which she is reluctant to discuss with her parents. Indeed, there is reason to suspect that her father was not very happy about their relationship. Arthur knew little about Henri's background and probably feared that Henri's poor health would make him a burden on his daughter. Katharine harbored no reservations when she said to her godmother, on 13 May 1920:

> My dear Marraine:
>
> As I told you, I am not telling any one of it—I could not have this great record in my heart, and not share it with you—and that you are happy about it adds unspeakably to my joy. Because, my dearest Marraine, as I have grown older, I have learned always better, how wonderful and sweet and kind and full of love and devotion you are. You can now know all you have meant to my life, for though I have tried to tell you, words are so weak when one feels all that I do about you.
>
> And so, that I am going to do something which makes you happy, is such great joy to me.
>
> I am sending you some pictures of Cahors and a letter of Henri's, all of which you can keep until I see you again. I feel as though you would get such a clear impression of him through the letter,—and the writing isn't as bad as it looks.

If you have the little blue book of my letters at hand
[*Letters from Two Hospitals by an American V.A.D.*], you
will find he appears on p. 14, 27 and 103.[40]

The decision to marry was soon made and on 27 July she
tells Mrs. Gardner that Henri, an "inherently modest" person,
was stationed with the Allied occupying force in Constantinople,
where she will go to get married. She left in December 1920. Her
father says the departure brought a great change. The Green
Street house was found to be too large for him and his wife.
Apartment buildings were going up all around,[41] so they thought
they would try apartment living and moved into an apartment at
102 Naples Road, just a few streets down from Green Street. Unfortunately, they soon found the move had been a mistake.
Apartment living was noisy and lacked the privacy they desired.
In 1925, they moved to their last residence, 158 Ridge Avenue,
Newton, which was fairly close to Newton Centre: "In our new
house we were practically on the edge of the real country away
from bricks, with sun and air and lovely views; and one felt that
as soon as one got there the city was left behind."[42]

Prior to their move to Ridge Avenue, the now married
Katharine wrote to Isabella Gardner from Constantinople on 20
March 1922. She says that her mother told her about the many
presents, including a cashmere shawl and an embroidered Japanese linen costume, from Mrs. Gardner that were being held for
her by her parents, pending her return. The return was immi-
nent. She and Henri Raffy were coming to live near her parents.
Unfortunately, her husband had not yet been able to shake off
his persistent tropical malaria.

Arthur Foote, that summer, "went up from the farm . . . to
Providence to meet the Fabre Line steamer 'Canada,' bringing
Katharine and her husband . . . [back] to Rest Harrow, where
they were to live permanently."[43] Perhaps Katharine's intention
was to bring about an improvement in Henri's health through
country living. We learn from a letter Mrs. Gardner sent to
Katharine on 30 November 1923 that the Raffys were trying out
farm life: "Thursday was made doubly thankful by the glorious
eggs from Amesbury. May good things come to you as you deserve, and, dear child, please always think kindly and lovingly of
me."[44] Sometime in the late twenties, the Raffys moved to Kezar

Falls, Maine, where they raised chickens and cultivated a tree farm. Henri died around 1954; Katharine on 5 March 1970.[45]

Pedagogy

In 1913 Oscar Sonneck gave a presentation, a survey of the state of American music that undoubtedly had musicians like Foote in mind:

> One has but to watch the growth, for instance, of the American Guild of Organists, with its high ideas and pretty stiff tests of efficiency, or to study the "Proceedings of the Music Teachers' National Association [Foote was an active member of both groups], to be impressed with the vigor, the knowledge, the methodical thoughtfulness of the new generation of the American musician and educator, who, though professedly in music as a business, is nevertheless an idealist. Not a dreamer, but a man who has visions of his peculiar country's peculiar needs and strives after these ideals with good old-fashioned practical common horse-sense.[46]

Foote was busy collecting and preparing keyboard music for publication by Schmidt during the new century: an *Etude Album* (1912), *Thirty-Five Two-Part Studies for Independent Part-Playing* (1913), *First-Year Bach: Twenty Compositions by J. S. Bach* (1914), *First-Year Handel: Twelve Compositions by G. F. Handel (1915)*, *Ten Sonatas for the Pianoforte* by Beethoven (1917), *Nine Sonatas for the Pianoforte* by Mozart (1918), *Twelve Studies for the Pianoforte* by Cramer (1918), *Instructive Album: Nineteen Short Piano Pieces* (1921) and augmented to twenty-two pieces in 1927, and *Ten Classical Pieces* (1932). All of this music had an educational purpose.

Foote authored *Some Practical Things in Piano Playing* (1909) and *Modulation and Related Harmonic Questions* (1919), both published by Schmidt. In addition, there was the unpublished "A Summary of the Principles of Harmony," which he wrote in 1932 for the instruction of his grandnephew Arthur Foote II.[47] Moses Smith states that the tract of 1909 on piano playing helped cure him of several weaknesses:

> It was not, very likely, that Foote had anything new or revolutionary to write on these subjects, but rather that his exposition of them was so clear, well reasoned, and forcefully simple.
>
> Those qualities, which are so apparent in his music and in his prose style, were also the marks of his pedagogy. In the latter case they were probably due to what are ordinarily regarded as the disadvantages of his kind of educational training. Remember that Foote was not only an eminent American musician who had had no European study; he was also largely self-taught.

Smith further states that Foote had a "first-rate intellect," which allowed him "to approach the subject of piano technic . . . with open eyes, ears, and muscles; and by dint of his hard thinking and recognition of the basis of his own difficulties he was thus enabled to pose the problems in their very essence before others similarly troubled."[48]

Foote had been urged at various times in the past to teach at the New England Conservatory of Music. He had feared to do so because he preferred to be his own master. After much persuasion from Chadwick, the head of the Conservatory, Foote finally agreed to teach there week-day mornings. In one place in his autobiography, he gives the date as 1921, but in another place he gives it as 1923, and he adds that in 1924 he commenced giving ten lectures a year on piano playing and teaching. This confusion of dates led me to Patrick Maxfield, catalog librarian at the New England Conservatory, who helped me to check on the dates. We found that Foote was first mentioned in the school's *Bulletin* of August 1920, which reports that he is to be a new faculty member and will offer "a special lecture course in Pianoforte Pedagogy." The school's catalogue for 1920–21 lists him as on the faculty and lecturer on "Piano Pedagogy." The *Bulletin* of October 1921 states that for the 1921–22 academic year, Frederick Shepherd Converse will give a new lecture course on "Musical Appreciation," free to students and scheduled for Thursdays at one o'clock. Foote's lecture course in "Pianoforte Pedagogy" would alternate with Converse's.[49] Presumably, the Foote course was also free. The 1922–23 catalogue enters him as not only giving the "Pianoforte Pedagogy" course but also teaching piano and on the applied-music faculty. After Maxfield had made an examination of all students graduating from the school, he concluded that Foote's piano students numbered about two a year and were majoring in pedagogy rather than piano performance. The last listing of one of his piano students occurs in the 1935 roll of graduates. Finally, the catalogue for 1935–36 includes a course description of "Pianoforte Pedagogy";

> Survey of technique (relaxation, arm-weight, finger-training, scales, arpeggios, double thirds, sixths, octaves, chords); good and bad habits, fingering. Phrasing and slurring; uses of the three pedals; touch (staccato, legato); rhythmical problems; how to learn to play expressively; the teaching of children. This is all with special reference to teaching. Mr. Foote, *one hour weekly for ten weeks, first half-year.*
>
> All pianoforte students intending to be candidates for the Junior Examination in any school year must attend these lectures from the beginning of the first semester.
>
> A fee of ten dollars will be charged for this course to students not pursuing the full Pianoforte Normal Course.[50]

Redfern Mason, in the *Boston Evening Transcript*, mentions the valuable criticism Foote gave to students at the conservatory. The teacher's commentaries were offered as fatherly counsel and without malice or for the sake of faultfinding:

> He could sum up the merits and demerits of a student in a few pithy words that told the truth and did not hurt. Horatio Parker found fault with MacDowell's "Indian Suite." "It has no Indian blood in it," he exclaimed. Foote said nothing; but his silence suggested that, when he reached home, he might make a few significant remarks to his beloved daughter.[51]

The Man and the Musician

To the people who knew him, the postwar Foote showed consistency in the high aims he kept in view, steady determination in the completion of what he had set out to do, and dedication to being a worthy musician. In addition, "loyalty was part of his nature," possibly carried "to a Quixotic excess." The Ditson publishing firm wanted him to edit a book of American songs, but he refused, saying: "I thank you for the honor you offer me, but I have never done any work editorially or offered my compositions to any publisher but Arthur P. Schmidt. I have been loyal to him from the beginning and I shall be loyal to him to the end." Redfern Mason insisted that qualities like these were essential for understanding the man. Mason also said:

> Arthur Foote had a trait which, in the eyes of the world, is a fault. He never blew his own trumpet, he was utterly unskilled in the art of crying up his own wares. Chadwick would try to stir him up, "When I want a work produced I go to Chicago and get Stock to do it," he would say. But Foote would shake his head. As William Arms Fisher says, "He made music for the joy and the love of it." The art of self-advertisement was something he was ashamed to learn. [52]

On the occasion of Foote's eightieth birthday in 1933 Koussevitzky and the Boston Symphony played the composer's *A Night Piece*. The composer wrote to Rosalie Housman; "Koussevitzky has put a little [?] on the programme of March 10—really I feel a little shy at all these compliments: it is a 'Night-piece' (I call it) for flute and strings." [53]

Another of Foote's strong suits was tolerance—a breadth of viewpoint and open-minded position concerning tenets and practices incompatible or colliding with his own. Not for him was the rigidity that often came with more advanced age. He always acted graciously to persons with views that he found unacceptable. Everett Truette stated in 1910 that "as a man, broad-minded, sympathetic, generous, modest, and always just, he is held in the greatest esteem by all who know him." [54]

He abhorred a few things. One was the rise of German Nazism and anti-Semitism and the destruction of what he had admired in Germany. He wrote to Rosalie Housman around 1933–34 denouncing "the hostility and folly and wickedness of the present day Germany," especially for one who knew what Germany had been like forty years before. In the same letter, he disclosed his staunch Republicanism: "I don't say anything about Roosevelt and his stump speech because this would be barred from the mail if I did."[55] Foote sent a letter to Mrs. Alfred Minsky on 14 February 1934 thanking her for an interesting communication concerning Jewish nationalism. He finds it "a strange speculation to think of what might have happened if long ago your [?] people had had a country of their own." He then writes of the "insanity" in Europe, which has become a "powder keg waiting for a match—which is sure to happen." Next, he talks about "the sources of anti-Semitism (which must go a great many years back). By the way, if you have a chance hear Bloch's (it must be great, for when the Jew in him is touched, he gives his best, which is mighty fine) Jewish service for the synagogue."[56]

After Foote died, an admirer, Moses Smith, said:

> He possessed that rare combination of intelligence, knowledge, and emotional stability which enabled him to examine the basis of his dislikes, justify them to the best of his power and then, above and beyond these things, realize the possibility of error and the advisability of postponing definitive judgment. He was not a man who vacillated from one point of view to another, like a frail leaf before the wind. Neither was he one who, arrived at a belief, hardened his mind and heart into a state of rigidity. . . .
>
> At eighty he could understand and sympathize with other people's ideals even though they were remote from his own. . . . He did not presume to judge the pattern that the lives of others who came after him should take.[57]

How did Foote view himself and his career? On 14 May 1935, Arthur Foote filled out and submitted to the New England Conservatory of Music a brief "faculty biography" with information written on a form provided by the school. The person named on the questionnaire, who was requesting the data, was, ironically, someone he had once helped get his feet on the first rungs of the career ladder, "Frederick S. Converse, Dean of the Faculty." Foote dates his faculty membership from "about 1922." Asked to name those he had studied with, he writes: "Harmony with Stephen A. Emery as a boy—Later at Harvard with John K. Paine; after graduation at Harvard—with B. J. Lang, piano, organ." Asked about his professional activities, he mentions, "Piano teaching in Boston since 1876; concerts chiefly in chamber music: also piano recitals and organ recitals—two or three times with orchestra." The final question on the form concerns important positions he has held. Foote writes: "President of American Guild of Organists. President of Cecilia Society (chorus). President of South End Music School. President Ditson Society for relief of needy musicians. One of the judges for Boott prize 'composition' at Harvard for many years."

The one obvious omission from the questionnaire was mention of his occupation as a composer. An indication of how he felt about creating music is contained in a letter he had sent on 24 June 1929 to his cousin, Eliza Orne White, author of over thirty books for children, of which twenty-four are still [1996] in circulation in greater Boston libraries. In the letter, he had reviewed what had happened to both of them after adolescence:

> You, too, at that time [the end of adolescence] would have been exceedingly astonished to be told what you were to accomplish—even though you knew you had talent for writing and inclination—and I think you sometimes can hardly believe it is you from whom came so many volumes and pages. I look with consternation at my array of fat works. We have both been fortunate in finding something which we like to do, and are successful in, which also gives pleasure to our lives. For instance, I should have been but a poor lawyer.

He was saddened by the loss of a number of his Harvard classmates. Yet, "I want to be the last survivor—as your father was."[58]

Foote wrote mostly the compositions he liked to write and, with commendable integrity, only that music he thought himself capable of writing. His grandnephew, Arthur II, states, "One day near his life's end, maybe 1932 or 3, I asked him why he hadn't composed symphonies; with his characteristic modesty and honest self-evaluation, he replied, 'Because I didn't have any symphonies to write.'"[59] At no time did he consider the artist to be the ultimate judge of what he did create. In his autobiography, he admits his satisfaction with only a few of his compositions, and disquiet with a great deal of what he had written. "This is the common lot of all composers, and I have not been perhaps so great a sinner as some. We are absorbed at the moment in the work we are doing, but lose interest in it after its completion, and it is hard for the author to estimate real values."[60]

Given his unpretentiousness and self-effacement, it is curious that he compiled the several scrapbooks on his professional life, which are held by the Boston Public Library, New England Conservatory of Music, Harvard Musical Association, and Music Division of the Library of Congress. Adding this activity to his willingness to have a bust of himself made by Courtenay Pollock (although this may have been Mrs. Foote's idea), one wonders if there was at least some anxiety about being forgotten. He may also have believed that his activities mirrored significant aspects of America's cultural history. Concerning the scrapbook in Washington, there is a letter to Oliver Strunk at the Music Division dated 2 November 1935, in which he offers the library a scrapbook mainly on "Boston and also largely personal," plus the manuscript of *A Night Piece* for flute and strings. Strunk replied that the library would be pleased to receive the two items. Foote sent the material along with a note pointing out that the scrapbook was not in good condition "and it is most likely that you will really have no use for it, I fear—in which case just destroy it—It is, also, of course, largely personal. But if it is of any good, I shall be glad."[61]

As always, Arthur Foote was avoiding any appearance of assertiveness.

Musical Views

When I speak of Foote's musical conservatism vis-à-vis the advanced styles of the twentieth century, I am referring to standards and preferences that he carefully considered and tested and that comply with what he concluded were permanent values rather than short-lived vogues. Asked what he considered to be the greatest masterpieces in 1924, Foote named works like Bach's Mass in B Minor, Mozart's Symphony no. 40 in G Minor ("One of the most perfect things in existence"), Brahms's Symphony no. 1 in C Minor, Beethoven's Piano Concerto no. 5 in E-flat Major, Schumann's *Fantasie in C Major* ("To me the greatest piano work of the last 100 Years"), Palestrina's *Pope Marcellus* Mass, Gluck's *Orpheus*, Wagner's *Die Meistersinger*, and Schubert's *Erlkönig*.[62]

There also grew within him a renewed desire to exclude romantic extravagance—whether lavish emotionality, retreat into spirituality, or delirious surrender of self—from the music he created. With great trepidation he witnessed the dissociation of the newest art music from the music public. The reasons for this, he saw, were various—the strengthening of mass culture, the fading of firmly held and shared musical principles, the dismissal of art music as a manifestation of elitism by intellectuals involved with societal ills, and, most of all, the emergence of young composers disillusioned by the tawdriness of modern life and opting for the alternative of self-expression. Self-expression meant indulging in extreme dissonance, weakening tonality to the point of abolishing it, and avoiding of melody as Foote and people of his generation understood it. He witnessed composers asserting their artistic independence, indulging in diverse acts of arbitrariness, and paying the price by losing their audiences.

Too many rising composers loved dissonance for its own sake, he said. A few musicians even considered some dissonance "an agreeable concord. . . . It is the old story of the cuckoo in the other bird's nest, and the driving out of the original inhabitants." He realized that music could not return to Mozart. On the other hand, there is a question of how far and how frequently a listener could meet with discordant tones, of "whether the melodic lines justify the dissonances." So much depended on "the sensitivity and keenness of ear of the composer and on his good sense." He himself could not foresee the results or tell what innovation would last: "It is nice to keep an open mind. But it must be admitted that it is sometimes rather hard to tell the gold from the tinsel. However, let us try."[63]

Modernists, he knew, were ignoring older American compos-

ers like him and his valuation of civilized culture. He could convince few of them that he was not ossified, that he was genuinely
trying to acknowledge merit in whatever place he could detect it.
Foote was concerned that the public was being driven elsewhere
for aesthetic satisfaction, no longer seeing a connected scheme
in the evolution of the art and sensing no possibility of achieving
the rich, transcending experiences it was led to believe came
with listening. Evolution in avant-garde circles stood for a negation of all that had gone before, "for which reason it seems to me
that, for instance, Schönberg, as seen in his later works, will have
not the slightest influence nor be considered in the future as
anything but a freak. It is not fair to lump Debussy with him, for
the former writes music as hitherto conceived, and I believe will
turn out to have had at least some effect permanently on our way
of thinking."[64]

After Foote became acquainted with "the [Arnold] Schönberg
5 pieces" [the *5 Klavierstücke*, op. 23, of 1923?], he wrote to Rosalie Housman: "It seemed such a terrible waste of immense
learning, cleverness and will power—to result in absolute piffle—
that's the worst of it—(or almost the worst)."[65] Debussy, in contrast, wrote a great deal of worthwhile music that acknowledged
"the presence of real voice-parts." Often his music was "not obviously polyphonic," but "real voice-parts" are found nevertheless.[66]

Foote did try to keep an open mind for changes and new developments in music, however much they flew "in the face of all
that one has cared for." He hoped he would not "become so hard-
ened in traditions as not to be honest toward what may seem to
be new and perhaps not of value." Nevertheless, since 1910, it
was increasingly difficult for him to remain readily receptive to
new ideas.[67] "It is not easy for [me] . . . to be unprejudiced, or to
find anything to prefer in the present upheaval; but, after all, do
we ask for a vacant mind except when obtaining a jury?"[68] Moses
Smith says that, around 1935, a friend of his once spent an
evening with Foote and found that the composer did not want to
talk about music of his day but about contemporary music. His
friend was "amazed by Foote's curiosity about what was happen-
ing among European composers of the advance guard, by his excellent knowledge of what was going on, and by his really
sympathetic interest. They discussed Alan [*sic*] Berg, a composer

whose training and artistic methods were at the furthest remove possible from those of Foote, and whose compositions in the twelve-tone system had been regarded as hideous monstrosities by younger men who have not had to live down a life-time of prejudice. Yet Foote's comments and questions were in the same vein of kindly interest and tolerance and alert curiosity."[69]

In his own day, Foote commented, the music of Brahms, Dvorák, Tschaikovsky, Franck, and Strauss were novelties. Nevertheless, at that time music had developed slowly and gradually, for example, in form, harmony, and instrumentation. To truly escape from tradition and to do so successfully called for an "uncommon skill and discretion that" no one seemed to have. Therefore he expected a short life for polytonality and atonality because they were illogical and a negation of all past musics. You either liked that sort of thing or you did not. He did not. As for Stravinsky's neoclassicism, this arguing for avoidance of expression altogether was not the antidote to the excesses of sentimentality to which some nineteenth-century composers had yielded.[70] It was like throwing the baby out with the bath water. Percussive writing for piano, as practiced by Bartok and Stravinsky, was something "we have been trying all these years to *keep out* of piano writing. It's a bad fashion—which must be very temporary indeed—and takes away beauty from piano playing."[71]

Foote said that his rhythms did not require percussive effects. In addition, his own harmonies had always been based on the triadic principle, building in thirds from the bass tone. "It has been proposed, however, to change this, and build upward by 4ths e.g., but there seems to be nothing in this." The pentatonic scale and the old modes "gave relief from the overworked major and minor" and composers have reverted to their use. But the attempts "by Bussoni and others to introduce scales based on smaller intervals than the half-step" have proved futile. "No doubt some results will come from these investigations: at present [1932] the modal scales are by no means yet overworked."[72]

Often Foote's words seem to come from a romanticist who was losing the argument to the modernists. However, he knew that the styles he espoused were heartily endorsed by the general music public. His sense of values and the way he chose to conduct his life as a man and musician were still shared by a large percentage of the American people. He was never completely cut off from the mainstream or out of fashion. In his music, he spoke strongly about and to the humanity in people, and, as before, he could appeal to a congenial audience. His listeners had not yet entirely succumbed to the views and dogmas of the mechanistic crowd, who preached the fall of old values and the need to discard old tastes in favor of the harsher sounds of "the real world" that the post-World War I period had ushered in.

Olin Downes, at the time of Foote's death in 1937, published a list of contemporary composers and their music about which Foote had commented. He said that Foote admired Strauss's music but found it did not age well. He liked the works of Bloch and Sibelius. Scriabin had worked himself into a cul-de-sac. Stravinsky had given the music public a "fine shock" with his *Rite of Spring*, but after that work he found nothing that engaged him. Honegger's mechanistic *Pacific 231* was not likable at all. Shostakovich's music and philosophy were both alien to him. Debussy's music he liked much more than he did Ravel's. And he truly enjoyed "the musical patois of" Gershwin.[73]

The mention of Gershwin, whose music Foote genuinely enjoyed, raises the question of nationalism in music.[74] What was "American" about American music was a hotly debated subject in the early twentieth century, with Arthur Farwell, Charles Wakefield Cadman, Henry Gilbert, John Powell, and John Alden Carpenter giving disparate answers (Amerindian, American minstrel, Anglo-Celtic derived American folk, traditional African-American, and jazz). In 1910, Foote said that when he had started off as a composer "the distinction between music that was or was not 'American' did not particularly trouble the composer of these parts." American composers then were taking valuable suggestions from Europe and assimilating what they had learned. Now Americans were growing more enterprising, and he was "an enthusiastic believer in the future of our national music."[75] The next year, in California, he cast some doubt on the final results of the five composers just mentioned and reasserted a long-held opinion: "If music takes a national form, it must do so unconsciously and without forethought on the part of the composer. . . . We can never have an American school of music by making up our minds to do so." We cannot have a national school based on one delimited style, such as Amerindian or African-American. If we were to bring about a national school, we first had to produce one great American composer. Indeed, it was likely that there would be several local American schools, since the country was large and widely separated.[76]

By 1924, jazz, both genuine and in various popular adaptations, was sweeping the country. The popular performances of the Original Dixieland Jazz Band and King Oliver's Band, Carpenter's *Krazy Kat* ballet (1921), and the celebrated "symphonic jazz" concert given by Paul Whiteman in New York City's Aeolian Hall on 12 February 1924 made several writers wonder if this was the most significant path leading to a national music. A few art music composers were queried for their reactions, among them Foote. Foote said he did not know much about jazz but the little he knew seemed to show that it was potentially a negative influence if not handled carefully. Appreciating jazz would not lead to an appreciation of art music. He concluded: "The truth may be that it is becoming increasingly difficult to find melodies and harmonies that are fresh (not to say new), that this interest in 'Jazz' means exploration of new and striking rhythmical dances—odd, but after centuries of musical development we should be returning to the primitive."[77]

Foote's knowledge and understanding of jazz increased over the next decade. In the 1930s, a new version of jazz, called swing, had gained popularity. By 1936, he had grown much less hostile to the idiom. Foote thought that possibly swing had gone "too far leftward," but its excesses would be corrected and it would add to our musical vocabulary, while what was foolish would be discarded.[78] Nevertheless, he continued to believe that a distinctive American art music would have to come into being unconsciously, aided and abetted by one or two great composers.

Notes

1.   Arthur Foote, "Arthur Foote, 1875 to 1881," Scrapbook at the New England Conservatory of Music, acquired from the estate of Moses Smith and the gift of Mrs. Gertrude Nissenbaum.

2.   Arthur Foote, *An Autobiography* (Norwood, Mass.: Plimpton Press, 1946), 113.

3. Susan Sinclair, archivist at the Gardner Museum, informed me about the hand; on the bas-relief, see W. H. L., "Girl Sculptor of Boston Makes Bas-Relief of Arthur Foote," *Musical America*, 27 January 1917, 27.

4. Newspaper clipping in Arthur Foote, Scrapbook III, Boston Public Library, shelf no. **ML. 46.F65.

5. Foote, *Autobiography*, 112.

6. "Presidents' Report" (Annual meeting of the Cecilia Society, Thursday, May 9, 1901, presented by Pres. Foote); in Arthur Foote, Scrapbook III, Boston Public Library, shelf no. **ML. 46.F65. Alongside the report is an article dated May 1901 on the twenty-fifth year of the society, which also talks about the Wage-Earners' Concerts.

7. Ibid.

8. Arthur Foote, "Letters Collected by Arthur Foote: Gift to the library in memory of Arthur Foote, April 16, 1940," Spaulding Library, New England Conservatory of Music, letters no. 45 and 87.

9. Eliot Forbes, *A History of Music at Harvard to 1972* (Cambridge: Department of Music, Harvard University, 1988), 17, 39–40.

10. Foote, "Letters Collected by Arthur Foote," letter no. 56.

11. Everett E. Truette, "Two American Organists and Composers," *The Musician* 15 (1910): 348.

12. Foote, *Autobiography*, 38–39.

13. The letter sent from Bridge Street, Dedham, is in the archives of the Gardner Museum.

14. Wilma Cipolla states that in 1908 Johanna Gadski "recorded 'An Irish Folk Song' for RCA Victor, the only recording of his music made during Foote's lifetime"; Wilma Reid Cipolla, "Chronology," in *A Catalog of the Works of Arthur Foote* (Detroit: Information Coordinators, 1980), xx.

15. Both letters, undated, are at the Boston Public Library, shelf no. M. Cab. 2.41.V2, p. 31.

16. Foote, "Letters collected by Arthur Foote," letter no. 38. The Tchaikovsky work was the Fifth Symphony; *Brigg Fair* is by Frederick Delius. The Trio no. 2 in B Major, op. 65, had been published in December 1909.

17. The letter is in the Arthur Foote Collection, Williams College, Williamstown, Massachusetts.

18. Arthur Foote, MS of lectures delivered at the University of California, Berkeley in 1911; now in the Boston Public Library, shelf no. **M.472.134.

19.   Foote, *An Autobiography*, 94–98.

20.   See Thomas Nunan, "Noted Composer Arrives at U. of C.," *San Francisco Examiner*, 3 June 1911, 3; mention of the two courses is also made in Frederick Kopp, "Arthur Foote: American Composer and Theorist," (Ph.D. diss., Eastman School of Music, University of Rochester, 1957), 108, 110.

21.   "Welcome is given to Arthur Foote," *San Francisco Examiner*, 7 June 1911, Education Section: 5.

22.   Thomas Nunan, "State Music Teachers Hold Convention," *San Francisco Examiner*, 6 July 1911, 5.

23.   Foote, "Music in the United States," MS of lecture delivered at the University of California, Boston Public Library, shelf no. **M.472.134, no. 1042, p. 23.

24.   Ibid., 29, 30.

25.   Ibid., 23–24.

26.   Thomas Nunan, "California will be a house of music culture," *San Francisco Examiner*, 30 July 1911, Education Section: 4.

27.   Thomas Nunan, "Arthur Foote's work at the summer school in Berkeley," *San Francisco Examiner*, 2 July 1911, Education Section, 4.

28.   Thomas Nunan, "Summer school lecturer declares that California will be a home of music culture," *San Francisco Examiner*, 30 July 1911, Education Section, "Music and Musicians," 4.

29.   Foote, *An Autobiography*, 98-99.

30.   Thomas Nunan, "Summer school lecturer declares that California will be a home of music culture," *San Francisco Examiner* (30 July 1911), Education Section: "Music and Musicians," 4.

31.   Letter in the *San Francisco Examiner*, 10 September 1911, Educational Section: 6.

32.   Foote, *An Autobiography*, 97.

33.   The record of the sale is at the Norfolk County Courthouse, Lib. 1198, Fol. 369.

34.   Foote, *An Autobiography*, 104.

35.   W. H. L., "Girl Sculptor of Boston Makes Bas-Relief of Arthur Foote," *Musical America*, 27 January 1917, 27.

36.   Foote, *An Autobiography*, 49, 100–01.

37.   The brief item is found in Foote, Scrapbook III.

38.   Everett E. Truette, "Two American Organists and Composers," *The Musician* (1910): 348.

39.   The letter is in the archives of the Gardner Museum.

40. This and the previous letter are in the archives of the Gardner Museum.

41. The street today is almost completely taken over by apartment buildings, including the lot where the Foote house had stood.

42. Foote, *An Autobiography*, 102. The house today is no longer "on the edge of the real country."

43. Ibid., 102.

44. The two letters are in the archives of the Gardner Museum. The Raffy move to Rest Harrow is mentioned in Foote, *Autobiography*, 102.

45. Letter from Rev. Arthur Foote II to Wilma Cipolla, 24 November 1974, now in the Arthur Foote Collection.

46. O. G. Sonneck, "A Survey of Music in America," in *Suum Cuique* (New York: Schirmer, 1916), 124.

47. Arthur Foote II has kindly provided me with a copy of the manuscript, now in the Arthur Foote Collection.

48. Moses Smith, "A Tribute to Arthur Foote," published with *Autobiography*, 118.

49. *The New England Conservatory of Music Bulletin*, August 1920, 1; *Bulletin*, October 1921, 1; *Year-Book, 1920–1921* of the New England Conservatory of Music, 11.

50. *Catalogue, 1935–36* of the New England Conservatory of Music, 64.

51. Redfern Mason, "The Passing of Arthur Foote," *Boston Evening Transcript"*, 17 April 1937, sec. 4, 6.

52. Mason, "The Passing of Arthur Foote," 6.

53. Arthur Foote, "Foote: Letters. Undated from Second [Rosalie] Housman Gift," Music Division of the Library of Congress, shelf no. ML 95.F77.

54. Truette, "Two American Organists and Composers," 349.

55. This undated letter, written ca. 1933–34, is in Foote, "Letters. Undated from Second [Rosalie] Housman Gift."

56. Letter to Mrs. Alfred Minsky ("Rebra") sent from Newton Centre, dated 14 February 1934, and now in the Arthur Foote Collection.

57. Moses Smith, "A Tribute to Arthur Foote," an address delivered at a memorial concert, Lasell Junior College, Auburndale, Mass., on 22 July 1937, and published with Foote, *An Autobiography*; 124, 126.

58. The letter is in the Arthur Foote Collection. Eliza was born in 1856; her father was William Orne White.

59. Letter from Rev. Arthur Foote II to Wilma Cipolla, 9 December 1980, now in the Arthur Foote Collection.

60.   Foote, *An Autobiography*, 59.

61.   The letters may be found in the Library of Congress, under "Music Div. Old Correspondence."

62.   *Etude* 42 (1924): 151.

63.   Arthur Foote, "The Relation of Consonance to Dissonance" *Etude* 55 (1937): 504.

64.   Arthur Foote, "Will the Music of Ultra-Modernists Survive?" *Etude* 34 (1916): 331.

65.   Undated letter, in Foote, "Foote: Letters. Undated from Second [Rosalie] Housman Gift."

66.   Arthur Foote, *Some Practical Things in Piano Playing* (Boston: Schmidt, 1909), 22.

67.   Foote, *An Autobiography*, 105–06.

68.   Arthur Foote, "You Like It or You Don't," clipping from an unidentified source, now in the Arthur Foote Collection.

69.   Smith, "A Tribute to Arthur Foote," 125–26.

70.   Ibid.; see also "As a Composer Regards His Craft," *Boston Evening Transcript*, 8 October 1936, clipping in the Arthur Foote Collection. The newspaper reprinted a report on the proceedings, prepared by the W.P.A. publicity department.

71.   Undated letter to Rosalie Housman in Foote, "Foote: Letters. Undated from Second [Rosalie] Housman Gift."

72.   Foote, "A Summary of the Principles of Harmony," 8, 10.

73.   Olin Downes, "Works of Arthur Foote," *New York Times* (18 April 1937), sec. 11, 5.

74.   Mason, "The Passing of Arthur Foote," 6. During my visit with him in Southwest Harbor, Maine, on 15–16 August 1995, Arthur Foote II mentioned twice that his granduncle had certainly enjoyed Gershwin's music,

75.   O. D., "How Can One Cherish Wagner and Equally Admire Strauss?" *Musical America*, 23 April 1910, 5.

76.   Thomas Nunan, "Foote tells Americans what national music is," *San Francisco Examiner*, 11 July 1911, Educational Section, 4.

77.   "Where is jazz leading America?" *Etude* 42 (1924): 517–18.

78.   Arthur Foote, "A Bostonian Remembers" *Musical Quarterly* 23 (1937): 44.

10

Making Music in a New Environment

A new art environment gradually came into being during the first third of the twentieth century, as the old moral, cultural, and artistic certainties gave way, and the arts turned their faces from common practices that had prevailed for centuries in order to examine radically different approaches to creativity. Throughout these years, Foote never repudiated the style that he had come to make his own. For critics dedicated to change, his music lost its contemporaneity and came to be regarded as conservative, or what was worse, as academic, imitative, and an example of boring *kapellmeistermusik*. That he was conservative is agreed. The rest of the adverse judgment I find untrue, as did the audiences of his day.

A composer who conjures up musical sounds while engaged in deep, reflective thought frequently incorporates his spirit into his music, whether his subject matter is light or substantial, his style conservative or advanced. Listening to Foote's late pieces affords an intimate and touching awareness of his temperament in the latter years of his life. Exactly why and in what measure his traits are disclosed is hard to say. Yet, his personality, like the late works he created, is permeated with a keen sense of personal values and an aversion to anything lacking in merit. His music's distinctively individual attributes, by force of circumstance, became more visible during the years of the twentieth century.

The Germanic character of Foote's work gradually diminished, as he became more receptive to French influences. This

307

change had begun during his stay at Bas-Meudon in 1897 and it continued in the following years. Furthermore, the unequivocal ambience of his own America now came forth, however understated, from Foote's most fully developed works. I know of no other major composer, European or otherwise, who could have composed works like the outer movements of the Suite in E for String Orchestra (1907), the song "Tranquillity" (1914), and the flute-string composition *A Night Piece* (1922).[1] Even in his slighter pieces, Foote achieved an agreeable composure of manner and a deftness of idea that qualify him for the highest respect as a composer. Self-possession and a warm glow of feeling predominate in quite a few of his late character pieces. These two characteristics help explain why musically educated listeners of his era relished his work. He presented a sophisticated consciousness of all musical literature, from Bach to Brahms to the American composers of his day. It is from this standpoint that we should understand comments like one made in 1906: "Few American composers have done more important work than Arthur Foote, a man who belongs most emphatically to those who have conscientiously endeavored to follow classical traditions."[2]

After 1901, he wrote about fifty-five solo songs, eight vocal duets, seven pieces for men's voices and nineteen for women's voices, including one motet with orchestra, and five secular and seven sacred compositions for mixed voices. His keyboard music included thirteen piano compositions, six of them containing more than one movement, and six organ compositions, four of them in two or more movements. He also produced ten instrumental chamber works and two pieces involving string orchestra.

Shortly after Foote died, Frederick Jacobi summarized the last years by saying that "Foote cared little for 'style' in the sense of 'modishness.' He did obviously care greatly for 'style' in the sense of purity of line, clarity of structure and unity in the mode of expression." The final works to be examined, like the person who wrote them, represent fine cultivation, intelligence, taste, and not a little charm. "Originality was expressed by the turn of a phrase, by the aggregate of his being, rather than by a striking or an arresting exterior." When desired, tenderness and warmth showed themselves "through an admirable web of New England tradition: a tradition which was the base of his cult of the restrained in art."[3] That tradition bespoke a sense of duty to his fellow humans, to his art, and to his God. This triple force lay behind every note that he set down and is understood in the discussion that follows.

Vocal Music

Foote continued to prefer lyric, rather than dramatic or rhetorical, poems for his song settings. However, the subject matter that now attracted him was more frequently involved in thoughts other than courtship and love. His solo songs turned increasingly to memories of the past, to longings for rest and serenity, to a growing consciousness of death, and to prayer. Several of them told a little story wrapped around a single emotion, which sometimes illustrated a moral of some sort. He remained aware that his songs sold well. Quite a few singers included them in recitals, and audiences liked hearing them. Whatever their artistic merits, the songs constantly reflect this awareness. The singer, not the pianist, is put at the forefront and given music that displays the voice attractively. The audience can easily respond to the vocal line without the distraction of rhythmic and harmonic complexity that calls attention to itself. Melodic and harmonic subtlety there is, but always unobtrusive and in aid of explicating the mood.

Usually, the listener senses a private world of feeling, more somber or sorrowing than celebrating. Foote is seeking to investigate and portray the hidden recesses of the human spirit by examining his own thoughts and feelings, his own sensory and subjective experiences, and universalizing them. He succeeds in doing this through the medium of song. Sympathetic to Foote's thinking is Thomas Eakins' painting *The Pathetic Song* (1881),[4] which shows a young feminine vocalist holding a song sheet as she sings. She stands physically present and to the fore, with people behind her. Yet, she remains psychologically isolated from the other figures in the painting, as she intently centers her whole being on the music and the imaginative world it creates. Her experiences and the composer's have become one—this is the effect that Foote hopes to induce in singer and listener.

A majority of texts are in three stanzas and set to three musical strains. Hardly any settings are strophic or ternary in structure. Most are through-composed, occasionally with a couple of measures of the first strain returning in a later strain. I have said that melody remains to the fore and planned with the singer in mind. Yet, in several songs the vocal line is not completely tuneful. It may turn declamatory and move mainly by repeated notes and skips that counteract lyricism, rather than by conjunct motion. While the vocal line in this last instance does remain the most prominent feature, it combines with harmony and rhythm to bring about a specific state of mind in the listener, which can be very gratifying. Thus, the tune by itself no longer makes or breaks a work. This represents a new departure for Foote.

The music in some strains (most often the first strain) or some songs may emphasize consonances and remain tonal and diatonic, with scarcely a chromatic alteration in the notes; in other strains (most often the middle strain) or other songs, it becomes far more dissonant and chromatic than ever before, often wandering through distant tonalities. Our understanding of his increased use of dissonance is enhanced by a comment he made in 1932:

> The use of dissonance has increased steadily since the day of the discovery of the dominant 7th, and to many of us today [it] seems to have exceeded reasonable limits, for a proper admixture of consonance and dissonance seems sensible, each setting the other off to advantage. . . . Today dissonances are sprinkled ad libitum throughout what is called by some "modern music" (e.g. Hindemith, etc.), *perhaps resulting in a monotony and tension still* [text unclear] who knows or can tell at this moment.
>
> The truth is that the ear becomes accustomed to dissonance, tolerates what at first it could not endure and finally perhaps likes it. E.g. compare the reception of Monteverdi's dominant 7th with that of today towards full of (to me) meaningless dissonance.[5]

Foote's tolerance of dissonance certainly increased and is demonstrated in the strands of tardily resolved or unresolved melodic dissonances and seventh and ninth chords that inhabit many passages of his late music.

Even though the composer employs harmony with delicacy and awareness of its varying nuances, he does not usually strive to invest his rhythms and piano accompaniments with the same kind of distinctiveness. The accompaniments still tend to be supportive, with no rhythmic or coloristic liberties that truly catch the listener's attention. As before, most keyboard introductions and conclusions may be perfunctory or completely absent. The curtain goes up swiftly on most songs and comes down as swiftly with the last word of the text.

The first songs we come upon are the *Four Songs*, op. 51 (1902): 1. "The Rose and the Gardener," text by Austin Dobson; 2. "Bisesa's Song," text by Rudyard Kipling; 3. "If Love Were What the Rose Is," text by Algernon Swinburne; 4. "Ashes of Roses," text by Elaine Goodale. Katharine Foote is known to have performed the first song in Boston, with her father at the keyboard, on 12 March 1902. It describes a prideful rose who complaisantly awaits the death of the ancient gardener, but dies before he does. The moral, stated in the final line, is that the rose, which represents beauty, fades quickly away, and the gardener, who represents time, buries it. The $^2/_4$ time signature and the E-flat major key are as expected. So also are the inconsequential two-measure prelude and postlude. However, the admonition at the beginning, "gracefully; not fast," is the first of many introductory captions to songs that are in English rather than Italian. Also unusual is the subdued dynamic range, almost entirely *p* or *pp*, which enhances the feeling of personal contemplation, even of spiritual reflection. The piece is through-composed and in three strains (each strain pausing on a held note), plus a concluding phrase at the very end. The first strain enters G minor but returns to E-flat; the second enters G major but again returns to E-flat; the third is in E-flat. The tune to these strains, most appropriately, is all innocence as the naïve rose exults in her youthful beauty in contrast to the rickety gardener who seems close to his demise. It strikes the ear like the singsong prattle of a child (example 27). In the third strain, the expression darkens. A wind blows the rose's petals to the ground; then the gardener gathers and buries them. The music sounds disquieted. The passage begins in A-flat minor and falls into E-flat minor and then B-flat major before closing in E-flat minor. The concluding music phrase, which sets the moral, is in E-flat major and entirely diatonic, save for a solitary A-natural in the bass. Its simplicity echoes the beginning and adds a touch of irony to the close.

"Bisesa's Song" is not as individual an utterance. The composer asks for a "strongly marked rhythm," and indeed the recurring one-measure piano figure that Foote introduces in the third measure is attractively rhythmic, with its upward sweep of thirty-second notes that alight on clipped eighth notes. The subject, regrettably, is hackneyed, and the music once or twice verges on the overripe. A maiden of the exotic East yearns for her adored warrior-sweetheart to cease his fighting and return to rescue her from her unhappy lot. Frequently resorting to the Dorian mode, measure after measure limns the young woman's longings with the familiar, if occasionally commonplace, melancholic exoticisms associated with this type of song. The fresh approach of the *Omar Khayyám* music is rarely evident. Nevertheless, the tune is pleasing, the musical background evocative, and the auditory sensation pleasant. The song was well received by contemporary audiences.

"If Love Were What the Rose Is" appears less clichéd. Its winning melody at times sounds suspiciously like an outgrowth from a popular song, which, of course, does not necessarily detract from its quality. The text tells us that two people who truly love, however different they may be, belong together, like rose and leaf, life and death, and words and music. The structure is ternary, the outer sections in bright D-flat major and the middle, which considers the tie binding life to death, in a hushed E minor.

I find the brief "Ashes of Roses"[6] to be a superior song to op. 51, nos. 2 and 3. The poem identifies the end of love with the ashes of roses. Only thirteen measures of $\frac{4}{4}$ time in F major are needed to set the two stanzas within an A A^1 structure. The entire tune is diatonic, save for one raised fifth that is heard as a neighboring tone. The harmonies underlying the melodic line harbor fewer chromatic alterations than those of the other three songs. Prelude and postlude are nonexistent. Foote shows an admirable sophistication when he proves that less is better. There is not a vestige of the mushy, sugary chromaticism or the bloated sonorities that can mar romantic songs of this kind. In fact, he excludes affectation of any sort from its two pages. This is an unadorned representation of feeling—not the passion of an emotionally troubled young lover, but the more subdued sensibility of an older person looking into himself. The creator of this composition is a more reserved individual than the man who wrote the Violin Sonata.

The piece begins by describing a sunset and likens its wan tinges of color to the ashes of roses. "Quietly, with rhythmical exactness" is the composer's admonition. The first section receives a serenade-like accompaniment as the piano sounds insouciant arpeggiated chords as a backdrop. The music remains resolutely diatonic throughout. The main event is the singer's tune that floats in on an offbeat, thus emulating the sunset's softness. It continues in elastic one-measure note groups until it completes its motion with a hold in the fifth measure. The notion of softness is compounded as the melody often moves through or alights on the mediant tone. When not in conjunct motion, the tune favors skips through a gentle minor third or unstartling hops through a sixth. Foote often shades the tune with the morose minor harmonies of the submediant, mediant, and supertonic. Dissonance is scarce. The music begins again. The second section changes from arpeggiated sounds to reiterated right-hand eighth-note chords, which add gravity and tension to the communication, for now love has set, its brightness dimmed and leaving ashes of roses. Dissonances in the piano and fleeting references to other keys disturb the tune. The voice ends with a melodic move from dominant to tonic tone, but the harmony underneath goes into two dissonant, chromatically altered chords before finally reaching the tonic (example 28).

In 1904, Schmidt issued Foote's *Three Songs*, op. 55: 1. "Constancy," text from an anonymous hand; 2. "The River Flows Forever," text by Philip Marston; 3. "Though All Betray," text by Marie van Vorst. With "Constancy," we see a definite stylistic change taking place, one already detectable in the first, third, and fourth songs of opus 51. Foote's debt to German *Lieder* has decreased considerably, replaced by increasing allusions to American popular song, Anglo-American folksong, and the hymnody that was a part of his New England inheritance. On occasion, the vocal line acquires *parlando* characteristics. The writing has become sparer in texture and more succinct in expression. Four-square and eight-square tunes may be replaced with three- or five-measure phrases and nine- to eleven-measure strains. If he can do without accidentals and an elaborate deployment of sophisticated techniques, Foote does not hesitate to choose simplicity. He finds no need to demonstrate the depths of his musical expertise or to remain on the beam of contemporary fashion. Emotion becomes more subtle, at times quite indirect; heated romantic expression is absent. Sentiments are more likely to remain muted than to be exposed. The composer's expressive intentions for a work gradually come together for the listener as he goes from beginning to end of a song. The auditor is left feeling deeply, without always knowing how and where the feeling took hold.

A relevant case is offered in what can be considered a representative Foote song, "Constancy," the testament of a steadfast lover. It is in ⁴/₄ and C major and directed to go "rather fast, with free diction." The musical form is ternary (A section in C major, B section in C minor, back to A). Like "Ashes of Roses," the A portion has the directness of a folk song and, except for one raised fifth tone, is completely diatonic. After the two-measure prelude, the accompaniment patters along in eighth-note figurations. The vocal strain is eleven measures long. The singer starts off jauntily, hopping down and up through triadic formations. By degrees, the melodic motion grows more conjunct, finally swelling upward step by step to climax on e″, before subsiding with longer note values to c′, on the words "I cannot help loving thee." What began buoyantly has somehow acquired an increased emotional overtone. The middle section, with the instruction to go "a little slower," has a ten-measure strain. As in "Ashes of Roses," reiterated eighth-note chords further the meaning of the text. The vocalist protests that whatever calamities nature brings forth, love will never cease. Before concluding, the tune drops an octave, leaping a minor seventh, down a perfect fourth, and up a diminished fifth in order to depict nature's excessive "growing, and blowing, and flowing." Longer notes and a drop of a perfect fifth illustrate the promise that the protagonist will "never cease loving thee." The final section returns to the airiness of the beginning, but not quite with the previous innocence, for there has come knowledge of "bloom or blight." Throughout, the music has hit a correct balance, being neither more profound in its aspiration than the subject warrants nor so superficial as to be of no account.

In 1906, there appeared *Two Songs with Violin Obbligato*, op. 59: 1. "Love Is a Bubble," text by Pearl Craigie; 2. "The Sun Is Low," text by Louise Moulton. The second work is especially attractive. In 1907, an outstanding song came out, "Requiem," to a poem by Robert Louis Stevenson.[7] Foote gives "Requiem" a ⁴/₄ meter and asks that it be performed maestoso, in order to bring out its exalted and dignified character. The music is in two strains (A B). The first strain starts in A minor and ends in C major; the second is in A major. Again a sincere simplicity prevails. We know he could have acted differently if he had chosen to do so. The first strain starts on the tone a' and gradually reaches higher and higher, going up to c'', to e'', to a climax on f'', then subsiding swiftly to a low c', on the words "and I laid me down with a will." Arpeggiated piano chords in both hands support the voice. The message, which is completed at the strain's end by means of a cadence in C major, is not meant to provoke easy tears, although the subject is death. The melody remains diatonic except for one raised sixth tone. The entire A strain is tinged with melancholy, to be sure, but there is no attempt to capitalize on emotion. The second strain, *poco più largamente*, must be performed more broadly to call attention to the epitaph: "Here he lies, / Where he longed to be; / Home is the sailor, home from the sea, / And the hunter home from the hill." Repeated eighth-note chords constitute the accompaniment. Now the phrases droop, acting the opposite of those in strain A. First, the music sinks from c-sharp$''$ to c-sharp$'$; next from c-sharp$''$ down to e', before gently ending on a'. Thus, the strain reaches equilibrium in the middle of the range, imparting a feeling of balance and repose. Further adding to the feeling of repose are the downward moving appoggiaturas, from dissonance to consonance on the last word of each line of verse, on the words "lies," "be," "sea," "home from the hill." The last dissonance is the most prolonged, achieving through its resolution a final achievement of peace. In the last two measures, the piano plays a plagal cadence, adding a musical "amen" to the proceedings (example 29).

Four Songs, op. 67, came out in 1908, published by Schmidt: 1. "Dew in the Heart of the Rose," text by James Kenyon; 2. "Love Guides the Roses," text by Thomas Lodge; 3. "Once at the Angelus," text by Austin Dobson; and 4. "Before Sunrise," text by Richard Gilder. The second and third songs are especially fine. "Love Guides the Roses" provides an example of a successful late song by Foote that does not aim at a studied simplicity. More elaborate music is required to encompass the sophisticated conceit of the Elizabethan poet Thomas Lodge. The poet, in three stanzas, likens love to a flying bee, to a boy building a bower in his beloved's eyes, and to a deity that can soften a beloved's heart. The music is in three strains, all different, except that the first measure of the first strain is reproduced in the first measure of the second strain. The piano accompaniment, although not technically difficult, is carefully elaborated and given some distinction. For example, the two-measure prelude introduction to the first strain contains a motive that will recur in the accompaniment throughout the song. Moreover, in measure after measure, we encounter chromaticism, appoggiatura chords, ninth chords, augmented chords, and sudden allusions to distant keys. To give one instance, on the words "If I approach, he forward skips, / And if I kiss, he stingeth," the harmony goes from a V^7 of IV to a N^6_4 to a V^7 of N to a VII^7 of V, before returning to the key of F. The tune reveals great rhythmic flexibility, the melody being given a different rhythmic pattern in every measure. The skill of the composer makes everything hang together with nothing sounding forced (example 30).

In 1909, Schmidt issued four songs by Foote: "O Love That Wilt Not Let Me Go," text by George Matheson; "I Am the Moth of the Night," text by Thomas Russell Sullivan; "All's Well," text by Harriet Kimball; and "There Sits a Bird on Every Tree," text by Charles Kingsley. Thomas Russell Sullivan gives evidence that contemporary poets of his acquaintance were pleased when Foote selected their verse for setting. In a letter headed "Nov. 24th [1909?], 382 Marlborough Street," he writes to thank "Arthur" for sending him published copies of the song and "observes with pride that his name appears no less than three times, once, too, in color! Fame descends upon him copiously, borne far and wide on the wings of the composer's tribute, and with attendant blushes he signs himself. Ever yours gratefully, T. S. Sullivan."[8]

"All's Well," which was composed in Dedham in 1908, is of particular interest because it is a prayer song asking God for forgiveness of all transgressions, for untroubled sleep, and ultimately for heavenly rest. "Quietly; not too slowly" is the direction. The tune does have some affiliation with hymns, but the harmony is much too chromatic and complex in structure for any work purporting to derive from hymnody. In addition, the verse setting is not strophic. The three strains have the form of A A^1 (the second half of the second strain differs from that of the first strain) B. Yet, the overall impression is one of humility. The music has charm and hides a great deal of expertise. The result is a supplication both moving and honest. Coming so soon after "Requiem," it indicates that the composer is setting off on a new road, at least in song.

"There Sits a Bird on Every Tree" is one of Foote's most delightful compositions. It is a lighthearted ditty on love and courtship. The accompaniment, in sixteenth-note triadic figuration, burbles blithely from beginning to end and in perfect accord with the tune's sentiment. Save in four measures, the texture never thickens. On the other hand, these four measures underscore the words "young maids must marry" with rising two-hand arpeggiated chords that add an expressive mellowness, not sentimental drivel, to the declaration. One would expect the song to be strophic. However, its three strains are all different, with the only duplication being the first measure and a half of the first two strains. A refrain, "sing heigh-ho!" returns repeatedly, each time treated differently, though always pertly. The words are tossed off as two staccato eighth notes followed by a longer note.

"Roses in Winter," text by Philip Marston, was completed and published in 1911. The next year, Schmidt published *Five Songs*, op. 72: 1. "I Know a Little Garden Path," text by Hildegard Hawthorne; 2. "Thistle-down," text by Richard Gilder; 3. "Song like a Rose Should Be," text by Frank Sherman; 4. "The Wanderer to His Heart's Desire," text by John Reed; 5. "A Song of Summer," text by Ellen Glines. Also published in 1912 was "There's a Ship Lies off Dunvegan," text by William Maclennan.

Foote considered "I Know a Little Garden Path" one of his best songs,[9] and contemporary audiences thoroughly enjoyed it. The composer wants it performed "quietly" and expressively ("espressivo"). As is common in the late songs, the protagonist is no longer young and aims at rest and quietude. The singer enters a garden at twilight, "hushed to deep repose . . . / And in the dark the garden fades, / And leaves memory." We find the usual

three strains with nothing repeated, except for the first two measures of the first strain recurring at the beginning of the second
strain. Strains one and two are in the minor; strain three, in the
major—a characteristic of Foote's late style. Also characteristic,
the old modes, alongside the normal major and minor tonalities,
are touched on. Now, more and more, we find him employing
the lowered seventh tone. Otherwise, he uses the seventh spar-
ingly as a leading tone, and this most often in the final measures
of the work. The same holds true for the perfect cadence. What
is most remarkable about this song is the high range of the accompaniment. Both hands play around middle C and above
(sometimes very high above), adding greatly to the evanescent,
time-in-suspense effect.

"The Wanderer to His Heart's Desire" has the protagonist
holding firmly to the memory of a beloved one, however wide
the distance separating them. If sent "a blown kiss in the wind's
long hair; / And though I sleep at the world's end, / Yet will it
find me there." Like the previous piece, it is through-composed
and is in the minor for the first two strains of the song, and in
the major for the final strain. Again, the perfect cadence in the
home key is avoided until the final measures. One surprise is the
close of the minor-key section, not in the anticipated home key,
but, after a sudden modulation, in the far removed major key
based on the lowered leading tone (in the low-voice version, not
A minor but A-flat major). Surprising, too, is the opening of the
last strain with two measures of melody similar to that of the
opening. An attractive feature of the accompaniment is the right
hand's running eighth-note figuration high in the treble clef,
which is heard during two-thirds of the song.

In several ways, "There's a Ship Lies off Dunvegan" is a de-
scendent of "An Irish Folk Song." It is strophic and arranged in
two stanzas, the music for each stanza having a minor-key first
section and a major-key second section. There is more than a
hint of dialect in the text. The musical setting receives a dollop
of modal melody and a simple chordal accompaniment. However, its harmony is richer and more varied than that of the earlier
song (example 31). The engaging tune, which is to be sung "with
freedom and expression," is the expression of someone old and
weary, who sees a ship beckoning him to board it and return to

his home in Dunvegan. The home referred to is ostensibly that of his childhood, but it could as easily be interpreted as his home in heaven.

In the years to come, we find the melodic curves and harmonic progressions becoming less predictable. More songs are preoccupied with thoughts of old age and death. Memory, prayer, and a seeking after serenity increasingly enter the subject matter. World War I, which began in 1914, with his beloved daughter Katharine across the submarine-infested Atlantic in France, reinforced these musings. The violent deaths of so many young men in the trenches agitated him. The high idealism and devotion to the arts in the Germany he had known being supplanted by the militarism of the modern German nation depressed him. Additionally, he confronted death face to face in his two serious bouts with illness.

In 1915, Schmidt published two songs that reflect Foote's preoccupations: "Rest," text by Hiram Wiley, and "Tranquillity," text by Mary van Orden. "Rest" is a prayer song, but not the very personal, subjective one of "All's Well!" There is no begging forgiveness for one individual's transgressions. The song embraces all humanity. "We" and "us" replaces "I" and "me." The lines of verse affirm a faith in God, however many the tribulations of human life. "Upward," God "leads us," though we feel fear and experience suffering, and He "will give us rest at last." The song opens like a hymn, "expressively, but not too slowly," in $^4/_4$ time and a D-flat major tonality, with each phrase closing on a long note. Unlike a hymn, the song is through-composed, not strophic. Nor are the three strains square-cut. An inconsequential two-measure prelude introduces the singer. The first strain, which is twenty-one measures long, approximates hymnal music. A two-measure piano interlude that mostly has the effect of marking time is heard. The second strain departs from the generalities about God's showing us the right path and instead deals with the disturbances, doubts, losses, and sorrows of existence. Its eighteen measures are filled out with increased dissonance and restless transits from one key to another. The music of the last strain, in order to encompass God's promised rest, stretches out to twenty-three measures, replacing the former feeling of pressure with peacefulness.

"Tranquillity" is undoubtedly one of Foote's finest songs. As in "I Know a Little Garden Path," the subject is solitude. Here serenity prevails, not nostalgia. Seagulls surround the protagonist and before him lies a city and the sea lighted up by the setting sun. "All the wrack of storm" has "passed into silent blue tranquility. / Seagulls about me and my heart at peace." The music reminds me of no previous song by Foote, nor by anyone else, for that matter. In no measure do I ask myself, "Where have I heard that before?" There is an impressionistic, dreamlike quality to the sound. The composition is in ¾ time and a B-flat major tonality. The music is in three musical strains and through-composed. The song's imposing start is both poignant and comforting. The notes allotted to the pianist's right hand remain high in range and lightly swing down and up, down and up, playing high eighth-note passages. The open sound of fourths, fifths, and sixths in these passages resembles the flutter of seagulls' wings. Even though the song seems to slip forth in a seamless surge of revelation, the music surely was exactingly fashioned, one measure at a time, during his pain-racked set-to with sickness. There is a restrained imperturbability about the vocal line, a far-offness that suggests profundity of feeling that cannot be approached too closely. The dynamics usually remain *p*, *pp*, or *ppp*. Only once does the music swell in volume to an *ff*, on the words "seagulls about me, and the sea stretching away like a great tourmaline." The change to loudness is telling because of the surrounding context of softness and the bold conduct of harmony from a V^9_0 of V to a V^7 of III (example 32). A hint of heartache lies concealed beneath the music's shimmering exterior.

After Grace Leslie sang "Tranquillity" in a recital in Berlin, Germany, on 3 October 1930, she sent Foote the program and wrote on it: "Debut beyond fondest hopes—fifteen recalls—many encores—Tranquillity made a great hit."[10]

Foote could now attain to an elegant and unpresuming depth of feeling of the sort commonly identified with the finest art-song composers. He could now accomplish this because his musical speech had long been exercised through the medium of the gentler and more lyrical works of his earlier years. The sound of his songs had always brought joy to the ear, but that of his late songs is far less easy to anticipate. Though the means are varied and the approaches are different, most songs, early and late, are distinguished essays into mood depiction, built on muted tints and exempt from easy rhetorical gestures.

In the years after his fiftieth birthday, he hewed mostly to the small number of themes already enumerated. From 1915 to 1919, six songs were published by Schmidt: "At Last," text by John Greenleaf Whittier (1916), "Drifting," text by Thomas Read (1917), "Lilac Time," text by Alfred Noyes (1917), "Mandalay," text by Rudyard Kipling (1917), "The Munster Fusiliers," text by N. H. Gibbins (1918), and "A Twilight Fear," text by Charles Blanden (1918). Of these, "Drifting" is one of the most successful. Again, a protagonist is described who is divorced from the surrounding world. At last free of the world's uproar, his soul is at peace. A sense of "drifting" arises from harmonies that stray from key to key, never really arriving at the home key until the end, and from a melodic line that roves from measure to measure, reluctant to retrace a rhythmic or tonal design. The work is in three strains and through-composed. The one recurrence is the music of the two-measure prelude, which reappears before the final strain.

I must confess to feeling uncomfortable about the music for "The Munster Fusiliers." The song is about intrepid soldiers from County Kerry who have died in battle. It is represented by two musical strains, each going from a minor to major tonality. Regrettably, the idiom is not too dissimilar from the marches written by David Braham for *The Mulligan Guard* revues presented by the comedy team Harrigan and Hart. In contrast, "A Twilight Fear" rings absolutely true. In it, darkness has arrived and with it vapors that reach out like ghostly hands. The protagonist, tormented by anxiety, wonders what it is they search to snatch away; is it his "love, the wilding rose, / By the old stone fence?" The entire song is only twenty measures long and in one strain. An immense measure of disturbance envelops the close of the song, as the singer intones the last phrase while the harmony moves by way of a chain of seventh chords to an unsettling dominant ninth of the dominant. After the voice is silent, it takes four measures of postlude for the piano to arrive at the tonic chord. William Treat Upton writes that "A Twilight Fear" contains music that is "simplicity itself. I commend it to our young writers as a model of expressive brevity, of artistic restraint."[11]

Of all the Foote songs, those that awaken the most distress-
ingly sharp emotions are the *Three Songs, 1914–1918*, op. 79,
which Schmidt published in 1919: 1. "In Flanders' Fields," text
by Lieutenant-Colonel John McCrae; 2. "The Soldier," text by Rupert Brooke; and 3. "Oh, Red is the English Rose," text by Dr.
Charles Richmond. The manuscript of the second song, now in
the Boston Public Library, has written on it, "For Katharine,
comp. Feb. 22, 1918." The subject of all three is the dead soldiers of World War I. The elegiac music was suggested to the
composer both by the deaths of actual people and by his meditation on the tragic aspects of existence. In the ordinary course of
things, the emotion would have been manifested as a dirge only.
Here, it takes comfort in the consideration of a few enduring beliefs like the commitment to duty, the strength of faith, and the
virtue of sacrifice.

Opus 79 was the closest that Foote ever came to writing a
song cycle, which this opus musically is not. No convincing connection can be established whether in tonality, musical themes,
or harmonic and rhythmic treatment. Indeed, Foote undoubtedly realized that there was no point in writing a song cycle. He
saw American songs normally presented to the public only one
or two at a time, sandwiched between instrumental numbers. An
all-song recital, the most likely setting for a lengthy song cycle,
was rarely given. Furthermore, professional singers did not want
native works to dominate their offerings; public bias leaned toward European creations. Besides, the attention span of the audience might not carry over to more than a couple of unfamiliar
American songs.

On the other hand, if any American art song composer could
arouse the music public, it was Foote. Furthermore, he was consistently successful in his single-song offerings. Each of the three
songs is through-composed and stirs the listener from beginning
to end. No maudlin sounds are heard, no lamentations in inces-
santly minor tonalities. Instead, the music of opus 79 takes on an
elevated noble quality. Although the vocal melodies of all three
songs are attractive, they are not by themselves the central interest. They do not comprise tunes that the listener goes away hum-
ming. Neither the half-cadence, tonic to dominant, nor the
perfect cadence, dominant to tonic, enter to knit the melodic

phrases together, as aids to remembrance. Disjunct motion lessens the lyricism. The progression of chords—simple triads, seventh chords, ninth chords, chromatically altered chords—as well as the companionable course of the piano accompaniment—sometimes seamlessly fluid, sometimes turning more rhythmic to make an emphatic point—are essential constituents of the music. Only when all three components fuse together in the mind do the songs acquire significance. It is not until the silence at the end of each number that listeners realize they have experienced a whole infinitely more meaningful than the details that had unfolded measure after measure. Of course, this might be said of many other fine songs, but it is especially true for these three.

To quote a few measures from a song is almost pointless, since the example would scarcely convey what is integral to the expression. Yet, the details are fascinating in their own way. One such detail occurs in the first song on the sentence "we are the dead." First, the singer intones the tonic note while the piano remains silent; next, on the word "dead," the piano enters very softly with a major triad based on the lowered submediant tone. The effect is both unforeseen and touching. In the second song, the soliloquy "if I should die, think only this of me" is conveyed judiciously through skips of a fourth or more in the conduct of the vocal line, and especially through the fall of minor sevenths. In the last song, the opening line, "Oh, red is the English rose / And the lilies of France are pale," is sung without a single accidental to alter the simple and euphonious harmonies. Later in the song, after the sensitive musical depiction of "ebbing pulses" in dying men, which "beat fainter and fainter and fail," the line returns. However, now sweetness is scoured out of the music, which has become chromatic and more discordant. The listener realizes that redness refers to spilled blood; paleness, to that of drained bodies. The musical change makes the impact that much greater.

Opus 79 was received enthusiastically. A reviewer, identified by the initials F. H. M., wrote in *Musical America* that various settings of all three poems already existed. However, "if for no other reason than that they stand for the musical reaction on the part of an American composer of such pre-eminent achievement as Arthur Foote to the great poems of the war, these fine songs should find an acknowledged place." They are "lofty" and "sincerely noble."[12] William Treat Upton agreed: "I doubt if anything finer in a musical way came out of the war than Mr. Foote's simple, sincere, heartfelt set of Three songs, Op. 79."[13]

Six more compositions round out the list of solo songs: "How Many Times Do I Love Thee," text by Thomas Beddoes (1919); "The Red Rose Whispers of Passion," text by John Boyle O'Reilly (1919); "The Lake Isle of Innisfree," text by William Butler Yeats (1921); "Ships That Pass in the Night," text by William Wadsworth Longfellow (1921); "Shadows," text by Estelle Potter (1921); and "The Song by the Mill," text by Ethel Clifford (1922). On the manuscript of the fourth song, now in the Boston Public Library, a fond father has touchingly written, "For Katharine to take away." They are all excellent works. The first is set strophically, has the most conventional harmony of the lot, and is highlighted with a readily recognizable tune. Foote cites the first, fourth, and fifth songs as among his best.[14] The second song was praised by William Treat Upton, who liked its simplicity and "the unaffected eloquence of the phrase 'And the white rose is a dove.'"[15] The famous singer John McCormack also liked it. He sang it, along with "The Song by the Mill" with some frequency.[16]

Foote also composed around ten unpublished songs. One of them is a strophic song in D minor, "Heart O'Love," text by Caroline Hazard, after Jean Richepin's "La Chanson de Marie-des-Anges." There is a letter dated 15 October 1909 in the library of the Harvard Musical Association, which is attached to the manuscript dated 31 July 1909.[17] It was sent by Caroline Hazard, from the "Office of the President/Wellesley College/Wellesley, Mass." She writes:

> Your most interesting setting of the Richepin Ballad came to me night before last, and you can imagine how eagerly I tried it over. I wish I could hear your daughter sing it, for I am sure she must get a splendid effect with it.
>
> I confess I was much interested to see how it struck you. It is of course possible to conceive of such a poem under two aspects—that of a folk song, with its grim straightforwardness, or, of a tragedy in little. If one conceives of it after the latter fashion a highly dramatic setting would be

possible, such as Loewe has given to some of the German ballads. Your setting [which is after the former fashion] is full of interest, and I long to hear it properly sung.

It was typical of Foote to choose the straightforward, folklike aspect. Nowhere in his solo-voice compositions is a highly dramatic setting found. This also holds true for his part-songs and choral music. Ingratiating, homophonic, and easy to sing are the secular and sacred pieces for men's, women's, or mixed voices. They have a functional purpose, and most were initially intended for local vocalists, singing associations, and church choirs. For the most part, they are lucid, sincere, expertly composed, and hew to plain melodies, homophony, and customary harmonic procedures. The music contributed to the maturation and sustenance of singers from diverse backgrounds and was allied directly to their customary needs and interests. Among the most interesting of these works are "Vita Nostra Plena Bellis," op. 47, a motet for unaccompanied mixed chorus (1901); the *Flower Songs*, op. 49, for women's voices (1902); "The Miller's Daughter," for unaccompanied four-part men's mixed chorus (1902); "O Zion, That Bringest Good Tidings," an anthem for mixed chorus (1903); the *Two Duets*, op. 64, for high voices (1908);[18] *Four Songs*, op. 68, for four-part chorus (1908); "The Gateway of Ispahan," for three-part women's chorus (1914); "Hear My Prayer, O God," for four-past men's chorus and organ (1914); "The One Eternal God," for four-part women's chorus and piano (1914); and "Recessional," for four-part men's chorus, trumpet and three trombones (1914). The lengthy motet demonstrates especially accomplished writing and in its day was sung frequently. On the occasion of its first performance by the Cecilia Society on 4 February 1902, a program note states that Foote is the Cecilia's president and that his musical influence has been great in Boston. Most significantly, it also states, "His chamber music perhaps represents his finest work as a composer."[19] "O Zion, That Bringest Good Tidings" is a fairly lengthy Christmas anthem that shows Foote at his most useful "best." It is through-composed, sectional, and somehow reminds us of the anthems of William Billings. Perhaps the reminder is attributable to the rather plain and frequently diatonic vocal passages, the open choral sonorities, and the contrasting divisions, each

allotted its own music. It begins with an SATB chorus singing homophonically in A-flat major and, for the most part, homorhyth-
mically about the bringing of good tidings. The next division, in
an expressive E major, has an alto soloist briefly narrate the birth
of Jesus; a tenor-bass contrapuntal duet asks where is the new-
born child; and the alto returns to describe the guiding star. The
third division, which goes from C-sharp minor to E major, contains the music of a *siciliana*, whose gently rocking triple rhythms
and dotted figures summon a pastoral atmosphere as a soprano
soloist and SATB chorus describe melodiously the "Christmas
morn when Christ was born." The final division, in A-flat again,
has the SATB chorus singing an exuberant song of praise, "Awake
up, my glory, awake lute and harp." The composer has attempted
to compose nothing outstandingly original; simply something
that will commemorate the occasion for which it was written with
festive and gratifying sound. Other sacred works that would be
useful during the church year and show a choir to advantage are
"Does the Road Wind Uphill All the Way?" (1903), "I Cannot Find
Thee" (1904), "The Law of the Lord Is Perfect" (1904), "Listen, O
Isles, unto Me" (1911), and "Be Thou My Guide" (1915). The
dates cited are those of publication.

While the music of "Recessional" is extremely well executed,
the present-day listener finds it difficult to relate to a text that refers to England's holding "dominion over palm and pine" and
that lauds the God of England's "farflung battleline." Compositions for men's voices that have more comfortable texts are "The
Miller's Daughter" (1901), "A Song of April" (1905), "Farewell to
Summer" (1911), "Hear My Prayer" (1914), "Seek and Ye Shall
Find" (1915), and "Magnificat" (1915). Note the turn to religious
topics during the time of his illness.

In the *Flower Songs*, we find the composer writing in his
most enjoyable and relaxed vein. In contrast, the most ambitious
vocal work of his late years was *Lygeia*, op. 58, for soloists, wom-
en's chorus, and orchestra (1906). Unfortunately, *Lygeia*
founders on an outmoded and overly sentimental text that includes some half-realized dramatic writing. Moreover, the style is
inconsistent. Foote does not convincingly reconcile his patches
of extremely complex harmonic writing, such as in the instrumental introduction (example 33), with the much simpler har-

monic means employed, say, for the solos sung by Lygeia and "the lover." Other works for women's voices that could be profitably explored are "The Green of Spring" (1906), "Mount Carmel" (1909), "Gray Twilight" (1909), "Tomorrow" (1911), "Through the Rushes by the River" (1913), "Sigh No More, Ladies" (1913), and "Constancy" (1928).

Finally, two rewarding duets intended for SA, or high and low, solo voices are "The Skylark" (1915) and "Lord of the Worlds Above" (1917).

Keyboard Music

Foote says in his autobiography that among "the most successful things" composed in 1900–1915 "were an Organ Suite; the little 'Twenty Preludes' for piano; [and] half a dozen organ pieces written after returning from California."[20] The success of the *Twenty Preludes for the Piano in the Form of Short Technical Studies*, op. 52, was attributable far more to their usefulness as training pieces than to their virtues as finished works of art. The edition published by Schmidt in 1903 includes a message at the bottom of the first page: "NOTE. It will be seen that some of the passages and figures found in these Preludes were suggested by other composers." Most of the preludes are one or two pages in length and single out one technical problem for exploration. The object is to discipline the fingers. There is absolutely no sense of adventure in harmony or rhythm and melody is absent in most of the selections. As a result, scarcely any offer a modicum of interest for the listener. Two do have appeal, no. 8 in B minor, which is set up in alternating $^5/_4$ and $^3/_4$ measures and discloses an amiable melody, and the extremely succinct no. 13 in B-flat major, to be played slowly and expressively.

In contrast, *Meditation*, op. 61, which Schmidt put out in 1907 in both a piano and an organ version, is one of Foote's finest keyboard pieces. As do several of his late songs, it looks inward, attempting to plumb and paint the more melancholic concerns of the human spirit. The piano version has a quotation under the title: "And leaves the world to darkness and to me." The organ version simply supplies a variant on the title: *Night: A Meditation*.

That is all; nothing is added to the title. The quotation comes from the first stanza of Thomas Gray's *Elegy to a Country Church-yard* (1750):

> The curfew tolls the knell of parting day,
> The lowing herd wend slowly o'er the lea,
> The ploughman homeward plods his weary way,
> And leaves the world to darkness and to me.

It is an uninterrupted soliloquy, a contemplative reverie charged with sadness of the sort most humans have experienced at one time or another. In ³/₄ and F major, the melody's first two measures contain the expressive kernel of the entire piece, in particular the half-step rise g′ to a-flat′, then the fall of a diminished seventh to a b-natural, which is immediately heard as an appoggiatura rising to c′ (example 34). The first strain, which is dressed with a great deal of chromaticism, is ten measures long and ends on the dominant. It is mainly ruminative but with an edge of yearning in its expression. The second strain, eleven measures long, starts with the same first measure as before, but a lovely and unexpected e-flat′ in its second measure signals the onset of a different and more eloquent commentary that eventually closes in the dominant minor. Yearning has changed to an ache, now laced with deepening grief. The third strain also starts with the same first measure as the other two, only transposed up a minor third. It begins in A-flat major but quickly winds through a number of keys on the flat side. Over its eighteen measures, texture thickens, volume increases, and feeling mounts to a climax. The final strain, *una corda*, reproduces the first five measures of the first strain. For the rest of its twelve measures, the music sounds softly, though not with any great degree of serenity. What is left is resignation. Nor is there a firm, affirmative close. We hear a discomforting dominant ninth of the dominant, then the dominant tone alone, then a wisp of a tonic harmony, and then the silence that comes afterwards.

No other late piano music approximates the seriousness and profound sentiment of *Meditation*. On the whole, the remaining music comprises brief character pieces, undemanding technically and meant to occupy idle moments pleasantly. Several had existed for some time prior to their publication by Schmidt. They include *Pieces at Twilight: Six Pianoforte Duets*, published in 1905 ("Church Bells," "Graceful Dance," "At Night," "The May-pole," "A Solemn March," "The Swing"); *Opus 60*, in 1907 ("Rev-ery," "A May Song"); *Opus 62*, in 1907 ("Whims," "Exaltation"); *Five Silhouettes*, op. 73, in 1913 ("Prelude," "Dusk," "Valse Triste," "Flying Cloud," "Oriental Dance"); the *Serenade in F Ma-jor*, revised edition of opus 45, in 1914 ("Aubade," "Air," "A Dance," "Finale and Toccatina"); *From Rest Harrow*, in 1922 ("Morning Glories," "Rain on the Garret Roof," "A Country Song," "Country Dance," "Alla Turca"). *Five Little Pieces* ("Cuck-oo," "A Little Waltz," "A Melody for a Young Musician," "Spinning Song," "Tarantelle") was composed at Rest Harrow in 1924. There also exist five brief works written purely with technical de-velopment in mind.

Each piece provides its own modest reward. "Prelude" of opus 73, for example, in its bold and loud assertiveness, is un-usual for Foote. It is in a D minor that contains more than a hint of modality. Reverberating chords are intertwined with upward sweeping sixty-fourth-note arpeggios. Also unusual for the com-poser is the end, where we hear the infrequently used dimin-ished seventh chord leading to a close on the tonic major chord.

When we examine the first four numbers of *From Rest Har-row*, we find miniature sketches. "Morning Glories," which is dedicated to Henri Raffy, features fast, somewhat eccentric, up-ward darting sixteenth-note movement in its outer sections and midrange lyricism at its center. "Rain on the Garret Roof" is quite inconsequential and made up mostly of single-line staccato eighth notes that the pianist taps out to approximate the patter of tiny raindrops. "A Country Song" involves a stretch of folksy melody, complete with a Scotch snap. "Country Dance," given one of Foote's favorite tempo indications, *allegro comodo*, is an enjoyable gavotte.

Although Foote was known as an organist for much of his life, he wrote few works for the instrument. Yet, the little he did compose was widely played, even by the celebrated organists of the United States and Europe. The late compositions for organ, compared to those for piano, are graver, more substantial, and more contrapuntal, though not overwhelmingly so. Most of them, without a doubt, were designed for use in church services. The predominant mood is exaltation. Elegance, which is made delightful through the grace, symmetry, and attractiveness of the sound, also forms a part of the essential nature of each piece, while mere brilliant exhibition is eschewed. Nowhere does he seek to win over the listener with the bravura of the music. The everyday pictorial-mood elements in most of the piano pieces are nowhere to be found.

Published by Schmidt, Foote's *Six Pieces*, op. 50 ("Meditation," "Pater Noster," "Offertory," "Intermezzo," "Prelude," and "Nocturne") bear a 1902 copyright. Copyrighted in 1904 was the Suite in D Major, op. 54 ("Maestoso," "Allegro energico," "Quasi minuetto," "Allegro comodo"); in 1907, the already mentioned *Night: A Meditation*; in 1910, *Compositions*, op. 71 ("Cantilena in G major," "Solemn March," "Sortie in C major," "Canzonetta," "Tempo di minuetto," "Communion," "Toccata"); and in 1919, *Christmas*, op. 80. Composed in 1912 and published in Paris in 1914 were *Deux Pièces* ("Marche, E-flat," "Communion, D Minor").

The *Six Pieces*, op. 50, show the composer almost entirely rapt in religious-musical thought. All are brief movements. Meditation is characterized by the attractive flow of four contrapuntal lines within a ternary structure (A B A^1). The first section moves from G to D major; the second section is less tonally stable and goes from B-flat major to E minor to C major; the third section more or less recapitulates the opening, except that whatever was in the dominant key is transposed to the tonic. In all, it is a reflective, rather withdrawn, creation, with a fairly even course of thought held to from beginning to end. No surge of emotion interrupts the quiet polyphonic discourse. The Pater Noster sustains a stately yet abstracted progress throughout. Though the piece begins ostensibly in an E-minor tonality, the Phrygian and Aeolian modes permeate the proceedings. This, plus a motion mostly in whole-, half-, and quarter-notes, gives the music an appearance of existing on another plane. It is intriguing to see the piece end with the antique modal transit of the D-minor triad to the A-minor triad, followed by the E-minor triad and D-minor triad, to close on the C-major triad—all in root position. Next comes the Offertory, whose measures are built on the same motive as that heard previously in the Quartet in E Major for Strings, op. 32 (example 20c).

The Intermezzo is pleasant to hear but is provided with less compelling ideas than those of the previous movements. More satisfying and supplied with ideas that are stronger than those of the Intermezzo, the Prelude unfolds with its different voices constantly in contrapuntal motion. The initial melodic line in the treble, which returns in the middle and the end of the piece, proceeds engagingly and even undergoes some development. The Nocturne is puzzling because stylistically it does not belong with the set. It is laid out like a Chopin nocturne and given a ternary form. The first and last sections are set up like the first section of Chopin's F-Minor Nocturne, op. 55, no. 4; the middle section, like the middle of Chopin's G-Minor Nocturne, op. 37 no. 1. The actual sound, however, is not at all in the style of Chopin. In ⁴/₄ and B minor, the movement begins with a fetching tune in the right hand accompanied by low single bass notes on beats one and three and higher chords on beats two and four of each measure. The middle section, in D major, is entirely a procession of solemn chords.

The Suite in D Major for Organ, op. 54, won widespread approval during the composer's lifetime. After Schmidt published it in 1904, movements from it were much performed in organ recitals and church services. For example, shortly after the work was published, the famous French organist Joseph Bonnet (1884–1944) chose to play its third movement during his first tour of the United States.[21]

It contains three movements: Maestoso-Allegro energico, Quasi minuetto, and Allegro comodo. The first movement opens with the stately motion of a French overture from two-hundred years before. In ⁴/₄ and D minor, it proceeds homophonically for fourteen measures on a dotted rhythm—a held note (dotted quarter plus a thirty-second note) and three rapidly descending thirty-second notes. The anticipated fast segment is not fugal, although portions of it are quite contrapuntal. It begins in D minor on a theme that could have nicely fit into the beginning of the Tchaikovsky Fifth Symphony (example 35a). However, it could as easily be taken as a direct descendant of the minor-mode tunes written by the late eighteenth-century New England singing-school composers. The second theme is in F major and commences with the falling fourth intervals that distinguish Horatio Parker's oratorio *Hora Novissima* of 1893. After the recapitulation of the first Allegro theme, the second one returns in D major. The Maestoso ending redeploys material from the very beginning.

The second movement in B-flat major is not the minuet that the title implies. For one, the time signature is ³/₄ (²/₄). The signature is meant to indicate that duple meter will interrupt the triple meter every now and again. For another, the notion of a minuet is quickly dispelled in the first thirteen measures, which could as easily have been barred in ²/₄ meter throughout. The rather eccentrically moving main idea is twice interrupted by a secondary subject that goes in sixteenth notes from F major to F minor and features a treble-to-bass give-and-take.

If the third movement, an andante *espressivo* in G minor, is to be taken as an "improvisation," the extemporization is based on a modal idea that, like the beginning of the first movement's *allegro*, sounds Russian or like old New England psalmody (example 35b). At any rate, the melody is heard four times and contrasted with a middle section in B-flat major that features a faster moving, jumpy staccato idea. The return to G minor at the end reintroduces both ideas in the home key, but briefly.

The last movement, in ³/₄ and D major, starts off like the Italian type of *courante* found in Baroque suites. The first subject is built expertly and mounts for eleven measures from d′ to a‴, over a running eighth-note figure until a climax is achieved, at which point the eighth notes unwind downward for four measures. The middle section is faster, its passages higher in range. The left hand plays chords in the treble clef while the right hand layers on eighth-note figurations an octave above. After a lengthy transition the first subject returns. The movement closes on a twenty-measure maestoso that is a return to and an extension of the music heard at the end of the first movement.

I find it difficult to describe the overall expression of the suite. It certainly is not highly charged music, nor preoccupied with romanticized emotion. Rather, there is a sense of detachment, of otherness, as if the composer were trying to efface himself, to retreat into prayer. Nevertheless, feeling there is—something like a grave and reverential coming closer to Divinity through music.

The seven compositions of *Opus 71*, though more involved with subjective emotion, do not completely abandon this sense of detachment. They are all strong works. The lovely "Cantilena in G major" is an arrangement of the Air from the Serenade for Strings, op. 25. It is one indication of several that Foote was now frequently looking back to and reassessing his earliest works. The Baroque accents audible in several of them now act as a spur to his twentieth-century efforts. The elements that would not reappear in his late years were the ardent and overbrimming emotional expressions of his young adulthood, as heard in the Trio no. 1, String Quartet no. 1, and Violin Sonata.

A highlight of the opus is the Solemn March in E Minor, whose straightforward first part builds to a powerful and choralelike *ff* and whose Trio in C Major establishes a hauntingly subdued mood, where no perfect cadence is heard and chords in root position evoke the era of Palestrina. The Canzonetta boasts one of Foote's most splendid tunes. In the first part, a lyric treble line flows forth over a simple chordal accompaniment in A minor (example 36a). The middle section, in F major, introduces a superb contrast in a solemn chantlike theme that has a link to the New England psalmody of the eighteenth century, at the same time sounding vaguely Russian (example 36b). Attributions of influence are often precarious, whether in this regard or in regard to other Foote compositions where a facile mention of Brahms occurs.

Not much need be said about the remaining organ compositions. Foote offers sturdy music that is appropriate for church use. "Christmas," which was dedicated to Joseph Bonnet, is a fantasy on three Christmas carols: "Listen, Lordlings unto Me," "What Child Is This," and "The First Noel." It is an effective and welcome piece for presentation during the Christmas season.

Chamber Music

The published chamber music that was written during the last thirty-five years of Foote's life add up to only four works: Trio no. 2 in B-flat, for Piano, Violin, and Cello, op. 65, was published by

Schmidt in1909; the Ballade in F Minor, for Violin and Piano, op. 69, in 1910; the Quartet in D for Strings, op. 70, in 1911; and *Opus 74* for violin and piano, consisting of a Canzonetta, and A Song of Sleep, in 1913. Remaining unpublished in his lifetime were *Legend* for violin and piano, op. 76 (1912?); *Aubade to Alwin Schroeder*, op. 77, for cello and piano (1912); Sonata in E Minor for Cello or Viola and Piano, op. 78 (between 1912 and 1918); Nocturne and Scherzo for flute and string quartet (1918); *At Dusk*, for flute, cello, and harp (1920);[22] and *Sarabande and Rigaudon*, for oboe or flute, viola or violin, and piano (1921).[23]

Ten chamber compositions, with so few of them offered to the public by the composer, is not a happy record. Although he was never a prolific composer, his manifold activities as a teacher, choir director, keyboard performer, and music entrepreneur had not left him much free time to author new compositions. However, after the age of fifty-five or so, he had begun to decrease these activities and, after the age of sixty, to eliminate most of them. Severe illness and resultant poor health had something to do with the scanty production. Eye problems commenced in the twenties, grew severe, and remained with him until his death. World War I came and went, taking with it the world he knew, altering the aesthetic, social, and moral values he held dear. Possibly the belief that history was passing him by, that the contemporary stage was increasingly being given over to younger musicians with radically different viewpoints and compositional practices contrary to his, led to his discouragement. Accusations against his artistry and denigration of the music that Foote espoused made by modernists had begun in the 1910s, but grew loud and persistent with the beginning of the 1920s.[24] He could not have been pleased over the charge that he was nothing but an unimaginative academic and that his music was genteel, overly polite, conventional, and insipid. Perhaps he was becoming musically played out, too tired to apply himself constantly to creative labor. Perhaps sales of his compositions had dropped, especially chamber and orchestral music. All of what I have just said is not mere conjecture. His autobiography, letters, and articles, and the commentaries of people who knew him all point to these inferences, especially for the years commencing with World War I.

The Trio No. 2 in B-flat Major, for Piano, Violin, and Cello, op. 65, was written between 1907 and 1908, premiered by Foote and the Kneisels at Isabella Gardner's Fenway Court on 8 December 1908, and published by Schmidt in 1909. The work contains three movements: Allegro Giocoso, Tranquillo, Allegro Molto. For the most part, the music appears rationally thought out, replete with inviting melodies that are expanded upon according to his fancy. There is about the work an unaffectedness and refinement of style reminiscent of eighteenth-century music. We also find a rejection of the struggle to achieve those big, momentous statements that inhabit the works of many late-nineteenth century composers. Throughout, we detect a technical competence entirely adequate to the demands of his creative vision.

Although the music is without question "romantic," it is not Central-European Romanticism that suffuses the movements. Distinctive American traits are added. Foote's manner of writing has relaxed somewhat regarding the rules of composition. He shows less concern about the consequences of unresolved dissonances, eccentric twists of melody, and unannounced modulations.

Foote does not assault the listener's sensibilities with one or two boldly stated emotions; indeed, his expressions are varied and subtly signified. Probably for these reasons, the new trio never made as strong an impression on the public as had the first trio. Foote's own assessment was that, though the second trio was a success in his estimation and was "less conventional and of greater interest harmonically and structurally than the one of twenty-five years before," it was "perhaps not so fresh."[25]

The initial subject of the first movement (in sonata-allegro form) is given a sprightly, rhythmic shape and by the thirteenth measure has become modulatory, as the composer works out his material during the transition from the home key to the secondary key. There is an American feeling to the jiggling way the violin tune jumps about in its first six measures. On balance, the music is not really as jocose as the composer's initial caption indicates. Dynamics that change from loud to very loud, chromatic alterations that have the harmony making darting references to secondary keys, the jar of a dissonance here and there, and a piano part that refuses to remain in a ³/₄ meter encourage emotions that go beyond mere jocundity (example 37a). The transition heightens the feeling of tension. The second subject area in the dominant key of F arrives as anticipated. However, what is decidedly unexpected is the veering away into the D-minor tonality and the introduction of a melodic idea in the Dorian mode that sounds Amerindian (example 37b). In the recapitulation, the two subject areas return reorchestrated and both in the home key, save for the "Amerindian" portion, which reappears in G minor. A seven-measure close marked *Tranquillo* resorts for a final time to the principal motive of the first subject, which is sounded twice, quietly and expressively. In this manner, the composer astutely prepares the listener for the second movement and provides a final touch to a movement that has refused to remain in a jocular vein.

The second movement is in D major—the mediant key is a common alternate tonality for composers of the nineteenth century. Here, the composer unveils a long, rambling melody, first stated by the cello, which though warm in feeling and abetted by suggestive chromatic inflections, does not communicate as immediately as do the tunes of his earlier slow movements. It shapes a communication that grows on the listener after a few hearings. Thirty-three measures later, in a section marked *largamente*, a new melody begins on the violin's G-string that impresses itself in the memory and refuses to leave. The music here is legato, mostly stepwise, and characterized by a double-dotted eighth note followed by two sixty-fourth notes (example 37c). It is especially lovely to listen to the piano, two octaves above the violin, giving a silvery edge to the sounds. The phrasing is compact, the communication direct, and the mood obviously designed to move emotions. There is a brief recapitulation of the two themes, the first in D, the second commencing in B-flat but ending in D.

The last movement, in sonata-allegro form, is very fast and begins in B-flat minor. A sense of urgency impels the principal melody forward. First the cello, next the cello and violin are given broad melodies that the staccato sixteenth-note piano accompaniment keeps on driving forward. A tumultuous climax results, after which comes an eloquent, even supplicatory, response, first a *marcato* in F minor, then a *poco largamente* in F major, where the piano alone holds forth for several measures— a rarity in Foote's chamber music with piano. The *poco largamente* idea returns in the recapitulation, but is heard in B-flat major. The final thirteen measures turn to the first theme of the first movement, which fills the air with resounding boldness to complete the trio. The musician in the audience comes away impressed by the attention to detail and the elaborate instrumental interchange of ideas in all three movements. The ordinary listener is won over by the wealth of sentiment and the kaleidoscopic array of melodies. The musical connoisseur enjoys the painstakingly readjusted frames of mind and feeling that follow one on another and the convincingly thought-out framework that holds the entire trio together.

Foote mentions the success of the several violin pieces he wrote after 1901, saying that of them all "the Ballade is the best."[26] The Ballade in F Minor for Violin and Piano, op. 69, was published in 1910, the year it was premiered. Like all of the late violin pieces, it is in ternary form and brings out the best in the string instrument. As was true for the second trio, the highly individualized ardor that emanated from the composer's own inner being, so evident in the earliest chamber compositions, has moderated. It is modified by the injection of a more reserved, less personalized display of feeling. Every now and again a modal quality permeates the measures. Yet, because equipped with a tender, sympathetic melody and given a swinging, triple-time motion, the music remains engaging throughout.

Foote may have started to compose the Quartet in D Major for Strings, op. 70, as early as 1907, but it was not until four years later that he completed it. In 1911, Schmidt saw to its publication, which included a dedication to the conductor of the Chicago Symphony, Frederick Stock. One of its earliest performances took place on 21 April 1912 at Schmidt's home. In many ways, the third quartet strikes the ear as one of Foote's best, most fully realized chamber compositions, every portion of it arrived at after slow and careful deliberation. Its superiority is shown in its planning, in the realization of his design in the score, and in the integration of every detail of its sound to enhance the whole. The music contains his furthest advances in harmony, whether in its construction or progression, in the free use of chromaticism, and in the application of dissonance for expressive purposes. The interchange of ideas between the instruments and the high incidence of contrapuntal activity are also outstanding attributes of the work.

Fascinating, too, is the way he manages a customary artistic medium so as to give the impression of freshness and renders his subject matter in a way that effectively imparts a rich variety of moods. R. D. Darrell writes about the quartet's "frankly romantic idiom" which "has little of the German accent," and about the employment of an accepted idiom, which nevertheless reveals "a saltily distinctive Yankee individuality, a freedom from clichés, a disdain of heart-on-sleeve sentimentality, and a fresh vitality."[27]

The first movement, an allegro in $\frac{4}{4}$ meter, is by no means in a clear-cut D major. Indeed, the focal point here, more than in any other of his works, is the selected tone itself, rather than a tonality regulating chords and tones. A confident, vigorous, and ecstatically ascending subject in the first violin reaches up to a very high b-flat''' before gradually subsiding into quietness (example 38a). The skip downward of a fifth in measure 3 should be noted, since it is a recurring sound. When combined with the three notes that come after, it is a recurring motto throughout the work. Foote makes certain that it catches the listener's attention from the beginning by underlining it with the chord of the dominant ninth (root missing) of the dominant. A measure like this one enhances an atmosphere of retrospection, of tender longing for a time that is no more. It is the first of many passages that seem to delineate a former life, whose moments of happiness and sadness, dreaming and desire, glide through the mind of the aging artist. He is intent on portraying these moments, for perhaps a final time, through sensitively realized, alternately bold and mournful sounds.

The idea of the falling fifth is not completely original with Foote, since Robert Schumann in his String Quartet in A, op. 41, no. 3, had also started off with the same falling f-sharp'' to b', and also over an unstable chord. The idea was not new to Schumann, since Beethoven, in his Piano Sonata in E-flat, op. 31, no. 3, had done the same in the first measure, a falling fifth, c'' to f', over a supertonic seventh chord. Foote's use of the idea, however, in no way parallels that of Schumann or Beethoven.

A variant on the motive enters in measure 26, in B minor, featuring at first the downward move of a diminished fourth, then a perfect fourth, but later expanding to a fifth. However, the context is that of a transition away from the first subject; the true second subject, in A major, does not arrive until measure 52. It also employs the downward skipping fifth, only the total setting is more conjunct, quieter, and lyric. A codetta that makes great use of a figure comprising two sixteenth-notes followed by an eighth note closes the sonata-allegro exposition. The development expertly exploits the material from the exposition, ringing all sorts of changes in expression. It is fairly brief, since Foote throughout the exposition had been constantly elaborating on his ideas. The recapitulation reorchestrates the material of the exposition. What was heard in B minor is now in F-sharp minor; what was heard in A, now in D. By the end of the movement, the listener is left remembering especially the affection that the composer showered on the pages, the warmhearted and stimulating musical speech patterns that resulted, and the fertile conjuring of a diversity of emotions.

The Scherzo movement is marked *capriccioso*, which refers to the whimsical moods that pass through the movement. A playful and weightless style prevails almost everywhere, characterized by rapid, detached, and precisely stressed figuration. Foote composed the measures with the delicacy that he was later to retain in a series of brief chamber works. The meter is $^3/_8$; the key is G minor. It begins with all instruments muted and playing high in their range, thus giving the tune an airy lightness. The distinguishing downward skip of a fifth, sometimes a fourth, returns, only now it adds a graceful lilt to the melody. Mutes are removed for the middle section, which is to go at a much faster clip (*molto più vivace*). The increased speed is important to Foote, since the expressive, legato nature of the melodic line might tempt the player to linger sentimentally on some of his notes. The fall of a fifth is a vital component of the transparent lyric line in C minor with which the second violin starts off (example 38b). If the first five measures of the melody are compared to the second to fourth measure of the first movement's opening subject, the connection becomes obvious. In both one hears a fall of a fifth, two conjunctly upward moving notes, and a third drop. The viola takes over from the second violin, and the cello from the viola, before the music returns to the material of the beginning.

The third movement is an *andante espressivo* in $^4/_4$ meter and B major. Often the music seems to envelop itself with a feeling of religious poignancy. It opens with the motto in the cello (a fall of a fifth, two stepwise notes moving upward, a third fall), which then plays an eloquent theme (example 38c). At first, composure has ruled. Yet swiftly, the tune is transfigured, in part owing to the rich harmonic atmosphere surrounding it and to the attractiveness of the chromaticism. The first violin takes over the melody in measure 6 and spins it out poetically until the arrival at the *animato* middle section. Tonally unstable and agitated, the spirited music achieves its climax quickly, after only eight measures, which Foote indicates by *ff*, half-step chromatic motion, double stops in the two middle instruments, a first violin that ranges up to g-sharp''', and a paradoxical *tranquillo* indication. True tranquillity, however, does not return until the restatement of the principal melody.

The final movement is introduced by a twenty-measure *andante espressivo* in ³/₄ meter, where the first violin sounds the motto (a fifth down, two upward steps, a third down) in the fourth and fifth measures. The dominant ninth of C, with root missing, that harmonizes the fall of the fifth, a' to d', in the melody, forms a direct link to the first movement. An *allegro non troppo marcato* follows in D minor. A taut theme with colorful downward leaps of a seventh, after staying on for eleven measures, then has an astonishing Debussy-like whole-tone continuation, during which the fifth drop of the motto is heard in the cello (example 38c). Eventually, a new, distinctly profiled theme is heard, first in D-flat major, later in F. The Debussy-like passage returns transposed up a half-step and becomes a transition back to the initial subject. At the close, the second subject returns in D major, blaringly loud and strongly affirmative in feeling, and twice refers to the motto before the movement (and the quartet) ends. The quartet ends, not with farewell gestures, but with the determination to live on.

The Sonata for Cello or Viola and the Nocturne and Scherzo aside, the remaining chamber works hardly ever probe deeply into the psyche. *Opus 74* gives us a supple "Canzonetta" and the calm warbling of "A Song of Sleep." *Legend*, op. 76, is more consequential. The violin begins with a recitative, then turns into a balladeer, as its declamatory, sometimes modal, melody builds in meditative fashion on a brief motive. The *Aubade*, op. 77, was written for Foote's friend, Alwin Schroeder, the principal cellist of the Boston Symphony, and hews to the same path as the *Legend*.

At Dusk boasts an unusual instrumental mix and sounds more emotional and gloomy than the previous three works. Could the Debussy Sonata for Flute, Viola, and Harp (1915) have directed Foote to the instrumental combination he uses? Foote's piece has a haunting, subdued opening, with the harp playing a series of rising diatonic chords in both hands, all in a modal E-flat minor. Then the cello lines out an elegiac melody, which remains diatonic and modal throughout. At measure 12, the flute enters on a phrase that sounds as if it could fit comfortably in Mahler's "Wenn mein Schatz Hochzeit macht" (the first of his *Lieder Eines Fahrenden Gesellen*, which date from the 1890s). The flute and cello, supported by the harp, then play a duet that glows with increasing heat until it achieves a fortissimo, after which the initial harp-cello-violin music returns.

In contrast to *At Dusk*, the *Sarabande and Rigaudon* contain tunes that give off purposely open, easy, and uncomplicated sentiments. It is as if the composer, in 1921 and toward the end of his creative life, had decided with premeditation to turn his face away from the present and look back to the distant past.

No one can say with certainty when the Sonata in E Minor for Cello [or viola], op. 78, was written. There is no evidence that it was ever performed during Foote's lifetime. The manuscript of the cello version, now in the Harvard Musical Association, bears no date. It is bound with other works that date from 1912 to 1922.[28] In the New England Conservatory of Music is a manuscript of the Sonata's viola version, which was written after the cello version. On its last page appears the date "1919." Also, it comes bound with an optional viola part for the *Melody*, op. 44, on which Foote has written: "Jan. 1918. Sent to E. Ferir— Adeline Packard." Douglas Moore, the authority on Foote's cello music, believes the original cello version was written after the *Aubade*, op. 77, probably in 1913.[29] With the pianist Frank Conlon, he presented what might have been its first performance, on 26 October 1976. There are three movements: 1. *Allegro appassionato* (cello and viola); 2. *Andantino con moto* (cello and viola); 3. *Vivace assai* (cello) and *Allegro comodo: con moto* (viola).

Douglas Moore has made a detailed comparison between the cello and viola versions, finding minor melodic, rhythmic, harmonic, and structural differences, but not much of major significance. The viola version clears up some confusing harmonies and eases uncomfortable piano passages.[30] After living with both versions for a while, I found the viola's timbre more suited to the nature of the music. The corrections in the 1919 manuscript give greater stature to the composition. For these reasons, it is from the viola version in particular that I draw the conclusions that follow.

An autumnal feeling surrounds the entire work, suggesting a last entry into the depths of musical feeling before the fires within the composer begin to diminish and he resigns himself to old age. The string instrument is the composer's own voice, constantly singing and supported by a mainly subordinate piano part. The sonata structure of the first movement, in $^2/_2$ meter, begins on a broad melody that needs space to expand, even as the emotion expands (example 39a). It starts on e and eventually rises two octaves to reach its zenith on e″, then subsides to e′. The piano alone introduces the second subject as a subdued hymn (example 39b). When the cello takes over, it brings with it greater melancholy, even a tinge of Brahmsian nostalgia. The contrasting of the expressive attitudes represented by the two subjects provide the material for everything that follows, as the movement takes on richer and richer meanings until the very end, when the string intsrument very quietly and ethereally rises from a low e to e‴.

The second movement is in $^4/_4$ meter and A-flat major. The employment of the key a major third above the tonic note (A-flat = G-sharp) for the second movement has already been seen in the second piano trio. In ternary form, the music starts with an ingratiating serenade-like melody (example 39c). The movement feels mostly serene and relaxed, although at times it has an elegiac quality. The last movement, in sonata form, has a first subject that is a straight-out tarantella in $^6/_8$ time. In contrast, the second subject in the relative major key, announced by the piano with the string instrument silent, takes on the expressive characteristics of the second subject of the first movement. When the second subject returns in the recapitulation, it is in E major, and in E major the movement ends.

Though much less adventurous in harmony and rhythm, and more subdued than the second piano trio and the third string quartet, the sonata, in the sum of all of its parts, wins the listener over through persuasion.

One final chamber work remains to be mentioned, the *Nocturne and Scherzo* for flute and string quartet. Its first movement, retitled as A Night Piece, was later arranged for flute and string orchestra. In his autobiography, Foote wrote:

> The last thing of consequence that I wrote was two pieces for flute and strings for Georges Laurent, the superlative first flute of the Boston Orchestra. He had formed a little society called the Flute Players' Club in 1920, at whose concerts a great deal of the newer chamber music (largely with wind instruments) had been played.[31]

That was around the year 1927. A few years later, on 11 March 1933, he said in a radio broadcast:

> A dozen years ago I was asked to write something for the San Francisco Chamber Music Society at the head of which was a well known flute player, Elias Hecht. The result was the "Night Piece." . . . The Chamber Music Society played it a good deal in its concerts, but I never heard it until later, when Georges Laurent, the distinguished first flute of our orchestra, placed it on a programme of the Flute Players' Club.[32]

The manuscript, now at the New England Conservatory of Music, is headed by the dedication "To the Chamber Music Society of San Francisco" at the top center of the first page. At the extreme right is written: "Arthur Foote, Rest Harrow, August 1918." The first movement bears no title. The second movement is entitled Caprice, and on its last page is the date "March 1918."[33] Elias Hecht and the society had requested a composition from Foote, and they received the *Nocturne and Scherzo* soon after its completion. It was premiered on 28 January 1919 by Hecht, on flute, and four string players in San Francisco.[34] Georges Laurent waited until 30 October 1921 to perform it in Boston.[35] In the early years of the composition's existence, the first movement was sometimes called A Night Piece, and the second, Caprice and A Night Piece.

Because the movement known as Nocturne or A Night Piece is one of the most outstanding compositions that Foote ever wrote, details on its first performances are required. Reviewing the San Francisco premiere, Ray Brown wrote in the *San Francisco Examiner:*

> The nocturne and scherzo for flute and strings by Arthur Foote, played for the first time anywhere, proved a surprise to those who believed that the composer had about written his talent out. The work was written last summer in Foote's sixty-fifth year, yet it shows not a trace of encroaching age. It is fresh and spontaneous, plentiful in melody and colored with beauty. The nocturne has nothing of the melancholy musings of disillusioned maturity, but is filled with the quickening impulses of spring, and the scherzo has a nimble and a joyous wit.[36]

The day after Laurent played the music in Boston, the *Transcript* music critic wrote that it was a contrast to the dullness of the Max Reger *Serenata*, which was also on the program. To this critic, Foote's composition demonstrated great technical knowledge and a superb imagination. Especially pleasing was the first movement, which the writer cites as "Night Piece." In rebuttal to those who saw no value in American compositions, this critic also writes: "However much the supercilious may rail against American music, and whatever reproaches it may incur, justly or unjustly, because of its lack of originality, its dependence upon some European idioms, one thing may be said for it—it is almost never dull. Perhaps it is the native sense of humor, an instinctive feeling for the fitness of things generally saves our composers."[37]

There is no need for me to talk about the music in the Scherzo, since it is an arrangement, with no important changes, of the second movement of the String Quartet no. 2, op. 32, which has already been discussed. I will take up the Nocturne in its reincarnation as A Night Piece, for flute and string orchestra.

The Two Last Works for Instrumental Ensemble

The same year, 1909, that Foote had his publisher Schmidt issue the Piano Trio no. 2, he also saw another composition go into print, the Suite in E Major for String Orchestra, op. 63, which he had started writing in 1907 alongside the trio. It is in three movements: Praeludium, Pizzicato and Adagietto, and Fugue. Originally he had included a movement consisting of a theme and variations in the suite, but it was eliminated just before publication.

Like the trio, the suite is carefully planned, is supplied with captivating music, and is realized by means of a mature and polished style. Not only do large portions of the suite look back to the eighteenth century, but they also recall and show affinities to the Suite no. 1 in E Major, for String Orchestra (1886), the Suite no. 2 in D Major for String Orchestra (1889), and the Serenade in E Major for String Orchestra (1891). However, no imitation results. Foote has gone back to his beginnings in order to scrutinize and reevaluate the creative road he has taken. In the new composition, he builds on the abundance of his experiences. Every idea in his third suite is newly refined within the mind of a fully developed artist.

The suite was premiered by Max Fiedler and the Boston Symphony Orchestra on 16 April 1909, and from the first hearing absolutely delighted audiences.[38] It immediately went on to fame and repeated performances by American and London orchestras. It was an especial favorite of Serge Koussevitsky after he assumed the conductorship of the Boston Symphony in 1924. When Koussevitsky and the Boston Symphony performed the work in New York in March 1929, Olin Downes gave his assessment of composer and music in the *New York Times*. His statement can be taken as a summation of most reviews written in the first three decades of the century:[39]

> [Foote is] one of the most modest and accomplished musicians of his group and generation, and, as the event proved, a composer of delightful music. . . . Nothing is rarer or pleasanter in these days of 1929 than to encounter in art or on the street a gentleman who is quietly himself, who never alters his manner for an occasion, and whose simplicity and self-possession are indexes to like qualities of his character. Mr. Foote makes his listeners think of these things. His music apes no other composer; it does not affect a modernity to which the author is not sympathetic; it does not rest on platitudes or academic

> devices to command the respect of the listener. The Suite
> is simply melodic; it is simply and well composed, and
> scored gracefully and in a transparent manner. . . . It holds
> the attention and it gratifies the listener by its melodious-
> ness, proportion, and workmanship.[40]

As expected of Foote, he composed for the strings with clear insight into their properties. What is more, he managed the musical lines after a fashion feasible solely for a musician who has absorbed an artistic heritage extending from the present (1909) back to Bach. The music has a concentrated quality and a continuously forceful forward motion to it; no extraneous matter intrudes. Emotion is always present, but never is it merely meretricious or excessively obtrusive. He achieves his effects with a comparatively modest ensemble, without needing a hundred players and a wide variety of instruments. The movements are spare and concentrate on a few basic ideas. Nowhere does dullness appear. Audiences were soon enamored of the entire work.

The brief Prelude, an *allegro comodo*, is in $^2/_2$ meter and E major. The entire movement is based on the first phrase of eighth notes (example 40a). The tune rocks gently back and forth between the tone b′ and e′. The mildly syncopated throb of the second violins and violas below is fetching and foreshadows the treatment found in much of the movement. From the first measure, we discover music with a graceful, melodious appearance, on balance homophonic, yet providing for some give and take among the parts. Unusual for Foote, relatively little chromaticism appears. The middle section begins in B major and generates a sense of urgency. The music grows more modulatory and contrapuntal, including some points of imitation, with short clipped phrases chasing one after another instead of a melodic line of any length. The opening section returns reorchestrated. The coda augments all note values, in effect slowing the tempo, and goes from an *ff* to a *ppp*. The piece ends exquisitely on an E-major triad in the high strings—the first violins divided *à* 3; the second violins and violas, *à* 2.

The movement entitled Pizzicato and Adagietto has the heading capriccioso allegretto for the first segment. Several writers have commented on the debt of the pizzicato section to the third movement of Tchaikovsky's Fourth Symphony, written in 1877. Indeed, there are some obvious similarities in the way the parts are handled. Still, the differences are considerable:

	Foote	*Tchaikovsky*
Key	A minor	F major
Tempo	Moderately fast	Fast
Meter	$^6/_8$ (middle $^3/_4$)	$^2/_4$ (middle: $^2/_4$)
Middle section	*Adagietto: un poco con moto,* muted strings	*Meno mosso,* open sounds
Expression of opening	Brisk charm	Nervous hurry
Expression of middle	Ruminative and probing	Frenetic march
Coda	Pizzicato, pacific, mostly *p*	March returns, aggressive, blatantly *ff*

When Foote labels the second movement's Pizzicato portion as capricious, he means it is whimsically changeable, subject to erratic behavior, but amiable as well. The second movement's Adagietto, ostensibly in F major, is the greatest distance Foote would travel toward out-and-out chromaticism. Indeed, he stands here almost at the cusp of atonality. The lyric line, touched with pathos, seems to be trying to free itself from the sharps and flats that hinder its uninhibited singing. The melody emerges in the first violins out of a chromatic morass and after nine measures of groping harmony. Example 40b shows the end of the Pizzicato section and the beginning of the Adagietto. F major is instated in measure ten, but lasts only for a couple of measures. Chromatic entanglement enmeshes the tune again. Briefly, the music enters C major. Again the ceaseless chromaticism returns. A final close in F major is heard before the return to the Pizzicato.

The Fugue in four voices is by no means stiff and academic (example 40c). It is an *allegro giusto* in $^4/_4$ meter and E-minor tonality. Foote does not attempt to establish his scholarly credentials through clever contrapuntal tricks, contrived strettos, and learned augmentations, diminutions, and inversions. There are even passages where he resorts to homophony rather than counterpoint. For example, the first episode, which begins at measure 15, is often, though not entirely, homophonic; the second episode, which begins at measure 25, is entirely homophonic. Strength, dignity, and invigorating gestures imbue the exposition of subject and answer, as well as the working out of motives derived from the subject in the episodes. A long dominant pedal introduces the subject for a final time, to ring out resoundingly until it finishes on an E-major chord.

Although Foote never tries to reach for bigness and earthshaking profundity, he has provided his music with fancy and freshness. He knows what he is capable of accomplishing. Individual expression abounds. It is not easy, for example, to locate elsewhere a true counterpart to the lovely imperturbable sound of the Prelude's first measures. He has confidently gone about erecting a work whose subtle conversion of resources to achieve his creative goal give the music a glorious, if not an extraordinary, lightness. This is true even in the Fugue, which abjures any thought of becoming gigantic. If murkiness exists, it is found only in the Adagietto. On the other hand, the Adagietto effectively contrasts and is surrounded at each end by the playful and featherweight Pizzicato. In short, the suite is the result of a genuine and perceptive artistry. Clearly, the composer preferred to produce a work of modest scope that is capably and commendably executed, rather than an ambitious opus that is pretentious and imperfect.

A Night Piece for flute and string orchestra, his last instrumental ensemble, allows for the same conclusion. Philip Hale writes of it: "This composition, which Mr. Foote with characteristic modesty calls 'a slight little thing' was composed in 1918 for the Chamber Music Society of San Francisco. . . ."[41] Nevertheless, this "slight little thing" is one of his finest and most loved compositions. It projects an ageless grace, a state of solemn fantasy, and a compassionate and touching tenderness that stands against the accelerated rate of change in twentieth-century existence and the several arts. John Burk, who had succeeded Hale as program annotator for the Boston Symphony, commented insightfully about the piece a few days after Foote's death in April 1937:

> The "Night Piece" may well be considered to typify Arthur
> Foote and his art. It has no concern to shake the world. It
> no more than searches the beauties of a certain tonal com-
> bination within the suitable confines of an accepted form.
> And this search is made with a neat skill, a sensitive re-
> sponse to beauty which has enabled him to capture a dis-
> tillation of sheer sensuous delight. It need hardly be
> added that the result is far more precious to the audiences
> of 1919 or 1937 than the more ambitious attempts of
> lesser men.[42]

While conductor of the Boston Symphony Orchestra, Pierre
Monteux had heard Georges Laurent play the *Nocturne and
Scherzo* for flute and string quartet at one of the Flute Players'
Club concerts. He liked the work and suggested to Foote that he
would welcome an arrangement of the nocturne for string orchestra. Foote says: "This required only partial rewriting of the
'cello and occasional addition of the double bass. The piece
made a real success at a Symphony concert [13 April 1923], and
Laurent of course played it exquisitely."[43] Like the Suite, op. 63,
A Night Piece went on to success after success. Schmidt finally
published it in 1934 with a dedication to Laurent.

On the first page of the published score for flute and string
orchestra, the bass is described as "optional" because it "is sufficient" to play only the parts for string quartet, "for which this
composition was originally written." The music, in $^3/_4$ meter, begins in G-sharp minor and ends in the major of its enharmonic
equivalent, A-flat. Foote requests that it be played *andante lan-
guido*, that is to say moderately slow and with a calm dreaminess.
A *Foote* style can be discerned when the flute melody is compared with the clarinet melody that opens the first movement of
Four Character Pieces after the Rubáiyát of Omar Khayyám—an
andante comodo in B major and also in $^3/_4$ meter. Both pieces include persistent but velvety rhythms and gossamery harmonies in
the background. *A Night Piece* also conveys an exotic character in
some measures, but the exoticism is so subtle that it is easily
missed. Both persuasively produce an elegiac atmosphere. The
Germanic manner of writing disappears from this nocturne. The
closest European equivalent to the Foote approach is French,

somewhere between the styles, say, of Fauré and Debussy. None-theless, the music, which goes on for about eight and a half minutes, could have come from no individual but Foote.

Example 41 gives the beginning of *A Night Piece*. Both expertise and poetic inspiration inform these first seven measures. Note how the melody in the first half-phrase begins with a half-step descent from d-sharp″ to c-double sharp″, then eventually droops to a low d′, in measure 4. This procedure is inverted in the second half-phrase with a half-step rise from f-sharp″ to g-natural″, and ultimately the music leaps upward to a high d-sharp‴, in measure 8. The sixteenth note at the beginning of the second and the sixth measure would have had only a prosaic, albeit pleasant, effect if it had been placed at the end of the previous measure. However, placed on the first beat and with the harmony given a sudden spin away from the home tonality, it gives an impetus to the half-phrase. The music lilts forward with an easy undulation that conveys the composer's intended expression to a remarkable degree.

The first melody continues to unfold for thirty-six measures. Then after a slight pause, a new tune begins *poco animato*, a convincing outcome of what has gone before. Triplet eighth notes cause the music to suggest $^9/_8$ rather than $^3/_4$ time. The tonality is F-sharp major. An elaboration of the tune through a series of modulations, with each new idea splitting off from a previous idea, continues until a flute cadenza announces the return of the first melody. After this tune reaches its end, the second theme returns in A-flat major until the piece comes to a quietly restful end.

We cannot help but accept the real seductiveness of the Foote music. The loving and adept scoring for the flute, heartfelt strains of flute song, and diaphanous murmurs from the strings collaborate to mesmerize the listener. When *A Night Piece* was presented at a Boston Symphony concert in March 1933, a reviewer called it "perfect in its kind and degree." The reviewer adds: "For the audience there was nothing left but round upon round of applause directed toward our eldest composer for his years, his work, his life."[44]

Notes

1. In this regard, see Oscar G. Sonneck, *Suum Cuique* (New York: Schirmer, 1916), 138.

2. Arthur Foote, Scrapbook III, Boston Public Library, shelf no. **ML. 46.F65. The publication and writer are unidentified.

3. Frederick Jacobi, "Homage to Arthur Foote," *Modern Music* 14 (1937): 198.

4. The painting is in the Corcoran Gallery of Art, Washington, D.C.

5. Arthur Foote, "A Summary of the Principles of Harmony," 1932, in the Arthur Foote Collection, Williams College, Williamstown, Massachusetts, pp. 4–5.

6. The Schmidt copyright on the first page of the song, reads "1905."

7. On the verso of the cover and the recto of the next page of a bound volume entitled *A.F. 1913*, now at the Harvard Musical Association, shelf no. MC F738, vol. 2, Foote has pasted in handwritten sheets of paper, headed "the best are in this list." Among other songs, he cites "The Rose and the Gardener," "Bisesa's Song," "Ashes of Roses," "The Sun Is Low," and "Requiem."

8. Ibid. The letter is pasted onto a copy of "I Am the Moth of the Night."

9. Ibid.

10. The program with her writing on it is in the Arthur Foote Collection.

11. William Treat Upton, "Some Recent Representative American Song-Composers," *Musical Quarterly* 11 (1925): 384.

12. F. H. M., "New Music," *Musical America* (1 May 1920), 42.

13. Upton, "Some Recent Representative American Song-Composers," 384.

14. See *A.F. 1913*.

15. Upton, "Some Recent Representative American Song-Composers," 384.

16. Arthur Foote, *An Autobiography* (Norwood, Mass.: Plimpton Press, 1946), 109.

17. The manuscript is in *A.F. 1913*.

18. "The Two Roses," op. 64, no. 1, is dedicated to "K.F. and K.F.," to wife Kate and daughter Katharine.

19.   The program with its notes may be found in Arthur Foote, Scrapbook III, Boston Public Library, shelf no. **ML. 46.F65.

20.   Foote, *Autobiography*, 58.

21.   Ibid., 109; Frederick Edward Kopp, "Arthur Foote: American Composer and Theorist" (Ph.D. diss., Eastman School of Music, University of Rochester, 1957), 103.

22.   It is now available in published form: *At Dusk,* ed. John Solum and Marilyn Costello (Boca Raton, Fla: Masters Music Publications, 1991).

23.   Now available as *Sarabande and Rigaudon,* ed. Stephen Kiser and Douglas B. Moore (Boca Raton, Fla: Masters Music Publications, 1991).

24.   For a very detailed account of this modernist attack on the more traditional composers, see Nicholas Tawa, *American Composers and Their Public* (Metuchen, N. J.: Scarecrow, 1995), chaps. 1–5.

25.   Foote, *Autobiography*, 58.

26.   Ibid., 58.

27.   R. D. Darrell, Notes, for *The Early String Quartet in the United States,* L.P. recording, Vox SVBX 5301.

28.   *Foote, 1925,* vol. 3, at the Harvard Musical Association, shelf no. MC F738. At the beginning of the volume is the information: "From estate, April 1943."

29.   Douglas Bryant Moore, "The Cello Music of Arthur Foote" (D.M.A. diss., Catholic University of America, 1976), 3.

30.   Ibid., 14–15.

31.   Foote, *Autobiography*, 111.

32.   This statement is typewritten on a sheet of paper on which Foote has written by hand: "W.B.Z. Broadcast Sat. Mar. 11. 1933 at 9*15* p.m. from Symphony Hall," now in the Arthur Foote Collection.

33.   The composition is item 3, in *Arthur Foote Mss. 1920,* a bound volume at the New England Conservatory of Music, Boston, Massachusetts. On the first blank page of the volumes there is written "Arthur Foote, April 1921."

34.   The announcement of its first performance by Hecht is pasted into *Arthur Foote Mss. 1920,* just before the score of the composition.

35.   The announcement of the Laurent concert, sponsored by the Boston Flute Players Club, is pasted underneath the announcement of the Hecht concert.

36.   Ray C. B. Brown, "S. F. Music Lovers Hear 2 Premieres," *San Francisco Examiner*, 29 January 1919, 9.

37. W. S. S., "Foote and Flutes," *Boston Evening Transcript*, 32 October 1921, 6.

38. H.T.P.[arker], "The Symphony Concert," *Boston Evening Transcript*, 17 April 1909, 4.

39. The clippings of several reviews are pasted in with the score of the suite, in Arthur Foote, *Op. 48, 63*, a bound volume of music in the library of the Harvard Musical Association, shelf no. 05.3 F738.1. At the end of the score, the composer has written, "Dedham, summer of 1907." He also gives the place and the year of twenty-one performances that had taken place up to April 1929.

40. Olin Downes, "Music," *New York Times*, 8 March 1929, 31.

41. Philip Hale, *Boston Symphony Orchestra Programme* no. 42, 13–14 April 1923, 1384.

42. John Burk, *Boston Symphony Orchestra Programme* no. 56, 16-17 April 1937, 1094, 1096.

43. Foote, *Autobiography*, 112.

44. "Concert of Contrasted Composers," *Boston Evening Transcript*, 11 March 1933, 4.

11

Epilogue

Arthur Foote was around seventy-four years old when he wrote:

> With some of the music contained in the bound volumes
> of my compositions I am even today satisfied; with more
> of it I'm not. This is the common lot of all composers, and
> I have not been perhaps so great a sinner as some. We are
> absorbed at the moment in the work we are doing, but
> lose interest in it after its completion, and it is hard for the
> author to estimate real values. As a result, practically all
> composers have left behind them too much that was pub-
> lished, instead of being torn up after the writing. Besides
> this, as one grows older, and has acquired greater techni-
> cal mastery, it is natural for a composer, writer, or painter
> to keep on producing long after he has said all that he had
> in him. In my time Saint-Saëns was a conspicuous ex-
> ample of this.[1]

By the mid-1920s, he had just about ceased composing any
new music, only rarely bestirring himself to make an arrangement
of something already composed. He had decided that he had "said
all that he had in him." Nevertheless, until the end of his life, he
continued to engage the social, political, and cultural world about
him. Foote remained sharp-witted and friendly, ever an agreeable
companion.

A Chronicle of the Thirties

Moses Smith gives us a picture of Foote at Boston's Common-wealth Pier, in the fall of 1930, awaiting the arrival of one of his oldest friends, George Henschel, the first conductor of the Boston Symphony. He was excited about meeting again with a man he loved and about learning what he had been thinking and doing in London and what the London music scene was like. Smith says that to his last hours, Foote took an interest "in the world of affairs rather than of dreams."[2] In the fall of 1930, the Boston Symphony celebrated its fiftieth anniversary. Foote commemorated the occasion on 9 October with an address, "Fifty Years in Fifty Minutes." At the beginning of the year, Nicolas Slonimsky had maintained in the pages of *Modern Music* that New England, especially Boston, was the birthplace of American music. He said further that two eminent New Englanders, Chadwick and Foote, had confirmed New England's distinction as a musical hub, although neither musician had felt it necessary to carve out a national style for himself.[3]

Foote continued to be involved with the world of music in 1932, writing "A Summary of the Principles of Harmony," as an unusual kindness for his grandnephew and namesake, Arthur Foote II.[4] Its forty-five pages showed in a meaningful way his pleasure in the grandnephew named after him. Reverend Henry W. Foote, II, nephew of Arthur Foote, had become the father of a boy on 18 January 1911, and had decided to name him after his uncle. Absolutely delighted by the act, Foote had immediately sent off a letter, saying: "I am going to begin the young Arthur's start in life with $500 in a savings bank book—(probably the Provident)."[5] Now, some twenty years later, he hoped to give young Arthur a start in his musical life. After his sophomore year at Harvard College, Arthur Foote II had conceived a tardy but enthusiastic curiosity about music. He had already arranged to take piano lessons from a young woman, when his granduncle learned about his new interest. Although he was now giving few piano lessons, the elderly musician graciously but adamantly declared that he himself would see to young Arthur's musical instruction. Reverend Arthur Foote II states in a letter he sent to me:

So for two winters (1931 and 2) I went to his home once a week. He was invariably kind, and, I think, pleased to get more intimately acquainted with the youngster who had been given his name. But I'm sure that he quickly realized that, despite my enthusiasm, I should not pursue a professional career in music. I was disappointed then, though I realized soon that he was right—that it was too late, that I lacked marked talent, and should limit myself to being "just a lover of music."[6]

Reverend Arthur Foote II testifies to his granduncle's many virtues, as he knew them:

I am immensely grateful for what he gave me; he was a truly lovable man, a superb teacher, with a fine sense of humor, and a wealth of musical information to pass along. Those forty or fifty evenings at his home were a richly rewarding experience. I do wish I had taken more of what he so freely offered me; but I was involved in college activities, academic and athletic, and deeply in love. Immediately after graduation in 1933 I got married, and my wife and I moved out to Chicago for my theological graduate studies.[7]

The composer invariably had a concern for what members of the music public thought of his music. This was especially so after he had grown old and wondered about the weight of his contributions to American culture and the musical legacy he would leave behind him. His eightieth birthday, 5 March 1933, occasioned a flurry of performances and more written responses than usual, all of them positive, from the music public. With pleasure, he clipped out of the *Boston Herald* (9 March 1933) a letter from Florence Wood Russell of Newton Centre, in which she makes public her delight in the Foote piano music played on the radio. She had admired his music for over forty years and took special pleasure in his songs, which were all "gems" to her. She cites "Eden Rose," "The Night Has a Thousand Eyes," and "Irish Folk Song" as her favorites, and also says she liked *Te Deum*.[8]

Two days later, a Robert Hughes Salomon of Mount Vernon, New York, sent a letter to the composer, which he preserved among his papers. It describes how meaningful Foote's music was to many ordinary listeners during a time of social and economic distress:

> Dear Mr. Foote:
>
> I think you might like to know how much happiness the playing of your "Night Piece" by Mr. Georges Laurent has brought to me. I am and have been for a considerable time unemployed. My resources are rapidly becoming depleted with no hope in sight. I was feeling very low when I turned on the radio to hear the Boston Symphony Concert. Then I heard your beautiful nocturne. It moved me from this wholly sordid world of materialism. It transferred me to my long sought for "land of quietness and peace." I imagined myself floating calmly down a beautiful landscaped river in a little boat. That single, clear flute tone rising steadily and true above the accompaniment of the orchestra was transcendent, I think.
>
> It is such beautiful creations which have the power to move such as yours moved me that should qualify for places in symphony programs, not these horrible series of dissonances that exist under the name of music.
>
> God bless you, sir, Thank you!
>> Your sincere admirer,
>> Robert Hughes Salomon.[9]

On 25 March 1933, a letter from Victor Harris appeared in the *Musical Courier*. Harris was a New York pianist, vocal coach, choral conductor, and composer of vocal music. He writes:

> The American public and the American composers especially are grateful to him [Foote] for the increased honor and prestige which he brought to them. He has lived up (always) to the highest standards and ideals adopted at the outset of his career, and all of us deeply appreciate the nobility and beauty and the sanity of his compositions in

all forms. I remember well my first reading of Go Lovely
Rose, over forty years ago. It appeared in one of my lessons during this past week, and I found that it had the
same originality, the same beauty and the same exquisite
taste as at my first reading.[10]

These testimonials demonstrate the public's long-standing
admiration for Foote, which showed no signs of abating. The
praise helped bolster his spirits in the face of his physical problems, many connected with the aging process. When Philip Hale
resigned as music critic for the *Boston Herald* and annotator for
the concert programs of the Boston Symphony in 1934, Foote
wrote to him:

Dear Phil,
When I called to see you at the Herald office, I was told
that you were out of town—and would be away for the
winter.
I wanted to tell you how truly I was sorry for the fact that
you had given up the Herald and the Symphony
programmes, for myself and countless others, and even
more for what this must mean to you—I wish you may understand how sorry I am—You have, too, been a power for
good all these years. . . . I was distressed when you told me,
the last time we met, of your arthritis—and so hope earnestly that you may before long find yourself better—and
more in good condition—The last would be good news. I
find it takes courage these last years of one's life. . . . With
the best wishes for you at this time and always. I am your
friend and colleague and yours faithfully,
Oct. 20, 1933   Arthur Foote
Don't bother yourself to reply—it is simply that I
wanted to write it to you.[11]

Despite the afflictions that arrived with old age, he occasionally had the strength to continue some familiar activities. As late
as December 1935, Foote still found the strength to conduct
one or two of his own compositions. On 16 December 1935, he

appeared before the Highland Glee Club of Newton to lead its
male members in his "Bedouin Song." The club's grateful director then sent him a brief note: "Thank you! Thank you! This
from every man in the Glee Club and from—Gratefully Yours,
Ralph Maclean."[12] When Foote's namesake, Arthur Foote II, was
ordained into the Unitarian ministry at his grandfather's church,
King Chapel, in September 1936, his granduncle played the organ for the service.[13]

Occasionally he was to be seen in the audience when his music was performed. That same December when the composer led
the Highland Glee Club, Fabien Sevitsky led the People's Symphony Orchestra in Boston for an all-Foote concert, with Foote
in attendance. The audience heard the Air from the Serenade for
Strings, the Fugue from the Suite for Strings in E Major, the *Four
Character Pieces after the Rubáiyát of Omar Khayyám*, and the
songs "Tranquility," "The Rose and the Gardener," and "Irish
Folk Song." The audience, says the *Transcript* reviewer, hailed
"this distinguished musician, whose quiet and courageous individuality" has been little appreciated and whose music "proved a
revelation" to those present and "gave pleasure to the general
listener." He was made to rise and bow to persistent applause.
Why were the listeners so delighted? The reviewer answered that
Foote struck the music public as being a genuine musician who
had no need to advocate a new theory, represent a new fashion,
or appear as a revolutionary through use of excessive percussion
and shocking harmony. He did "uphold the single ideal of beauty" with which the audience sympathized. Additionally:

> The audience of the People's Symphony is no exception
> to the rule that the public cares nothing at all for style in
> composition as such. All listeners enjoy new thrills in mu-
> sic when they are the spontaneous result of sincere cre-
> ative effort. They are frankly bored with deliberate at-
> tempts to be "different."
>
> Deserved honor is gradually creeping up on Arthur
> Foote for digging away in his own field in his own way, let
> the bombshells of fame burst where they may. His music is
> no less individual because of its simplicity and lack of pre-
> tension.[14]

Foote was still an active and competent musician in 1936. He and Walter Spalding revised and enlarged the book *Modern Harmony* by adding two chapters on recent tendencies in music theory.[15] He received an application and a letter dated 3 December 1936 from the American Society of Composers, Authors, and Publishers, urging him to join the association despite the unexplained opposition of Arthur P. Schmidt and Henry Austin. Even though Foote would be eighty-four years old in three months, he decided to join. At the bottom of the letter, Foote wrote in pencil, "Filled out."[16]

Denouement

Foote once said to Philip Hale, "I find it takes courage these last years of one's life." Of courage, he had plenty. In the final months of his life he demonstrated again and again an ingrained capability for confronting problems with grit, moral strength, and the ability to rebound in spirit and intellect.

In December 1936, he wrote to Willis Kopes of Salem apologizing for not writing to him due to eye strain, which forced him to use his eyes "as little as possible." he wrote the same apology to Mrs. Rebra Paeff Mirsky, saying he was "ordered to write and read only what is absolutely necessary."[17] He had developed cataracts, which had gradually clouded the lenses of his eyes and made reading and writing difficult chores.

On the other hand, his friend Olin Downes says that from the summer of 1936 until his death, Foote had been restudying keyboard music like the Bach *Italian Concerto* and the Brahms piano music. Despite his poor vision, he tried to maintain an active correspondence and avidly read the clippings sent by friends and pupils from the world over. Downes visited him in his modest white, two-story house in Newton, which was garbed in flowers during the warmer months, and found the composer cognizant of what was going on with contemporary composers and heard him express firm opinions about their music. He loved Gershwin. Arnold Dolmetsch's activities in early music still proved fascinating to him.[18]

Another friend, Redfern Mason, reported that "in spirit he

was young till the day of his death. Up to the last he attended the concerts of the Symphony and he took as much pleasure in its performances in his ninth decade as he did in the eighties of last century."[19]

A report on Foote's final days has come to us from Edith Lane, a woman who studied with him years before. Her lines hint at a man who was delighted to receive congenial visitors and reluctant to see his callers leave. She writes:

> Time flitted by and one evening in 1937 our family was having a musical evening and Mr. Foote's name came into the conversation. It had been probably fifteen years since I had last studied with him—he was now 84 years old. I wrote to ask him if I could have a few lessons. He told me to come—We had several very happy afternoons at the piano, for it wasn't a question of a half-hour or hour—it usually was an entire afternoon. In fact, when I arrived at what was a seemly time to me, he asked me to come earlier so that we could have more time. He said there was so much musical literature to go over. These hours are a cherished memory. I had expected to go for a lesson the last week of his life but the sad news came that he had suddenly gone on to the greater music of the spheres."[20]

Foote came down with acute pneumonia early in 1937 and died at Massachusetts General Hospital on 8 April 1937. His nephew Henry W. Foote, Jr., wrote to his son, Arthur Foote II, about the event and his sincere love for his uncle:[21]

> Uncle Arthur's death was as peaceful and easy as could be desired. He was ill four days with pneumonia, was taken to Phillips House [of the Massachusetts General Hospital] and died there, April 8. . . . Katharine and Henri Raffy report that a few hours before he died he knew them, how that most of the time he lay quietly, eyes closed, his fingers moving across the coverings as though he were playing the piano, or his hand beating time while his head was cocked as tho listening to an orchestra.

Henry W. Foote, II, says that he had called on his uncle three weeks before his death and had "a delightful chat" with him, although his uncle looked frail and was greatly bothered by the cataracts in his eyes. He then tells his son Arthur:

> I don't think I've known another man so widely and
> deeply loved, as well as honored for his gifts and graces.
> And he was the soul of integrity and honor. It was a happi-
> ness to him that *you* bear his name,—be worthy of it!

A large number of pupils and friends attended the funeral. The service at Mount Auburn Chapel was conducted by Rev. Henry W. Foote Jr. and Rev. Charles E. Park, the minister of the church where Arthur Foote had served for so many years as organist and music director. The composer's remains were buried in Mount Auburn Cemetery.[22]

Arthur Foote's wife, Kate Grant Knowlton Foote, also died on 8 April. The *Polk's Newton City Directory* states: "Foote, Kate wid Arth died Apr 8. 1943." She had still been living at 158 Ridge Avenue.[23] She was buried next to her husband. His daughter Katharine and her husband, Henri Raffy, had moved to Kezar Falls, Maine, where they operated a chicken farm and later a tree farm. Katharine died 5 March 1970 in a Portland, Maine, nursing home, writes Rev. Arthur Foote II. "The Arthur Foote line ends with Cousin Katharine's death, leaving no child."[24]

A Summation of a Musical Life

Younger, more change-minded, and more adventuresome musicians have criticized Foote's work in the years after his death. One criticism is that because he is an American composer who built his music on established criteria, his style must be considered unacceptably imitative of musical methods already employed by one or more European composers. However excellent his craftsmanship and serious his purpose, his music is considered stale, humdrum, excessively polite, safely mediocre—something belonging in a museum. Even the relatively tolerant Aaron

Copland shared this view, as evidenced in his *Music and Imagination*.[25] But the rationale for this adverse judgment was more subjective than objective. Moreover, it represented the opposite of what the general music public believed to be true.[26] Whatever the case, the negative argument influenced individual performers, vocal and instrumental groups, conductors, academics, and music critics to such an extent that Foote and composers of his persuasion, went into eclipse after the 1940s.

Yet, as I have tried to show, he was judged an exceptional composer by competent contemporary writers on music. They confirmed his art's musical merits, which they tried to define more clearly in terms of professional craftsmanship than would be the case later. They resisted applying only personal responses to Foote's artistic aims, preferring to make judgments based on commonly accepted musical standards. Considerable unanimity on standards had existed among composers and other musicians who claimed a proficiency in their complicated art. On balance, they agreed about what made up a capably finished composition and what measurements were just and reasonable to apply. They were not fully addicted to sweeping impressionistic declarations that demoted the strict, professional knowledge possessed by an artist like Foote to secondary importance. They held that the existence of music as a viable art relied on discipline.

Foote was no hidebound reactionary. His style was considered up-to-date during his youthful and middle years. He did base his activities on a bedrock of principles, laid down after mature consideration. The question is, should the principles used for measurement rest on tradition, or should they be laid down anew by every new crop of composers bent on innovation or by any individual who sets himself or herself up as a self-referential judge? Foote and a majority of listeners held to a discernment and enjoyment of excellence in music that they deemed valid, however much it kept faith with the past.

Convinced of Foote's merits as a person and artist, Arthur Foote II and Katharine Raffy tried to advance his cause. As Foote told me:

> Not long after Uncle Arthur's death, with Cousin Katharine Raffy's help, I began building the collection of

his published music. This in part was to repay him for what he had given me, but gradually came a deepening love of, and respect for, his compositions. I came to regard his compositions, especially his chamber music and larger orchestral works, as not only of markedly superior musicianship, but of having some hard to define "extra" that makes his work more durable and interesting than most of his [American] contemporaries.[27]

Their efforts were repaid more with lip service than deeds. For example, on the one-hundredth anniversary of the composer's birth, Katharine Raffy informed the Harvard Music Department of the fact. She received a reply from the department chairman, Randall Thompson:

Professor Woodworth turned over to me your very kind note about the 100th anniversary of your father's birth. It so happened that we were having a department meeting that day and I read my colleagues your letter. Doctor Davison, Professor Piston, Professor Woodworth, and I all knew and loved your father and have the highest admiration for his music. He made a permanent contribution to music of this country and was always a loyal friend of this department.[28]

The hope that Harvard, the Boston Symphony, the New England Conservatory of Music, or others would schedule a composition or two to commemorate the anniversary met with little success. Homer Humphrey wrote to Katharine in July that he had learned to dislike Charles Munch, music director of the Boston Symphony, and hoped that he would be removed from his position. He had tried to get this orchestral conductor and the Boston Symphony to play at least one Foote work but failed. Munch, he said, had no excuse and might easily have done something if he had wanted to. Humphrey was also talking with the conservatory people, but could report no results.[29] If Koussevitzky, that outstanding champion of American music, had been alive, he would certainly have scheduled one or more compositions to commemorate the anniversary. He had a high respect for Foote's abilities and, not surprisingly for the maestro, sometimes indicated that he understood Foote's music better than did the composer. Lawrence Dame once reported in the *Boston Herald*:

> Dr. Koussevitsky related . . . that he once surprised . . . Arthur Foote by saying, "You know Mr. Foote, there is something of jazz in your suite [in E major]." Foote jumped with astonishment, but Dr. Koussevitsky proved his point by softly repeating yesterday, "Maree de rump pouff, maree de rump pouff!"[30]

Months later, on 6 January 1954, the New England Conservatory of Music did a few songs as a birthday commemoration, in a concert sponsored by the IOTA chapter of Pi Kappa Lambda, whose president Foote once was. There was also a broadcast of the music and a talk by Chester W. William over Boston's radio station WHDH on 4 February. For the most part, however, the anniversary of Foote's birth went unnoticed.

Nevertheless, Foote and his compositions were and still are eminently worthy of notice. His music continues to reveal a forthright and appealing individual, who is expert in his calling and has the power and faculty to assert himself in a lucid and sensible musical fashion. One hears no assertive Americanisms in his scores, Koussevitsky's comment about jazz in the suite notwithstanding. Indeed, the present age is beginning to realize, as Foote realized years before, that a widely accepted American identity in music is difficult to establish in a country with diverse races and ethnic groups. Regarding the issue of musical nationalism, Arthur Weld wrote in 1964:

> That which appears most undeniable at present is that those who hope in that direction are in far too great a hurry. All we can possibly say at this time is that we have some eminent musicians who were born in this country, and why go further? Why ask more? Why not be merely glad and proud that George Chadwick and Arthur Foote, being citizens of these United States, write the beautiful music that they do without bothering our head as to the "lack of nationality" . . . in that same beautiful music?[31]

To the end of his creative life, Foote allowed no radical innovations or painstaking resurrections of ancient procedures to prevail in his measures, preferring instead melodic openness, superior craftsmanship, and independence of spirit. He was not "original" in the sense of being on the cutting edge of his art and trying to sound disconnected from anyone who had gone before; he *was* "original" in sounding consistently like himself. Homer Humphrey once complained to Katharine Raffy how critics often missed that whatever Foote wrote was entirely his own, reminiscent of no one, belonging solely to him.[32] Humphrey's claim is exaggerated, since Foote's music here and there may suggest music by Schumann or Brahms, for example. Foote was certainly aware of his stylistic debts to other composers. Nor did he consider himself to have sinned. He would have agreed with Oscar Sonneck's assertion that every composer, "even the wildest anarchist," writes music based on someone else and "is demonstrably descended from one or more masters." Whatever his resultant style, said Sonneck, the composer had to be, above all, sincere in what he was doing.[33] Sincere, Foote decidedly was.

A distinct Foote style does exist, if we accept the usual meaning of the term, which can be defined as an especially characteristic technique and manner typical of the composer. His style is an outgrowth of Central European practices to be sure, but by the late nineties he was looking toward France and Russia, even as he refined his chromatic usage. Slowly his melodies turned more modal. Seventh tones were either avoided or lowered in pitch so as not to act as leading tones to the tonic. As the years went by, he was less apt to use half-steps in the ordinary course of the primary melodic line. As I have pointed out, New England psalmody, British-American folk song, musical stage ditties lie half-concealed in the background of many a tune.

He likes songlike lines that are expandable or incorporate motives suitable for development, especially when writing within a sonata-allegro structure. Melodic phrases normally are balanced. A move or skip in one direction is answered with an opposite move or skip. S-curves are often seen. Quite a few melodies may include, toward their beginning, a leap downward to a chromatically raised note, which acts as an appoggiatura rising a half-step for its resolution. Even taking this leap into consideration,

joltingly jagged disjunct linear motion through ninths, major sevenths, diminished fifths, and augmented fourths are rare. The
most frequent melodic syncopations are those associated with
the English language, like the stressed-short and unstressed-long
syllables of "*mo*-ther," whose musical equivalent is an eighth note
occurring on, possibly, a first half-beat of a measure followed by a
quarter or dotted-quarter note.

Foote's harmony embraces all the resources of late nineteenth-century romanticism—secondary seventh and ninth constructions, altered-tone augmented chords, continuous passing
allusions to other keys, modulation to the flat side and recur-
rently to the key a major or minor third above or below the tonic. Every now and again, he is apt to suddenly shift to a distant
key, perhaps through enharmonic means. Very often after the
first measure, he is fond of making prominent use of the mediant and the submediant chords, usually in their minor configurations. He injects an intimation of ancient practices when
concordant diatonic triads, all in root position and without relation to tonal function, succeed one another to close a phrase or
strain without invoking a perfect cadence.

His prevalent homophonic context takes the form either of
melody plus clearly subordinate accompaniment that is given a
slight rhythmic impulse or of activated harmony, which may give
the impression of contrapuntally moving parts. Accompaniments
may resort to mild syncopation, but the syncopations never in-
trude on the melodic statement. Again and again one finds what
might be denominated organ-stop thinking, with passages of
some length maintaining a similar coloration. The lucidity of his
tonal arrangements is scarcely ever marred by complex, murky
textures.

Foote eschews bravura writing—to dazzle is never his aim.
Virtuosic demands on players are rare, the one major exception
being the solo part of the Cello Concerto. Yet, even here, the
tendency is more to lyricism than to display. To let a cello, violin,
or flute simply sing eloquently is dear to his heart. Contrary to
the practices of other nineteenth-century pianist-composers,
Foote does not allow the piano to dominate the other instruments in any chamber composition that includes it.

Almost everything that has just been said is true for his

songs. Voice and piano are in no way equal partners; the voice is indisputably to the fore. Even instrumental preludes, interludes, and postludes are usually inconsequential, if they exist at all. Despite the fact that a couple of his most successful songs are strophic, most are through-composed and in three strains. A measure or two of the first strain may recur later, but that is the only redundancy.

Because they complement his lyrical inclinations, his instrumental forms are mainly in ternary or theme-and-variations structures. Rondos are disfavored. Sonata-allegro movements turn up in multimovemented compositions descended from Classical genres—sonatas, trios, quartets, and quintets. A cyclical element may enter, when occasionally portions of earlier movements recur in the finale. Sometimes a motive wends its way from one movement to another. However, a majority of his multimovemented compositions are not descended from classical-sonata genres but appear as loosely joined suites. Most often, they contain two or more unrelated movements in ternary or variation form. Once in a while, Foote spins out a single idea from beginning to end of a movement, gradually deviating from a home tonality but ultimately returning to it. Very occasionally, a fugue or a preluding on a brief initial idea is heard.

The scherzo type of movement—fleet, brusque, and relentlessly forward pushing—is not for Foote, even when he so entitles a movement. A movement that is labeled as a Scherzo tends toward the light and frolicsome, and harbors touches of whimsy. Foote always leaned toward moderation, tempering an allegro, allegretto, or andante with the modifiers *moderato, non troppo,* or *comodo.* When he turned to a new idea that might tempt the performer to play with lingering sentiment during a movement, he more often than not wrote *più mosso* in order to counter the temptation.

Two expressive tendencies predominate in most of the music, though not necessarily in the light poetic character pieces for piano that are given fanciful titles. One is inward, self-searching, intimately emotional, and quite melodious. The other is outwardly directed, devotional, and given the stately progression of a hymn. These expressions are found as early as in the first trio and first quartet, where Foote undertakes an exposure and development of the two expressions, ultimately allowing the second to win out. They persist as late as the final songs and the cello-viola sonata.

In short, Foote's style was both individual and consistent. It was sound in construction and pinned to melody, and not given to extremes. His musical expressions were attractive and easy to understand. This was the secret behind his popularity with contemporary audiences. Quite distinctive and worthy of the highest respect are several songs, the violin sonata, the two trios, the three string quartets, the piano quartet and quintet, and the suites for piano and for organ. Equally fine are the Serenade in E for string orchestra, the Prologue to *Francesca da Rimini* for full orchestra, the Suite in D Minor for full orchestra, the *Four Character Pieces after the Rubáiyát of Omar Khayyám* for full orchestra, the Suite in E for string orchestra, and *A Night Piece* for flute and strings.

Foote can again win renown if given a fair rehearing. The new artistic movements that have dominated twentieth-century music have produced music that is no more comprehensive, much less universally accepted, and not usually as durable as the music of Foote. In banishing Foote's music from the current repertoire, we have taken away much that was good under the delusion that it was not good enough. In art music's transit from one generation to another, it is constantly abandoning previous strengths it needs and eventually will have to rediscover. No period in music history, no matter how seemingly outdated and barren, is entirely and hopelessly inferior, leastwise the period of Paine, Chadwick, MacDowell, and Foote. Although the innovative musical styles of subsequent periods were more adequate to the requirements of a different set of composers, they did not for the most part meet the needs and desires of listeners.

It may be that after so much commendation of experiment and excess in the twentieth century, simplicity such as Foote's is getting to be an attractive alternative for mature and cultivated music lovers. It is time to poke into the ashes of the past to see if there are glowing embers that can ignite fresh musical fires and inspire a host of listeners disconsolate over the present state of music. If such an investigation is undertaken, it is likely to end with success.

Foote's music exemplifies a time-honored era in American music writing. Once his compositions are restored to the concert hall, they will win an increasing following with repeated performances. Such music as Foote's can form an important part of the base for an American repertoire. It is not enough to have the works of more recent composers like Aaron Copland and Samuel Barber, fine as they are. We need to go back further to the roots of American art music, roots that we have so assiduously and mistakenly tried to pull up. American art music will then acquire a respectable history and will gain a wholeness that we deny it when we discommend what has gone before and find value only in what is in the present and future. Art music must free itself of its ephemeral status and win a larger circle of dedicated supporters in order to survive.

Foote avoided the emotional excesses of late romanticism by holding a firm rein on his feelings. He helped insure a future for art music by respecting the need for sureness of technique and logicality of structure. Nothing he wrote was ripped off at the spur of the moment. He thoroughly scrutinized every new work before it was made public. Yet, rushing from teaching job to church position to concert performance to his study in order to compose forced him to forfeit much of his leisure and served to deny him the full domestic life he desired. Fortunately, the music he wrote shows no sign of haste or impatience.

"Faithfully yours," he signed himself in the letters he sent out. He showed this faithfulness in his dedication to duty and his firm commitment to whatever he engaged himself to do. Whether in his life or in his music, he gave unstinting loyalty to what he felt bound to by ties of ancestry, religion, art, and to fellowship with all members of the music world. It is this sincere faithfulness that affirms his music's capacity to endure.

Notes

1. Arthur Foote, *An Autobiography* (Norwood, Mass.: Plimpton Press, 1946), 59.

2. Moses Smith, "A Tribute to Arthur Foote," (address delivered at a memorial concert, Lasell Junior College, Auburndale, Mass., on 22 July 1937), published with Foote, *An Autobiography*; see p. 123.

3.   Nicolas Slonimsky, "Composers of New England," *Modern Music*, January-February 1930, 24, 26. In this year, the periodical was paginated by issue.

4.   The summary is now in the Arthur Foote Collection, Williams College, Williamstown, Massachusetts. The occasion for its writing is contained in a letter from Arthur Foote II to Douglas Moore, dated 20 August 1988, now in the Arthur Foote Collection.

5.   The letter is in the Arthur Foote Collection.

6.   Letter sent to me, dated 1 October 1994.

7.   Ibid.

8.   The newspaper clipping is in the Arthur Foote Collection.

9.   The letter is in the Arthur Foote Collection.

10.   Victor Harris, letter on Foote's eightieth birthday, *Musical Courier*, 25 March 1933, 22.

11.   The letter, written from his Newton home on Ridge Avenue, is in the Boston Public Library, shelf no. MS Mus. 508.

12.   The undated note may be found in the Arthur Foote Collection.

13.   Letter from Arthur Foote II to me, dated 4 January 1996.

14.   N. M. J., "Foote's Music from People's Orchestra," *Boston Evening Transcript* (9 December 1935), 4.

15.   Arthur W. Foote and Walter R. Spalding, *Modern Harmony in Its Theory and Practice*, aug. and rev. ed. (Boston: Schmidt, 1936).

16.   The letter alone is in the Arthur Foote Collection. The application had been filled out and returned.

17.   The letter to Willis Kopes bears no date, but the post office stamp on the envelope is 17 December 1936; it is in the Essex Institute, Salem, Massachusetts, filed under "Foote Family Mss." The letter to Mrs. Mirsky, dated 22 December 1936, is in the Arthur Foote Collection.

18.   Olin Downes, "Works of Arthur Foote," *New York Times* (18 April 1937), sec. 11, p. 5.

19.   Redfern Mason, "The Passing of Arthur Foote," *Boston Evening Transcript* (17 April 1937), sec. 4, p. 6.

20.   Edith Lane, "Arthur Foote, Massachusetts' Own Musician," typewritten MS, p. 9, now in the Essex Institute, Shelf no. E F688.3L 19–. The year "1937" is written in pencil on the manuscript. In a letter that Arthur Foote II sent to me, 4 January 1996, he says of Lane's report: "On first reading I found it confusing; then I realized that her 'very happy afternoons at the piano' had been 15 years earlier than 1937, about a decade earlier than my happy evenings with him."

21. The letter, dated 16 April 1937, is in the Arthur Foote Collection.

22. The letter of Henry W. Foote, Jr., describes the funeral; so also does a clipping entitled Vale Arthur Foote, on which is handwritten "Musical Leader. May 8, 1937," now in the Arthur Foote Collection.

23. *Polk's Newton City Directory* 39, for 1943 (Boston: R. L. Polk, 1943), 233.

24. Arthur Foote II, letter to me, 4 November 1994.

25. Aaron Copland, *Music and Imagination* (New York: Mentor, 1959), 107–08. It should be noted that Copland seemed to have altered his opinion when he approved issuing his flute music with Foote's, on Northeastern CD 227, which came out in 1987.

26. A book-length discussion of the differing viewpoints of the music modernists and the general music public may be found in Nicholas Tawa, *American Composers and Their Public* (Metuchen, N. J.: Scarecrow, 1995).

27. Letter from Arthur Foote II to me, dated 1 October 1994.

28. Letter of Randall Thompson to Katharine Raffy, dated 30 March 1953, now in the Arthur Foote Collection.

29. Letter from Homer Humphrey to Katharine Raffy, dated 23 July 1953, now in the Arthur Foote Collection.

30. Lawrence Dame, "U. S. Music Held Greatest," *Boston Herald*, 28 September 1939, clipping in the Arthur Foote Collection.

31. Arthur Weld, "A Contribution to the Discussion of 'Americanism' in Music," *Music* 5 (1964): 639.

32. Letter from Humphrey to Raffy, 23 July 1953.

33. Oscar Sonneck, *Suum Cuique* (New York: Schirmer, 1916), 4–5.

Bibliography

Adams, James Donald. *Copy of Harvard*. Boston: Houghton Mifflin, 1960.

Allen, Una L. "The Composer's Corner, No. 18—Arthur Foote." *The Musician*, March 1931, 31.

Alviani, Doric. "The Choral Church Music of Arthur William Foote." S.M.D. diss., Union Theological Seminary, 1962.

Amory, Cleveland. *The Proper Bostonians*. New York: Dutton, 1947.

Apthorp, William Foster. *By the Way*. 2 vols. Boston: Copland & Day, 1898.

____. *Musicians and Music Lovers*. New York: Scribner's Sons, 1894.

"A. P. Schmidt, Pioneer Publisher of American Music, Is Dead." *Musical America*, 14 May 1921, 55.

"Arthur Foote and the Flowering of American Music." Sermon, First Church Unitarian, Boston, 8 November 1953. Probably delivered by Rev. Duncan Clark.

"Arthur Foote, Programs and Clippings, Feb. 1, 1879–April 17, 1937." Compiled by the Music Department, Boston Public Library. Shelf no. **ML.46.B6F6.

"As a Composer Regards His Craft." *Boston Evening Transcript*, 8 October 1936. Clipping in the "Arthur Foote Collection," Williams College, Williamstown, Massachusetts.

Bates, Arlo. *The Pagans*. Boston: Ticknor, 1888.

____. *The Philistines*. Boston: Ticknor, 1889.

Bispham, David. *A Quaker Singer's Recollections*. New York: Macmillan, 1920.

Blackwell, Alice Stone. *Growing Up in Boston's Gilded Age: The Journal of Alice Stone Blackwell, 1872–1874*. Edited by

Marlene Deahl Merrill. New Haven: Yale University Press, 1990.

Bowen, Catherine Drinker. *Yankee from Olympus*. New York: Bantam Books, 1960.

Brooks, Van Wyck. *New England Indian Summer: 1865–1915*. New York: Dutton, 1940.

Brown, Allan A., comp. "Boston Symphony Orchestra. Clippings and Reviews." Boston Public Library. Shelf no. **M.125.5.

Carter, Morris. *Isabella Steward Gardner and Fenway Court*. Boston: Houghton Mifflin, 1925.

Cipolla, Wilma Reid. "Foote, Arthur (William)." In *New Grove Dictionary of American Music*, ed. H. Wiley Hitchcock and Stanley Sadie. London: Macmillan, 1986.

____. *A Catalog of the Works of Arthur Foote*. Bibliographies in American Music, 6. Detroit: Information Coordinators, 1980.

Cooke, George Willis. *John Sullivan Dwight*. Boston: Small, Maynard, 1898.

Downes, Olin. "Works of Arthur Foote." *New York Times*, 18 April 1937, sec. 11, p. 5.

Dunham, Henry Morton. *The Life of a Musician*. New York: Mrs. Henry M. Dunham, 1931, 74, 77.

Dwight, John Sullivan. *Music in Boston*. Vol. 4 of *The Memorial History of Boston*. Edited by Justin Winsor. Boston: Ticknor, 1881.

Ellinwood, Leonard. *The History of American Church Music*. Rev. ed. New York: Da Capo, 1970.

Elson, Louis C. *The History of American Music*. Revised to 1925 by Arthur Elson. New York: Macmillan, 1925.

____. *The Realm of Music*, 3rd ed. Boston: New England Conservatory of Music, 1897.

Ewen, David. "Foote, Arthur William." In *American Composers*. New York: Putnam's Sons, 1982.

Fairbrother, Trevor J. *The Bostonians, Painters of an Elegant Age, 1870–1930*. Boston: Museum of Fine Arts, 1986.

Farwell, Arthur, and W. Dermot Darby, eds. *Music in America*. Vol. 4 of *The Art of Music*. New York: National Society of Music, 1915.

Finck, Henry T. *My Adventures in the Golden Age of Music*. New York: Funk & Wagnalls, 1926.

Foote, Arthur. *An Autobiography*. Norwood, Mass.: Plimpton Press, 1946. Reprint, with notes by Wilma Reid Cipolla. New York: Da Capo, 1979.

———. "A Bostonian Remembers." *Musical Quarterly* 23 (1937): 37–44.

———. "A.F. 1913." Bound volume of music and clippings. Harvard Musical Association, Shelf no. MC F738, volume 2.

———. "Arthur Foote: Three Scrapbooks, 1881-1907." Boston Public Library. Shelf no. **ML.46.F65.

———. "The Development of the Secular Style in Music." M.A. diss. Harvard University, 1875. Now in Harvard Archives.

———. "Foote 1925." Bound volume of music and clippings. Harvard Musical Association. Shelf no. MC F738, vol. 3.

———. "Foote. Op. 24, 25, 28." Bound volume of music and clippings. Harvard Musical Association. Shelf no. O5.1 F738.1.

———. "Foote. Op. 48, 63." Bound volume of music and clippings. Harvard Musical Association. Shelf no. O5.3 F738.1.

———. "Foote I." Bound volume of music and clippings. Harvard Musical Association. Shelf no. MC F738, vol. 1.

———. "Letters Collected by Arthur Foote: Gift to the Library in Memory of Arthur Foote, April 16 , 1940." In a bound volume. Spaulding Library, New England Conservatory of Music.

———. "Letters. Undated from Second [Rosalie] Housman Gift." Library of Congress, Shelf no. ML.95.F77.

———. *Modulation and Related Harmonic Questions*. Boston: Schmidt, 1919.

———. Manuscript of lectures delivered at University of California, 1911. Boston Public Library. Shelf no. **M.472.134. No. 1042 is entitled "Music in the United States."

———. Scrapbook. New England Conservatory of Music.

———. "A Near View of Mr. Lang." *Boston Evening Transcript*, 1 May 1909, pt 3, p. 4.

———. Scrapbook, 1869–76. Harvard University Archives. Shelf no. HUD 874.27F.

_____. *Some Practical Things in Piano Playing*. Boston: Schmidt, 1909.

_____. "A Summary of the Principles of Harmony," for Arthur Foote II. Manuscript, 1932. Arthur Foote Collection, Williams College, Williamstown, Massachusetts.

_____. "Then and Now, Thirty Years of Advance in Musical America" *Etude*, January 1913, 19.

_____. "You Like It or You Don't." Clipping in the Arthur Foote Collection, Williams College, Williamstown, Massachusetts.

Foote, Arthur, and Walter R. Spalding. *Modern Harmony in Its Theory and Practice*. Boston: Schmidt, 1905.

"Foote, Arthur." In *The National Cyclopedia of American Biography*. Vol. 27. New York: White, 1939.

Foote, Rev. Arthur, II. *Henry Wilder Foote, Hymnologist*. The Papers of the Hymn Society, no. 26. New York: Hymn Society of America, 1968.

Forbes, Elliot. *A History of Music at Harvard to 1972*. Cambridge: Department of Music, Harvard University, 1988.

Gilman, Lawrence. *Edward MacDowell*. New York: Lane, 1908.

Goldman, Richard Franko. "Those Forgotten American Composers." *HiFi / Stereo Review*, February 1968, 114–15.

Green, Martin. *The Mount Vernon Street Warrens, A Boston Story, 1860–1910*. New York: Scribner's Sons, 1989.

Hall, Constance Huntington, and Helen Ingersoll Tetlow, eds. *Helen Hopekirk, 1856–1945*. Cambridge, Massachusetts: privately printed, 1954.

Henschel, Sir George. *Musings & Memories of a Musician*. London: Macmillan, 1918.

Henschel, Helen. *When Soft Voices Die*. London: Westhouse, 1944.

Howard, John Tasker. *Our American Music*. 4th ed. New York: Crowell, 1965.

Howe, Helen. *The Gentle Americans, 1864–1960*. New York: Harper & Row, 1965.

Howe, M. A. DeWolfe. *Barrett Wendell and His Letters*. Boston: Atlantic Monthly Press, 1924.

_____. *The Boston Symphony Orchestra*. Boston: Houghton Mifflin, 1914.

_____. *Boston, The Place and the People*. New York: Macmillan, 1903.

_____. *John Jay Chapman and His Letters*. Boston: Houghton Mifflin, 1937.

_____. *Memories of a Hostess*. Boston: Atlantic Monthly Press, 1922.

_____. *Semi-Centennial History of the Tavern Club, 1884–1934*. Boston: The Tavern Club, 1934.

_____. *A Venture in Remembrance*. Boston: Little, Brown, 1941.

Hughes, Rupert. *Contemporary American Composers*. Boston: Page, 1900.

James, Henry. *The American Scene*. Bloomington: Indiana University Press, 1968.

Johns, Clayton. *Reminiscences of a Musician*. Cambridge, Mass: Washburn & Thomas, 1929.

Kearns, William K. *Horatio Parker, 1863–1919*. Metuchen, N. J.: Scarecrow, 1990.

Knight, Ellen. *Charles Martin Loeffler*. Urbana: University of Illinois Press, 1993.

Kopp, Frederick Edward. "Arthur Foote: American Composer and Theorist." Ph.D. diss., Eastman School of Music, Rochester University, 1957.

Lane, Edith. "Arthur Foote, Massachusetts' Own Musician." Manuscript at the Essex Institute, Salem, Mass. Shelf no. F688.3L 19–.

Mason, Daniel Gregory. *The Dilemma of American Music*. New York: Macmillan, 1928.

Mason, Redfern. "The Passing of Arthur Foote." *Boston Evening Transcript*, 17 April 1937, sec. 4, p. 6.

Milligan, Harold Vincent. "Organ Works of Arthur Foote." *The Diapason*, April 1919. Clipping in "A.F. 1913." Harvard Musical Association.

Moore, Douglas Bryant. "The Cello Music of Arthur Foote." D.M.A. diss., Catholic University, 1976.

"Mrs. Mary W. Foote." *Salem Gazette*, 29 December 1857. Clipping at the Essex Institute, Salem, Massachusetts, Shelf no. BR 920.F68.

Parker, H. T. *Eighth Notes*. New York: Dodd, Mead, 1922.

Patch, Ira J., comp. "Abstracts from Wills, Inventories, etc. on file in the Office of Clerk of Courts, Salem, Mass." *Historical Collections of the Essex Institute*. Vol. 2. Salem, Mass.: Essex Institute, 1860.

"A Prolific Composer of Boston." *The Music Leader* 46 (1923): 273.

Raffy, Katharine Foote. "2 West Cedar Street, 1882–1895." Manuscript, a photocopy of which was sent to me by Arthur Foote II.

"Reminiscences of the Revolution, Prison Letters and Sea Journal of Caleb Foot: Born, 1750, Died 1787." Compiled by his grandson and namesake, Caleb Foote. *Historical Collections of the Essex Institute*. Vol. 26. Salem, Mass.: Essex Institute, 1889.

Rogers, Clara Kathleen. *Memories of a Musical Career*. Boston: Little, Brown, 1919.

_____. *The Story of Two Lives*. Boston: Plimpton Press, 1932.

Ryan, Thomas. *Recollections of an Old Musician*. New York: Dutton, 1899.

Schmidt, John C. *The Life and Works of John Knowles Paine*. Ann Arbor, Mich.: UMI Research Press, 1980.

Semler, Isabel Parker. *Horatio Parker*. New York: Putnam's Sons, 1942.

Shand-Tucci, Douglas. *Boston Bohemia, 1881–1900*. Amherst: University of Massachusetts Press, 1995.

Smith, Moses. "A Tribute to Arthur Foote." An address delivered at a memorial concert, Lasell Junior College, Auburndale, Massachusetts, 22 July 1937. Published with Foote, *An Autobiography*, 117–30.

Smith, Warren Storey. "Pianoforte Works of Arthur Foote." *The Musician*, May 1923, 10, 27; June 1923, 15.

Sonneck, Oscar G. *Suum Cuique*. New York: Schirmer, 1916.

Spalding, Walter. *Music at Harvard*. New York: Coward McCann, 1935.

Sturgis, Mrs. Elizabeth Orne (Paine). "Recollections of the 'Old Tucker House,' 28 Chestnut Street, Salem." *Historical Collections of the Essex Institute*. Vol. 74. Salem, Mass.: Essex Institute, 1928.

Stutsman, Grace May. "Bostonians Honor Memory of Foote." *Musical America*, 10 May 1937, 30.

Sullivan, T. R. *Boston, New and Old*. Boston: Houghton Mifflin, 1912.

Thomas, Theodore. "Musical Possibilities in America." In [Thomas, Theodore] *Musical Autobiography*. Edited by George P. Upton. Chicago: McClurg, 1905.

Thompson, Vance. *The Life of Ethelbert Nevin*. Boston: Boston Music, 1913.

Tileston, Mary Wilder, ed. *Caleb and Mary Wilder Foote, Reminiscences and Letters*. Boston: Houghton Mifflin, 1918.

Truette, Everett E. "Two American Organists and Composers." *The Musician* 15 (1910): 347-48.

Upton, William Treat. *Art-Song in America*. Boston: Ditson, 1930.

____. "Some Recent Representative American Song-Composers." *Musical Quarterly* 11 (1925): 385–417.

Urrows, David Francis. "Apollo in Athens: Otto Dresel and Boston, 1850–90." *American Music*, 12 (1994): 345–88.

Whipple, George M. "A Sketch of the Musical Societies of Salem." *Historical Collections of the Essex Institute*. Vol. 23. Salem, Mass.: Essex Institute, 1886.

Musical Examples

Example 1a. "Andante" (15 May 1869)

Example 1b. "The Sands of Dee" (16 July 1869)

Example 2a. *Drei Stücke* for Piano and Cello, op. 1, no. 2

2.

Example 2b. *Drei Stücke* for Piano and Cello, op. 1, no. 3

3.

Example 3a. Trio in C minor for Piano, Violin, and Cello, op. 3, mvt. 1, theme 1

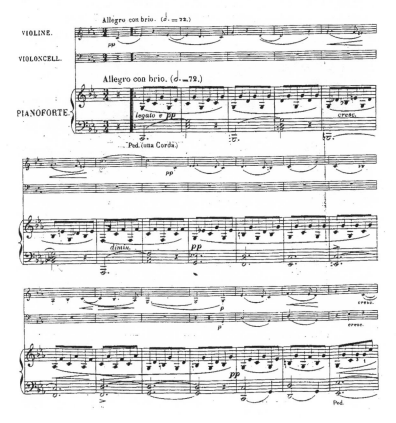

Example 3b. Trio in C Minor, mvt. 1, theme 2, mm. 96-110

Example 3c. Trio in C Minor, mvt. 2, theme 1

Example 3d. Trio in C Minor, mvt. 2, theme 2, mm. 161-176

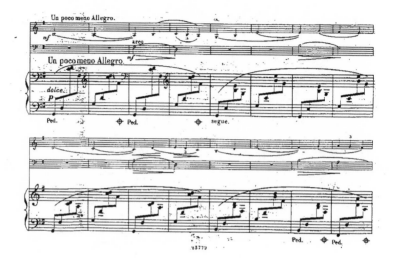

Example 3e. Trio in C Minor, mvt. 3, theme 1

III

Example 3f. Trio in C Minor, mvt. 4, theme 1

IV

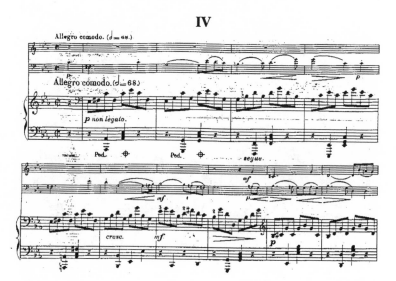

Example 4a. Quartet in G Minor for Strings, op. 4, mvt. 1, theme 1

Example 4b. Quartet in G Minor for Strings, op. 4, mvt. 1, theme 2, mm. 48-55

Example 4c. Quartet in G Minor for Strings, op. 4, mvt. 3, theme 1

Example 5. Song: "Go Lovely Rose"

"GO, LOVELY ROSE!"

ARTHUR FOOTE.

Example 6. Song: "I'm Wearing Awa' to the Land O' the Leal"

To Mrs. Caroline Washburn Rockwood.

"I'M WEARING AWA' TO THE LAND O' THE LEAL"

ARTHUR FOOTE.

Op. 13, Nº 2.

Example 7. Eclogue for Piano, op. 8, no. 2

ECLOGUE.

Example 8. Suite in D Minor for Piano, op. 15, Fugue

Example 9a. Sonata for Piano and Violin op. 20, mvt. 1, theme 1

SONATE.

I

ARTHUR FOOTE OP. 20.

Example 9b. Sonata for Piano and Violin, op. 20, mvt. 1, theme 2, mm. 24-34

Example 9c. Sonata for Piano and Violin, op. 20, mvt. 2, theme 1

Example 9d. Sonata for Piano and Violin, op. 20, mvt. 3, closing measures

Example 9e. Sonata for Piano and Violin, op. 20, mvt. 4, theme 1

A. P. S. 2690

Example 9f. Sonata for Piano and Violin, op. 20, mvt. 4, theme 2, mm. 68-92

Example 10. Overture *In The Mountains*, op. 14

Example 11. Song: "On the Way to Kew"

The Poem by WILLIAM ERNEST HENLEY.

ARTHUR FOOTE.

A. P. S. 7172

Example 12. Song: "Elaine's Song"

Example 13. Song: "Memnon"

The Poem by ARLO BATES

ARTHUR FOOTE.

Example 14. Song: "An Irish Folk Song"

Example 14. Song: "An Irish Folk Song" (continued)

Example 15. Song: "A Ditty"

Example 16. Song: "In Picardie"

Example 17a. Zweite Suite in C Moll for Piano, op. 30, mvt. 1, theme 1

Zweite Suite.

Example 17b. Zweite Suite in C Moll for Piano, op. 30, mvt. 2, theme 1

Example 18. *Festival March,* op. 29, no. 1, for Organ

1.
Festival March.

Arthur Foote, Op. 29. No. 1

Example 19a. Quartet in C Major for Piano and Strings, op. 23, mvt. 1, theme 1

Example 19b. Quartet in C Major for Piano and Strings, op. 23, mvt. 3, theme 1

III.

Example 19c. Quartet in C Major for Piano and Strings, op. 23, mvt. 4, theme 1

Example 19d. Quartet in C Major for Piano and Strings, op. 23, mvt. 4, mm. 23–33
The hymn begins in the fifth measure of the example.

Example 20a. Quartet in E Major for Strings, op. 32, mvt. 2, trio

Example 20b. Quartet in E Major for Strings, op. 32, mvt. 3, theme

Example 20c. Quartet in E Major for Strings, op. 32, mvt. 3, variation 4

Example 21a. Quintet in A Minor for Piano and Strings, op. 38, mvt. 1, theme 1

Quintett.
I.

Example 21b. Quintet in A Minor for Piano and Strings, op. 38, mvt. 2, theme 1

II.
Intermezzo.

Example 21c. Quintet in A Minor for Piano and Strings, op. 38, mvt. 3, theme 1

III.
Scherzo.

Example 21d. Quintet in A Minor for Piano and Strings, op. 38, mvt 4, theme 1

Example 22a. Serenade in E for String Orchestra, op. 25, mvt. 1, theme 1

SERENADE
in E-dur
für Streich-Orchester.

I. Praeludium.

ARTHUR FOOTE, OP. 25.

... ... (⁴ᵃ ⁱ ᵖ)ᵒdur viarto Satz("R o m a n z e") kann, wenn nothwendig, ausgelassen werden.

Example 22b. Serenade in E for String Orchestra, op. 25, mvt. 2, theme 1

II. Air.

Example 22c. Serenade in E for String Orchestra, op. 25, mvt. 3, theme 1

III. Intermezzo.

Example 22d. Serenade in E for String Orchestra, op. 25, mvt. 3, middle section

Example 22e. Serenade in E for String Orchestra, op. 25, mvt. 4, theme 1

Example 23a. Symphonic prologue: *Francesca da Rimini*, op. 24,
for full orchestra, opening

Symphonischer Prolog:
"Francesca da Rimini."

Arthur Foote, Op. 24.

Example 23b. Symphonic prologue: *Francesca da Rimini*, op. 24,
theme 2, mm. 171–84

Example 23c. Symphonic prologue: *Francesca da Rimini,* op. 24,
episode 2, mm. 233–44

Example 24a. Concerto in G Minor for Cello and Orchestra,
op. 33, mvt. 1, opening

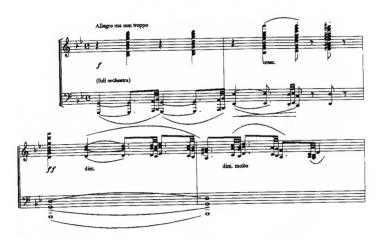

Example 24b. Concerto in G Minor for Cello and Orchestra,
op. 33, mvt. 1, theme 1, mm. 48–51

Example 24c. Concerto in G Minor for Cello and Orchestra,
op. 33, mvt. 2, theme 1

Example 24d. Concerto in G Minor for Cello and Orchestra,
op. 33, mvt. 3, theme 1

Example 24e. Concerto in G Minor for Cello and Orchestra,
op. 33, mvt. 3, theme 1, part 2, mm. 16–21

Example 25a. Suite in D Minor for Full Orchestra , op. 36, mvt. 1, theme 1

Suite in D Moll.
I.

ARTHUR FOOTE, Op. 36.

Example 25b. Suite in D Minor for Full Orchestra , op. 36, mvt. 1,
theme 2, mm. 101–8

Example 25c. Suite in D Minor for Full Orchestra , op. 36, mvt. 2, theme 1

Example 25d. Suite in D Minor for Full Orchestra , op. 36, mvt. 2, mm. 61–69

Example 25e. Suite in D Minor for Full Orchestra , op. 36, mvt. 3, variation 7

Example 25f. Suite in D Minor for Full Orchestra, op. 36, mvt. 4, theme 1

Example 25g. Suite in D Minor for Full Orchestra, op. 36, mvt. 4,
theme 2, mm. 101–13

Example 25g. Suite in D Minor, op. 36, mvt. 4, theme 2, mm. 101–13 (continued)

139

Example 26a. *Four Character Pieces after the Rubáiyát of Omar Khayyam*
op. 48, mvt. 1, theme 1

Four Character Pieces
after the Rubáiyát of Omar Khayyám.

I.

Iran indeed is gone with all his Rose,
And Jamshyd's Sev'n-ring'd Cup where no one knows;
But still a Ruby kindles in the Vine,
And many a garden by the Water blows

ARTHUR FOOTE, Op. 48.

Example 26b. *Four Character Pieces after the Rubáiyát of Omar Khayyám*
op. 48, mvt. 2, theme 1

II.

They say the lion and the lizard keep
The Courts where Jamshyd gloried and drank deep:
And Bahrám, that great Hunter—the Wild Ass
Stamps o'er his head, but cannot break his Sleep.

Example 26c. *Four Character Pieces after the Rubáiyát of Omar Khayyám*
op. 48, mvt. 2, middle section

Yet ah, that Spring should vanish with the Rose!
That Youth's sweet-scented manuscript should close!
The Nightingale that in the branches sang,
Ah whence, and whither flown again, who knows!

Example 26d. *Four Character Pieces after the Rubáiyát of Omar Khayyám*
op. 48, mvt. 3, theme 1

III.

A Book of Verses underneath the Bough,
A Jug of Wine, a Loaf of Bread—and Thou
Beside me singing in the Wilderness—
Oh, Wilderness, were Paradise enow!

Example 26e. *Four Character Pieces after the Rubáiyát of Omar Khayyám*
op. 48, mvt. 4, middle section

Waste not your Hour, nor in the vain pursuit
Of This and That endeavor and dispute;
Better be jocund with the fruitful Grape
Than sadden after none, or bitter, Fruit

Example 26f. *Four Character Pieces after the Rubáiyát of Omar Khayyám* op. 48, mvt. 4, return of theme 1

Example 27. Song: "The Rose and the Gardener"

ARTHUR FOOTE, OP. 51. Nº 1.

Example 28. Song: "Ashes of Roses," mm. 7–13

Example 29. Song: "Requiem," last 18 measures

Example 30. Song: "Love Guides the Roses"

Example 31. Song: "There's a Ship Lies off Dunvegan"

Example 32. Song: "Tranquillity," mm. 15–24

Example 33. *Lygeia,* introduction

LYGEIA.

ARTHUR FOOTE, Op. 58.

**The Poem by
Gertrude Rogers.**

Example 34. *Meditation,* for Piano

Meditation.

"And leaves the world to darkness and to me."

ARTHUR FOOTE, Op. 61.

Example 35a. Suite in D major for Organ, op. 54, mvt. 1, mm. 15–22

Example 35b. Suite in D major for Organ, op. 54, mvt. 3

Example 36a. Canzonetta for Organ, op. 71, no. 4, opening

Example 36b. Canzonetta for Organ, op. 71, no. 4, mm. 51–61

Example 37a. Trio no. 2 in B-flat Major, op. 65, mvt. 1, theme 1

I.

ARTHUR FOOTE, Op. 65

Example 37b. Trio no. 2 in B-flat Major, op. 65, mvt. 1, mm. 65–76

Example 37c. Trio no. 2 in B-flat Major, op. 65, mvt. 2, mm. 32–35

Example 38a. Quartet in D Major for Strings, op. 70, mvt. 1, theme 1

I.

ARTHUR FOOTE, Op. 70.

Example 38b. Quartet in D Major for Strings, op. 70, mvt. 2, middle section

Example 38c. Quartet in D Major for Strings, op. 70, mvt. 4, mm. 28–37

Example 39a. Sonata in E. Minor for Piano and Viola [or cello],
op. 78, mvt. 1, theme 1

Example 39b. Sonata in E Minor for Piano and Viola [or cello],
op. 78, mvt. 1, mm. 56–73

Example 39b. Sonata in E Minor for Piano and Viola [or cello],
op. 78, mvt. 2, opening

Example 40a. Suite in E Major for String Orchestra, op. 63, mvt. 1, opening

Suite in E dur.
I.
Praeludium.

Arthur Foote, Op. 63.

Example 40b. Suite in E Major for String Orchestra, op. 63, mvt. 2, mm. 63–107

Example 40b. Suite in E Major for String Orchestra,
op. 63, mvt. 2, mm. 63–107 (continued)

Example 40c. Suite in E Major for String Orchestra, op. 63, mvt. 3, opening

III.
Fuge.

Example 41. *A Night Piece* for Flute and Strings, opening

(As the Basso is optional, the String Quartet, for which this composition was originally written, is sufficient.)

Index

About the Author

Nicholas E. Tawa is professor emeritus of music at the University of Massachusetts, Boston. He received his doctorate in musicology from Harvard, has taught in New York state and New England, and has composed award-winning works for instrumental groups. His other books on American Music are *Sweet Songs for Gentle Americans: The Parlor Song in America, 1790–1860*; *A Sound of Strangers: Musical Acculturation and the post-Civil War Ethnic American*, *A Music for the Millions: Antebellum Democratic Attitudes and the Birth of American Popular Music*, *A Most Wondrous Babble: American Art Composers, Their Music, and the American Scene, 1950–1985*, *Art Music in the American Society: The Condition of Art Music in the Late Twentieth Century*, *The Way to Tin Pan Alley: American Popular Song, 1866–1910*, *The Coming of Age of American Art Music: New England's Classical Romanticists*, *Mainstream Music of Early Twentieth Century America*, *American Composers and Their Public*. He is co-founder of the Sonneck Society, an organization devoted to the study of American music and music in America.